Managing Information and Knowledge in Organizations

Knowledge is increasingly regarded as central both to the successful functioning of organizations and to their strategic direction. *Managing Information and Knowledge in Organizations* explores the nature and place of knowledge in contemporary organizations, paying particular attention to the management of information and data and to the crucial enabling role played by information and communication technology. Mutch draws on a wide range of literature spanning the disciplines of business, management, information management and information systems. This material is located in a framework based on critical realism but covering the full range of contemporary debates.

Managing Information and Knowledge in Organizations distinguishes itself by:

- Taking a process-based approach centered around the notion of 'information literacy'
- Giving more attention to issues of data and information than other texts
- Emphasizing the importance of technology while continuing to stress the centrality of social and organizational factors
- Placing issues of organizational and national culture in a broader politico-economic context.

With such useful features as chapter objectives, mini-cases, chapter summaries and suggestions for further reading, this text is ideal for advanced undergraduate and graduate students in Knowledge Management, Information Management and Management of Information Systems courses and modules.

Alistair Mutch is Professor of Information and Learning in the Department of Information Management and Systems, The Nottingham Trent University. He is the author of several books and numerous papers in the field of information management.

Routledge Series in Information Systems

Edited by Steve Clarke (Hull University Business School, UK),
M. Adam Mahmood (University of Texas at El Paso, USA),
Morten Thanning Vendelø (Copenhagen Business School, Denmark)
and Andrew Wenn (Victoria University of Technology, Australia)

The overall aim of the series is to provide a range of text books for advanced undergraduate and postgraduate study and to satisfy the advanced undergraduate and postgraduate markets, with a focus on key areas of those curricula.

The key to success lies in delivering the correct balance between organizational, managerial, technological, theoretical and practical aspects. In particular, the interaction between, and interdependence of, these often different perspectives is an important theme. All texts demonstrate a 'theory into practice' perspective, whereby the relevant theory is discussed only in so far as it contributes to the applied nature of the domain. The objective here is to offer a balanced approach to theory and practice.

Information Systems is a rapidly developing and changing domain, and any book series needs to reflect current developments. It is also a global domain, and a specific aim of this series, as reflected in the international composition of the editorial team, is to reflect its global nature. The purpose is to combine state-of-the-art topics with global perspectives.

Information Systems Strategic Management 2nd edition

An integrated approach
Steve Clarke

Managing Information and Knowledge in Organizations: A Literacy Approach

Alistair Mutch

Managing Information and Knowledge in Organizations

A Literacy Approach

Alistair Mutch

 Routledge
Taylor & Francis Group

NEW YORK AND LONDON

First published 2008
by Routledge
711 Third Ave, New York, NY 10017

Simultaneously published in the UK
by Routledge
2 Park Square, Milton Park, Abingdon, Oxon OX14 4RN

Routledge is an imprint of the Taylor & Francis Group, an informa business

© 2008 Alistair Mutch

Typeset in Perpetua and Bell Gothic by
Florence Production Ltd, Stoodleigh, Devon

Library of Congress Cataloging in Publication Data
Mutch, Alistair, 1954–
    Managing information and knowledge in organizations: a literacy
    approach/Alistair Mutch.
        p. cm. – (Routledge series in information systems)
    Includes bibliographical references and index.
    1. Knowledge management.   2. Information technology – Management.
    3. Organizational learning.   I. Title.
    HD30.2.M95 2008
    658.4′038 – dc22   2007040844

ISBN10: 0–415–41725–2 (hbk)
ISBN10: 0–415–41726–0 (pbk)
ISBN10: 0–203–93317–6 (ebk)

ISBN13: 978–0–415–41725–9 (hbk)
ISBN13: 978–0–415–41726–6 (pbk)
ISBN13: 978–0–203–93317–6 (ebk)

To Kath

Contents

CONTENTS

Figures

Tables

Preface

This book has its origins in the ten years I spent working as an auditor, management accountant and computer modeller for British Telecommunications in the 1980s. That decade saw the advent of commercially available personal computers and I was involved in the extraction of data from mainframe computers in order to model it on personal computers using early generation spreadsheets. This experience and the changes that I witnessed gave me an interest in the information from a user's perspective that I have been fortunate enough to be able to develop in my time at Nottingham Business School. During this time I have been exposed not only to a range of literature but also to the experiences and opinions of many students at both undergraduate and postgraduate level. Some of this book derives from trying to explain the importance of information, both 'traditional' and ICT-enabled, to undergraduate students who perhaps started with rather naïve views about the magic of computers. Other parts are informed by the many managers who have certainly experienced the frustrations of computers but who have tended to take the information they use for granted. Many of their experiences are reflected in this book and I thank all my students, past and present, for the ways in which they, probably without realizing it, have shaped my thinking. The other group of people who have helped shape that thinking are the colleagues with whom I have been fortunate to work during this period. A number of them have worked closely with me and have been good enough to read parts or all of this book in draft form. I thank Melanie Currie, John Orley, Carole Tansley, Chris Cramphorn, Karl Knox and Shirley Walker for taking time to do this. On a broader stage, a number of other colleagues have been very helpful to me as I struggled to negotiate the boundaries between information systems and organizational theory. During the writing of this book I have had particularly useful conversations with Rick Delbridge, Marc Ventresca, Hari Tsoukas, Tony Watson and Bernard Leca. Nancy Hale and Felisa Salvago-Keyes from Routledge guided me through the publishing process and series editors Andrew Wenn and Morten Thanning Vandelo supplied extremely helpful feedback at the draft stage. None of these people, of course, bear any responsibility for the final shape of the book. However, without Kath's support I would never have made this journey at all, so she will have to bear full responsibility! The dedication is a small token of my thanks.

Thanks are due to the following for permission to reproduce material:

Academy of Management Review for a figure from Daft, R. L., and Weick, K. E. (1984) 'Toward a Model of Organizations as Interpretation Systems', *Academy of Management Review* 9(2): 284–295.

Blackwells for a table from Schwenk, C. (1988) 'The Cognitive Perspective on Strategic Decision Making', *Journal of Management Studies*, 25(1): 41–55.

Cambridge University Press for a figure from Archer, M. (1995) *Realist Social Theory: The Morphogenetic Approach*. Cambridge, Cambridge University Press.

Elsevier for a passage from Westerman, P. (2001) *Data Warehousing: Using the Wal-Mart Model*. San Francisco, Morgan Kaufmann; and for a table from Bruce C. (1999) 'Workplace experiences of information literacy', *International Journal of Information Management* 19(1): 33–47.

IBM Systems Journal for figures from Henderson J. C. and Venkatraman, N. (1993) 'Strategic Alignment: Leveraging Information Technology for Transforming Organizations', *IBM Systems Journal* 32(1): 472–484.

Oxford University Press for figures from Nonaka , I. and Takeuchi, H. (1995) *The Knowledge-Creating Company: How Japanese Companies Create the Dynamics of Innovation*. New York, Oxford University Press; Venkatraman N. (1991) 'IT-Induced Business Reconfiguration' in M. Scott-Morton (ed.) *The Corporation of the 1990s*. New York: Oxford University Press; and Scott-Morton, M. 'Introduction' in M. Scott-Morton (ed.) *The Corporation of the 1990s*. New York: Oxford University Press.

Pearson Education for the adaptation of a figure from Earl, M. (2000) 'Every Business is an Information Business', in T. Davenport and D. Marchand (eds) *Mastering Information Management*. London: FT Management.

Introduction

WHAT IS THIS BOOK ABOUT AND WHO IS IT AIMED AT?

'Knowledge' is a central concern in both organizational theory and practice in the contemporary world. This book is aimed at those who wish to get a better understanding of the many factors which can impinge on the creation, sharing and use of knowledge in the world of organizations. It is aimed primarily at those who either are or aspire to be in a position of management responsibility in organizations in the private, public or voluntary sectors. We will look at the nature of management in a little more detail during the course of the book, but just for now we will work with the assumption that managers have some interest in and ability to influence the actions which their organizations adopt. Of course, the degree to which this can happen in practice varies enormously, but we will assume for now that you are interested in exploring knowledge in organizations not just for purely abstract reasons but because it, and your actions, can have some real effect in your organization.

If we examine the terms used in the title we can see what distinguishes the approach taken from other authors you may have come across. The active verb 'managing' is used in the title to stress the need for activity. In this, I am adopting the stress that many writers about organizations lay on what they term a 'processual' view. That is, a traditional view of organizations is to see them as composed of entities like 'structure', 'department' or 'function'. The task of another entity 'strategy' is then seen as being the articulation of these entities with the 'environment'. However, many writers have suggested that this focus on abstract entities leads to a fairly sterile form of analysis which underplays the role of human activity in creating and changing these entities. For example, some writers on organizational strategy (one, for example, is Henry Mintzberg) have suggested that what is important is not the strategy itself but the process of arriving at it. In this book, I seek to marry this focus on the importance of process – that is, a focus on what it is that people actually *do* when involved with knowledge – with a concern to place this process in a broader context. That implies a particular set of assumptions which are bound up with the theories that inform my approach – but more of that shortly.

So far, I have used the term 'knowledge' as a shorthand. In the title I couple this with the term 'information', which suggests that I want to draw a distinction between these two terms. Indeed I do, and there is a reason for this. It is that much writing on 'knowledge management' often turns out to be more about information management. Indeed, I could have added the term 'data' to the title (but titles often work best when they are not a long list of terms!). One claim I make for this book is that I pay more attention to the importance of data and information in organizations than some other writers in the area. I think managers need to be concerned with aspects of both which are often neglected when more glamorous terms like 'knowledge' are used. Much of the book will be devoted to teasing out these differences and their practical consequences.

Another term which does not appear in the title is 'technology'. While I agree that in most cases it is problems with, broadly, 'people' rather than technical issues which prevent the full use of information in organizations, the problem with this truism is that it can blind us to the fact that technical choices can profoundly influence what we can do with information. Again, while a task of this book will be to explore just what the impact of technology is, for now we can note that I intend to place rather more emphasis here than some other treatments on the nature and place of information technology do. However, I have no intention of going into technical detail. Rather, my focus will be on the implications for information use. I will try to use examples that indicate the technical choices that organizations have made and their consequences, and in so doing point you to sources should you wish to find out more detail. It is my contention, however, that as actual or aspiring managers you need to at least know something about the potential offered by technology and some of the pitfalls that it presents.

Some of the complexities involved in exploring knowledge are presented in the diagrams in Figure 0:1. The first set of overlapping circles (Figure 0:1a) refers to the academic disciplines which I will be drawing upon. The area for my particular concern is that where the three circles intersect, but it is clear that there is a vast body of material outside this intersection which sets the context for our discussions. I will talk about some of the problems this brings with it in the next section. The second diagram (Figure 0:1b) refers to the overlapping set of interests within organizations, and you will notice here that the three circles do not map directly across on to each other. The closest parallel is between the information systems areas, as there is often a close relationship here between the predominantly technical concerns in the world of work and those in some aspects of the discipline in universities. However, there is no such direct match for library and information science, as librarians and their concerns are often fairly marginal in the world of work. This should remind us that just because ideas exist and are helpful, that is no guarantee that they are applied. Ideas are often most effective when embedded in social practices or associated with particular roles or institutions. As we will see, there is much of value in the discipline area of library and information science, but this often struggles to find an organizational home. In turn, the academic discipline often tends to downplay the practical aspects of organizing, which here are split into two. The area of business strategy is present to remind us that information and knowledge are used in organizations for a purpose – even if that purpose is often unclear or very debatable. Indeed, much of the discussion in organizations tends to be about the intersection between organizational strategy and IS strategy, so much so that the human relations contribution is also marginalized. Part of the task of this book is to make sure that you are aware of the different perspectives that can be trained upon this subject both theoretically and practically.

This mention of alternatives should indicate that there are many choices to be made in this area of organizational endeavour. You don't have to agree with the choices that are made to seek to try to understand them; indeed, such understanding might be felt to be a necessary

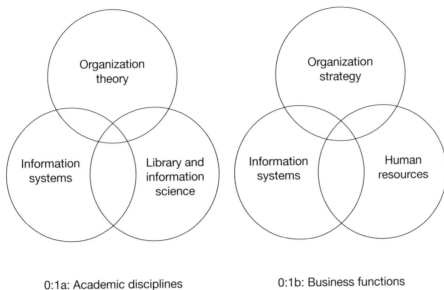

0:1a: Academic disciplines   0:1b: Business functions

Figure 0:1 *The focus of study*

precondition to challenging them. I seek to adopt a critical, questioning approach, which does not assume that because something *is* that that is the way that it *should* be, nor to shut down the possibility that it might be done differently. The widespread focus on knowledge has brought with it some interesting questions about sources of value and power in organizational life. It follows from this approach that this book seeks to offer explanation, not prescription. There are many books available that suggest to you that if you only adopt the particular course of action they advocate then you will meet with success. The furthest I want to go towards prescription is to suggest that it is likely that any approach will fail if not contextualized properly and that, in undertaking this, careful reflection on, and awareness of choices, are vital.

WHERE DOES THE MATERIAL COME FROM?

In seeking to prompt you to ask questions I will be using a range of examples. I will largely draw on the research literature to do this, because I want to use material that has been through an extensive process of 'quality control'. What I am reliant on here is your relating of this material to that which you have encountered elsewhere in your studies or through prolonged experience. I will be supplying extensive references which you can follow up if you want to explore issues in more detail. However, it is not my intention to reproduce material which you may have met elsewhere. Most of you, for example, will at some point encounter ideas about organizational strategy. I will be referring to this material, but only to draw out what I see are the implications for knowledge. I need you, that is, to understand the basics of these areas, just as I won't go into the finer details of, for example, human resource management policies. This means that you might frequently encounter me saying that 'there is an extensive literature' on a particular topic, for which I apologize now. The purpose of this book is to focus on the information dimension of a particular discussion, but this is often so central to so many areas that a complete treatment would result in an enormous book. So I try to supply sufficient references and guidance to further reading for you to be able to explore topics in more depth. I also supply examples drawn from practice which I hope you can relate to organizational contexts known to you.

Having said that I will refer you predominantly to academic literature as the support for my arguments and as the source of further material. I also have to recognize that at certain points this is not possible: academic literature has its own particular gaps and omissions. In part this is because the very processes of quality control which make it more reliable also make it less up to date in this area than one might wish. In addition, as we will see, there are certain preferences for areas of study which mean that I have to draw upon other sources. For example, there is surprisingly little on the impact of the intensive use of data on patterns of organizational learning, and yet such data intensive systems are very important in practice. One can, for instance, read many articles about 'business intelligence' in the trade press which confirm that this is an important topic for practising managers, yet the academic coverage is rather slight. Accordingly, I also draw upon the trade press and my own experience for examples. Of course, we have to be careful here in that what strikes a journalist as being worthy of attention in the short term may prove not to have importance in the long term. However, such sources are often a good guide to emerging trends and practical concerns. If we can combine them with rather more enduring bodies of theory then they can be helpful in fleshing out our understanding. One such body of work is that on the concept of information literacy. This suggests that awareness of sources of information and how they might be used are as important in an age dominated by information and communication technology (ICT) as traditional skills of reading and writing. We will subject these claims to critical attention throughout the book, but in the next section I explore the way in which this concept is addressed.

INFORMATION LITERACY: EXPLAINING A THEME

In this section I explain why the book is structured in the way it is, which requires that I consider the nature of the theoretical assumptions that it rests on. You might at this point choose to skip to the overview of contents, but I hope that you don't (or at least, if you do, I hope you return to this section later). This is because learning should not be a matter of a simple procession of facts. Indeed, it cannot be, for, as we will see, even the most basic of data are profoundly shaped by our theories of the world. From the focus I identified above I have chosen to structure the book around the notion of information literacy. This is one which might be unfamiliar to you and I will explain it in more detail in the next chapter. I have chosen it because it seems an interesting but rather neglected response which has emerged from the library and information science discipline but which seems to have wider applicability. However, as I will explain, it does seem to neglect certain aspects of organizational life which means that as a concept it cannot simply be transferred from the domain of higher education. It is these aspects – the nature of management, the impact of organizational culture and structure, the question of power – that form much of the latter part of the book.

This approach flows from my own theoretical assumptions, which I need to explain briefly. I intend, as I touched on previously, to explore these towards the end of the book, but for now let's introduce some working assumptions. I assume that there is a real world which exists independently of our knowing of it. Our knowledge of that world is always mediated through concepts, hence the importance of discussing theory at this early stage. The social world is constructed by people, but they do so in circumstances not of their own choosing. That is, there is such a thing as 'society' and it consists of structures, like organizations, and ideas, such as theories of management, which have been created by people who may not be now present. That is, all our social activity is both constrained and enabled by forces external to the actors who engage in it. What is important is to examine the inter-relationship between context and action over time. These ideas are derived from a complex tradition of thought known as critical realism, which I think provides us with a rich set of ideas for looking at organizational life. However, this is also difficult material on first acquaintance, so rather than starting with a detailed exposition of these ideas, I have drawn upon the rich tradition of socio-technical approaches to the study of technology in organizations to help me structure the book. This approach is explained in more detail in Chapter 4, but a brief introduction is in order at this point.

In the 1950s researchers at the Tavistock Institute, part of the University of London, formulated an approach to the investigation of technology in work organizations labelled the socio-technical approach. Based in part on an exploration of changes in coal mining, which we explore in more detail in Chapter 4, this suggested technology, roles and structures of work needed to be aligned if the best results were to be obtained. This approach has been an influential one, although the subsequent developments of work humanization were more taken up in other areas of the world, notably the Scandinavian countries, than in the country of origin. Two observations might be made about this approach. One is that some charge it with a tendency towards technological determinism, that is, assuming that certain consequences inevitably flow from the use of particular forms of technology. This is an often over-stated criticism, but the approach here is one which seeks to set technology, and specifically ICT, in its complex social and organizational context. A second is that approaches which continue in this tradition tend to rather underplay debates about the nature of data, information and knowledge, so in the early sections of the book I spend rather more time discussing these concepts in the context of managerial work than is often the case. In the next section I explain the structure of the book in a little more detail in order to give you a sense of what you will encounter in each chapter.

OVERVIEW

Part 1: Setting the scene

In this section I start to develop some working definitions through a discussion of the context in which organizations operate. The first chapter introduces you to the concept of information literacy in the context of a discussion of the 'knowledge economy'. We then, in Chapter 2, consider the way in which information has been considered in accounts of the nature of management. This leads us to a discussion in Chapter 3 of the distinctions between data, information and knowledge. By the end of this section of the book you should have a good grasp of some key terms.

Part 2: Possibilities and constraints

Chapter 4 starts this section with an examination of some of the possibilities that technological developments bring for our manager aspiring to information literacy. This means that I have first to outline some ways of conceptualizing technology. The rest of this chapter then focuses on data intensive applications. Chapter 5 continues our consideration of the development of technology by looking at those applications which have a particular impact on communication. This gives us a sense of possibilities which we can then carry over into the consideration of strategy in Chapter 6. In this chapter we focus in particular on the notion of information strategy, rather than the relationship between Information Systems (IS) and business strategy which is covered in much more detail in the companion volume in this series. In Chapters 7 and 8 we look in turn at structural and individual impacts on the use of information.

Part 3: Culture, power and information

We will have seen that approaches derived from a socio-technical approach tend to neglect or downplay concerns with the impact of culture and power on the use of information, but these can be seen in our discussion in Chapter 9 to be of major importance. However, one concern will be that some of the discussion of these issues has tended to reside within organizational boundaries, without locating those organizations in a wider setting. Accordingly, Chapter 10 considers institutionalist perspectives which relate the workings of organizations to aspects of their setting. This is done in part through the development of the critical realist framework that was touched upon above.

Part 4: Conclusion

The final chapter provides an opportunity to pull together some of the concepts which have been introduced throughout the book, reinforcing the major themes and suggesting some areas for further investigation.

STRUCTURE AND DISTINCTIVE FEATURES OF THE BOOK

The layout followed is standard for the Routledge Information Systems Series. The aim of this is to provide a basis for courses of academic study at the levels identified within its target audience.

- At the beginning of each of the three parts, key questions to be answered by each chapter within that part are identified.
- Each chapter begins with clear learning objectives.
- International perspectives are identified for each of the key topics.
- Case examples are provided.
- Each chapter concludes with a chapter summary.

- Review questions and discussion questions are given towards the end of each chapter.
- A case exercise is given for each of the main topic areas.
- Further reading is suggested at the end of each chapter.

The book crosses the boundaries between the academic disciplines of information systems, organization theory, and library and information sciences, with the aim of providing a focus on questions of knowledge, information and data which are neglected in texts which stay within these boundaries. Information literacy is used as a focal concept.

USE OF THE BOOK FOR TEACHING

As we have seen, each part of the book has specific objectives. The book has been designed as an integrated text but, depending on the aim of the course of study, students may be directed towards the different parts. Courses with limited time might focus on the central part of the book, while those with greater resources might wish to spend more time on the definitional issues in Part One. Where interest is mainly on practical issues, Chapter 11 can be ignored without prejudicing understanding of the rest of the text.

In terms of specific pedagogical features:

- Each chapter begins with learning objectives. Chapters are summarized, and key words and phrases listed. Questions for review and questions for discussion are given towards the end of each chapter.
- Suggested further reading, with a guide as to the relevance of the reading suggested, and references, appear at the end of each chapter.
- A glossary is provided at the end of the book.

Part One

The knowledge economy and managerial work

CHAPTER SUMMARY

KEY QUESTIONS

Chapter 1 Being information literate in the knowledge economy

■ What are the claims made for the knowledge economy, in particular with relation to work organizations?
■ What particular implications are there for skills and competences at work?
■ How can we define the notion of information literacy and how is it shaped by its origins?
■ Do we need to modify information literacy to be able to use it in the context of work organizations?

Chapter 2 Managers and information

■ How do managers use information?
■ How are our views of managerial use of information shaped by looking at managers as decision makers?
■ How are views on information use changed by considering management as communication and negotiation?
■ Can an examination of the function of management help our understanding?

Chapter 3 Data, information and knowledge

■ How can we best characterize data, information and knowledge?
■ What is the importance of data quality and ownership for use within organizations?
■ How important are informal networks in the sharing of information?
■ What is the distinction between tacit and explicit knowledge and how important is it?
■ How can we conceptualize systems of knowing in organizations?

Chapter 1

Being information literate in the knowledge economy

INTRODUCTION

The title to this chapter contains two terms, both of which need careful treatment. The notion that we are in a 'knowledge economy' is a fairly widely used one; information literacy is a little less familiar. However, both are important in setting the context for our later discussions. The idea that we are, at least in the 'developed' world, in a post-industrial age in which information rather than land, capital or labour is the prime input is a staple of much contemporary debate. There are no doubt significant changes at work in the balance of the world economy, but we must be careful not to over-exaggerate these. In many cases the discussion is based on rather vague notions about the nature of information and on an over-emphasis on the potential of information and communication technology (ICT). In this chapter we look at some of the claims that are made in order to set the scene for our deeper consideration of organizational issues.

Whatever our assessment of some of the wilder claims, there seems no doubt that these broader changes have implications for those who work in organizations. One of these implications is, some argue, with the way in which work is approached, particularly at managerial levels. We will discuss some of these claims throughout the book, but one useful notion is that which claims that all employees, and especially managers, in the world of work which is shaped by the knowledge economy will have to be 'information literate'. This is a useful notion in that it takes our attention away from an often obsessive concentration on technology and shifts it to central questions such as what do we mean by information and what counts as being literate in its use? Our discussions of the origins and nature of the concept of information literacy will lead us to question its applicability in the workplace. It will also help set the agenda for the rest of the book.

This chapter will examine:

- the claims made for the knowledge economy
- the implications for those at work in organizations
- the origins of information literacy and its applicability in the workplace
- some of the factors which influence the development of information literacy at work, with particular reference to the managerial use of information

THINKING ABOUT THE KNOWLEDGE ECONOMY

One of the problems with considering the knowledge economy is the plethora of terms which are used. We have the 'information age', the 'digital divide', the 'weightless economy', the 'network age' and so on. These terms are closely bound up with important debates about changes in the nature of the world economy. One is the notion that we are entering a 'post industrial' phase of development, in which the nature of productive activity undergoes a profound shift from manufacturing to services. A second is the idea of globalization, the emergence of a world system of products and services. Of course, these terms are contentious and their very definition remains a topic of debate. Globalization, for example, relates both to increases in world trade and to shifts towards globally organized production systems. While such trends are hotly debated, not only in terms of their consequences but also in terms of the empirical evidence for their existence, there is little doubt that there have been some significant moves in the balance of activities across the world. The term 'post-industrial' can be profoundly misleading, as those involved in the manufacture of goods are at the highest level ever as a proportion of the world's workforce. What the term in fact refers to is the change in the nature of the economy in the so-called 'developed' countries of the world. There has been a massive shift of basic manufacturing to the East, specifically to China, which emerged in the final years of the twentieth century as the manufacturing powerhouse of the world. We have to be careful in assuming that this means the death of manufacturing jobs in the traditional countries of the Industrial Revolution. However, it certainly means significant changes in the balance of those economies. In particular, the shift has been towards both service industries and to those areas of economic activity based on the exploitation of scientific and other knowledge. It is these trends which are summarised in the broad heading of the knowledge economy (Powell and Snellman 2004).

These shifts have attracted attention at the highest level of policy making, with governments in the countries affected anxious to promote both scientific based inquiry in areas such as biotechnology and a considerable increase in the number of those participating in levels of higher education. One of the concerns that we will explore below is that these initiatives tend to overlook the impact of longer term trends across the economy as a whole by focusing on particular sectors with distinctive characteristics. There is also a tendency to rather overplay the impact of technology, with many responses envisaging that simple investment in new forms of ICT by itself will bring about change. So it is important to look at some of the broader trends. One of the key thinkers in this area has been Anthony Giddens. A prominent social theorist, he has also been involved in debates at the policy level, with his formulation of the notion of the 'third way' between capitalism and socialism (Giddens 1998). He has collaborated with the journalist Will Hutton to examine some of the trends in employment and economy (Hutton and Giddens 2000), but his work has suggested some deeper trends. In his *The consequences of modernity* (Giddens 1990) he argues that what he terms 'late modernity', that is, the current phase of development, is characterized by what he terms 'disembedded systems'. These are systems of operation which are removed from the situations of co-presence which characterize other, often earlier, forms of social organization. That is, much of modern life, facilitated by technology, is conducted at different times and in different places from those with whom we share it. This has a number of consequences, not least in making questions of information and knowledge more salient. Giddens suggests four features contributing to the importance of knowledge in the context of such systems:

- larger organizations;
- globalization;
- new forms of organization, particularly regulation;
- expert systems.

Larger organizations demand new styles of management, styles which are often heavily dependent on performance information (in turn enabled by ICT) to monitor and control operations. These organizations often operate in a global fashion, which both makes the use of standard information more important and raises new barriers to its existence, by way of local meaning systems which conflict with the desire for one global picture. Trends, generally summarized under the heading of 'neo-liberalism', have seen new forms of economic regulation, which often depend on the use of data to represent the affairs of organizations, notably those in the public sector or the recently privatized utilities. Hence the widespread use of league tables of performance, where summarized indicators are made available for public consumption in the belief that these will engender competition and so raise standards. Finally, Giddens refers to the way in which we are all increasingly dependent on expert knowledge, often built in to the products and services we use. So, for example, it was once possible for the average motor car driver to diagnose and fix basic problems with their car's engine. Now that these are controlled by sophisticated engine management systems this is no longer possible.

Technology, of course, is central to many of these developments. It has led to some claiming that we are now in a 'network age' in which the nature and shape of organizations is radically changed (Castells 2000). We will examine some of this evidence in a little more detail later, but the work of Giddens and others is often characterized by a rather sweeping approach to the evidence of what is actually happening in organizations (Jones, Orlikowski and Munir 2004). In order to explore this, we need to consider some of the claims that are made about the changing nature of both the products and services organizations provide and the nature of employment. The comments which follow are largely based on experience in the developed countries, as this is where these trends are claimed to have operated with most effect. One starting point might be with the nature of the products on offer. While much attention has been focused on the large shifts in basic manufacturing, there have also been changes in the nature of the more complex manufactured products, changes which impact on the importance of information and knowledge in work organizations.

This shift from products to services and, within products, from simple products to complex ones containing much information, is mirrored in broader shifts in the nature of economic outputs. IBM, for example, is a company which was founded on the production of computer hardware, but now makes more money from its move to services such as consultancy. These service industries are often associated with what Leadbetter (1999) has termed the 'weightless society'. That is, using the power of ICT to overcome barriers of time and distance, much economic activity is involved with the manipulation of representations rather than with the production of tangible outputs. The classic example is the financial services sector, where money does not physically change hands but is represented by symbols which can be exchanged electronically. Coupled with the trends which Giddens identified, this has tended to place more emphasis on the sharing of explicit knowledge, meaning knowledge which can be taken

MANUFACTURING TRAINS: FROM PRODUCTS TO SERVICES

The production of locomotives and rolling stock to run on railways involves the production of large, expensive and complex pieces of machinery. In traditional railway operation, such large items were often manufactured by the railway company which operated them, thus ensuring a close relationship between the machine and the conditions in which it operated. If they did not build the stock themselves, railway companies often closely specified their requirements. Once delivered, stock was maintained by another division of the railway company, which owned and operated extensive repair facilities, often capable of substantially rebuilding equipment. However, conditions of operation in the railway industry have changed, with the emergence of specialist rolling stock manufacturers and, often, the separation of elements of operation of the railway. In the UK, for example, rolling stock is now purchased from specialist manufacturers by leasing companies. These lease the stock to train operating companies, who in turn buy access from the operators of the rail infrastructure. This is an example of the new forms of operation that Giddens discusses, with a complex regulatory regime based on detailed performance measurement.

The consequence for the rolling stock manufacturers is that they no longer simply sell a product, but they also sell services. Most contracts now include not only the delivery of the stock, but also the signing of a maintenance contract, in which the manufacturer undertakes to maintain the equipment for a period of years. This means that the manufacturer now has a direct interest in how the train runs. They use sophisticated on-board software to monitor running and pass back data for diagnostic purposes. There needs to be a two way flow of information and knowledge between the production and maintenance functions. Maintenance will need to know how the trains were constructed, for this will help them in better fault finding and correction. In turn, the lessons that maintenance learn in practice can be of immense value in building trains which will not be so prone to failure. In this way, the organization becomes more connected, with the information produced in one part being of value to others. This *systemic* nature of information use will be seen to be of considerable importance.

Source: Haigh 2000; Wolmar 2001

from its original context and represented in forms which can circulate widely around organizations. This is not without its problems, as we will see in Chapter 3.

However, these changes in the nature of economic outputs also have implications for the nature of employment. Reich (1991) has drawn attention to the importance of what he terms 'symbolic analysts', that is those, classically in the financial sector, who work only with electronic representations. Their skill lies in combining their knowledge of what the symbols represent with their broader knowledge to take action, action which is also dependent on the ICT available to them. The nature of the work means that it is not necessary for it to be tied to one particular place (Knorr-Cetina and Preda 2005). Although this might technically be the case, in practice much of the more skilled work still takes place in particular physical locations, because it also depends on a clustering of expertise, reinforced by more tacit personal relationships. What can be shifted is the 'back office' work, where the symbolic analysts are complemented by a legion of low paid data workers. One major trend has been the 'off shoring' of much of this type of work to economies such as India which possess not only an educated workforce but much lower costs.

Changes in employment also don't only come about because of the nature of the products or services on offer. In addition, we have noted that a major policy commitment of many governments has been to the increased participation of the economically active population in higher education. This is intended to produce a workforce matched to the perceived demands of a knowledge economy. There is some doubt, as we will see below, about the extent to which these demands actually match the supply of the newly qualified (Brown and Hesketh 2004). But what this produces is a workforce with higher levels of educational credentials than before. What this suggests is that styles of management based on command and control are unlikely to be as effective with a workforce that might be looking for more involvement in decision making. This change in workforce composition is significant for our review of the nature of management which we undertake in the next chapter.

However, the example of shifts in the financial services sector should make us pause before celebrating the vision of a high skilled economy. One problem is a matter of definition. Many attempts have been made to show that the balance of the workforce is shifting towards 'knowledge workers', but such attempts are fraught with problems of definition. It is often hard to disentangle manufacturing from services (particularly in areas such as distribution) but even harder to take out the 'information' elements from jobs. This is because all human activity involves some use of information and the application of some knowledge, even (and one might say especially) in more 'traditional' applications (Mutch 1998). The problem here is that we tend to equate information with that which can be stored in a computer, thus downplaying the tacit knowledge acquired through means such as the apprenticeship. Thus, in a review which still has much relevance, David Lyons (1988) cast considerable doubt on attempts to show that a particular proportion of a nation's workforce could be classified as undertaking 'information work'. He noted that some of these definitions stretched credibility and diverted our attention away from the way in which information plays a role in most occupations. This concern to relate information too closely to technology in a direct sense also diverted our attention away from the growth in occupations such as those in distribution, where a key barrier to the growth of the information economy lay in the shortage of, for example, lorry drivers. In other words, the 'weightless' economy depended very much on some very weighty, that is, very much physical, occupations.

Part of the problem, then, with some of these discussions is that they pay too much attention to particular occupations. In part this glosses over the fact that divergent changes can be happening within the same organizations. Thus, Burris (1993) points to increasing polarization within work organizations, with highly paid 'symbolic analysts' sharing the organization (if not the workspace) with considerable numbers of workers carrying out highly routine tasks. Since her work, this phenomenon has been emphasized by the growth of call centre work, work which is often highly scripted and tightly monitored, offering none of the responsibility afforded to the classic 'knowledge worker' – yet this work is centrally implicated in questions of information and knowledge. Another problem with these discussions is that they tend to focus on particular types of organization, often under the heading of the 'knowledge intensive firm' (Alvesson 2004). Often applied to organizations such as consultancies and advertising agencies, this can have the impact of not only glossing over internal divisions within organizations, but also of diverting our attention away from organizations operating in a more 'traditional' style. As we will see, such organizations often use intensive data analysis to support their activities, but this style of operation is one which we can often overlook. In our discussions, then, we will need to be sensitive to the full range of occupations and organizations which are affected by the broader shifts we have discussed.

To summarize this part of the discussion, we have seen that changes in the nature of economic outputs have had an impact on the importance of information and knowledge in work organizations. However, this discussion has been at the level of national economies: what implications do these trends have for those inside organizations, especially those seeking to manage them? We will review the nature of the managerial use of information in the next chapter but for now we can note that the changes we have reviewed seem to place greater stress on the ability of managers to interpret their world. This need for interpretation has led some to suggest that information literacy might be a useful way of conceptualizing some of the skills required.

INFORMATION LITERACY: ORIGINS AND APPLICATION

It was Peter Drucker, one of the first to identify the changes which were to be labelled as 'knowledge work', who suggested that '[t]o be information literate, you need to begin with learning what it is you need to know'. He went on to argue that '[n]ow that knowledge is taking the place of capital as the driving force in organizations worldwide, it is all too easy to confuse data with knowledge and information technology with information' (Harris 1993: 120). These comments are echoed elsewhere. For example, in a book about information technology, aimed at practising managers, N. Caroline Daniels (1994: 67) argues that, '[r]elatively few people are information literate and even fewer understand the relevance of information to their business visions'. The problem with such statements is that they do not begin to specify what information literacy might be. However, there is a domain of inquiry in which this question has been taken up in some detail, and in which it remains a concern of some importance. This is the discipline of library and information science (LIS).

The roots of the concern with information literacy on the part of librarians can be traced in large part to the threats posed by the opening up of new routes to information by ICT. The by-passing of traditional skills of locating information meant a concern to probe just what these skills consisted of. In the process, a body of work has been built up which suggests that using information involves far more than simply knowing where to look (Mutch 1997). This work was pursued in particular in the arena of higher education, where the perceived threat to the status and jobs of librarians was at its highest. It was recognized that this expanded definition meant that librarians needed to work in partnership with others, notably academics, in building information skills into course provision. This resulted in the concern with information literacy spreading its appeal, a process which went furthest in Australia. The influential Candy report (Candy, Crebert and O'Leary 1994) suggested that all graduates from Australian universities ought to possess a number of skills, among which was information literacy. An information literate graduate would possess the following attributes:

- knowledge of major current resources;
- ability to frame researchable questions;
- ability to locate, evaluate, manage and use information in a range of contexts;
- ability to retrieve information using a variety of media;
- ability to decode information in a variety of forms;
- critical evaluation of information.

One point to note immediately about these attributes is that they are not dependent on, or even explicit about, the use of ICT. This draws a clear contrast with the related notion of computer literacy, unlike some other accounts which confuse the two. For example Kanter, in arguing that the concept of information literacy 'will be mandatory', envisages it as comprising:

An understanding of the general concepts of information processing; how computer systems support and shape a person's job function, the tradeoffs between investment and benefits, time expended, and time saved; and the application areas that will give a company a strategic advantage.

(Kanter 1992: 373)

While we might agree that these are important areas for development, they are shaped by a heritage in the domain of what is known in computer science as 'end-user computing'. This is a specialized area of endeavour, in which computer users build applications using packages

USING PAPER-BASED INFORMATION EFFECTIVELY

Butterfly World in Stockton-on-Tees in the UK is a small tourist attraction in the north of England which was concerned to increase its visitor numbers. Its advertising was initially based on visitors to the region, but an examination of a customer survey indicated that large numbers came from the immediate locality. It was decided to refocus advertising, monitor response rates and use the results in deciding future policies. All this was done using a paper based system.

Source: Hanage 1994

such as spreadsheets or databases. However, there are many more people using computers to help them generate information and many examples of information which are not dependent on computers at all.

The problem with definitions which emphasize the use of ICT is that they tend to fall into a view of information as something object-like, rather than involving processes of human-centred meaning creation. Christine Bruce (1997) draws out this distinction in her work which suggests that among her respondents in higher education seven conceptions (which she termed seven 'faces') of what it meant to be information literate could be teased out. The first four of these very much corresponded to an 'objective' view of information, exposing roots not only in computer science but also in other disciplines – including in the library, where a tradition of the custodianship of books could engender similar notions. Bruce places these conceptions on a continuum, contrasting them with more subjective ideas which emphasized the overlap with what we might term 'critical thinking'. This placed much more emphasis, as we have seen Drucker do, on the formulation of questions. This, then, would suggest that the information literate manager might start with what they needed to know, rather than with the information available. Bruce went on to suggest how the seven faces that she identified might be linked to workplace experiences, as summarized in Table 1.1.

So, for example, a view which relates information literacy entirely to the effective use of ICT might produce a focus on the use of tools like the Internet to derive information about the environment within which the organization operates. The problem here is that this is likely to place a premium on skills of information retrieval rather than on the evaluation of the material gathered. It is as we move from this conceptualization that we might start to get more such evaluation and in the process draw on different resources. So if we adopt an information control perspective, for example, we may use librarians and their skills for the more effective cataloguing and recording of information. It could be argued, however, that this would give us little guidance as to how the information might be used. As we move through the conceptualizations, so we find more emphasis placed on what we might term 'systems of knowing'. These

Table 1.1 *Seven faces of information literacy*

Workplace processes that correspond to the seven faces of information literacy	
The seven faces of IL [Individual]	Workplace processes [Organizational]
The information technology experience	Environmental scanning
The information sources experience	Provision of in-house and external information resources and services
The information process experience	Information processing; packaging for internal/external consumption
The information control experience	Information/records management, archiving
The knowledge construction experience	Corporate memory
The knowledge extension experience	Research and development
The wisdom experience	Professional ethics/codes of conduct

Source: Bruce 1999: 43; reproduced by permission of Elsevier

emanate in the 'wisdom' face, for example, from outside the organization and draw on aspects of professional socialization.

It is fair to point out that these are tentative steps and in this book we will explore both the value of a focus on systems of knowing and the limitations of a focus on information literacy. Bruce (1999) has indeed argued that there is a need to generalize work on information literacy, which has been developed almost exclusively in the domain of higher education, to the world of the workplace. She points out that it cannot be assumed that the attributes which can be developed in higher education can be transferred into work organizations. Despite some limited work, there has been relatively little investigation of the notion of information literacy in the workplace (Bruce and Candy 2000; O'Sullivan 2002). In part this is because, as we have seen in the preface, the issue is one which falls between discipline areas. In part, also, it is because there are people with specific roles in the world of higher education who have an interest in the agenda posed by information literacy and sufficient position to get it taken seriously. By contrast, those with an LIS background who go into broader work organizations often find their position a rather marginal one, in which it is difficult to influence wider debates. However, a further reason might be because of some very sharp distinctions between the nature of information use at work and within education, distinctions which we look at in the next section.

INFORMATION LITERACY AND MANAGERIAL WORK

In this section I will draw on some work I have done with a group of managers which I have used to indicate some of the key differences between the use of information in higher education and that in the workplace (Mutch 1999). The two are not altogether divorced, for this group of managers was one which I encountered during the delivery of a course which was intended to get them thinking about their use of information. They were a group of fairly experienced junior and middle managers, many of whom had very little formal education beyond secondary school. They worked in a diverse range of functions within a food manufacturing company, a company working in a sector characterized by tight margins and insistent time pressure. The first difference to which they can draw our attention is summed up in the following:

> I have been a production manager at . . . for 17 months and worked in production for a total of 4.5 years, during this time I have never really thought about what information I required and what information I supply, while performing my daily tasks.
>
> (Mutch 1999: 325)

By contrast with higher education, where information is required for a specific task, the parameters of which are often supplied and defined in some detail, these managers had to structure their own information needs. This often meant that they assumed that the information they got was the information they needed.

The point of the story in the box overleaf is that not only might information be produced in organizations that has no purpose, but also that its existence produces explanations. It is taken for granted that existence means that it is legitimate (especially if computer produced) and that its limitations are put up with. Often it is difficult for busy managers to challenge the

THE CASE OF THE UNOPENED ENVELOPE

When carrying out research on the ways in which public house managers in the UK used information, I asked one manager to retain a month's correspondence for me and indicate what he did with it – did he action it, dispose of it, file it? When I examined the bundle, I came across a brown envelope, unopened, marked 'file'. When I asked the manager about what appeared to be an unusual action he explained that this was an invoice for the beer he had had delivered from the brewery which owned the pub. He had no choice about where he got his beer from, he explained, and he already had checked off quantities and prices against the delivery note which had accompanied the beer. So he felt that the invoice was of no value to him, but he had better retain it just in case it might be called for. This seemed a little wasteful, so on my next visit to the head office I asked about why the invoice was needed. 'Ah, that's for the auditors,' I was told, 'they need it when they visit the pub to check stocks against the till.' I was visiting a few pubs, so on my next visit I put this to the joint managers, a very well organized couple whose pub was one of the top performers in the country. 'Well,' I was informed, 'we never use it and we've just had an audit visit. They never used it either – they had all they needed on their laptops.' And so I pursued the mystery of the unopened envelope across the company, being told plausible stories about the need for its existence and getting equally plausible rebuttals from those 'on the ground'. Finally I reached the office of the information director. On being told about the unused invoices, he simply thanked me for reminding him that he had needed for some time to stop its production – it had been seen as a good idea once, but was recognized by senior managers as being redundant.

Source: Mutch 2001

necessity for information, or to get it reformulated into something which they can use. So managers face a different world from students, one in which they not only have to determine for themselves what information is needed, but also have little time (or perhaps inclination) to reflect on what might be needed. In such a situation they tend to fall back on what is already in existence, assuming that this is what they ought to use. Our information literate manager might need to start, that is, by recognizing the existence of this situation, something which is very difficult when they have other competing pressures on their time. (We explore some more theoretical conceptualizations of this situation in the following chapter.)

A further consideration can be illustrated by words from another manager in this group:

I have always, . . . thought of the information as 'operational' [now] . . . I am aware that not only do I receive operational information but tactical information, and strategic information, each to a lesser degree.

(Mutch 1999: 326)

For most of the tasks which students are set, not only has the initial questioning already been done, but also there are clear criteria about what information might be relevant. In particular, there is a hierarchy of quality, related to control mechanisms such as peer review, which gives an initial measure of suitability. This can be further enhanced by knowledge of other indicators, such as citation measures. There is an elaborate set of conventions to do with the referencing of evidence which can give some degree of reassurance about fitness for purpose. These indicators do not always exist in the workplace, in particular because the same information can serve different purposes. This context then shapes the type of information which is required. Without an awareness that different sorts of information might be relevant in different contexts, information appears as an undifferentiated mass. This can lead to the phenomenon of information overload, in which users are paralysed by the sheer volume of what is on offer. Keegan reports the words of one sufferer:

> 'They didn't give me any training in how to manage the information, or what was important', she says. 'If you ask for help you think you are failing. I wish now that I had, but there was so much pressure to succeed. I had to work 13 or 14 hours a day coping with thick wodges of computer printouts, emails, 30 to 40 memos a day and notes.'
>
> (Keegan 1996: 2)

One approach to tackling this is to seek to reduce the volume of information on offer. However, a more productive approach might be to place more emphasis on the quality of the questions asked. This can prompt the awareness that much of what is on offer is simply irrelevant and can be safely put to one side. Our information literate manager needs to have some means of sifting what is relevant from the mass of material which demands their attention.

Another consideration is the form that information takes. While in higher education this is predominantly in the shape of pre-formed material, stored and accessible in particular locations, in the workplace it is much more likely to be bound up in a web of social relationships. Indeed, it could be that the key skills for information literate managers are ones of persuasion and communication. As we will see, some argue that it is communicative competence which is most important for managers, something touched upon by another from our group of managers, who observed that she recognized 'the need to provide information rather than data, by actively taking into consideration the end users' needs' (Mutch 1999: 327).

This is another consideration which distinguishes information use in the workplace. While a key part of the student's skill is the rendering of information in the appropriate form, be that an essay, an examination or a presentation, these forms tend to be tightly specified in advance. The judgement is often not on what new information has been transferred but on how well existing information has been sourced and collated. The focus here, as one might expect from the roots in the library, is on awareness of sources and effective access to them. By contrast, in the workplace the focus might be on what is done with the information produced, with many people being at the start rather than the end of the chain of use. While some might argue that technological developments will see this information supply role diminish, we will see that studies of use indicate that it is, in particular, middle managers who play a pivotal role in filtering and shaping information for use by others. In such endeavours a key skill might be that of ascertaining the needs of others, something that we will see in the context of managerial use of information is no easy task.

The final consideration arising from our group of managers, and we might consider it the most significant one, is that of power. Expressing this in terms of 'strong cultural influences' this manager observed that information use:

. . . arises from a strong need for control and to invite comments from the department's more junior staff, let alone customers, would be high risk as it might lead to a challenge, which would not be welcome, of the status quo.

(Mutch 1999: 327)

While there are clearly questions of control in educational relationships (as in any relationship) such questions are often mediated by checks and balances in the educational context. In particular, there is a high premium placed, in name at least, on the reflexive discussion of such issues. In the workplace the question of power, either on an individual or an organizational level, is often not directly raised but something of which participants are often acutely aware.

CONCLUSION

There are, then, some important differences between the use of information in educational settings and in the workplace which mean that we cannot simply transfer the concept without modification. In the same way, we might want to argue that these differences place some limits on the extent to which skills of information literacy learned during higher education are transferable to work organizations. However, for all these caveats, the idea remains a useful one, in drawing our attention to a range of considerations far beyond the technical. In particular, it raises a number of questions that we need to address in the discussion that follows. These can be summarized as follows:

- The use of information has been seen to be embedded in context. This shapes, in particular, the questions which are to be asked, which we have seen as perhaps the most important of the attributes associated with information literacy. In many cases this context is complex and difficult to establish, with the result perhaps being that what exists is taken for granted. This is a consideration that we need to take into our discussion of the managerial use of information in the next chapter.
- The nature of information is itself a matter of some interpretation. As we have seen, managers may feel themselves not necessarily aware of distinctions, so we need to pursue these questions a little further.
- While information literacy is not to be reduced to computer literacy, ICT remains an important consideration and our information literate manager needs an awareness of the impact of technology on the information available to her.
- What counts as information in the context of the work organization is shaped by the nature of that organization. Information literacy is not therefore simply a matter of an individual set of skills, but is profoundly embedded in a web of relations, some of which appear as external to and constraining of individual action. We need, in particular, to be concerned with how questions of power within organizations affect the nature of information use.
- Finally, if we have assumed that information literacy skills cannot simply be transferred from other forms of education and that they need forms of translation to be effective in the workplace, then training ought to be a prime consideration.

SUMMARY

- Changes in the nature of the world economy have meant that questions of information and knowledge have become more salient in work organizations. These changes relate not only to the nature of products and services, but also to the characteristics of the workforce. Policy commitments to higher participation in formal education have meant an increased emphasis on credentials and challenges to styles of management.

- While these changes are important, too much attention to specific occupations or to specific forms of organization can blind us to the nature of changes taking place across occupations and organizations. In particular, there has been a good deal of work on emerging forms of organization which tends to neglect equally important changes in more traditional organizations. Here, the use of intensive data capture and manipulation seems significant.

- Information literacy is one way of thinking about some of the shifts in skills required to operate in contemporary organizations. The concept has been developed in the education world, particularly in higher education, but its focus on information broadly drawn, as opposed to information technology, offers a valuable corrective to an over emphasis on technological considerations.

- There are significant differences between information use at work and in higher education which means that we need further work to make the concept useful for us. In particular, these differences relate to the embeddedness of managers in an existing context, their lack of time for reflection on alternatives, their positioning in a complex web of relationships and the influence of power on their use of information.

REVIEW QUESTIONS

1 What is the knowledge economy?

2 What are the key dimensions of information literacy?

3 What factors might differentiate information literacy at work from that in higher education?

DISCUSSION QUESTIONS

1 Apply the ideas about the knowledge economy to an industry with which you are familiar. Can you think of products that have knowledge embedded in them?

2 Can you apply the ideas about information literacy to an industry with which you are familiar?

CASE EXERCISE

Shorko is a French manufacturer of packaging film. It upgraded its process control system to control inputs automatically, with the results being displayed on screens in a central control room. The data from the system were stored in a separate system which enabled the production of information about trends and relationships between particular inputs and the quality of outputs. (We will encounter aspects of the Shorko case in later chapters; here it is introduced to help you think through the implications of the discussion in this chapter.)

1 What implications for the information literacy required of process workers and managers might there be?

2 How does the increasing importance of data and information to the firm fit with the idea of the knowledge economy?

FURTHER READING

Brown, J. S. and Duguid, P. (2002) *The Social Life of Information*. Harvard Business School Press, Cambridge, MA.

A very accessible discussion of some of the issues raised by the increased availability of information, with some sceptical comments about those enthusiastic for technological solutions.

Bruce C. (1997) *Seven Faces of Information Literacy*. Adelaide, AUSLIB Press.

While this book is about higher education, it should be read in conjunction with her article about information literacy in the workplace to get a full grasp of the complexity involved in the concept.

Dutton, W. (1999) *Society on the Line: Information Politics in the Digital Age*. Oxford University Press, Oxford.

An overview by the director of a major research project into the broader impacts of ICT with a number of short essays contributed by other researchers on the project. A very good introduction to some of the broader aspects of the changes considered in this chapter.

REFERENCES

Alvesson, M. (2004) *Knowledge Work and Knowledge-Intensive Firms*. Oxford, Oxford University Press.

Brown, P. and Hesketh, A. (2004) *The Mismanagement of Talent: Employability and Jobs in the Knowledge Economy*. Oxford, Oxford University Press.

Bruce, C. (1997) *Seven Faces of Information Literacy*. Adelaide, AUSLIB Press.

Bruce, C. (1999) 'Workplace experiences of information literacy', *International Journal of Information Management*, 19(1): 33–47.

Bruce, C. and Candy, P. (2000) *Information Literacy: Advances in Programs and Research*. Wagga Wagga NSW, Charles Sturt University.

Burris, B. (1993) *Technocracy at Work*, Albany, State University of New York Press.

Candy, P. C., Crebert, G. and O'Leary, J. (1994) *Developing Lifelong Learners Through Undergraduate Education*. Canberra, Australian Government Publishing Service.

Castells, M. (2000) *The Rise of the Network Society*. Oxford, Blackwell.

Daniels, N. C. (1994) *Information Technology: The Management Challenge*. Wokingham, Addison-Wesley.

Giddens, A. (1990) *The Consequences of Modernity*. Cambridge, Polity.

Giddens, A. (1998) *The Third Way: The Renewal of Social Democracy*. Cambridge, Polity.

Haigh, P. (2000) 'The Unacceptable Face of Train Acceptance?', *Rail*, 379: 36–40.

Hanage, R. (1994) *Making Information Work for You: A Briefing for Senior Managers of Small and Medium-Sized Companies*. London, Department of Trade and Industry.

Harris, T. G. (1993) 'The Post-Capitalist Executive: An Interview with Peter F. Drucker', *Harvard Business Review*, 71(3): 115–122.

Hutton, W. and Giddens, A. (2000) *On the Edge: Living with Global Capitalism*. London, Chatto & Windus.

Jones, M., Orlikowski, W. and Munir, K. (2004) 'Structuration Theory and Information Systems: A Critical Reappraisal', in J. Mingers and L. Willcocks (eds) *Social Theory and Philosophy for Information Systems*. Chichester, Wiley: 297–328.

Kanter, J. (1992) *Managing with Information*. New Jersey, Prentice Hall.

Keegan, V. (1996) 'Brain storms', *The Guardian (Online supplement)*, 5 November: 2–3.

Knorr-Cetina, K. and Preda, A. (2005) *The Sociology of Financial Markets*. Oxford, Oxford University Press.

Leadbetter, C. (1999) *Living on Thin Air: The New Economy*. London, Viking.

Lyon, D. (1988) *The Information Society: Issues and Illusions*. Cambridge, Polity.

Mutch, A. (1997) 'Information Literacy: An Exploration', *International Journal of Information Management*, 17(5): 377–386.

Mutch, A. (1998) 'The Impact of Information Technology on 'Traditional' Occupations: The Case of Welding', *New Technology, Work and Employment*, 13(2): 140–149.

Mutch, A. (1999) 'Critical Realism, Managers and Information', *British Journal of Management*, 10: 323–333.

Mutch, A. (2001) 'Information and Agency: The Case of the Unopened Envelope', in R. Roberts, M. Moulton, S. Hand and C. Adams (eds) *Information Systems in the Digital World*. Manchester, Zeus: 66–75.

O'Sullivan, C. (2002) 'Is Information Literacy Relevant in the Real World?' *Reference Services Review*, 30(1): 7–14.

Powell, W. W. and Snellman, K. (2004) 'The Knowledge Economy', *Annual Review of Sociology*, 30: 199–220.

Reich, R. (1991) *The Work of Nations: Preparing Ourselves for 21st Century Capitalism*. New York, Knopf.

Wolmar, C. (2001) *Broken Rails: How Privatisation Wrecked Britain's Railways*. London, Aurum.

25

Chapter 2

Managers and information

INTRODUCTION

There is, of course, extensive literature on the nature of management, literature in which questions of data, information and knowledge often figure. These questions, though, are often treated rather implicitly. In this chapter, we look at some important discussions of the nature of management, with a view to bringing such questions to the fore. Our discussion will frame many of the issues which are dealt with in the following chapters.

This chapter will examine:

■ the manager as decision maker, with the image of information as structured data
■ the manager as communicator and negotiator, with the focus on information as emergent and relational
■ the function of the manager, with a particular focus on the importance of interpretation

We do this through a review of how some major writers have conceived of management and how information has figured in these conceptions. We start by reviewing the contribution of management science.

THE MANAGER AS DECISION MAKER

A very important theme in much writing about managers and information is that management is about decision making and that information is used to reduce uncertainty. We will question both of these focuses in our discussion, but we need to start with the development of this very important school of thought. By looking at its development, we can see the roots of these powerful ideas, ideas which persist in much of the writing about these issues. However, these ideas are increasingly questioned from a number of directions. In particular, the reliance of these ideas on a particular view of the application of the scientific method needs to be placed in the conditions which brought them into being.

While many of the ideas that underlay the development of what we can broadly term management science were developed in embryonic form before the Second World War (1939–45), it was the experience of the logistical challenges of that massive conflict that brought them to prominence. Mathematical techniques such as linear programming and queuing theory, often collectively known under the heading of operations research, were used to plan operations such as the extensive Allied bombing raids over Germany. The prestige which this brought to such techniques and the practical knowledge that was gained made them attractive in the booming conditions of American industry after the war (Locke 1989). Not faced with the ruined factories and industrial infrastructures of Europe and Asia, and with highly productive facilities converted from war use, these were the years of the massive expansion of the bureaucratic industrial corporation in the USA. Such corporations were faced with the twin challenges of mass production and mass consumption, challenges which seemed ideal for the application of new mathematical techniques. In parallel, the war effort had also seen the development of computing technology, initially for the work of code breaking. Such technology gradually became available for commercial applications. These two related practical developments were also paralleled by developments in thinking about management.

Such thinking had its roots in broader concerns about the nature of decision making, concerns associated in particular with the work of Herbert Simon and his collaborators. Simon was an economist who won the Nobel Prize for Economics in 1978, but his interests lay in the synthesis of an array of ideas to understand decision making in organizations. He drew upon developments in cognitive psychology and computing to lay the foundations of developments in artificial intelligence. These foundations led him to draw a distinction between programmed and unprogrammed decisions (Simon 1977). Programmed decisions were those decisions which were taken on a routine and regular basis. The detailed rules that underlay those decisions could be formulated, often in mathematical terms, and followed to give similar (and if followed properly, optimum) results in each case. For example, stock control models work on the basis of determining the cost of holding stock, the time taken to replenish it and the level of demand. Once these are available, then they can be placed into a mathematical model and the decision taken automatically. It is not a great step from this to place such a model in a computer program, and programs of this type are widespread in many basic business applications. One example is credit scoring models, which automate many lending decisions by specifying particular variables and the rules which connect them. This brought radical changes to the position of bank branch manager, from taking lending decisions to managing sales teams.

Simon distinguished such decisions from those which were unprogrammed. Such decisions were those which happened infrequently and required the exercise of judgement. Because of this, no rules existed which could be refined in mathematical terms – or, at least, this is how it might appear on the surface. For Simon, the challenge was to get behind the surface and discover underlying patterns. It might be, he argued, that unprogrammed decisions were in fact the result of chains of what could be programmed decisions. The challenge therefore, was to break down these complex decisions to find the underlying patterns, patterns which could

27

then be simulated using the power of computing. We will return to the problems with this view of human thinking when we look in a little more detail at artificial intelligence in Chapter 5, but it has to seen in the context of a very optimistic view about the development of cognitive science. This was, moreover, what one might term a reductionist form of science, in which specific parts of the brain would be responsible for particular patterns of thought. However, the subsequent development of brain science suggests that such a reductionist programme needs to be rejected in favour of a more holistic approach (Rose 1993). This debate continues, but it suggests some limitations on Simon's enthusiasm for technological developments. This enthusiasm lay behind his prediction in 1977 that '[w]e are gradually acquiring the technological means, through these techniques, to automate all management decisions, nonprogrammed as well as programmed' (Simon 1977: 30). This vision was placed in a strictly hierarchical view of decision making, in which decisions taken at operational and tactical levels would increasingly be taken by computer, with a limited number of unprogrammed decisions being reserved for senior managers at the strategic level.

However, Simon did recognize some limits to this perspective. These limits were, he argued, economic and social rather than technological. However, there is a sense in which the other activities in which managers were engaged were underplayed, with the limits being those of human cognition rather than organizational context. In sketching out these limits, Simon and his collaborators were informed by developments in cognitive psychology. These indicated the limits on human decision making expressed in the term that Simon developed, 'bounded rationality'. This held that while humans sought to take decisions in a rational fashion, rationality had limits because of the cognitive limits on the ability to process information. That is, a purely 'rational' decision would demand that all alternatives be assessed in order to arrive at the optimum solution, with the collection and analysis of all the appropriate information. However, for most significant decisions the range of potential alternatives and the volumes of information required were beyond human capacities to comprehend. Rather, then, than optimize, Simon argued that human decision makers 'satisficied'. That is, they selected decision alternatives on the basis of those with which they were familiar and which lay close to the decision space and they processed just enough information to be able to select between this narrower range of options. The challenge was then to ensure that the right alternatives were selected, the appropriate information collected and the analysis done in an appropriate way.

Much of the effort in cognitive psychology in this tradition has been expended on exploring the types of bias to which human beings are prone and which affect these processes. Schwenk (1988) uses this literature to point to a number of biases which might impact on strategic decision making (Table 2.1). For example, he draws attention to the availability bias, whereby we recall particularly vivid events (which may very well be atypical) and generalize inappropriately from them. The overall conclusion might be that human beings make very poor intuitive statisticians, being prone to find patterns where none exist or to miss those which are present because they do not fit existing models (Hodgkinson and Sparrow 2002).

Pursuing an approach based on cognitive psychology means that the emphasis of our analysis will tend to be on individual characteristics. The challenges in such an approach are the identification of common cognitive patterns and action taken to correct or enhance these as appropriate, which tends to neglect the influence of the social setting in which these attributes are developed and applied. It also produces a particular image of information, as clearly expressed in the following:

Table 2.1 *Selected heuristics in strategic decision making*

Bias	Effects
Availability	Judgements of probability of easily-recalled events distorted
Selective perception	Expectations may bias observations of variables relevant to strategy
Illusory correlation	Encourages belief that unrelated variables are correlated
Conservatism	Failure sufficiently to revise forecasts based on new information
Law of small numbers	Overestimation of the degree to which small samples are representative of populations
Regression bias	Failure to allow for regression to the mean
Wishful thinking	Probability of desired outcomes judged to be inappropriately high
Illusion of control	Overestimation of personal control over outcomes
Logical reconstruction	'Logical' reconstruction of events which cannot be accurately recalled
Hindsight bias	Overestimation of predictability of past events

Source: Adapted from Schwenk 1988: 44

Nowadays, with computers everywhere, we can think of information as something almost tangible: strings of symbols which, like strips of steel or plastic ribbons, can be processed – changed from one form to another. We can think of white-collar organization as factories for processing information.

(Simon, 1977: 45)

This is the image of information as structured data. It places the computer at the centre, with information being that which can be processed and stored in mechanical form. Many would argue that this is to confuse information with data, something which we will return to in the next chapter. And it is an image of information, and the role of managers in its creation and use, that is at considerable odds with many other views of management. There are two major lines of objection to the manager as decision maker tradition. One, which we will consider in much more detail in the next section, is that it misrepresents what managers actually do. This tradition, developed through studies of what managers actually do rather than what they are supposed to do, can be extended to challenge the very notion of decision making. However, there is another line of work which accepts that decision making is important but questions some of the approaches that we have discussed. This is the focus on naturalistic decision making.

Those who look at naturalistic decision making argue that decision making needs to be studied in context (Lipshitz, Klein and Carroll 2006). That is, much of the knowledge which underpins the decision making approach has been gained from laboratory experiments. In these settings research subjects, often students volunteering for course credits, are presented with simulated settings and their responses measured. While this can yield much useful information for some subjects, the concern is that what we learn, at best, is how a particular population (and not necessarily a typical one) reacts to artificial tasks. By contrast, in organizations both the participants and the context may be considerably different. Organizational contexts for decisions may not present themselves clearly. The demand for a decision may occur in conditions of stress, producing heightened emotions which might alter the response to stimulus. In other cases the information might simply not be available.

For example, in an extensive review of the use of information for performance appraisals, DeNisi (1996) noted that much of the information that rating was based on was historical information. It might be information that was never formally recorded, as it was not anticipated that it would be used for another purpose and so was subject to problems with recall. 'The critical realization,' he argues, 'though, was that *most* of the information raters used for making appraisal decision, had to be acquired in a way that would make it difficult for that information to be organized in memory' (DeNisi 1996: 67; emphasis in original). This could lead different raters using an identical rating instrument to rate the same candidate very differently. This suggested to DeNisi that the problem was that much research had focused on processes of micro-cognition, but that the need was 'to consider organization-level contextual variables, and even consider the environment beyond the organization when we study HR practices such as appraisals' (DeNisi 1996: 185–186). This raises an important tension that we will need to be aware of throughout, the delicate balance between individual and organizational factors. While we need to be aware of the cognitive limitations of human beings, such cognitions are shaped by and used in organizational contexts which also have a profound effect on their content. It is to the study of managers in context that we turn next.

MANAGERS IN CONTEXT: COMMUNICATION AND NEGOTIATION

The prestige of both management science in industrial and commercial practice and of scientific approaches in universities lent a good deal of weight to the decision making tradition. It coincided with attempts to lay out structural theories for organizations which spelled out the optimum size and scope of operations. However, even within such traditions some questions started to be raised. In the late 1960s, for example, a leading management science researcher, Russell Ackoff, raised some concerns about the direction of inquiries which are still pertinent. They centred round the increasing emphasis on the importance of computing technology and the associated attitudes. He suggested that there were five conventional assumptions about managers and information which were misleading, if not completely wrong. These were, as expressed in his abstract:

> (1) the critical deficiency under which most managers operate is the lack of relevant information, (2) the manager needs the information he wants, (3) if a manager has the information he needs his decision making will improve, (4) better communication between managers improves organizational performance, and (5) a manager does not have to understand how his information system works, only how to use it.
>
> (Ackoff 1967: 147)

By contrast, argued Ackoff, many managers suffered from an excess of information, information which they lacked the ability to filter effectively. Even if they could get the information they required, there was no necessary correlation between possession or access and use. This challenge to the hegemony of computerized decision systems was taken further by others who challenged the decision making tradition in more radical ways. They formed part of a tradition which reacted against what they saw was the reductionist and prescriptive bent of much theorizing, abstracting as it did from the lived experience of managers. They were concerned to look at what it was that managers actually did in practice, not what they said they did in questionnaires or what their organizations (and their consultants) said they should do. Of particular importance here was the work of Henry Mintzberg.

In the early 1970s Mintzberg carried out detailed observation on five senior managers (Mintzberg 1973). His observations were that such managers had a fragmented work pattern, unable to spend long on any task and prone to interruption. As well as having to switch from task to task, they seemed to display a preference for an action orientation, one which was not given to the detailed examination of routine reports. Rather, they often depended on subordinates to get information for them and preferred to get this orally. They gained a good deal of their information through informal means, such as discussions at the beginning and end of meetings. Much of their work involved engagements outside the organization, in which they gleaned information through their networks. This paints a very different picture of the manager from that we get from the decision making school. While confined in this case to senior managers, these type of findings seem to hold good for many managers.

Kurke and Aldrich (1978) found that the same patterns held true when they replicated the study with four managers in 1978. Over a decade later Stephens (1993), in an echo of the original research, followed five chief information officers around for a period of a week each and found patterns which were remarkably similar, in particular the frantic pace of work and the action orientation. One shift which clearly represented developments since the early 1970s was the importance of electronic mail, although even here much of the work was done by personal assistants applying filters. Boisot and Liang (1992), in a study of six Chinese enterprise directors found similar behavioural patterns, although they stressed the very different institutional setting. Finally, Moss-Jones (1990) observed that ICT, rather than giving managers more time for reflection, was in fact increasing the pace and fragmentation of work. Thus, there seems strong support for the argument that when managers are observed in the field that their patterns of information use are at a considerable distance from that envisaged in the decision making tradition. In particular, the use of information as structured data seems a relatively minor part of activity.

Mintzberg continued to develop his thinking in this area, although his work shifted more into the areas of strategic planning and, more recently, management education. However, in 1994 he attempted to provide a synthesis of his ideas on the nature of managerial work which placed the nature of managerial information use in context. In 'Rounding out the manager's job' he suggested that there were three ways in which a manager could control and influence activities: through information, through people or through action (Mintzberg 1994). The action dimension was where managers got directly involved in the execution of tasks. The people dimension was where tasks were delegated to people and the manager's role was the delegation and monitoring of activity. The least direct method was by managing through information, but this was an orientation of significant importance.

Mintzberg suggests that all three roles are present in managerial activity but the variety comes in which are preferred and how they are performed. He further notes that while some of the informational role, the controlling of people and through them tasks through information, reflects the prescriptive emphasis of early writers on management with their emphasis on administrative functions (planning, budgeting, etc.), it also is related to more recent concerns with performance management. The informational role is divided into two, communication and control, with the former, as illustrated in his earlier work, by far the most significant. One comment is significant in our context and worthy of further attention:

> Managers scan their environment, they monitor their own units, and they share with and disseminate to others considerable amounts of the information they pick up. A point worth emphasizing, and one emphasized in almost every serious study of managerial work, is that the *formal information – in other words, information capable of being processed in a computer –* does not play a particularly dominant role here. Oral information – much of it too early or too 'soft' to formalize – and even nonverbal information, namely what is seen and 'felt' but not heard, forms a critical part of every serious managerial job (or, at least, every managerial job performed seriously).
>
> (Mintzberg 1994: 16; emphasis added)

What is interesting here is the way that Mintzberg tends to ignore some of the more recent impacts of ICT, not least by a certain sleight of hand in equating 'formal' information with that 'processed in a computer'. We will investigate the forms of information that can be so processed in much more detail in Chapters 4 and 5, but it is worth suggesting that one can have formal information without it being computerized and that not all information handled by a computer is formal. In order to see this, it is necessary to consider the notion of formal information in a little more detail.

In a helpful review, Preston (1986) suggests that formal information is the 'official', legitimate version of events. It is often associated with a particular office, that is, it is produced by a particular, authorized set of persons and it is conveyed via 'the proper channels'. It is often routine and regular in character and as such is particularly amenable to computerization. A classic example in many organizations is the monthly budget report, produced by management accounts at the same time each month and covering a standard period according to standard rules. However, not all formal information is conveyed in this fashion. The information passed on ('cascaded') in team meetings is designed to be the official, formal version of what is to be known. It can be reinforced by newsletters and notice boards. So computers are not essential for information to be formal; the seal of approval is. By contrast, with the spread of technologies like email, groupware and instant messaging, especially with their capability to handle a wide variety of data types (such as sound and pictures as well as text), much of the gossip in organizations is actually spread through computers. One might well argue that this affects its character in so far as participants are aware of the 'textualization' that we will discuss below, but these examples suggest that perhaps Mintzberg underestimates the impact of such developments, which we will return to when we look at features such as data warehousing and virtual teams.

The focus on communication is, however, one which is continued in other more recent and detailed accounts of the nature of managerial work, most notably in Tony Watson's (1994) ethnographic study *In search of management*. This work places considerable emphasis on the skills of managers in achieving outcomes through negotiation, not only with subordinates and superiors but most importantly among themselves. Such an approach places a premium on the skilled use of language and it is noticeable that in a study of a high tech workplace ICT is only mentioned once, and that a passing mention of email. However, in an interesting echo of our concern with information literacy, Watson reports the competency scheme for managers that was being constructed, which included the following interesting passage:

> Good managers are constantly collecting and sifting information from a variety of sources and work hard to maintain an information network which will continually feed them with knowledge and intelligence of both a formal and informal nature.
>
> Bad managers either (i) limit themselves to a few, usually formal, sources of information so that they have little knowledge of or 'feel for' what is going on around them, or (ii) allow themselves to be swamped with indiscriminately received information so that they quickly become dazed and out of touch.
>
> (Watson 1994: 226)

The focus on managerial activity and the importance of communication is taken further in Lucas Introna's (1997) *Management, information and power*, a book which uses a philosophical framework drawn from the work of Heidegger. From this difficult and challenging body of ideas he takes the notion of managers being 'thrown', as we all are, into particular contexts. Rather, that is, than being the detached, dispassionate analyst of the decision making tradition the manager is already part of an ongoing context. In such a context many decisions are not 'made', they simply flow from the ongoing pattern of events in which the manager is caught up. Decisions only happen in conditions of breakdown, during which linguistic resources are drawn upon to effect repairs.

This is a very different perspective on managing, one in which the focus is on communicative competence rather than information and in which the computer tends to fade into the background. Thus Winograd and Flores (1986) are deeply critical of conventional models of artificial intelligence, expressing a need for training in 'communicative competence'. Such competence is the need to recognize that communicating effectively in a particular situation, that is, making sure that there is optimum understanding on the behalf of all participants, requires us to be clear about what is being communicated and why. Most people, Winograd and Flores argue, are not conscious of their ongoing achievements in maintaining the web of commitments in which they are bound. Rather than worrying about better use of computers, they argue, more important is the ability to be conscious of the capacity to act with language. And in a challenge to notions of information literacy, they suggest that, if we accept their focus on the importance of 'thrownness', meaning the being-in-the-world that does not distinguish between individual and context, 'it becomes clear that the unexpected and unintended encounters one has in browsing can at times be of much greater importance than efficient precise recall' (Winograd and Flores 1986: 167).

There is another important approach to the impact of information on managers, one which also draws on studies of managerial activity in context but one which retains focus on both the importance of ICT and the manager in context. This is the work of Shosahna Zuboff (1988). Drawing on extensive ethnographic studies of workers in paper mills and offices, Zuboff suggested that the difference between ICT and other forms of technology was the capacity of ICT to supply information about the way operations had been carried out. She termed this capacity 'informate' and we will explore this term a little more in the next chapter. However, Zuboff suggested that the capacity to use the information made available by ICT was one with profound consequences for managers. She placed this in context by presenting a historical account of the unfolding of management over the twentieth century, one which she suggested was characterized by a concern to remove the manual aspects of the job. Managers then came to be seen as legitimate because of their command of the 'intellective' elements of the job.

However, the effective use of ICT demands that such intellective skills – more abstract forms of reasoning – are employed by those directly using the system. That is, those who are working with the data produced by an ICT-enabled system need to apply their own reasoning to the data in order to learn from it, rather than relying on managers for the answers. In order to do this they need to be able to frame appropriate questions. This represents, argues Zuboff, a direct challenge to managerial legitimacy, thus explaining why they might respond with anger to changes which require that workers take more responsibility for the information they use. She suggests that:

> Questions, in a fundamental way, are inimical to authority. The question values change over tradition, doubt over reverence, fact over faith. The question responds to knowledge and creates new knowledge. The question initiates and reflects learning. The question is incompatible with the unity of imperative control. Yet the question is essential if information is to yield its full value.
>
> (Zuboff 1988: 290)

The implications for managers are two-fold, which we can consider under the headings of reintegration and diffusion. On the one hand, ICT means a *reintegration* into their jobs of elements that had previously been expunged. Thus managers used to getting others to do their data analysis might now have direct access to the tools with which to do it themselves. Email is perhaps the aspect of ICT that has seen the most direct examples of this form of reintegration, as communications formerly handled by secretaries and personal assistants become part of the managerial task, raising questions about levels of communicative competence. So, rather than getting somebody else to worry about the formatting of messages, managers now are directly concerned in the selection and use of a range of communication media. As we will see in Chapter 5, such selection is not a straightforward matter. On the other hand, at the same time as this reintegration is taking place, there can also be elements of *diffusion* as databases allow for direct access to material which was once the sole province of the manager. In addition, Zuboff argues that ICT 'textualizes' much of the flow of information (again, seen very clearly in the trails left by email discussions) so that the nature of managerial action is laid more open to view. Both the perspective of management as communicative competence, rather than decision making, and the suggestions by Zuboff of trends to both reintegration and diffusion of managerial activities suggest some of the changes that ICT brings to management. However, their focus is largely on managerial activity, a focus which has been questioned by some commentators. It is this critique that we turn to next.

MANAGERS AND INTERPRETATION

One concern that has been expressed is that as a result of all this research activity we know a good deal about *what* managers do but not *why* they do it (Hales 2001). Put trenchantly by Armstrong this argument is that:

The writings of modern empiricists (such as Mintzberg) represent a retreat even from this modest level of interpretation, in that the activities of managers are there portrayed as quite arbitrary sets of roles with little suggestion as to why they are as they are, what purpose or circumstance gives them coherence, or how they might vary. The assumption would appear to be that management is simply there, unchanging in essentials, and to be taken for granted by practical men.

(Armstrong 1986: 19)

One of the problems is that while activities can be seen, functions cannot (Thomas 2003). That is, the notion of managers having a function is an analytical device, in which the carrying out of a function requires activity on the part of a number of managers in a web of relations. However, Watson (1994) suggests that one useful way of looking at management is to see it through three lenses – as activity, as a group of people and as function. In this section we will look a little more at the final category, which seeks to address the question, what is management for? This becomes particularly important as new forms of information access enabled by ICT challenge what managers do. We have already reviewed the impact of information on managerial activity and this will be a theme throughout the rest of the book. We will look at the impact on managers as a group of people in our chapter on structure, but we can briefly raise one paradox now. This is that at the same time that some would argue that the trend to diffusion identified above calls into question the whole notion of managers as a specialized group of people, 'managers' appear to be the fastest growing occupational group. What this paradox does call into question are simplistic notions of technological determinism in which managers will be replaced either by machines or by their 'empowered' workforce. The persistence of management does suggest the need to look a little more at what function they fill for organizations.

While those looking at managerial activity have often tended to take for granted the nature of the organizations they manage, other more radical critics start from the outside of organizations in order to derive the functions of management. Thus they would start from the premise of competition and capital accumulation in a capitalist economy to argue for two functions of management, functions which have the potential for tension. Starting from the premise that workers, whether manual or mental, sell their capacity to labour rather than their labour itself, Carchedi (1977) argues that one key function of management is that of global capital; that it is in the interest of capital for the maximum value to be extracted from the work of those employed and it falls to managers to ensure that this happens. This then places emphasis on *control* as the key function of management.

However, Carchedi also argues that the development of modern industry has seen the knowledge level of work expand, with managers being drawn into this process as part of the function of collective labour. Their function here is particularly to *coordinate* work, which is not just about the giving of orders but increasingly demands involvement in the work itself. This reflects growing levels of expertise within the ranks of management and also an emerging tension. This is because managers themselves are employees who also wish to preserve their own positions. Some would argue that this compromises the very notion of functions, as managers put their own interests ahead of their function on behalf of the owners of the firm (Willmott 1998). For example, managers who carry out particular roles for a short period of time often focus on the achievement of short term goals which enhance their own career progression rather than on activities which will bear more fruit for the organization in the longer term. Thus, they may prefer short term investments with immediate return over longer term capital expenditure which will bring success for those who occupy the role in future years. However, another way of exploring the issue is by focusing on the notion of another function, that of interpretation.

This starts from the observation that what seems inherent in the notion of the functions of management as discussed is that the demands of the market are clear and require no translation. This is a view which downplays the importance of the management of organizations and sees them instead as almost automata which respond to market signals. An alternative perspective can be taken if we return to the work of Karl Marx which forms the inspiration for many of these radical accounts and reminds ourselves of what, for him, distinguishes human labour from that in the natural world:

> A spider conducts operations that resemble those of a weaver, and a bee puts to shame many an architect in the construction of her cells. But what distinguishes the worst architect from the best of bees is this, that the architect raises his structure in imagination before he erects it in reality. At the end of every labour-process, we get a result that already existed in the imagination of the labourer at its commencement.
>
> (Marx 1998: 257)

Marx's argument points to something which he saw as a feature of human existence. In earlier periods of existence, it could be seen that the ability to interpret the world and translate such interpretation directly into productive work were two sides of the same coin. This is the condition of the craft worker where there is a direct link between conceptions of the world and operations. But one of the critiques of modern capitalism is that it saw a divorce between conception and execution. This lies at the heart of accounts of the work of F. W. Taylor, whose schemes for the rationalization of work depended on the creation of specific routines for the carrying out of work which were the property of the planning office, to be carried out to the letter by those who were employed just to labour (Braverman 1974).

However, this critique tends to see the role of management as simply an expropriation of the knowledge which workers already have. A more complex picture is obtained if we see some of the knowledge that Taylor saw as being the monopoly of management coming from outside the organization, in particular from the advances which science was bringing to, for example, machine tool design. This suggests that organizations, especially under conditions of intense competition, engage in a constant process of interpretation of the external environment and it is this, as much as the capturing of tacit knowledge, that marks the function of management in modern capitalism. With the separation of the direct producers from the means of production we have also a separation of interpretative effort. This gives to managers a creative aspect, as expressed in Hales' notion of 'preconceptualisation'. Hales develops this concept from the practice of design engineers and managers in chemical process industries. He conceives it as a creative process in which managers (compared, at any rate, to direct process workers) 'have a well-developed idea of how the physical and social organization of the new process is likely to work' (Hales 1980: 96). Drawing on these interpretations and on various bodies of knowledge they then produce products in the form of both documents and learning, both of which form the material, both physical and mental, on which process workers draw. This is not to deny the existence of interpretative skill on the part of direct workers, but this tacit knowledge is hemmed and circumscribed by the preconceptualization process; in Hales' words, 'preconceptualisation systematically determines the relative power of different workers in different labour processes, by determining, objectively, their ability to know' (Hales 1980: 97). The great advantage of this formulation is on its introducing a relationship between the interpretative function and the interpretative activity which goes on within the collective labourer.

An important function of management under capitalism can therefore be argued to be to interpret various signals from both the internal and external environment and translate them into some form of action, be that action a policy, a decision or some other expression of learning. This is a creative act which goes beyond the expropriation of the knowledge of the direct producer, although this is part of the equation. It rests on a system in which the direct producer does not have access to these types of signals, in which interpretations about the nature of the environment and how to respond to them are largely reserved for the owners of the means of production and to their agents. Managers as agents for capital have to respond to its dynamics, either in reaction or in anticipation, and using a range of interpretative strategies. The tone for these strategies is determined by a range of factors, some internal to the organization and its history, some external in the shape of such factors as the education system. This function of interpretation is seen as being a distinct and important function of management, which is in a position of tension with the other functions of control and co-ordination. That the function might work best with informal information, for example, clashes with hierarchical principles of organization:

> This isn't a democracy. Firstly, you have to get used to [the Chairman], because if he wants to know something, he will pick a telephone up and he will ask somebody. If he wants something about a guy who works two levels below me doing something, he will phone him. I might find out three days later, or I might never find out at all . . . I think that . . . an hierarchical approach gets in the way.
>
> (Macdonald 1998: 275)

Yet that hierarchical approach is in turn related to the need for control within a divided economy and society and to meet the incessant demands for capital accumulation. What we need is an approach which neither dissolves every activity into interpretation nor resolutely insists that control is the only concern of management. As we will see, there is increasing focus in the research literature on the central role played by middle managers in particular in such processes of interpretation, a focus which becomes clearer if we consider interpretation as a key function of management in relation with their other functions of control and coordination.

CONCLUSION

Information, broadly defined, forms an important part of theories of what management is and how it is carried out, although it is often implicit. By reviewing the material with a focus on information we bring this importance into relief. Our discussion indicates that rather than being a feature of the 'knowledge economy', information has always been a central part of the definition of what it is to manage. However, the nature and importance of types of information in the role has shifted over time and with the influence of different contexts. This is why we have considered that managers need to be information literate. Of course, much depends on the facet of management that we are examining. If, as has been argued above, much of the focus has been on the activity of managing, then certain aspects tend to be overlooked. However, the contemporary focus on tacit knowledge has brought out much more clearly the important place of certain groups of managers, notably those termed 'middle managers' in surfacing and articulating such knowledge in organizations. This requires more discussion, and we explore the terms we have been using rather loosely so far in more detail in the next chapter. In particular, we tackle the thorny problem of the nature of tacit knowledge. We will also return to the notion of the function of the middle manager in Chapter 7.

SUMMARY

- Information forms an important part of the literature on management, even if it has often not taken centre stage. Some of the major traditions give us very different views on the types of information that managers are likely to use.

- The management as decision making school focuses on information as structured data, with use being a matter of appropriate selection in order to come to decisions. The tendency is to focus on decision making as a technical process subject to individual cognitive limitations and to abstract this from the organizational context.

- The emphasis on the manager as communicator and negotiator, based on detailed examinations of managerial work, places its stress on communicative competence, sometimes to the neglect of questions raised by contemporary use of ICT. In some incarnations, the issue of information tends to disappear altogether, which rather underplays the importance of intensive data use in contemporary organizations.

- An examination of what managers do reveals the importance of informal information in many situations, that is information not officially sanctioned and embedded in social relationships.

- A focus on the function of management reinforces the importance of management as interpretation and can help us make sense of the continuing importance of management in a context of concern with the articulation of tacit knowledge.

- Our information literate manager will need to be aware of a wide range of types of information utilized in a range of contexts. An exclusive focus on a particular type or source is likely to be profoundly limiting.

REVIEW QUESTIONS

1 What is the distinction between programmed and unprogrammed decisions?

2 What are the cognitive biases which can affect decision making?

3 Distinguish between informal and formal information.

DISCUSSION QUESTIONS

1 Does formal information have to be that which is stored in a computer? What, for example, of team briefings? Can you think of other examples?

2 How might the requirement for communicative competence be affected by changes in communication channels brought about by technological change?

FURTHER READING

Ackoff, R. (1967) 'Management Misinformation Systems', *Management Science*, 14(4): 147–156.

This is an early classic article which retains much of its relevance today, especially in countering the notion that the answer to all problems is more information.

Watson, T. (1994) *In Search of Management: Culture, Chaos and Control in Managerial Work*. London, Routledge.

Extremely lucid and engaging account drawn from first hand observation of managerial practice. Contains surprisingly little on the impact of ICT, but valuable as an overview of the broader literature in the context of closely observed practice.

REFERENCES

Ackoff, R. (1967) 'Management Misinformation Systems', *Management Science*, 14(4): 147–156.

Armstrong, P. (1986) 'Management Control Strategies and Inter-Professional Competition: The Cases of Accountancy and Personnel Management', in D. Knights and H. Willmott (eds) *Managing the labour process*. Aldershot, Gower: 19–43.

Boisot, M. and Liang, X. G. (1992) 'The Nature of Managerial Work in the Chinese Enterprise Reforms: A Study of Six Directors', *Organization Studies*, 13(2): 161–184.

Braverman, H. (1974) *Labour and Monopoly Capital: The Degradation of Work in the Twentieth Century*. New York, Monthly Review Press.

Carchedi, G. (1977) *On the Economic Identification of Social Classes*. London, Routledge.

DeNisi, A. S. (1996) *A Cognitive Approach to Performance Appraisal: A Program of Research*. London, Routledge.

Hales, C. (2001) 'Does it matter what managers do?' *Business Strategy Review*, 12(2), 50–58.

Hales, M. (1980) *Living Thinkwork: Where do Labour Processes Come From?* London, CSE Books.

Hodgkinson, G. P. and Sparrow, P. R. (2002) *The Competent Organization: A Psychological Analysis of the Strategic Management Process*. Buckingham, Open University Press.

Introna, L. D. (1997) *Management, Information and Power*. London, Macmillan.

Kurke, L. B. and Aldrich, H. E. (1983) 'Mintzberg Was Right!: A Replication and Extension of *The Nature of Managerial Work*', *Management Science*, 29(8): 975–984.

Lipshitz, R., Klein, G. and Carroll, J. S. (2006) 'Naturalistic Decision Making and Organizational Decision Making: Exploring the Intersections', *Organization Studies*, 27(7): 917–923.

Locke, R. R. (1989) *Management and Higher Education Since 1940: The Influence of America and Japan on West Germany, Great Britain and France*. Cambridge, Cambridge University Press.

Macdonald, S. (1998) *Information for Innovation: Managing Change from an Information Perspective.* Oxford, Oxford University Press.

Marx, K. (1998) *Capital Vol 1.* London, ElecBook.

Mintzberg, H. (1973) *The Nature of Managerial Work.* London, Harper and Row.

Mintzberg, H. (1994) 'Rounding Out the Manager's Job', *Sloan Management Review*, 36(1): 11–26.

Moss-Jones, J. (1990) *Automating Managers – The Implications of Information Technology for Managers.* London, Pinter.

Preston, A. (1986) 'Interactions and Arrangements in the Process of Informing', *Accounting, Organisations and Society*, 11(6): 521–540.

Rose, S. (1993) *The Making of Memory: From Molecules to Mind.* London, Bantam.

Schwenk, C. (1988) 'The Cognitive Perspective on Strategic Decision Making', *Journal of Management Studies*, 25(1): 41–55.

Simon, H. (1977) *The New Science of Management Decision.* New Jersey, Prentice Hall.

Stephens, C. S. (1993) 'Five CIO's at Work: Folklore and Fact Revisited', *Journal of Systems Management*, March: 34–40.

Thomas, A. B. (2003) *Controversies in Management: Issues, Debates, Answers.* London, Routledge.

Watson, T. (1994) *In Search of Management: Culture, Chaos and Control in Managerial Work.* London, Routledge.

Willmott, H. C. (1998) 'Rethinking Management and Managerial Work: Capitalism, Control and Subjectivity', *Human Relations*, 50(11): 1329–1359.

Winograd, T. and Flores, F. (1986) *Understanding Computers and Cognition: A New Foundation for Design.* Reading, Addison-Wesley.

Zuboff, S. (1988) *In the Age of the Smart Machine: The Future of Work and Power.* London, Heinemann.

Chapter 3

Data, information and knowledge

INTRODUCTION

In this chapter we look at some of the issues connected with the increased focus on knowledge in organizational life. In order to do this, I have used a common division between 'data', 'information' and 'knowledge'. As we will see, it is sometimes difficult to draw clear lines between these terms. For example, it can be argued that use of a term like 'knowledge' often seems to refer more to information. However, in order to reach some sort of judgement on these practices it is first necessary that we discuss some of the attributes of the different terms. While it is helpful to view these terms as lying on a continuum, rather than being sharply distinguished from each other, it is also helpful for pragmatic reasons to maintain the distinctions. As the discussion progresses we will see that keeping these classifications is also helpful in pointing our attention to different types of problem that might in turn suggest different types of remedy.

However, before getting into the detail of this discussion, it is worth considering some of the reasons that might lie behind the contemporary interest in knowledge in organizations. One way of commencing this discussion is by considering the following lines from a poem by T. S. Eliot (1934):

Where is the wisdom we have lost in knowledge?
Where is the knowledge we have lost in information?

These lines, published in 1934, should remind us that knowledge is not a recent discovery of management consultancies, but rather a fundamental part of human existence. Many years before the advent of what we now call information processing technology, Eliot was concerned by the relentless piling up of facts, the product of scientific investigation and a burgeoning mass media. This was, of course, well before the full impact of media such as television, but Eliot was concerned that in the midst of what then seemed an abundance of information, knowledge was becoming lost. However, simply having knowledge in the form of an abstract commodity was insufficient: we also needed the wisdom to apply what we knew appropriately. For Eliot, such wisdom was to be found in faith and belief; there were simply some things which could not be known and the key to living was in religious belief.

What is helpful here is not only the reminder that these are long enduring issues, but that they are also questions connected with what it is to be human. That is, we seek knowledge not only for its own sake but in order to make sense of our existence (Midgley 1989). It is therefore not surprising that what it is to know has been a central concern of philosophers. Their debates about the nature of the world and what it is to know it are not our central concern, but we need to acknowledge the nature of the debates that have endured over many centuries. In particular, philosophers have debated the nature of 'truth' and its connection with knowledge. What is clear is that this is a slippery and elusive category, and that the course of history has cast considerable doubt on both the existence of, and the striving to find, 'the' truth. That is, our knowledge is founded on some reasons, but those reasons are always provisional and revisable in the light of new evidence. In the discussion that follows it is important to keep this more modest aim in mind. Our concern is to look at knowledge in a more sociological light, but the connections with these deeper debates should be kept in the back of your mind. With this, let us explore some of the reasons why knowledge might be a topic of contemporary concern in organizational life. We do this in order to give some context to the later discussion.

 This chapter will examine:

- some broad trends in knowledge, building on the facets we explored in Chapter 1
- the nature of data use in organizations, with a particular focus on its relation to systems of knowing. This section also considers questions of data quality and ownership
- the distinction between information as product and information as process. The impact of ICT is discussed through a look at Zuboff's notion of 'informate'. We pay particular attention to questions of informal information sharing
- some important distinctions with regard to knowledge in organizations, with special attention paid to the idea of 'tacit knowledge'. A stress on the importance of systems of knowing in organizations leads us to consider some ways of conceptualizing such systems

---

SOME KNOWLEDGE TRENDS

One simple response to the question of why knowledge is now of importance is to point to the cumulative impact of the introduction of information technology into work organizations. This has generated, so the argument goes, a vast amount of knowledge that companies simply did not possess before; the challenge is simply to exploit this new resource. There is something to this, for, as we will see, while there have been other 'information technologies' in the past, they have not generated the same volume of information nor made it so easy for this to be transported across barriers of time and space. However, a counter to this argument is to point out that the simple possession of volumes of information does not constitute knowledge. These type of arguments, often expressed in the language of advertising which promises faster and better decision making, lead to the cynical perspective that knowledge management is simply the latest management fashion. It is the product of a rebranding exercise by software companies with a vested interest in pushing their products (Wilson 2002). The label of information management is no longer sufficiently attractive and so it is replaced with knowledge management. This promises seductively attractive benefits to hard-pressed executives and so achieves the status of management fashion, becoming the latest 'must have' acquisition (Scarbrough and Swan 2001).

There is a degree of truth in such accusations. The fashionable status of knowledge management, as pressed by management consultancies and inscribed into software, has proved to be a successful selling point. Further, it could be argued that this marketing effort has itself shaped perceptions of what knowledge is, reducing it to those things capable of storage in technology. However, to leave it at this would be to under-estimate some more important trends which do suggest that a focus on knowledge is a real response to challenges which face contemporary organizations. For example, while knowledge management has been seen as a trend that gathered pace in the 1990s, as early as 1972 the chairman of the multinational consumer goods company Unilever could state at his company's annual general meeting that much of the knowledge his company used was not to be found in books, being 'the result of cumulative learning, and multifaceted and tacit' (cited in Wilson and Thomson 2006: 5). As we will see, this was an observation which foreshadowed much later discussion on the matter, suggesting that there are indeed changes which go beyond simple fashion. We have already reviewed the changing nature of the workforce and shifts in the nature of products and services; it can also be useful to consider some deeper changes in the nature of knowledge creation itself.

We have seen that T. S. Eliot suggested that religious belief was one response to the explosion of knowledge created by the scientific revolution in the West in the nineteenth and early twentieth centuries. It is perhaps worth exploring these developments in a little more detail, because they have shaped much of what we take for knowledge in the modern world. This is not to downplay alternative traditions of knowledge, but the developments that I discuss are so much at the heart of the modern knowledge economy, especially because of the power and prestige of US forms of organizing, that a brief discussion should help you get a better sense of the context in which we will be looking in more detail at data, information and knowledge. The Western scientific revolution had its roots in a challenge to a particular form of knowledge creation, that which saw knowledge as the property of a limited group, priests in the church, authorized by their position in a system of belief that alone claimed to have the keys to knowledge. Against this monopoly of religious belief the Enlightenment tradition in Western Europe counter-posed intellectual scepticism, detailed empirical investigation and the power of Reason. The main agency for the development of this new approach was the university which, in different forms according to national tradition, became the authorized source of knowledge.

However, this position in some cases involved a degree of distancing from the concerns of organizations. In particular, it tended to rather downplay vocational and practical knowledge, notably in the Oxbridge tradition in the UK. Because of this, industrial corporations, especially in the chemicals industries which were becoming particularly important in the late nineteenth century, began to develop their own research and development capabilities. This is not to say that universities did not also contribute to knowledge here, although this was often in the form of basic research which was then contextualized within companies. However, what did happen was the growth of knowledge creation agencies outside the university. At the same time technologies for diffusing that knowledge, in the form of the growth of a specialist press, were expanding on the basis of developments in printing technology. This process really flowered in the years following the Second World War, when the development of the management consultancy saw the growth of agencies devoted to the creation and dissemination of knowledge about business processes themselves (Locke 1989). Now, we can debate the efficacy of the advice that consultancies give, but the way in which large companies, such as IBM, now make more money from advice about the use of their products than from their products themselves is an indicator of the mushrooming of agencies for knowledge production. The development of the Internet simply affords better access to this explosion of knowledge, something which in turn can be seen to have contributed to an increase in anxiety and uncertainty. When knowledge production was limited, there was relatively little choice; now, faced with an overwhelming volume of knowledge (or information posing as knowledge, as we shall see), managers can be forgiven for seeking certainty in the advice literature and the recommendations of the consultancies.

The increasing interest in knowledge is, then, the result of a number of factors. While there are elements of fashion involved, there are real shifts in the nature of productive activity. These include not only the shift from products to services but also the changing nature of products themselves, which often are the result of and contain significant bodies of knowledge. In addition, there has been an explosion of agencies devoted to the creation of knowledge and of channels for its dissemination. This renewed interest in perennial problems brings to light issues that had often been taken for granted. One of the difficulties that many face in looking at this area is the degree to which questions of data, information and knowledge are embedded in other activities. Success in, for example, accounting, marketing or human resource management demands the effective negotiation of questions of data, information and knowledge, but this is often taken for granted. So, if a marketing person seeks to use a particular piece of data they will do so with the primary purpose of meeting a marketing objective, not as an exercise in information management. This might mean that questions to do with data quality or ownership are not generalized beyond the particular instance to become a wider concern for marketing staff; rather they are often assumed to be the province of other specialists (if they are treated at all). By default those specialists have often been within information systems. Their expertise, however, is in technical rather than organizational matters. That is, as we saw in the preface, many of the questions fall between the responsibility of different functions and so never get the attention they deserve. It is to a more detailed consideration of some of these complexities we turn now, starting with data.

DATA

Data selection: the importance of the initial question

Data is a term that we tend to take for granted. In our everyday speech we often refer to 'raw data' which we speak of 'collecting' or 'gathering'. This gives us the impression that data is simply 'out there' waiting for us to obtain it. However, a closer look will indicate that there are important processes of definition and selection at work. Take one piece of data as an example: NJ630117. This could be a stock code or a customer reference number; it is in fact a British National Grid reference. Using a map (or mapping software) we can attach this reference to a farm called Culthibbert in Aberdeenshire, Scotland. Of course, if we were interested in the nature of the geology, or the scale of the buildings, or the type of crop production, this would be of little help. My interest in it comes from it being the site of a croft which some of my family lived on in the nineteenth century. So the selection of this particular piece of data out of the great mass of data about that part of the world has been an active process of selection, guided by broader knowledge that tells me why that data is important as part of a larger scheme. This process of selection is so important, but so often overlooked, that Peter Checkland and Sue Holwell (1998) suggest that we need a new word, 'capta' to indicate that part of data which we have chosen to focus on.

Data are then sense impressions of the world shaped by our questioning of that world. What we choose to regard as important is conditioned by the questions that we start with. This places considerable importance on the nature of the questions that we ask, rather than on our capacity to collect data. In organizational terms we very often take data for granted, something compounded by the ever increasing capacity we have in the form of IT to capture greater quantities of data. This can now happen as a routine by-product of customer transactions. Whether this be in the form of frequent flyer programmes, customer loyalty schemes in supermarkets or logs of visits to websites, we can gather increasing volumes of detail. However, such data may not be that which we require to answer the really important questions. The nature of this need for data can change with business conditions, as in the box below.

The nature of the data required and the means of obtaining it were changed by the changing organizational circumstances. Data is thus affected by both the questions that we ask and the way in which we ask them. Simply gathering more and more data by ever more sophisticated

NEW CONDITIONS, NEW DATA: TRAIN ACCEPTANCE PROBLEMS IN THE UK

There was a persistent problem following rail privatization in the UK of new trains not being accepted into service for many months. At the heart of the problem lay the new organizational arrangements. For most of the period when the railways were a nationalized operation, run by British Rail, new trains were built by an in-house engineering division. When the railways were privatized, with a separation between those who built the trains, those who owned and maintained the structures on which they ran, and those who operated them, questions of data came to the fore. The train manufacturers required data on the assets of the railway, such as the length of platforms and how close they stood to the rail. Such data simply did not exist, as train builders had historically 'learned by doing' – in other words, they had run trains on the network and observed whether the necessary clearance was available. (In some cases by attaching polystyrene to the outside of the trains and observing the results!) Such a course of action was, of course, no longer available to a legally separate body.

Source: Haigh 2000

means may not be the appropriate response. One example of this is the contrast that Cawson, Haddon and Miles (1995) draw between Japanese and European methods of market research in connection with advanced technology for home use. The European approach of intensive market research is contrasted with the Japanese approach of the rapid release of prototypes using the consumer as a testing ground. The problem they point to is the difficulty that consumers have in imagining how they would use new forms of technology, to which we could add the imaginative flexibility with which innovations, such as Short Messaging Service (SMS or 'texting') are taken up, often in ways that could not be envisaged by market researchers (Leonard 2007). That is, the way in which we ask questions conditions the sort of data that we can generate.

In addition, the suggestion from the Japanese experience is that structures are needed 'to collect and interpret data on market characteristics, and feed it continuously into the innovation process' (Cawson, Haddon and Miles 1995: 264). The success of the Sony Walkman, for example, is seen as owing much to the way that data on consumer preferences was fed rapidly into the design process. That is, it is not enough simply to generate data; we then need mechanisms to ensure that they get to and are understood by those who need them. Data are, then, selected on the basis of particular ways of knowing which generate specific questions and are conditioned by the way in which we go about answering those questions. Such considerations become more important when data are used in systemic fashion across an organization, something which we look at in more detail in the next section.

Data quality

Review the case in the box below. What underlies this example is the broader issue of the systemic nature of contemporary business. What is meant here is the way in which changes in business processes and technology have had the impact of tying parts of organizations more

DATA USE AND QUALITY IN THE BANK OF SCOTLAND

In 1997 the Bank of Scotland was reported to have used an analysis tool to search their customer database, their aim being to pinpoint suitable targets for marketing. They had 'assumed data quality would be good, but it was a much bigger task than we thought', according to the strategic analysis manager (Amos 1997: 8). What they found was that staff inputting data to create customer accounts had done enough to get those accounts accepted, even if the data were inappropriate (such as patently infeasible dates of birth, for example). This was fine as long as the data were only used to create accounts, but as soon as the data were used for another purpose problems with their quality were revealed. The response in the Bank of Scotland was to tie data quality to the bonus of the branch manager and to ensure that staff was aware of the impact of their actions: 'Training in data awareness is now part of our core competencies for all staff and makes a huge difference to data quality' (Goodwin 1999: 48).

Source: Amos 1997; Goodwin 1999

closely together. A clear example, and one which is not dependent on advanced technology, is the implementation of just-in-time production systems. Historically, production systems have contained 'buffers', generally in the form of stock, which contain shocks in one part of the system from impacting on activities in another part. However, the removal of these buffers means that events in one part of a system have an almost immediate impact in other parts, parts which might be far distant from the original cause. One only has to think of the impact of strikes in parts of those car manufacturers who organize production on a global scale to see how a dispute in one part of the production chain can very rapidly affect activity elsewhere. In a similar way, data can often ripple straight through a company and can come to be relied on by those who have a very different purpose in mind. Some authors (Senge 1990) have suggested that what is required by managers in particular is an appreciation of the broader picture. This is an issue we will return to at the end of the chapter, but for our current focus on data it suggests that many more managers than before need to take an interest in issues of data quality.

In the next chapter we explore IT applications like data warehousing in further depth. However, for the current discussion it is sufficient to acknowledge that developments like this have dramatically improved the capacity of organizations to store and manipulate vast amounts of data. The skills needed to analyse that data are part of our later discussion, but what such developments have made of much more importance is the quality of the data that is being used in such systems. The cliché is 'garbage in, garbage out'; the challenge is what to do about it. There are two ways of approaching data quality, which can be summarized under the headings of inspecting quality in or building it in, terms which might be familiar to you from your broader knowledge of approaches to quality. Briefly, the first approach is that which seeks to check work to ensure that it is of an acceptable standard. Of course, the problem with data in many organizations is the sheer volume. Customer databases, for example, rapidly become out of date and inspection of these is time consuming and expensive given the volumes. What is more important is ensuring that data are of sufficient quality at the beginning and that they remain of such a quality throughout their lifecycle.

Redman (1995) argues that this necessitates a view of data as a process. There are a number of important stages in this process. The first comes with specifying what attributes data ought to have at the outset. This means, for example, that if we wish to use them for marketing as well as operational purposes that seemingly trivial matters, such as salutation, should be specified at the outset. The process of capturing the data then needs some attention. Increasingly this is taken care of by automated recording devices using, for example, bar codes and scanners. This has dramatically improved the quality of data in many supply chain operations, for example by the electronic booking in of stock to warehouses. However, in many areas data are still gathered and entered by people, and it is here that the issues of training and reward that we saw in the Bank of Scotland example are important.

Finally, much of the problem with data quality lies not with the initial capture but on the transfer of data between different systems. These interface problems are one of the reasons why many organizations are investing in systems, such as Enterprise Resource Planning (ERP) systems which seek to avoid such interfaces. We will look at these and the challenges that they pose in the next chapter. However, the message in the current context is that data quality is an often neglected area but one that should be a concern for many managers. In particular, the adequate specification of the attributes of data at the beginning of a process or project rather than as an afterthought can be crucial in ensuring that the data can be used effectively.

47

This is often referred to as the provision of *meta data* — data about data. For example, it can be vital that we know how and when data have been collected to ensure that subsequent comparisons are being carried out on a like for like basis. However, ensuring that data are of adequate quality does not mean that they are used effectively: a further area for our consideration is that of data ownership.

Data ownership

The widespread use of computer enabled systems which have facilitated broader access to data has raised important concerns about data ownership. In particular, studies of data warehouses, systems for the storage and manipulation of data for decision making processes that we consider in more detail in the next chapter, have indicated that a prime reason for failure is that those with control over data have been unwilling to share that data. By default, data have been seen as coming under the ownership of the area where they have been created. As we have seen, the systemic use of data across an organization means that there needs to be consideration of the wider use of data, something which those in charge of their creation may not be equipped or ready to consider. One argument is that data should now be regarded as a corporate resource, but this simply raises new questions about the formulation of organizational policy. We will need to return to this point in our chapter on strategy, but one important consideration that informs such policies is that of data definition.

Once again, many data are defined by default to meet the requirements of the particular area in which they are used. However, once they are used in a more systemic fashion, then it is important that definitions are clear. Davenport, for example, gives the example of the Union Pacific Railroad company which, he reports, had different definitions for a train depending on different parts of the organization. 'Is it,' he asks, 'a locomotive, all cars actually pulled from an origin to a destination, or an abstract scheduling entity?' (Davenport 1994: 122). Now, clearly it would be difficult to have precise definitions for every item of data employed in an organization. However, those key elements that are shared across internal boundaries are worthy of some debate.

Data summary

Our brief discussion of data has raised some important issues that we will need to carry forward in our discussion. It is possible to argue that data are relatively neglected in organizations, despite being taken for granted as the foundation of further activities. It may be, as we will see, that when we talk of 'information management' we are often raising issues that fall more in the areas we have discussed above. In particular, the following points seem to be of some importance:

■ The emphasis in many organizations seems to be on collecting more and more data. The assumption seems to be that more is better and that answers will emerge from the data. By contrast, we have suggested that data are selected in an active process that places more stress on the importance of formulating the question; that data are shaped by the nature

TAKING IT FOR GRANTED: DATA DEFINITION AND RAIL SAFETY

Track repair engineers working on the UK railways require a 'possession' in order to be able to work, which specifies the safe limits within which they can work. This prevents the movement of trains through the area while the maintenance gang has possession of the area. In 2006 a maintenance gang was working on track which ran through Thirsk station when they cut a rail which was not intended. The subsequent investigation found that the person in charge of the possession had two possessions from points north and south of the station. He assumed that the two possessions ran back to back, that they covered all the track in the station, whereas local staff had always thought that they extended only to points north and south of the station not to the track in the station itself. The inquiry recommended that future possessions were defined by mileages rather than named locations.

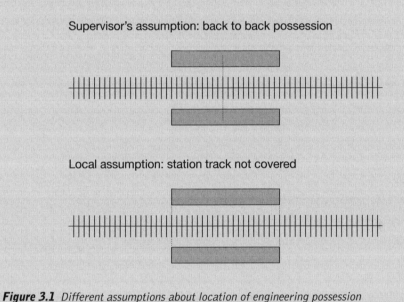

Figure 3.1 *Different assumptions about location of engineering possession*

Source: *Rail* 2006: 6

of the questions that are asked. This is a theme we will return to at a number of points in this chapter.

- The nature of these questions, and hence the data required, varies with changing conditions. New conditions demand the creation and use of different sorts of data. Using data collected for other purposes may simply give misleading results.
- Data are now used in many more parts of organizations than just the area in which they originate due to the systemic nature of contemporary organizations. This raises important questions about the attributes of data that are best addressed by considering data creation and use as a process. Once again, we see the importance of a processual approach.

■ As part of this processual approach, issues of ownership and definition are raised which seem to demand an organizational level response. By default, however, it can be argued that such questions are either left to the departments where data originate or to specialists, like IS departments. Neither is satisfactory if data are to be seen as an organizational resource.

INFORMATION

Information as process

In our everyday use of the term we often consider 'information' as a 'product'. So, for example, if I ask for tourist information on a particular area, I generally receive a set of leaflets that constitute the 'information'. Consider the following observation, which you may have encountered in other contexts:

> A weekday edition of the New York Times contains more information than the average person was likely to come across in a lifetime in seventeenth century England.
>
> (Wurman 1991: 32)

At first glance, this seems unexceptionable and might express what many of us feel intuitively. However, if we consider it a little further, we may think that there are some problems which illustrate nicely some problems of considering information as a product:

■ To what extent does the content of the newspaper constitute 'information'? If it has no interest for me and, importantly, if I don't understand it when I access it, perhaps over the Internet (because, say, of its local context), to what extent is it 'information' as opposed to data?

■ Doesn't this statement tend to privilege particular forms of information, namely text? The implication seems to be that because there were not mass newspapers in seventeenth-century England (although this would be to ignore the explosion of tracts that distinguished the Civil War period in particular) that therefore there was no information. There is a hidden assumption here that print equals information.

■ Does such an assumption underplay the existence of different forms of information, information which may be lost to dwellers in a print-dominated world? Might, for example, the inhabitants of seventeenth-century England have information about the curative properties of plants lost to us? For example, Alasdair Maclean's elegy to vanishing peasant life in Ardnamurchan points to this:

> That particular rock, let us say, halfway to a certain peat moss, conveniently sited and shaped, where the homeward-bound carriers sat for a moment to ease their burdens, has suffered with the rest. The name that named it, that very likely commemorated its use and value, has disappeared. Indeed you may say that the rock itself has been obliterated for it is no longer significantly there.
>
> (Maclean 1986: 184)

This suggests the knowledge about particular features of the landscape is bound up with a particular way of life. Once the way of life disappears, so too does the knowledge. This might be very valuable knowledge, suggesting that we should be careful not to simply assume that more information means knowing more. (For an argument on these lines about developing countries, see Goontilake (1991).)

This notion of information as a product is given powerful reinforcement by the notion that information is that which can be processed by a computer. This is given support, as we have seen, by linguistic usage such as 'information technology' and by organizational arrangements, such as the common reporting arrangement of information systems specialists to the finance director. All of this tends to privilege a particular view of information as structured data.

This perspective on information was given particular support by the movement known as 'information resource management'. This powerful metaphor, which sought to compare information to the other resources used in organizations, such as people and tools, arose out of challenges to the accumulation of material by US governmental agencies. The huge volume of information gathered at considerable cost by such agencies, often without being used, gave rise to attempts to exploit what was seen as an underused resource in order to realize some value from it. However, the problem with this particular use of metaphor was that information differs in a number of crucial respects from other resources used in organizational life. For one thing, it does not get depleted or worn out in use, like other assets. Rather, it can expand its value in use. Similarly, time is of great moment in trying to put a value on information. In some situations information can have enormous value at one time, when it is initially possessed, and virtually none soon after, when it becomes common knowledge (the most vivid being information about market conditions in stock valuation). However, a key dimension is that information by itself implies nothing about the value which can be realized from it. That is, excellent decisions might be made with incomplete information and very poor ones when the decision maker might be considered to have a full range of information. These distinctions, argue Eaton and Bawden (1991), make the concept of managing information as a resource a tenuous one and perhaps suggest our attention ought to be more focused on the process by which meaning is derived from information.

We might want to consider information as a process in two ways. One is the process of interpretation that we undergo when faced with any data – the way in which we assimilate them to our existing knowledge patterns, for example, or cross-refer them to other data to place them in context. A second is the organizational process that is engaged in, where often data are created in one place, processed in another, manipulated in a third and used in a fourth. It is such considerations that lay behind Boland's assertion that:

> Information is not a resource to be stockpiled as one more factor of production. It is meaning, and can only be achieved through dialogue in a human community. Information is not a commodity. It is a skilled human accomplishment.
>
> (Boland 1987: 377)

Such an approach shifts the emphasis away from the attributes of the information itself and towards the processes by which it is created. In particular, it suggests that we need to look at the theories which are brought to bear in the process of meaning creation and at the organizational context in which these processes take place. These are valuable suggestions which will inform much of the discussion that follows.

However, there is a danger with a purely processual approach that we lose sight of the status of that which is created. The process does create, in various forms, entities which we call information and which enter other processes with that status. They are subject then to further processes of interpretation, but what is important here is the relationship between these successive rounds of production and use. This is caught in the literature on organizational learning by Etienne Wenger's (1999) focus on what he terms 'reification' and 'participation'. By 'reification' he means the rendering in material form of the processes of participation – perhaps, say, in the production of procedure manuals from the results of brainstorming about how best to carry out certain actions. (This, it should be noted, is a rather specialized use of the term reification, which has other uses in the sociological literature.) 'Participation', then, relates to our use of 'process' and what is important, Wenger argues, is the relationship between the two:

> Participation and reification must be in such proportion and relation as to compensate for their respective shortcomings. When too much reliance is placed on one at the expense of the other, the continuity of meaning is likely to become problematic in practice.
>
> (Wenger 1999: 65)

That is, the rendering of learning from process into a concrete form ('information') is important in that it can then be transferred into different contexts where new forms of participation may follow. From this we take a notion that what is important is the viewing of information as both process and product, in which we are concerned about the relationship between the two. You should note that these are analytical distinctions that we are making here – in practice, it may be difficult to see the distinction, but it can help you to think in this way if you are challenging the taken for granted use of the term 'information'. One challenge is the wider use of the term in the context of ICT; we need to consider this a little further.

'Informate'

You could argue, and you would be right, that the processes of information creation and use that we have been discussing exist without any form of technology. Further, technology other than that which we currently view as being 'IT' (that is, digital computers, as explored in the next chapter) has long had an impact on such processes. The invention of the typewriter and the filing cabinet, for example, had a considerable impact in changing information use, not least by facilitating the bureaucratic organizations that characterized much of the twentieth century (Beninger 1986; Yates 1989). However, it is possible to argue that IT is different and it is here that it is useful to reflect on the arguments of Shoshana Zuboff (1988). Based on investigations in work organizations, most notably in paper mills, she argued that we needed to draw a distinction between the impacts of different types of technology. Take the example of machine tools. An automatic lathe will essentially reproduce human actions, but it will do so in a more reliable and consistent fashion. However, it makes few changes to the nature of work – these tend to come from associated practices, such as grouping similar machines together and instituting flow line work processes. By contrast, a computer controlled lathe not only fulfils all the functions of an automatic lathe, but it also records details of the process that it has engaged in. Zuboff uses the terms 'automate' and 'informate' to distinguish between these different effects.

We might be able to see from our discussions so far that 'datamate' might have been a more useful term. If we distinguish between data and information, a distinction elided in the term 'informate', we can see that IT does indeed possess the power to produce masses of data that will tell us about the processes engaged in. You could relate this to the examples we raised before – the frequent flyers programs, the supermarket transaction data, the logs of web use. In each case, the data are collected as an automatic by-product of processing operational transactions. However, whether they are discarded, stored or used is dependent on a range of factors – awareness that they are there to be used, for example, or broader schemes of knowledge in which to place the data. For Zuboff, this is the distinction between simply using ICT to automate existing processes or using the data which it produces to create information. There is some confusion in Zuboff's account as to whether this is an inevitable function of the application of ICT or whether it represents potential. However, using this data to create information requires considerable changes, she argues. Thus, based on her experience in the paper mills, she argues that:

> It encompasses a shift away from physical cues, towards sense-making based more exclusively on abstract cues; explicit inferential reasoning used both inductively and deductively; and procedural, systemic thinking.
>
> (Zuboff 1988: 95)

These are important considerations to which we will return when we look more closely at training. For now, it is important to recognize that 'informate' is best thought of as a potential rather than a necessary consequence of the application of IT, one that moreover depends on organizational choices. The ways in which such choices are influenced by existing power structures will be considered later; for now, it might be useful to consider a little more the ways in which information use is embedded in organizational relationships by a closer look at information sharing.

Information sharing: formal and informal information

One problem that managers have with considering questions to do with information is the extent to which they are taken for granted. Because they are embedded in existing routines which serve towards the completion of other goals, questions about information are often hidden and only come to light when new systems are introduced. So, for example, when social work managers in a Dutch authority were asked for the information they would like from a new system they faced such problems in defining their requirements that they included everything they might need. This resulted in a system containing over 150 screens, more than half of which were never used (Phillips and Berman 1995: 110). This might reflect the extent to which managers depend on informal information for achieving their tasks. As we saw in the previous chapter, formal information is that which is officially sanctioned by the organization. It tends to be associated with particular offices which have the responsibility of producing it on a regular basis and it is often disseminated through established channels of communication.

A good example would be monthly management accounting reports. We should be careful not to associate all formal information with this example – a briefing session, for example, is formal because it is the legitimate, approved version. However, formal information tends towards the production of regular and clearly defined reports, which bring with them problems of rigidity and lack of relevance.

It is for this reason that informal information is so important in organizations. We could give this other names – gossip, the grapevine – but what these tend to do is downgrade the importance of these channels. We can see this well illustrated in a fascinating exploration by Alistair Preston (1986) of the use of information by managers in a plastics factory. Based on a year's observation, Preston's observations started from the position that the formal Management Information System was almost never used by managers in their day-to-day activities. Rather, they constructed elaborate systems in order to keep themselves informed. These took two forms. One form was the personal information system, in which officially held records were duplicated because managers didn't trust them. The second was arrangements to keep themselves informed which depended on a network of contacts in the plant. This involved important social dimensions and, importantly, excluded senior plant management. If managers wanted to know the latest stock situation, for example, they would ignore official systems and go direct to their trusted contacts. What we see here is the importance of trust and social relationships in information use and sharing – these managers would simply not share the information with those outside their networks.

In this example, it was not that the formal information systems were entirely ignored. They were considered useful in constructing a historic record of events, but they had almost no impact on everyday information use. Now, we could argue that this happened, as Preston discusses, for one of two reasons. It could be *because* of the faults of the existing system. That is, many production managers often need information in real-time in order to take decisions, whereas many formal systems are geared to longer reporting cycles. If this were the case, then the answer might be the construction of better formal systems, perhaps by the deployment of more modern technology. However, another argument might be that managers used their informal systems *despite* the formal systems. That is, it might be that the factors of trust and social relationships that are found in the use of informal information sharing are more important, which is something that would direct our attention away from purely technical solutions and towards other organizational arrangements, ones which, for example, facilitate rather than obstruct informal sharing. We will return to this question later, but let us summarize what we have learned so far about information.

Information summary

One feature which our discussion of information shares with that on data is the importance of schemes of knowing, something which we will return to in the next section. Other features which seem worthy of note are:

- The importance of seeing information as a relationship between product and process. Stressing the relational character of information directs our attention away from purely technological answers and towards organizational arrangements.

- However, Zuboff's work suggests why it is important not to ignore technology in our analyses, for the 'informating' power of computer-enabled systems has significant implications for the use of information in organizations. We might want to argue that what is produced is data rather than information, but the impact is still important.
- A focus on the social relations in which information use is embedded draws out the importance of trust and networks. It also suggests that arrangements which encourage the sharing of informal information might be a powerful move, one which would balance effort put into formal systems and recognize the importance in practice of such information.

KNOWLEDGE

Knowledge in theory and practice

From our discussion so far, we might want to make a distinction between knowing and knowledge. Much of that which passes for the latter in organizations might be better described as information; indeed, we can see information as a product as the concrete realization of processes of knowing. Elizabeth Orna (2005) suggests that seeing this form of packaged knowledge as 'information products' directs attention towards the more effective creation of such products. In particular, she argues for the need for greater attention to be paid to the design of information products. As we have seen, what is often important in the creation of data and information is the theory which informs the questions that we ask. However, this mention of theory perhaps raises an important question about the nature of what it is to know. The notion of theory suggests abstraction from everyday practices and an association with agencies, such as universities and consultancies, outside the normal run of business. Indeed, one could argue that such a divorce has been a feature of what has been taken as knowledge over the period that has seen the development of industrialized economies from the eighteenth century onwards. Some have argued that the prestige of science in this development has seen the downgrading of practical knowledge and the privileging of abstract knowledge (Bernstein 1996). This is a general observation, but we can make this a little more concrete in terms of organizations by looking at two particular developments.

One with which you might already be familiar is the movement known as 'Scientific Management' and associated with the work of F. W. Taylor in the USA at the turn of the twentieth century. Also known as 'Taylorism', this approach, which sought to adopt a 'scientific' approach to questions of work organization, had at its heart a particular conception of knowledge. This was one in which knowledge was the property of a particular social group, managers, operating in organizations. Rather than learning from practice, workers were to follow schemes laid down for them by experts. Now, the full impact of Scientific Management is open to considerable debate in the field of the history of management, but the approach can be seen in the assembly lines developed by Henry Ford and the development of time and motion studies. What is important for our discussion is the assumption that knowledge was to be divorced from those carrying out work – the separation of conception and execution. Of course, the tenets of Scientific Management were challenged from within management thinking as well as by organized labour, but the model of knowing contained in it remained powerful.

As we have seen, it received a further fillip from the success of techniques broadly known as 'Operational Research' in the Second World War. Success in applying mathematical and statistical techniques to large scale military operations saw a considerable increase in prestige to those operating under the banner of 'Management Science' and many of these techniques came to be applied in the large corporations of the post-war period. This movement had considerable success in the USA in particular, and with it long-lasting impacts on management education. The focus of many MBAs, for example, on the detailed analysis of bodies of financial and other data can be seen to reflect the prestige of planning in this period, as can the emphasis on planning in much work on strategy. The impact of management science was also important in the development of computing in organizations, directing a considerable amount of attention towards techniques such as Artificial Intelligence. This tended to reinforce a conception of knowledge as a commodity produced by experts working on the basis of abstract bodies of knowledge, preferably those based on models derived from the natural sciences. However, changes in both intellectual currents and economic fortunes have placed a greater emphasis on practical knowledge. In terms of organizations, the most important focus in recent years has been that on tacit knowledge.

Tacit knowledge

The emphasis on the importance of tacit, as opposed to explicit, knowledge first emerged in the work of the scientist and philosopher Michael Polanyi (1958; 1967). For Polanyi, we know more than we can say. Certain forms of knowledge are acquired in an almost unconscious fashion and once learned can be used to produce an effective performance. However, such knowledge is not immediately accessible to us and can be difficult to communicate to others. The most well-known application of this to knowing in organizations has been the work of Nonaka and Takeuchi (1995).

Nonaka and Takeuchi use the example in the box opposite, and others, to suggest what has become widely referred to as the SECI model (Figure 3.2). They suggest that much knowledge is held tacitly and can only be acquired through extensive periods of *socialization*. It is this knowledge which could only be acquired by the software developer through the actual process of work when the stretching and twisting action became apparent. Once this had been recognized, then the knowledge could be *externalized*, in this case by a particular concept which made it explicit in character. This could then be *combined* with other forms of knowledge which already existed in explicit form. Finally, a key stage would be making the new forms of knowledge taken for granted through *internalization*.

There are parallels in this account with the stress in material on organizational learning on the importance of learning from experience. In their influential work on *Situated Learning*, Lave and Wenger (1991) draw on accounts of learning in apprenticeships to develop their notion of 'legitimate peripheral participation'. This refers to the learning that takes place when newcomers begin to participate in a 'community of practice'. What is important here is not the formal learning process, but learning to act and talk as a member of the community. In such a process tacit knowledge is acquired and shared. In the context of knowledge in organizations this suggests that questions of identity are central. That is, rather than placing

EXTERNALIZING TACIT KNOWLEDGE: THE MATSUSHITA HOME BAKERY

One of Nonaka and Takeuchi's key examples is the development of the 'Home Bakery' by the Matsushita Company. This development of an automated bread making machine ran into particular problems when trying to replicate the quality and taste of traditionally made breads. The problem was solved only when a software developer went to work alongside the head baker at Osaka International Hotel, where she learned the secrets of kneading dough. Her experience indicated to her that there was a simultaneous twisting and stretching movement which needed to be replicated in the machine. This was then translated into a machine which met with considerable success on its introduction in 1987. Nonaka and Takeuchi suggest that a key process here was the learning that occurred when the developer was actively engaged in learning. Simple observation was insufficient, as was asking the baker to explain the process of kneading. This was because the knowledge had been acquired through long experience and was tacit. It could only be passed on through the socialization that lies at the heart of the apprenticeship model of learning. However, when acquired by somebody with an external purpose, it could be externalized into explicit knowledge which could be used by others. In this case, what was needed was a concept, in this case the phrase 'twisting stretch' which could be translated into mechanical specifications by engineers. Here the new explicit knowledge could be combined with other forms of explicit knowledge about, for example, the properties of particular components to create new knowledge. The cycle is completed when this external knowledge is internalized, perhaps through training, in order to form part of the 'taken for granted' ways of operating.

Source: Nonaka and Takeuchi 1995

Figure 3.2 *The SECI model*

the emphasis on forms of technology, the focus should be on methods of socialization into communities of practice (Gherardi 2006). Again, we see the emphasis that is placed in both approaches on forms of knowledge that do not fit into conceptions drawn from formal models of theories and education. In a sense we can see a reversal of the process of abstraction from practical life that we alluded to in our account of the development of agencies for knowledge creation. This focus on the importance of practical, experiential knowledge is a welcome one, but it carries with it a number of problems.

One is that both approaches pay relatively little attention to questions of power and authority. While knowledge may be tacit because people cannot tell what they know, the reasons for not telling may not be simply down to problems of articulation. The history of artificial intelligence, with its focus on 'knowledge elicitation', is that people may be unwilling to share what they know. This may well be because they fear that once shared the benefits accrue to others and that it leaves them in a poorer position. In both approaches the nature of organizations and the purposes they follow tend to be taken for granted and the impact of organizational hierarchy underplayed. These are important questions to which we will return. However, others have suggested some further concerns with the notion of tacit knowledge. As Tsoukas (2003) has pointed out, the use of Polanyi by Nonaka and Takeuchi is based on a particular reading of his work, a reading which can be challenged. Tsoukas argues that tacit knowledge is an integral part of the creation of knowledge for Polanyi and so cannot be divorced from explicit forms of knowing; that is, the division between tacit and explicit knowledge is an invalid one. Spender (1998), by contrast, has drawn a contrast between 'tacit' and 'implicit' knowledge. Tacit knowledge is that which is not said, either because it cannot or will not be said. Implicit knowledge is that which exists, argues Spender, in a pre-conscious state at both an individual and a collective level and which is instantiated in action. This is knowledge, therefore, that is inherent in routines but because of its taken-for-granted nature cannot be articulated without effort. However, the possibility exists of explicating it, unlike tacit knowledge which remains inaccessible because of its unconscious operation. We will tend to favour the term 'implicit' because of its recognition of this distinction, while recognizing that much of the literature persists in using the term 'tacit'. This can be extended further to consider the ways in which such knowledge can be related to social or national backgrounds. Again, these are considerations to which we will return when we look in more detail at culture in Chapter 9. However, the focus on activity and the range of knowledge in organizations is at the heart of a very useful overview, that of Frank Blackler (1995).

Based on an extensive review of the literature, Blackler argues that knowledge can be seen in a number of ways, which he classifies in various ways as summarized in Table 3.1. These distinctions suggest that knowledge is not just a matter of cognition. There are forms of knowing other than the 'embrained'. Blackler goes on to suggest that certain forms of knowledge may be associated with particular types of organization, although he recognizes that this identification is provisional and tentative. The traditional sense of knowledge as embrained is one which we tend to associate with universities and other places of learning, but if we treat this as the only form of knowing then we restrict our attention. However, what he suggests is that rather than focus on types of knowledge we should look at ways of knowing. Based on activity theory he suggests that such ways of knowing should be seen as mediated, situated, provisional, pragmatic and contested. This is rather in the form of setting out an agenda for research than as supplying definitive answers, but it does suggest that:

Table 3.1 *Forms of organizational knowing*

Form	Characteristics
Embrained	Dependent on conceptual skills and cognitive abilities
Embodied	Action oriented
Encultured	Shared understandings and meanings
Embedded	Resides in organizational routines
Encoded	Conveyed by signs and symbols

Source: Adapted from Blackler 1995

The analysis of activity systems involves the identification of the linguistic, social and material infrastructures that make knowing possible. It emphasizes that knowledge is culturally situated, technologically mediated and socially distributed, and that it occurs within and between 'communities of knowing'.

(Blackler 1995: 78)

This suggests that we look more closely at ways of knowing and forms of conceptualization of these, because of the way in which these are shaped by their organizational setting and in turn shape what it is to know in those organizations.

Ways of knowing in organizations

Daft and Weick (1984) suggest that we can locate organizational ways of knowing, which they term interpretive systems, against two sets of assumptions (Figure 3.3).

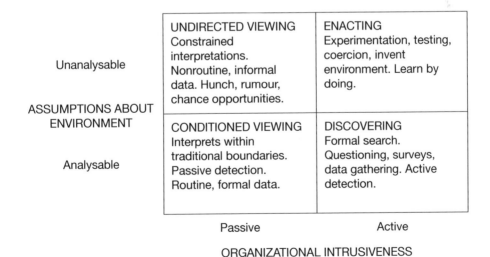

Figure 3.3 *Organizations as interpretation systems*

On the one hand are the assumptions that organizations make about the nature of the context in which they operate. For many companies, this appears as simply something that is given to them and which cannot be analysed. Many smaller companies fall into this assumption, one which is often closely related to their position relative to other larger organizations, for example, as very junior partners in a supply chain. This means that they may feel that they have little choice in their environment and so do not undertake any formal analysis. This could be contrasted to many larger organizations which conduct extensive analyses of their environment in a formal sense. However, the ways in which these analyses are conducted can also be conditioned by their assumptions about the degree to which they can change that environment. So many companies simply rely on their internal management information, as they do not reach out into their external environment. This gives them a very backward looking set of information on which to base their decisions. For example, a survey by Harris Research in 1990 found that 59 per cent of companies surveyed relied on management accounting data to take strategic decisions – data which by their nature are better suited to monitoring internal practice than forecasting the external future (KPMG 1990). By contrast, many large companies, especially those in the Fast Moving Consumer Goods (FMCG) sector conduct extensive market research. However, as we have already seen, this might be good at revealing established preferences, but not at assessing new demands. For this, an approach which learns through doing might be more appropriate. We saw something of this in our earlier discussions of Japanese processes of the fast release of prototypes to learn about consumer acceptance. The inter-pretation systems which this approach suggests organizations possess might not be those formally acknowledged, but they will condition organizational action.

One criticism of this approach is that it tends to assume a unitary form of organization. In practice we know that organizations are made up of often competing sub-cultures, each of which may possess its own ways of knowing. Sackmann's (1991) detailed investigations in one organization found a number of competing and overlapping logics at work. In the organization she studied, Sackmann found seven groupings which were particularly associated with differing definitions, that is, with what she termed 'dictionary' knowledge. We have already seen how definitions of trains differed within one large organization and how important such definitions can be. In Sackmann's company, different definitions were held even within functions which shared similar characteristics. There were, for example, three groupings with different sets of definitions within production and two concerned with aspects of marketing. Top management had its own set of definitions, as did those concerned with co-ordinating activity. This suggests that even within groupings which we might think from the outside might share the same definitions, such as production, there could be important differences. By contrast, Sackmann found a common conception of what she termed 'directory' knowledge, that is, assumptions about how things get done. For example, organizational members could share a common commitment to active forms of knowing, of the type which encourages active experimentation in order to develop knowledge. By contrast, more formal attempts to express this knowledge in the form of what she termed 'axiomatic' knowledge, of the type often expressed in mission statements and the like, had relatively little importance outside the ranks of top management. This led her to suggest that:

[b]y differentiating the kinds of cultural knowledge, a homogeneous quality of culture or cultural synergy emerged in regard to directory knowledge, whereas several cultural

groupings emerged in regard to dictionary knowledge, and a different grouping surfaced in regard to axiomatic knowledge.

(Sackmann 1991: 166)

This approach is interesting in suggesting the need to break down forms of knowing. It does, however, suggest that particular companies acquire forms of practice that can influence disparate sets of activities. Patriotta (2003), in his study of the Italian car manufacturer Fiat, also found that it was important that forms of knowing were institutionalized into sets of practices, which might be carried in artefacts such as blueprints or encapsulated in commonly told stories. What such approaches appear to neglect, however, is the focus on intellective skills, that is on more abstract forms of reasoning. This seemed as important for Patriotta's car workers as it did for Zuboff's paper mill workers:

. . . the numbers and messages displayed on electronic boards have important cognitive implications for shopfloor operators. The capacity to read the data displayed on electronic boards and make inferences from them indicates the presence of systemic maps at the cognitive level.

(Patriotta 2003: 138)

However, this insight is not followed up, creating as it does a tension between the common sense experiential learning which Patriotta suggests characterizes the shopfloor and a more abstract form of reasoning which seems to be what is required.

FAILED LOGICS IN MENSWEAR RETAILING: FOSTER BROTHERS

Foster Brothers was a successful menswear retailer in the UK until the early 1980s. It built its success on the provision of cheap clothing in convenient locations to a market which was relatively unsophisticated. Its dominant logic was a buying one. That is, it had strong capabilities in the sourcing of material at cheap prices. An important and contending logic, but always a subordinate one, was a logic of location. That is, it also had the ability to locate and obtain retail sites at low cost. Neither of these logics paid much attention to the needs of the customer, rather taking these for granted. When a new marketing director arrived in the early 1980s he commissioned market research, the first in the company's history. This research indicated that customers were heavily critical of both the merchandise and the stores, finding both to be cheap and dowdy. However, the initial response to the research was to attack it on the grounds of the authors' perceived lack of retailing experience. By the time changes were made, it was too late. New competitors entered the market, having perceived a demand for well made, fashionable menswear at reasonable prices but presented in attractive retail settings. Foster Brothers was taken over and many of its outlets closed down. Its dominant logic had not only failed to change to meet changing circumstances, but had prevented the need for such change being realized until too late.

Source: Johnson 1987

One means of conceptualizing such systems of knowing is that suggested by Prahalad and Bettis (1986) with their notion of the 'dominant logic'. This is 'a mind set or world view or conceptualization of the business' (Prahald and Bettis 1986: 491) which is formed over time. While it can be a source of advantage, it can also be problematic when, for example, an organization moves into unrelated areas. What is helpful here is the notion of 'dominance', suggesting that other logics might also exist but connecting us to authoritative control over the organization's resources. In addition, logic suggests a set of propositions which can be transferable across content and context.

While it is useful to conceive of experiences such as those of Foster Brothers under the heading of the playing out of a dominant logic, one reservation about the term is that it suffers from the excessively internal focus that writing on organizational strategy often has, in which the world outside the organization is conceptualized as the 'environment' to which the organization reacts, rather than as a set of structures in which the organization is inextricably embedded. One consequence is that dominant logics are seen almost entirely as a product of those within the organization itself, rather than being in dynamic relationship with ideas produced within the particular domain within which the organization operates. In examining industries as diverse as foundries, dairying and fork lift rentals, J.C. Spender (1989) suggests the notion of 'industry recipes'. He argues that managers in these industries exhibited a 'pattern of judgements', 'a way of looking at their situations that is widely shared within their industry' (Spender 1989: 188). This pattern of judgements tended to be at senior levels, which suggests that it was based on shared experience. What we might want to do is to explore the interplay between these patterns of judgements and broader sets of logics. In the brewing industry in the UK, for example, there was a shift between 1950 and 1990 on the part of the major companies in the industry from a dominant logic of production, in which public houses were seen as part of a distribution network, to one of retailing in which pubs were seen as the key point of contact with the customer (Mutch 2006). This process owed a great deal to the rise of a broader logic of retailing in society, in which the success of the major supermarkets brought a new respectability to retailing. Because of this, retailing ideas percolated through a range of organizations with which they were not historically associated (such as financial services as well as brewing) and so transformed their dominant logic. This brings us back to our starting point, the broader shifts in what it means to know in society more generally.

Knowledge summary

As we have seen in the sections on data and information, the notion of ways of knowing is an important one. In our discussion of knowledge, we have seen that:

- While scientific knowledge has enjoyed immense prestige in the years since the Second World War, there has been a renewed emphasis in recent years of different forms of knowing. In particular, there has been a concern with tacit knowledge.
- One problem with this new focus might be a tendency to underplay what we might term 'practical reasoning'. That is, the types of skill isolated by Zuboff in her discussion of intellective skill seem to be rather underplayed. We will return to this neglect at several points.

■ Knowing in organizations is not just a matter of individual cognition. It is also shaped by what counts as knowing within the organization, something shaped over time and encapsulated in the idea of a 'dominant logic'.

CONCLUSION

In a discussion of ways of knowing in organizations David Marchand issues a caution which is worth reproducing:

> . . . with all of the academic and managerial interest in 'knowledge management' today, it is important that the role of information use and sharing in a company should not be overlooked or confused with 'knowledge development'. As important as knowledge development is to organizational learning and change, information is the means or vehicle that companies employ to express, convey and share knowledge retained among their people. Thus, a company's capabilities to manage information provide the means through which knowledge development and management are possible.
>
> (Marchand 1998: 267)

We could add here the need to also take data seriously. This is why in this chapter I have tried to address each of the categories in turn. What are the key messages that we can take forward?

■ In each section we have seen the importance of ways of knowing. In more traditional accounts we could depict the relationship between them as follows:

Data ➔ Information ➔ Knowledge

Our discussion suggests that we would be better reversing the direction, as follows:

Knowledge ➔ Information ➔ Data

That is, rather than information somehow emerging out of data and creating knowledge, it is knowledge that suggests the data that we need and the information that we will draw from it. This places a particular stress, as we discussed in Chapter 1, on the ability to ask questions.

■ We could note a persistent tendency to rather conflate the terms that we use. Thus, many discussions of information management seem to refer to data processing activities, and much of the discussion about knowledge confuses information as a product of knowing with bodies of knowledge. Part of this 'linguistic inflation' can be related to the claims of those with vested interest in improving their status. It can be far more prestigious, for example, to be an information systems specialist rather than a data processing expert, and it can seem far simpler to sell a knowledge management rather than an information management product, even if in both cases there is little or no change to the underlying activity or functionality. However, what this tendency can lead to is an under-estimation of continuing problems with, for example, data quality or information literacy.

I hope that this chapter has clarified matters somewhat. Of course, what I have done is to raise a large number of issues which require further discussion. We start that further discussion in the next chapter by considering the impact of ICT on all of the categories we have been discussing here.

SUMMARY

- Knowledge is not simply the accumulation of more material. Indeed, the very success of forms of inquiry and the snowballing of agencies for the dissemination of the results has, arguably, resulted in more uncertainty. In such a world certainty might be found in the comfort of management fashion.

- Data are not simply waiting to be found but are created by the questions which we ask, questions which can change with changing conditions. The widespread availability of data through new means of capture raises important questions about data quality and ownership.

- We can view information as both process and product, although one helpful way of viewing it is as packaged knowledge. Such packaging requires an active process, a process which is influenced by ICT by the way in which it creates new sources – a process Zuboff terms 'informate'. However, such processes also involve a web of relations, something revealed by a contrast between formal and informal information.

- While much of what we term knowledge in organizations can be better conceived of as information products, it is still the product of systems of knowing. There are various ways of conceptualizing this, but the notion of the dominate logic is a particularly useful one, both for its stress on the 'rules' rather than the content and for its recognition of the continuing importance of those with control over the allocation of resources.

REVIEW QUESTIONS

1 What do you understand by the terms data, information and knowledge in the light of the discussion in this chapter?

2 Distinguish between tacit and explicit knowledge and outline the process by which, according to Nonaka and Takeuchi, one is turned into the other.

3 Is 'informate' an inevitable process or merely potential?

DISCUSSION QUESTIONS

1 Review the example given in this chapter of the different assumptions about railway engineering locations using the SECI model of Nonaka and Takeuchi as a guide. How might

tacit knowledge about local conditions be turned into explicit knowledge? Are these terms helpful?

2 Apply the Daft and Weick model of organizations as interpretation systems to the example of Foster Brothers. Can you place the company on the grid and what difficulties does this pose? How might you suggest the company change its positioning?

FURTHER READING

Davenport, T. with Prusak, L. (1997) *Information Ecology: Mastering the Information and Knowledge Environment*. New York, Oxford University Press.

Very accessible account from an author who spans the academic/consultancy divide and has been associated with some influential fashions (such as Business Process Re-engineering). Stresses the importance of seeing information in context.

Nonaka, I. and Takeuchi, H. (1995) *The Knowledge-Creating Company: How Japanese Companies Create the Dynamics of Innovation*. New York, Oxford University Press.

Massively influential work which brought the use of the term 'tacit' to the wider debate. The use of such terms is open to some question as are some other details of the work (it tends to downplay similar insights which had already been presented), but there is no doubting its influence. Many interesting examples drawn from experience in Japanese companies.

Tsoukas, H. (2004) *Complex Knowledge: Studies in Organizational Epistemology*. Oxford, Oxford University Press.

Rich collection of papers, full of interest and insight which challenge much of the work on knowledge management. Contains, in particular, the challenge to the way in which tacit knowledge has been widely used in a way which is not faithful, he argues, to the way in which Polanyi intended.

Zuboff, S. (1989) *In the Age of the Smart Machine: The Future of Work and Power*. London, Heinemann.

Full of rich detail drawn from ethnographic work in paper mills and insurance offices, this book develops Zuboff's ideas about the 'informating' potential of ICT.

REFERENCES

Amos, S. (1997) 'Bank Boosts Sales Through Profiling', *Computer Weekly*, 13 November: 8.

Beninger, J. R. (1986) *The Control Revolution: Technological and Economic Origins of the Information Society*. Cambridge, MA: Harvard University Press.

Bernstein, B. (1996) *Pedagogy, Symbolic Control and Identity: Theory, Research, Critique*. London, Taylor & Francis.

Blackler, F. (1995) 'Knowledge, Knowledge Work and Organizations: An Overview and Interpretation', *Organization Studies*, 16(6): 1021–1046.

Boland, R. J. (1987) 'The In-Formation of Information Systems', in R. Boland and R. Hirschheim (eds) *Critical Issues in Information Systems Research*. Chichester, Wiley: 363–380.

Cawson, A., Haddon, L. and Miles, I. (1995) *The Shape Of Things to Consume: Delivering Information Technology into the Home*. Aldershot, Avebury.

Checkland, P. and Holwell, S. (1998) *Information, Systems and Information Systems: Making Sense of the Field*. Chichester, Wiley.

Daft, R. L. and Weick, K. E. (1984) 'Toward a Model of Organizations as Interpretation Systems', *Academy of Management Review*, 9(2): 284–295.

Davenport, T. (1994) 'Saving IT's Soul: Human-Centred Information Management', *Harvard Business Review*, 72(2): 119–131.

Eaton, J. J. and Bawden, D. (1991) 'What Kind of Resource is Information?' *International Journal of Information Management*, 11: 156–165.

Eliot, T. S. (1934) *The Rock*. London, Faber & Faber.

Gherardi, S. (2006) *Organizational Knowledge: The Texture of Workplace Learning*. Oxford, Blackwell.

Goodwin, C. (1999) 'Ignorance Isn't Always Bliss', *Computing*, 24 June: 43–48.

Goontilake, S. (1991) *The Evolution of Information: Lineages in Gene, Culture and Artefact*. London, Pinter.

Haigh, P. (2000) 'The Unacceptable Face of Train Acceptance?' *Rail*, 379: 36–40.

Johnson, G. (1987) *Strategic Change and the Management Process*. Oxford, Blackwell.

KPMG (1990) *Information for Strategic Management: A Survey of Leading Companies*. London, KPMG.

Lave, J. and Wenger, E. (1991) *Situated Learning: Legitimate Peripheral Participation*. Cambridge, Cambridge University Press.

Leonard, D. (2007) 'Market Research in Product Development', in K. Ichijo and I. Nonaka, *Knowledge Creation and Management: New Challenges for Managers*. Oxford, Oxford University Press.

Locke, R. R. (1989) *Management and Higher Education Since 1940: The Influence of America and Japan on West Germany, Great Britain and France*. Cambridge, Cambridge University Press.

Maclean, A. (1986) *Night falls on Ardnamurchan: The Twilight of a Crofting Family*, Harmonsdworth: Penguin.

Marchand, D. (1998) 'Competing with Intellectual Capital', in G. von Krogh, G. Roos and D. Kleine *Knowing in Firms*. London, Sage: 253–268.

Midgley, M. (1989) *Wisdom, Information and Wonder: What is Knowledge for?* London, Routledge.

Mutch, A. (2006) *Strategic and Organizational Change: From Production to Retailing in UK Brewing 1950–1990*. London, Routledge.

Nonaka, I. and Takeuchi, H. (1995) *The Knowledge-Creating Company: How Japanese Companies Create the Dynamics of Innovation*. New York, Oxford University Press.

Orna, E. (2005) *Making Knowledge Visible: Communicating Knowledge Through Information Products*. Aldershot, Gower.

Patriotta, G. (2003) *Organizational Knowledge in the Making: How Firms Create, Use and Institutionalize Knowledge*. Oxford, Oxford University Press.

Phillips, D. and Berman, Y. (1995) *Human Services in the Age of New Technology: Harmonising Social Work and Computerisation*. Aldershot, Avebury.

Polanyi, M. (1958) *Personal Knowledge: Towards a Post-Critical Philosophy*. London, Routledge & Kegan Paul.

Polanyi, M. (1967) *The Tacit Dimension*. London, Routledge & Kegan Paul.

Prahalad, C. K. and Bettis, R. A. (1986) 'The Dominant Logic: A New Linkage Between Diversity and Performance', *Strategic Management Journal*, 7: 485–501.

Preston, A. (1986) 'Interactions and Arrangements in the Process of Informing', *Accounting, Organisations and Society*, 11(6): 521–540.

Rail (2006) 'Rail Cut as Train Came Near, RAIB Finds', *Rail*, 548: 6.

Redman, T. C. (1995) 'Improve Data Quality for Competitive Advantage', *Sloan Management Review*, 36(2): 99–107.

Sackmann, S. (1991) *Cultural Knowledge in Organizations: Exploring the Collective Mind*. Newbury Park, CA, Sage.

Scarbrough, H. and Swan, J. (2001) 'Explaining the Diffusion of Knowledge Management: The Role of Fashion', *British Journal of Management*, 12(1): 3–12.

Senge, P. M. (1990) *The Fifth Discipline: The Art and Practice of the Learning Organization.* New York, Doubleday.

Spender, J. (1989) *Industry Recipes: An Enquiry into the Nature and Sources of Managerial Judgement.* Oxford, Blackwell.

Spender, J. (1998) 'The Dynamics of Individual and Organizational Knowledge', in C. Eden and J.C. Spender (eds) *Managerial and Organizational Cognition: Theory, Methods and Research.* London, Sage: 13–39.

Tsoukas, H. (2003) 'Do We Really Understand Tacit Knowledge?' in M. Easterby-Smith and M Lyles (eds) *The Blackwell Handbook of Organizational Learning and Knowledge Management.* Oxford, Blackwell: 410–427.

Wenger, E. (1999) *Communities of Practice: Learning, Meaning and Identity.* Cambridge, Cambridge University Press.

Wilson, J. and Thomson, A. (2006) *The Making of Modern Management: British Management in Historical Perspective.* Oxford, Oxford University Press.

Wilson, T. (2002) 'The Nonsense of "Knowledge Management"', *Information Research*, 8(10) [available at http://InformationR.net/ir/8–1/paper144.html] paper no. 144.

Wurman, R. S. (1991) *Information Anxiety.* London, Pan.

Yates, J. (1989) *Control Through Communication: The Rise of System in American Management.* Baltimore, The Johns Hopkins University Press.

Zuboff, S. (1988) *In the Age of the Smart Machine: The Future of Work and Power.* London, Heinemann.

Part Two

Technology, structure and individuals

CHAPTER SUMMARY

KEY QUESTIONS

Chapter 4 Technology 1: Definitions and data

- What is a useful way of conceptualizing information and communication technology?
- Why are databases important to organizations and what are their limitations?
- How does the storage and manipulation of large bodies of data in data warehouses impact on managers?
- Have Executive Information Systems failed or been transformed into different systems of continuing importance?
- What other significant systems are there which assist in the handling of large bodies of data?

Chapter 5 Technology 2: ICT and communication

- Are there ways of selecting the appropriate medium for communication?
- In what ways has ICT changed the media available for communication and how can they best be characterized?
- Why is groupware often not used to its full potential?
- How useful is the notion of communication genres in understanding the success of email?
- What are the characteristics and limitations of systems aimed at managing knowledge?

Chapter 6 Strategy, information and ICT

- What are the differences between the positioning and resource-based views of strategy and how does information impinge on each?
- Is the impact on strategy primarily from ICT or from information?
- In what ways might the impact of information on strategy be more clearly recognized?
- How can ICT be aligned with business strategy and is this either a feasible or desirable target?

Chapter 7 Structure and information

- What is the position of the middle manager given the widespread use of ICT?
- Have ICT and developments such as Business Process Re-engineering removed functional boundaries in organizations?
- What is the distinction between project teams and communities of practice and how do each impinge on knowing in organizations?
- Are the external boundaries between organizations becoming increasingly blurred?

Chapter 8 Roles, responsibilities and change

- How can the applications discussed already be better used with training which goes beyond application specific features?
- What changes in roles and responsibilities might be needed to take full advantage of new potential?
- What new features might need to be taken into account in recruitment processes?
- Are there any specific features associated with ICT-enabled organizational change?

Chapter 4

Technology 1:
Definitions and data

INTRODUCTION

For our information literate manager, the concern with technology is the impact that it has on the information she deals with. But in order to understand this, we need to characterize technology effectively. Such effective characterization is and has been the stuff of major debate. This chapter reviews these debates before moving on to look in a little more detail at applications of ICT particularly aimed at handling large volumes of data. However, first consider the case in the box below.

Was this problem a 'technical' one . . . or was it one of individual training or organizational policy? As we will see below it is generally impossible to isolate out an issue as 'just' a 'technical' problem. This suggests that managers need some awareness of the impact of ICT, not least on

USING DATABASES: PROBLEMS IN PRACTICE

Country Holidays is the leading holiday cottage letting agency in the UK. From its earliest years it has been an enthusiastic adopter of technology to deal with a large volume of properties and booking transactions. In the early 1990s it adopted a database to store such details, a database which was designed to handle operational transactions but which also contained a query tool. This query tool allowed non-specialists to write queries which would search the database for the data desired – say the number of properties of a particular classification still available for let in a particular area during a specified time period. However, one such query, inexpertly constructed, ran through the entire database. While it was at work, it slowed down the entire system to such an extent that bookings could no longer be taken. As a business which relied almost entirely on telephone bookings at the time of inquiry this was unacceptable; such queries were banned during working hours. However, the results of such queries promise considerable benefit if the results can be acted on.

Source: interviews with the IT manager and information in Mutch (1993)

the nature of the information that they use. As we will see over the course of the next two chapters, the sheer variety of ICT-enabled applications brings into question Mintzberg's confident assertion, examined in Chapter 2, that computer information is unimportant to managers.

 This chapter will examine:

- some important ways of looking at technology in order to come up with a working definition of ICT
- the impact of some systems which are particularly aimed at the management of large volumes of data

---

Our starting point is with defining just what we mean by technology and its impacts.

DEFINING TECHNOLOGY

The definition of technology may seem initially an easy matter but, as we have seen in the short case above, when we examine it a little more closely it becomes more complicated. It has been at the centre of some important debates in the organizational literature, debates which we review below. We look at the following:

- The case for 'technological determinism', which is found to be often over-stated but raises some important points about the material properties of technology.
- The important response based on structuration theory from Wanda Orlikowski, which is of significant influence but, it is argued, underplays the material properties of technology.
- Another important set of ideas under the label of 'actor–network theory' which force us to 'be specific about technology' but which tend to over-emphasize the role of technology.
- An alternative, based on a number of perspectives, which seeks to achieve a balance between the specifics of the technology and the importance of human agency.

We look first at the notion of technological determinism.

Technological determinism: over-stressing the case

Before looking at some of the perspectives which are often encompassed under this label, we ought first of all to consider the very notion of 'determinism'. This is most often met within the context of 'economic determinism', the idea, often associated with certain versions of Marxism, that economic mechanisms determine the nature of society. A more recent version is 'genetic determinism', the notion that particular genes exist to govern specific behaviours. Determinism, then, suggests a very direct causal link between a particular explanatory variable and a particular result. As such, it is widely discredited in many areas of investigation in favour of more multi-causal models. 'Technological determinism', then, is the notion that particular forms of technology induce particular results, and only those results. As Grint and Woolgar (1997) point out, such a charge is hard to sustain, although many have been accused of it. Approaches which suggest a strong shaping or conditioning of activity are not in themselves 'determinist' and in many ways this is too easy a label to throw about. However, a number of influential approaches have been so labelled and it is worth reviewing them in a little more detail.

Another important consideration in our context is that the studies discussed here are not ones of ICT but of technology more broadly. As we will see, it is necessary to be specific about particular technological forms, for different features shape or suggest different actions. However, these studies give a more abstract approach which has been important. One of these approaches is that adopted by Joan Woodward, who examined the relationship between technological forms and organizational structure in 1950s Britain. Based on studies of a number of manufacturing plants, she argued that particular forms of technology were associated with particular organizational arrangements. This argument brought technology firmly on to the stage, conflicting as it did with some of the tenets of the classical management school that stressed 'one best way' of organization. It also led to extensive debates about whether size or technology was the key explanatory variable, debates which were to form the basis of the 'Aston School'. This is a debate which is beyond the scope of this book, but the importance of Woodward's ideas was in bringing technology firmly into the debate (Guillen 1994).

At the same time, some significant investigations were being carried out into the use of technology in mining by researchers at the Tavistock Institute of the University of London under the leadership of Eric Trist. The problem that these researchers sought to address was the paradox of declining productivity following increased use of coal mining machinery.

SOCIO-TECHNICAL SYSTEMS IN COAL MINING

The deep mined coal industry in Britain had been nationalized in 1948. One of the reasons for this had been a chronic lack of capital investment in the industry over many years, notably in the challenging physical conditions of coal fields with narrow seams. However, the introduction of mechanized means of getting coal did not have the desired result. On further investigation, Trist found that the machinery had been implemented in a fashion that ignored the previous forms of work organization, forms of organization which had a strong social dimension. In a dangerous working environment, strong group bonds had grown up, reinforced by both living patterns (mines were often located in isolated pit villages) and by organizational arrangements (there had been a tradition of payment to the leader of the group, who then paid other group members, who were often related). These group bonds had given rise to a strong collective ethos in which, for example, it was considered important to leave the coal face in a tidy state for the next shift to begin working. The introduction of the new machinery had disrupted these bonds, with jobs allocated according to the perceived technical logic of the machinery. Reductions in productivity could be in part attributed to, for example, the need for new shifts to spend substantial amounts of time in clearing up the mess left by the previous shift prior to being able to start work.

Source: Trist 1963

What the Tavistock researchers argued was that work was not simply a matter of technical arrangements. Rather, it carried important social and individual meanings, and such meanings had to be addressed in the context of new working arrangements. New technology simply intruded into existing social and organizational arrangements was unlikely to be successful. This 'socio-technical systems' approach combined aspects of organizational structure and individual training with technological features. It was a particularly influential perspective in the 'quality of working life' movement in the Scandinavian countries in the 1960s and 1970s. This movement saw significant experiments in, for example, car and truck production at Volvo plants, in which there was a move away from assembly line production towards the completion of more significant assemblies in production cells.

The work of Trist and his collaborators played an important role in the development of self-managed work teams and contributed to the development of action research and other process based theories of learning. However, its close association with systems theory saw it associated with a focus on structural arrangements which was a feature of the intellectual milieu of the time. The focus on management science meant that technology was seen as a variable in forms of analysis which underplayed questions of human agency, notably ones of power and politics in organizations. Some of this legacy was carried forward in the influence of the socio-technical perspective on a significant approach of the early 1990s, that deployed by a team of investigators drawn largely from the Massachusetts Institute of Technology in their study of the impact of information technology on business organizations (Scott-Morton 1991). Funded by a number of large corporations, from both the US and the UK, this project sought to suggest that if the 'Corporation of the 90s' (the title of the book that reported their findings) was to gain full benefit from advances in information technology they needed to take account of a number of factors. They used a model (the 'MIT Model') to display these factors in diagrammatic form and it is reproduced in Figure 2.

The continuing influence of the socio-technical approach can be seen in three dimensions of the MIT model, those of technology, roles and responsibilities, and structure. However, the MIT team saw the need to develop their model still further. One important consideration for them was the need to adjust organizational strategy appropriately to align with the other elements. The main concern of the Tavistock team was to optimize effort within a strategy which was already given; however, from an organizational perspective this cannot be taken as a given, but needs to be incorporated in processes of choice and change. The concern of the MIT team was also not just with analysis but with action, and their addition of the factor labelled 'management processes' reflects the shift in thinking towards a more processual approach that we have already discussed.

The dotted line in the diagram represents the inside and outside of the organization and reminds us that all organizations are embedded in a wider context with which they interact. Organizational members, for example, do not change their concerns completely when they enter the world of the organization, but bring attitudes and values from their broader life with them. Culture was seen as an emergent property of the relationship between structures and individual roles and responsibilities, but the model has no explicit place for the exercise of power. It also fails to address questions of the nature of knowledge and information directly. Some would see it as, in common with the broader socio-technical perspective, being still marked by elements of technological determinism. This brought with it a reaction which can

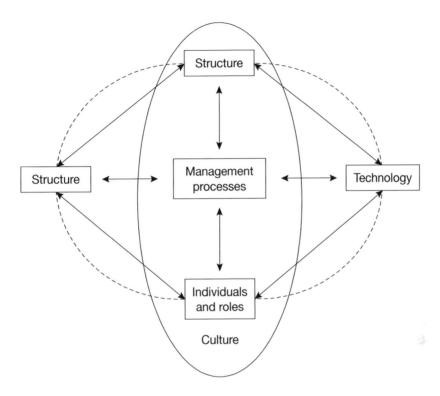

Figure 4.1 *The MIT model*

be traced in the next perspective, the application by Orlikowski of structuration theory to the domain of technology.

Orlikowski and structuration theory: over-emphasizing agency?

In 1992 Wanda Orlikowksi published what was to be a very significant article in the journal *Organization Science*. Titled '[t]he duality of technology: rethinking the concept of technology in organizations', this sought to build on the work of the social theorist Anthony Giddens and, in particular, on his notion of structuration. Giddens' (1984) argument was that social theory was bedevilled by a persistent argument between two opposing camps. On the one side were the structuralists, who emphasized enduring structures such as economic arrangements. This led, he argued, to an impoverished view of human action, in which human intention was reduced to being the bearers of structural properties, thus ruling out active choice. On the other hand were those who so emphasized individual choice that more enduring patterns, such as language, were seen to have little impact. In particular, he argued that those in the latter camp often had a restricted view of structures, viewing them only as constraints on action. Rather, he argued, we should see that without enduring structures no action would be possible and so such structures should be seen as enabling as well as constraining action. Accordingly he proposed a model which emphasized the duality of social action, action which contained both human agency and structural properties in the same moment. Now this is a complex theory developed at quite an abstract level and it has been subject to extensive critique (especially in Archer 1995). However, for our purpose what is important is its influence on Orlikowski's views of technology (given, in particular, that Giddens says little about technology himself).

Against those who might be perceived as technological determinists, Orlikowski (1992) is anxious to stress an approach in which technology is a dynamic factor shaped by human perceptions and actions. She draws our attention to an important distinction between technology *scope* and *role*. Scope refers to the way in which we define the material artefact of technology. There had been, she argued, a tendency to include ever more under the heading of 'technology' (for example the work processes which accompanied a particular artefact). She was concerned to restrict our attention to just the material artefact, which she took for ICT to be a particular bundle of hardware and software. The role of technology referred to the way in which it was perceived and used, and here she wished to place much greater stress on creative imagination and activity. Arguing at this point that technology could be an important structural component of organizational life, she sought to explore the interplay between technology and how it might be used. This sparked a whole series of important empirical investigations, many of which centred round the use of emerging groupware technologies (Yates and Orlikowski 1992; Orlikowski and Yates 1994; Orlikowski and Gash 1994; Kellogg, Orlikowski and Yates 2006). We will review some of these in the next chapter.

However, in the course of developing these ideas, Orlikowski received some criticism which caused her to rethink her ideas. In particular, Grint and Woolgar (1997: 22) were concerned to suggest that her argument that technologies had some material properties which influenced organizational activity 'misses the point, since what counts as material and structural is itself a social construction'. In addition, others had pointed out some difficulties with deploying Giddens' work, especially given his notion of structures as 'memory traces' only instantiated in action (Whittington 1992; Jones 1999). This caused Orlikowski to suggest that an approach which claims:

> that technologies 'embody' social structures – is problematic from a structurational perspective, because it situates structures within technological artifacts. This is a departure from Giddens' (1984) view of structures as having only a virtual existence, that is, as having 'no reality except as they are instantiated in activity' (Whittington 1992: 696). Seeing structures as embodied in artifacts thus ascribes a material existence to structures which Giddens explicitly denies.
>
> (Orlikowski, 2000: 406)

Thus she moved to a perspective which underplayed the material properties of the technology in favour of a focus on the interpretive flexibility (that is, the variety of ways in which ICT can be perceived) with which human actors approached it. She conceptualized structures of technology in use as 'technologies-in-practice' and placed her emphasis on a practice centred approach which privileged human agency. For many this simply emphasized the dangers already present in Giddens' account, in which structures tended to fade into the background (Jones, Orlikowski and Munir 2004). Certainly this has been the tendency of much of the work of both Orlikowski herself and those who have followed her lead. While, then, this has been an influential approach, it is one which seems to downplay the specific characteristics of the technology. Accordingly we need to look at other perspectives which give more weight to these properties.

Actor–network theory: privileging technology?

The approach we explore next is one which might seem eccentric or odd on first encounter. It is one which stresses the importance of the network and sees such networks as being comprised of both human and non-human actors (the latter sometimes being termed 'actants' to distinguish them). This school of thought is particularly associated with the French sociologist of technology Bruno Latour (1987, 1993, 1999). He suggests that we delegate some of our tasks to inanimate objects which then play a causal role in our affairs. This can be even mundane artefacts, like door closers or hotel keys. Latour argues for there being many more such artefacts involved in our daily doings and that we need to operate with a principle of 'symmetry' in our analysis of them. That is, we need to place equal attention and weight on material artefacts, for they play an important role in the construction and maintenance of networks of action. In the context of ICT, for example, one might think of the automated selling systems on stock exchanges which have been held responsible for stock market crashes (Beunza, Hardie and MacKenzie 2006).

Drawing on such examples, Latour and his followers have suggested a language for exploring the process whereby actions happen. Rather than operating with a notion of 'diffusion', in which a particular artefact or idea is seen to pass unchanged from inventor to user, they suggest that we need to examine processes of enrolment and translation. In enrolment a person or artefact becomes successful to the extent to which they can enrol others in their network. Once they are established as a key part of a network, an 'obligatory passage point', then they can be 'stabilized' to form part of what is taken for granted. For this to happen, however, ideas or artefacts developed at one site might need to be 'translated', to undergo an active process of being rendered in terms which are acceptable. These ideas have been extensively deployed in studies of information systems (Walsham, 1997). One particularly important result has been the injunction of Monteiro and Hanseth (1996) to 'be specific' about technology. This is something which is often not done and which we will need to address in our own definition. However, while actor–network theory has provided us with a very useful language for thinking about the process of the embedding of technology in organizations, there are a number of concerns with it. One is that it is so different in its language with its talk of material artefacts having agency that it can seem outlandish. In the hands of some of its less skilled proponents it can be, but it is worth persevering with to get a very different way of thinking about technology. However, on occasion it is pushed too far. The following is drawn from a discussion of the Swedish ball bearing firm SKF.

In considering the production process, which involves the machining of steel rings the following is what Dahlbom, Hanseth and Ljoungberg (2000) argue:

Information about what should be done with the individual pieces is written directly on the material: any area that contains a defect is marked (using a piece of chalk); the area is then

77

checked later to see if the defect disappears as the material is cut down; after the cutting process, inner and outer rings are paired together and given identifiers (post-it notes are stuck to the surface); after the grinding process the rings are marked (with ink pen) to indicate how much extra material there is left before the polishing.

(Dahlbom, Hanseth and Ljoungberg 2000: 95)

The conclusion drawn is that '[i]n this way the steel rings are not only the objects to be worked on and 'manufactured'; they take an active part in the production process, informing the operators what to do' (Dahlbom, Hanseth and Ljoungberg 2000: 95).

We might want to look more closely at the assertion here that it is the steel rings that are taking an 'active' part in 'informing' operators. Such a closer look would suggest that the rings are at best carriers of other marks – chalk, post-it notes, ink pens – that are doing the process of informing. While an actor–network perspective is useful in drawing to our attention the importance of such varied means of informing, what it tends to do is downplay the active involvement of human agents in both providing the marks and interpreting them. This is not to address the very serious reservations that many have with the notion of material agency, with its connotations of interest and intentionality (Mutch 2002). However, what such perspectives draw our attention to very forcibly are the material properties of technology. These do not have to be active to have an impact. For example, Ciborra (2002) draws our attention to the importance of the 'installed base'. This can be not just assemblages of machines but importantly, as we will see, accumulations of existing data and associated structures. While such bases may be amenable to change this might be over a relatively long time period. In the intervening period they form an important constraint on what is possible.

LOOKING AT TECHNOLOGY FROM A MORPHOGENETIC PERSPECTIVE

We have, then, noted a number of important features of technology as well as some problems with existing approaches. From each of the approaches discussed we can take the following:

- From the socio-technical approach the notion that there is a *relationship* between technology and organization.
- From the structurationist approach the importance of distinguishing between the scope and the role of technology:
  - For the former, the scope should be confined to material artefacts
  - For the latter, the perceptions of those using technology are important in how technology is used.
- From actor–network theory the need to be specific about technology and the importance of material properties.

The morphogenetic approach is that associated with Margaret Archer (1995), which we cover in more detail in Chapter 10. Archer, just like Giddens, has little to say about technology. However, her realist approach suggests that, contrary to the social constructivism of Grint and Woolgar (1997), there is a world independent of our knowing of it. This suggests that technology can possess material properties whether or not these are perceived by the user. Her morphogenetic approach also suggests that technology is not to be seen as a structure in its own right, but as a bearer of the marks of wider structures. Thus, for example, functional boundaries can be inscribed into software and in the process appear to future users as real constraints which limit their freedom of action. We will see this in operation later in this chapter. This approach also suggests that we need to look at levels of technology (as developed in Whyte 2005). In terms of ICT we can suggest a number of levels, each of which could be sub-divided. We could suggest that there is a hardware level, which draws our attention to particular arrangements of physical artefacts, which constrain and enable the software which can run on them. We will see an example of the constraining nature of physical arrangements in our review of data warehousing shortly.

We could split the software level into a number of sub levels. From a user perspective (as opposed to systems development) the important layers are probably those of the operating system, the applications software and the interface. Clearly, there are overlaps between these but what is important is the degree to which these are manipulable by the user and over what time period. For most users the operating system is a given, not open to change except at the organizational level, and even here the choice is in practice between a limited set of options determined elsewhere. There is more choice at the level of the application, where we might also include the data structures that are enacted. The level often most malleable by the user is that which they interface with, where to a greater or lesser degree there is the ability to customize screens and reports. For example, as we will see with the groupware that is so much a feature of the work of Orlikowski and collaborators, there is the capability to radically customize software.

For the purpose of the discussion which follows we are going to focus on three levels as organizing principles: hardware, software and interfaces. This is to simplify matters, but also to draw attention to the very different pace at which these can change and which influence the nature of the information produced. As part of the interface we will include the nature of the data represented by the system. Later we will see how Ciborra and Patriotta (1996) refer to this as the 'infostructure'. Such an infostructure often appears to users as representations on the screen or on pieces of paper produced by computer programs. Such representations often only take material form when brought together as the result of the rules built into software, rules which in turn are dependent on definitions agreed as an outcome of organizational debate (or created by default). While such representations might not bear a direct relation to the physical forms in which they are stored, their 'logical' relations (to use the term often encountered in the language of computer specialists) is what is most important. As Hutchby observes:

> materiality here need not be thought of only in physical terms. We may, for instance, be able to conceive of the telephone as having a materiality affecting the distribution of interactional space through the promotion of what I will call conversational 'intimacy at a distance' . . . Likewise, we can conceive of the interfaces of expert systems or Internet conferencing software as having a materiality affecting navigation through a technically bounded interactional space as people attempt to orient themselves in the sequential order of a particular interaction.
>
> (Hutchby 2001: 3)

However, it is not enough to simply distinguish between levels. If we are to 'be specific' about technology it is important that we distinguish between the features which different applications possess (Jasperson, Carter and Zmud 2005). This can often be difficult, in part because different applications can overlap and be made to perform the same function. For example, one can produce a list in word processing, spreadsheet or database packages. We might argue that one of these packages is best able to fulfil that function, but the others can be made to stretch to it. Groupware packages, for example, are enabled to facilitate collaborative work using shared databases and discussion boards, but intranet systems can be made, if not always as efficiently and securely, to meet the same function. This blurring is further confused by the practice of software vendors of re-badging products and making large claims for their capabilities.

However, if one sets data warehouses, which feature the large scale manipulation of huge volumes of data, against the ability of groupware packages to handle unstructured databases then we get an indication of the need to be clear about features. That is, one feature set is optimized for high volume data manipulation, the other for unstructured information sharing, a distinction which we will illustrate later. For now, our working definition of ICT will be 'technologies for the processing, storage and transmission of digital material, consisting of ensembles of hardware and software with distinctive feature sets allowing for the physical storage and logical representation of different forms of data'. You will notice that in this definition we have avoided both the terms 'information' and 'communication'. This is because these are profoundly human acts in which interpretation and context are of central importance. The problem with the use of the terms information and communication in 'ICT' is that we run the risk of reducing these activities to matters of technology. However, the term 'ICT' is a widely used one in everyday discourse that we need to work with, and so is used as a convenient shorthand throughout.

APPLICATIONS AND DATA

This next section is about those applications which are particularly optimized for and aimed at the intensive manipulation of data. As with all of our discussion of technology, the focus is on the implications for our information literate manager, rather than on technical features in and of themselves. However, we need to consider the impact of such features in so far as they both constrain and enable particular uses. In order to set this in context we need some basic appreciation of the ways in which data can be handled by ICT. Accordingly, this section covers the following:

- The emergence and use of databases.
- The use of data warehouses for intensive data analysis.
- The application of terms such as Executive Information Systems and Business Intelligence to enable particular forms of access to data.
- Other applications which also rely on and supply extensive types of data:
  - Product Data Management
  - Customer Relationship Management
  - Workflow.

From data to database

Our starting point in considering the ways in which data are handled by ICT is the distinction between data as an integral part of an application and data maintained in a distinct form. In many early systems, some of which still run, data was created by and modified by the applications in which it was used. This meant that, for example, an organization might have several different systems, all with their own separate records for customer names and addresses. While this might enable the individual applications to run, incompatible formats meant that it was difficult, if not impossible, to relate records to each other. Many major banks, for example, found that when their market place shifted from a focus on accounts to one on customers their existing systems prevented them from responding (Ennew, Watkins and Wright 1995); it prevented them from developing effective cross-selling, as they had no way of knowing what customers received which services. The consequence was a shift to a database form of organization. In such a form of organization, the data is kept independent from the applications which use it. There is therefore one customer name and address record, which is drawn upon as required by applications, but maintained independent of them. This allows for the easier cross-referencing of data.

However, we have to appreciate that simply having data organized in this fashion does not solve all data access problems. Indeed, the Country Holidays example at the beginning of this chapter illustrates something of the elusive promise of databases. We have to distinguish here between forms of database which are optimized to run operations and those which are best for running queries, as the two are not necessarily the same. Some forms of database are *hierarchical* in form, where data relationships are determined in advance and written into the structure of the database. This leads to very fast processing but makes changes extremely difficult. A new report, for example, which combines data items from different parts of the hierarchy may require extensive restructuring of the database. There are ways round this, but a key one was the development of the *relational* database.

This will be familiar on a small scale to those who have used a desktop database like Microsoft Access, where data are organized in tables and relationships can be established between fields in those tables. However, it is important to realize that such a structure requires careful analysis and design when millions of items of data are being handled. Sophisticated techniques have been devised to construct tables and the relationships between them in order to enable speedy response and processing. It is just such speedy response that Country Holidays required to enable them to check availability and confirm bookings on the telephone. However, such data structures are not the best for in-depth queries. Their structure means that logic can be hard to follow and queries constructed in the wrong fashion can cause immense processing problems. Hence many organizations with extensive data volumes and a desire to analyse that data started to look for alternative ways of organizing them. This leads us to a consideration of the data warehouse.

Data warehousing

One of the responses to the problem of the incompatibility between data organized for operations and the desire to use them for analytical purposes was to take a copy of the data

Table 4.1 *Data warehouses*

Level	Features
Data	Large volumes of transaction data, transferred from operational systems
Software	Online Analytical Processing (OLAP) allowing for multi-dimensional views of data. Transfer and cleansing applications
Hardware	Standalone specialist processors. Parallel processing

and move them to another machine (Westerman 2001). In this way, queries could be run which would not interfere with day to day operations. As part of this shift an important development was the availability of new forms of hardware which would enable the processing of large volumes of data. While this had traditionally been done on mainframe computers, large machines designed to handle such tasks, these faced the same problem that faced all computer architecture, that of sequential processing. That is, traditional computer architectures execute one task at a time and, regardless of the speed of the processor, this places a limit on the volume of transactions that can be processed. However, new developments in computer architecture resulted in the design of parallel processing, that is, where a computer consisted of a number of processors running in parallel. When tasks could be split up that could benefit from such an arrangement, such as extensive data processing, then considerable gains in speed could be obtained. In the earlier years of data warehousing such specialist machines were at the heart of developments and one continues to be the foundation for the running of the world's largest civilian data warehouse, that run by Wal-Mart in the USA (Westerman 2001). Developments in computing power have meant that smaller volumes of data can be run on less specialized hardware, but the availability of the right hardware is still an important consideration.

We also need to bear in mind that the data warehouse also depends on the existence of other hardware components. The networking of computers both to supply access and to enable the transfer of data is important, but the widespread growth of technologies for the automatic capture of data is what feeds the volumes of data that make analysis effective. These have been particularly prominent in retail operations, where the associated developments of bar codes on products and scanning software to read them have enabled the automatic collection of sales data. Such technologies have been applied in a wide range of other situations, notably in many parts of supply chain operations. This means that items can be tracked in their progress through operations and as a consequence create records that can be stored. This produces data which are less susceptible to problems such as mistranscription. It also produces an enormous volume of data. Such volumes necessitate the type of specialist processing which we have already met. Until such specialist processing was available, it proved difficult for many organizations, especially those with high volumes of low value transactions to analyse their data. However, data warehousing is not just about particular types of hardware. It is also, and most importantly, a way of defining particular types of data. We can get a better insight to this by examining a little further the definition supplied by Bill Inmon, a key player in the development of the concept. His definition is that 'a data warehouse is a subject oriented, integrated, non volatile, time variant collection of data designed to support management DSS needs' (Inmon 2001).

Let us work through the elements of this definition in turn to see how specialized this particular application is. The *subject oriented* part suggests that data warehouses are built for a purpose, that they are not just a collection of all the data that an organization possesses, but rather are of a selection of that data chosen for particular need, needs which will vary according to the approach taken by the organization. Thus in the Wal-Mart case there is a particular orientation on supplier information, because the data is used in supplier negotiations to reduce cost. In the case of Tesco, another significant adopter, the focus is on customer data. Data warehouses often start off by collecting data to answer a specific set of questions and then grow and develop to take in further types of data. One key problem which arises is when the project is treated as a technical one in which the aim is to get all the data together and then see what questions can be asked. For example, Humby, Hunt and Phillips (2003: 4) report that the response of one UK supermarket, Waitrose, to their attempts to use a data warehouse was that 'trying to analyse all the data is madness'. Their argument would be that this demonstrates that one should start with the questions rather than with either the data or the technology. There are debates within the literature (Westerman 2001) about the best form of organization of data warehouses, with some favouring the creation of smaller data marts. The advantage of the latter is that processing times are reduced and the data can be better fitted to particular needs. However, the benefit of being able to make relationships with other pieces of data is curtailed and there are risks of developing inconsistent islands of data out of step with each other. This is not a matter for our detailed consideration, but it does suggest that our information literate manager will need to take some interest in broad principles of design, as these are likely to affect the nature and type of data available.

Of course, data in organizations are unlikely to be captured by just one system. In most organizations a range of systems capture and process data. Often the most value is obtained when such data are cross-referenced, as it is only then that important patterns emerge. However, such data are often inconsistent. In data warehousing terms they have to be 'cleansed' before they can be used. This means the conversion into compatible format and, often, the tagging of data to indicate their source. Such operations are time consuming and often the Achilles Heel of the process. However, it is this to which Inmon is referring when considering the data in warehouses to be *integrated*. This means that they have been merged from supporting sub-systems in such a fashion that relationships can be established. Another distinction, and one that is necessary in order for analysis to take place at all, is that such data are *non-volatile*. This means that once in the warehouse they are not subject to change, unlike in an operational system. One of the penalties of using operational data for decision making is that they are always liable to change. Thus, two analyses conducted at even slightly different times are likely to come up with different answers. The benefit of having data which stand apart from operations is that they represent a snapshot in time (or elements of trend data) which can be more relied on.

Data are transferred to the warehouse at particular points in time – they are *time variant*. Dependent both on the nature of the business and the questions which are being asked, this might be on a daily, a weekly or even a monthly basis. This means that analysts have to be clear about how time matters in relation to the data which they are using. While many operational decisions require real time data, many other decisions can use aggregated data on longer time periods. There is a clear trade off here between the increased accuracy gained with finer levels of detail and the processing and storage overheads incurred. It might be that the 'accuracy' is spurious, in that too much detail clouds underlying patterns. This can be particularly the case with the

USING HISTORIC DATA IN A SUPERMARKET

During the process of developing their data warehouse, Tesco faced price competition. The traditional response to such moves by a competitor might be to lower prices across the board. However, this might mean that in order to retain price sensitive customers (those likely to defect to another store on the grounds of price alone) the company might be giving discounts on products bought by customers who were not likely to defect anyway. In other words, the selection of products was important if the company was not simply to waste money by giving ineffective incentives. Using their Clubcard data they had segmented their customer base on the basis of shopping patterns over a period of time. From this they were able to establish products which were bought largely by price conscious customers. If they could offer discounts on these products this would retain these customers without giving discounts to those who did not need them to stay loyal. They selected Tesco Value Brand Margarine, as they identified from their data that this was bought only by those customers likely to defect on grounds of price alone. A price cut on this product was relatively cheap but had the desired effect.

Source: adapted from Humby, Hunt and Phillips 2003: 147

other aspect of time, that of the use of historical data to determine trends. This is often where the greatest value is realized, but it means that data needs to be clearly assigned to a particular time period and rules developed about how such data are aggregated.

The example of Tesco Value Brand Margarine suggests the value that might be derived from an analysis of historical data. However, the extraction of such value is not a trivial matter. The literature is replete with stories of failed data warehouses, stories which rest more on organizational than technical issues. However, some of these still have a technical component. One of these is the data structure adopted. For example, one manager comments:

> Entity Relationship Modelling [ERM] normalization is a great technique for reducing data redundancy, and a great technique for ensuring an optimum database design for flexibility etc. However, it is the worst possible technique for ensuring a queryable database.
>
> (Finnegan and Sammon 2002: 205)

That is, a particular technique, in this case ERM, can be used to ensure that the way data are stored is optimized to get the fastest response possible for operational uses. These techniques are used to produce particular patterns of data which are technically appropriate. However, their use then produces a confusing form of organization for those who wish to ask questions of the data. Of course, the decision about which techniques to use is an organizational one, but once made it constrains what can be achieved. Similarly, the choice of software which enables particular types of query is important. For example, queries often wish to address multiple dimensions simultaneously (time, product, space, responsibility – for example, think about the marketing manager who wishes to determine which product has sold most in which area in a particular time period, sorted by manager). There are particular tools which facilitate this process but their use poses further questions, some of which we will address in later chapters.

A particularly specialized application in this area is that of *data mining*. Data mining involves the use of specialist pieces of software which search for patterns in data, patterns which would be difficult if not impossible for a human being to ascertain, given the volumes of data with which we are dealing. It is here that many of the techniques derived from research in artificial intelligence have been applied most effectively. Artificial intelligence is that class of applications which seek to model human problem solving techniques and encode them. Such applications have brought a measure of success in the limited domain of expert systems. These are computer systems which work on the basis of rules derived from expert practice. While there are many problems with eliciting such rules (both because experts find it difficult to say what such rules are and because of their reluctance to share them) such systems have been implemented in a wide range of problem areas. These are notably those areas where there are clear boundaries and a limited number of cases, most of which follow standard rules. For example, credit card providers use such systems, based on statistical analysis of spending patterns, to identify potential fraud (Bolton and Hand, 2002). Such cases can then be reported out for further investigation. However, our mention of statistical techniques points to one area of concern for managers facing data warehouses, that of training and skills. There are a number of other such concerns which we will need to consider later. Briefly these are:

- Questions of power and data ownership. Many projects fail not for technical reasons but because they raise questions of data ownership, which in turn can be related to particular positions. These are returned to in Chapter 9.
- Even if questions of ownership are resolved, data warehouses raise important questions about data quality. We have reviewed some of these above, but they raise concerns about policy which we return to in Chapter 6.
- There are questions about training, roles and responsibilities. In particular issues are raised by widespread data manipulation:
  - Is such manipulation best left to statistical experts or is statistical training needed by those who use warehousing systems?
  - Effective use also requires some knowledge and skills in specialized computer applications. Are these best left to computer specialists or can they be developed in so-called 'power users'?
  - What is the relationship between these specialists and other users?
  - What are the ethical concerns raised by the collection and analysis of such extensive bodies of personal information?

These questions are discussed in Chapter 8. Meanwhile, however, you should have enough detail to appreciate how important such applications can be and how they raise new questions for our information literate manager. The spread of such applications has lead to a resurgence of applications which draw on such data to deliver information to more senior managers, now often under the label of Business Intelligence.

Executive Information Systems and Business Intelligence

The 1970s saw many advances in the automation of many basic tasks, but considerable frustration at the information available to senior managers. The applications in use were based

Table 4.2 *Executive Information Systems*

Level	Features
Data	Operational data from internal systems, feeds from external data providers (e.g. share prices, raw material prices)
Software	Drill down capacity, often via graphical representation, from high level figures to source data. Presentation of data
Hardware	Touchscreens. Often dedicated hardware with data feeds from operational systems

on rather rigid mainframe systems, with reporting in the form of standard paper reports. Some work had been done on management information systems and decision support systems, but these seemed to be aimed largely at operational systems. They were not particularly user friendly and produced large volumes of data in which it was difficult to see what counted. In particular, the feeling was that the systems pushed data out, rather than allowing for direct access to the significant data. It was in this environment that John Rockart (1979) published his influential article in *Harvard Business Review*, 'Chief executives define their own data needs'. In this he suggested that the decreasing cost and expanding power of computers could enable direct access by senior managers to operational data. To facilitate this he suggested a methodology based on the notion of critical success factors and key performance indicators. What was important about this was that such success factors would be set by senior managers themselves. In other words, the aim was that information needs would be determined by the objectives set by senior managers rather than by the features of the data.

The instantiation of these ideas in terms of applications was the development of the Executive Information System (EIS). Some might argue that these were a product of their time, soon to be forgotten, but this would be to dismiss them rather too easily. Tracking the development of such systems actually indicates not only some enduring features but also some important underlying trends. Dismissing the EIS too quickly is symptomatic of the lack of attention to data in the literature purporting to look at organizational information use. What, then, were the key features of an EIS? The central design feature was one of direct access to operational systems, enabling executives to 'drill down' into the data. So, rather than asking for reports from support staff, reports which could be time consuming to produce and subject to omissions and distortions in their compilation, executives could obtain the data they required directly. This would be done through a system of exception reporting. Thus levels of acceptability would be set for key indicators and status would be indicated visually. Typically this meant that acceptable figures would be displayed in green, missed targets in red. The executive, alerted to problems in this fashion, would be able to investigate the problem by looking at the contributory data. If, for example, sales failed to reach target, the executive could work down through various levels to ascertain the cause. Of particular importance in selling such systems was the presentation of the data. Much was made of newly available computing power to use features such as touch screens which would enable a direct connection to be made without the mediation of devices such as keyboards. A number of such systems were installed with some success, but rather more such applications failed, bringing the whole concept into some disrepute (Houdeshei and Watson 1987; Cottrell and Rapley 1991; Belcher and Watson 1993; Allison 1996).

Two key factors seemed to lie behind many of the failures. One was the state of operational data. The success of EIS was predicated on the existence of appropriate operational data systems, but many organizations found that in practice their data was not in a satisfactory state. We need to bear in mind that these developments occurred when many companies operated with disparate data systems lacking common data definitions. As we will see, developments associated with data warehouses may have helped ease this concern. The second was that such systems did not match the way the majority of the target audience operated. This was not a matter of technophobia (although some of that may well have existed). Rather, if we turn back to Mintzberg's (1973) pioneering work on *The Nature of Managerial Work* we find that the executives that he studied worked in a responsive manner in which they were continually interrupted. As we saw in Chapter 2, rather than having the time to analyse figures in detail, they had remarkably little time to pay attention to any particular problem. They depended on others to provide the data they required and operated with much more action centred information. Such findings have been replicated in other studies of senior management, and suggest that the ideal of the data driven 'rational' manager which Rockart had in mind was far from what was obtained in practice. However, we need to be careful in dismissing EIS too hastily because it failed on these two counts. The relative lack of attention given to them after a peak of interest in the late 1980s could be down to a number of factors:

- They may indeed have been completely unsuccessful and have been replaced with more appropriate systems – or with nothing at all.
- They may have escaped academic attention because of the persistent focus on implementation problems. In other words, the failure of EIS may be as much an artefact of academic investigation as it is of practice.
- They may have transformed into other applications, perhaps under a different name, based on the learning from early experience.

That the latter contention may have some validity can be seen if we return to the ideas underlying Rockart's original formulations. These were, stripped of any direct relationship with ICT, that senior managers ought to be determining information needs by starting from critical success factors. Defined as the key elements which would have to happen in order for an organization to be successful, these in fact became a widespread management technique. One early problem with this approach was that, given the state of existing data systems, it tended to place a focus on those elements within an organization which could be measured. Given the widespread early computerization of accounting systems, this meant that in practice many early key performance indicators were financial in nature. This drew a critical reaction on the grounds that it tended to downplay other areas essential for organizational survival such as having the right expertise and engaging in successful research and development. The advocates of the 'balanced scorecard' suggested ways of correcting this imbalance, often instantiated in new forms of ICT-enabled applications such as 'executive dashboards' (Kaplan and Norton 1993).

This form of thinking has been remarkably influential and not only within organizations. The development of a performance management culture, founded on numerical indicators, has been a feature of many aspects of public life. Many aspects of human activity, such as education and health, are now subject to the publication of league tables which purport to show performance and to rank it. That such measures can often be profoundly misleading, reducing as they do often complex and difficult questions to simple numbers, is a matter for considerable debate. However, it does explain why systems such as 'Business Intelligence' replicate many of the features of the EIS in new guise. Indeed, in an overview of the restructuring of contemporary business, Ackroyd (2002) argues, although without the detail that we have supplied here, that much coordination in major multinationals is enabled by just the systems we have been discussing here. As a complement to such systems, 'not a chance discovery of a better way of organizing, or the benign expression of goodwill of employers' (Ackroyd 2002: 174), comes the requirement to foster more collaborative ways of working. In their desire to focus on resistance and failure, many critical accounts have perhaps tended to ignore the importance of such systems.

Part of what has happened to EIS, therefore, is that they have mutated into other forms of system – variously termed 'Everybody's Information System' or more formally 'Enterprise Information Systems'. As we will see below, the initial failures have prompted further developments. However, the newer systems, often termed 'Business Intelligence', have benefited from other developments. The work done in many organizations under the push to develop data warehouses has had the impact of improving sources of operational data. Indeed, the data warehouse itself can supply one unified source of data, so that it can be used as the basis for performance management reports as well as for analytical queries. In addition, developments at the level of the interface have meant that such systems are more accessible. Some use familiar business analysis tools, like the spreadsheet, as their means of access, thus allowing additional manipulation. In other settings the use of intranet browsers as an access channel enables wider access. These developments, as Ackroyd (2002) points out, have implications for the way in which organizations are run, implications which we will return to when we explore organizational structure in more detail. For now, however, we also need to consider in a little less detail some further applications which also extend the range of data available to our information literate manager.

FROM 'EXECUTIVE INFORMATION SYSTEM' TO 'EVERYBODY'S INFORMATION SYSTEM'

A major steel corporation, responding to the enthusiasm of a senior executive, created an EIS in 1984. Allowing access to familiar reports but with improved graphics capability, this was used by other executives until the original sponsor left the company. Its use then withered away, with executives preferring to ask others to provide the information they needed. They found the system limited and inflexible; as their information needs were unpredictable and triggered by events, they preferred to ask others to provide them with what they needed. However, the system proved of considerable value to more junior managers and improved access saw the level of queries rise dramatically. The system fitted with the work patterns and information requirements of these managers much more closely.

Source: Wheeler, Chang and Thomas (1993)

Making data visible: varieties of enterprise data

Enterprise Resource Planning

Enterprise Resource Planning (ERP) systems are the latest attempt to realize the elusive promise of databases: the provision of a common set of data operating across all an enterprise's operations (Davenport 1998). For many companies the problem was that they could obtain applications which shared common data, but these applications might not be the most suited to operational needs. If they sought the applications which best suited their operations, they might end up with the problems that databases were designed to avoid: functional islands of data. ERP systems offer the prospect of addressing these problems by their modular design. They arose out of manufacturing solutions such as Materials Resource Planning (MRP) and have clear lineages in the tradition of regarding information as a key 'resource'. They were associated in particular with two developments. One was the management technique known as Business Process Re-engineering, which we will cover in more detail later, but in essence suggested that new forms of IT could support radically new forms of working which were structured according to process rather than function. The second was the panic around the year 2000 problem: many organizations were concerned that their ageing systems would not be able to cope with the date change of the new millennium having been programmed only with two characters for dates (and so 01 would come before, not after 99). As a consequence, they decided to replace their systems with what they perceived as an integrated system.

Much of the focus on ERP systems has been on the implications for work processes. The systems tend to suggest particular ways of working – indeed, much of the attraction for many senior decision makers is that such systems seem an ideal way of enforcing 'best practice' (Benders, Batenburg and Van der Blonk 2006). They need to work this way if extensive (and expensive) attempts are to be avoided to customize them. Much of the criticism has centred on the way that such a perspective ignores the often implicit aspects of existing working practices and has sought to demonstrate the way that in practice users have resisted attempts to change such practices (Boudreau and Robey 2005). In addition, the association of ERP with many failed attempts to carry through BPR has led to a form of guilt by association. These concerns are all valid, but they perhaps tend to underplay the impact on data in organizations. Again, much of the critical attention has been on the initial implementation period, when many problems do seem to have called into question the value of ERP. Investigations following the bedding in of such systems are needed to determine what the longer term consequences for data availability and use are. However, such systems certainly bring to the fore questions of data quality that we will consider in Chapter 6 when looking at strategy.

Table 4.3 *Enterprise Resource Planning*

Level	Features
Data	Single view of data across operations; require adoption of standard processes or extensive customization
Software	Modular design with modules for major business processes
Hardware	Client-server with mainframe for central data storage

ERP AND DATA QUALITY

In 2004 the UK furniture retailer MFI hit the headlines when major problems were reported with its implementation of an ERP system. The system was designed to automate its supply chain, but the new system in practice meant that customer orders were not being fulfilled. ERP systems have their roots in manufacturing, where the business processes, and so the associated data, are relatively straightforward. However, implementing such systems in retailing has to deal with changing priorities and large volumes of data. The problems in MFI appeared to be ones of data quality, with the system depending on the disciplined entry of data at source.

'Most of the issues you get when doing SAP are about the transition of data from old systems into new systems,' said an MFI source close to the project. 'You get issues around managing the data – data disciplines at depots, for example – or the quality of data put into the system by people. The other issues you get are around process and procedural robustness,' he says. 'You are asking a lot of people to change the way they work and this takes time.'

The problems with the system were eventually to cost the company £80 million and saw the chief executive leave.

Source: Ballard (2004); Thompson (2006)

Product Data Management/Shopfloor Capture and Data Analysis

One case where we do have a detailed investigation of a system with impacts on data capture and subsequent use is that on a set of applications known as Product Data Management (PDM). Luciana D'Adderio (2004) investigated such a system in some depth and concluded that accounts which solely focused on resistance and failure were not sufficient to understand such systems. What she noted in particular was the way in which such systems brought to the fore previously hidden or latent disputes over just what terms meant. PDM systems are designed to assemble the vast amount of data that is generated about a product during its manufacture, ranging from initial design to specification and production. Such data are becoming of more importance given changes in product markets. We have seen, for example, how train manufacturers are now not simply selling trains but also taking responsibility for extended periods of maintenance. In such circumstances it is important for maintenance engineers to have access to data which have been generated during design and production phases, not only

Table 4.4 *Product Data Management/SCADA*

Level	Features
Data	Automated data capture from sensors and control devices; design data
Software	Data capture from operational and design systems; mapping and monitoring of processes
Hardware	Client-server; specialist design workstations

to fix immediate problems but also to suggest changes in manufacturing processes which might make future maintenance easier. By the same token, success in pharmaceutical markets may depend on how quickly regulatory approval can be obtained (McKinlay 2002). Such approval requires the generation of masses of data from not only manufacturing but also from field trials. Being able to access such data rapidly can be of considerable importance. Data like these may traditionally have been generated in a number of different formats. For example, an engineering drawing may need to be converted into a bill of materials to enable purchasing to take place. The increasing use of ICT at various stages, such as Computer Aided Design, makes it more possible to collect such data and 'attach' it to products throughout their lifecycle.

What D'Adderio noted, however, was that this process was far from being just a 'technical' one; it in fact uncovered major differences in the way different functions perceived the world. She observes that:

> The PDM-EPL [Engineering Parts List] configuration is information for engineering because they have the knowledge required to interpret it. Production instead comes from a differ-ent sub-disciplinary background and is unable to make sense of the data contained in the engineering EPL.
>
> (D'Adderio 2004: 117)

The desire was to use the same EPL in both functions, containing the same data, in order to have a smoother flow of work between the two functions. However, this failed to recognize the importance of often implicit theories in making sense of data. The problem in this organ-ization was that the gap in meaning meant that they were unable to spot mistakes made in automated conversions from design to production systems, so resulting in more inefficiencies than before the software was implemented. D'Adderio concludes that:

> supporting the formation of shared meanings across the organization is not simply about ensuring smooth information and communication flows across functions, but also, and most importantly, about integrating meaning structures.
>
> (D'Adderio 2004: 121)

This is an important consideration that we will return to. However, it is also worth at this stage recognizing a further source of data in the manufacturing process, that of the automated collection of data on the operation of processes.

Such systems are often grouped under the acronym SCADA (Supervisory Control and Data Acquisition) and are to be found in many process industries. They consist of the control of processes through sensors which produce data on current states, data often represented on monitors in central control rooms. Of course, as we will see later, the realization of such benefits depended on having the training to both recognize and utilize such data, but this observation mirrors those made by Zuboff (1988) in her study of working practices in paper mills. This is the process she refers to as 'informate'; the making visible of data on not only what has been produced but how it has been produced. Many systems, from supermarket tills to websites, automatically produce data which can be subsequently analysed for patterns and trends. One key such system in the Country Holidays case was the Automatic Call Distribution (ACD) system which managed telephone traffic. Not only did this route traffic to the appropriate

COLLECTING DATA THROUGH ICT

Shorko was a manufacturer of plastic packaging films which implemented a new automated production process control system. Rather than shopfloor workers manually turning valves to change inputs, these were now automated and controlled semi-automatically from a central control room. This made production cheaper and more efficient, but the crucial difference was the data that were acquired on the production process. This enabled learning about the different composition of films and enabled the organization to move into new areas of specialist packaging material.

Source: Earl 1994

team, but it could also collect data on patterns of customer response. The widespread use of such systems in call centres has led in part to the development of systems which will store and manage data on customers.

Customer Relationship Management

As with so many aspects of ICT in organizations, we face problems of definition when considering Customer Relationship Management (CRM). For some it applies just to specific examples of technology designed to store customer data, for others it is a broad philosophy which seeks to emphasize the importance of a single and consistent view of the customer relationship (Payne and Frow 2005). It can be applied to the data acquired through loyalty schemes, to that which is generated through call centres or to that which is created when visits to websites are monitored. It can also be applied to systems such as sales force automation, where ICT is applied to automatically record contacts. In many cases, the data are generated automatically and, indeed, can be adjusted by customers themselves. For example, under the latter category come recommendation systems on sites such as Amazon, which use opportunities to gather data about preferences from customers directly (rather than using purchasing patterns to infer such preferences). However, in many cases such data are not so readily available. Hayes and Walsham (2000) cover sales force resistance to the use of a contact recording system, which was seen as generating extra work for sales representatives. Not only was this perceived to have little additional value for them, but also it raised the spectre of closer monitoring of their activities.

This concern with surveillance is an important facet of much use of ICT to which we will return in Chapter 9. However, from a data-centric perspective the concern might be to draw

Table 4.5 *Customer Relationship Management*

Level	Features
Data	Transaction data from sales systems, web systems and sales contact systems
Software	Analysis of relationships
Hardware	Client-server with mainframe for data volumes

a distinction between these applications and those we explored above in the section on data warehouses. Drawing on his research with sales reps, Walsham (2001: 601) comments 'if we recognized the complexity of these processes a little more, we might have less data warehouses which nobody visits'. However, as we have seen, a crucial distinguishing point here is the method of data capture. Data warehouses, as with several of the systems that we have discussed, rely on automated methods of data capture. Such methods generate large bodies of data which can be analysed to suggest patterns and relationships. Of course, much data in organizations does not take such a form. CRM applications operate somewhere on the boundary between the type of structured data generated in data warehouses and other rather less structured forms. It was this blurring that led Payton and Zahay (2003) to observe that marketing operations frequently do not use data warehouses. In particular the desire was for more external data. Such data might often be available for purchase externally, as in the use by the credit card company Capital One of extensive bodies of demographic data. However, the importance here was the recognition of the need and the capacity to integrate such data with internal operations (Day 2003). This capacity for integration is also important in the final system we discuss, one which also sits on the boundary between the structured data systems we have been reviewing and the more unstructured systems we consider in the next chapter.

Workflow

Workflow systems are those which use ICT to automatically route work. The reason why they cross the boundaries is that they are often reliant on document management systems, systems which operate on the premise that much of the data in organizations is contained not in transaction data but in documents of various types. However, such documents can also be part of intensive workflow systems which can be modelled, configured and controlled using ICT. Workflow systems are particularly applicable in document intensive operations where routine operations have to be carried out in particular orders, often involving elements of parallel processing. For example, an insurance claim often needs to be approved in particular stages. Some of these stages can be carried out in parallel. Using a paper claim means that such processes take time, both with the same file being needed by different groups at the same time and with the file being in transit. Workflow systems, in which details of the claim are entered in the application, can eliminate these delays. Claims can be routed automatically to the next available agent, taking into account work on hand and expertise. Several such agents can work on the same claim in parallel, using their specialist expertise. From a data perspective, this once again creates data about how a process operates, identifying time taken to process claims at different stages. Of course, this raises an important question about power and surveillance to which we

Table 4.6 *Workflow management*

Level	Features
Data	Document handling; data on workloads and competencies
Software	Process mapping and monitoring; automatic allocation of tasks
Hardware	Document scanning and handling; client-server network

THE POTENTIAL OF DATA

Using the capacity given to them by their telephone system, Country Holidays attached a different telephone number to each media source in which they advertised. This meant that telephone queries automatically carried with them an indicator of source, enabling the company to maintain records of the number of brochure requests generated by a particular source. This record was then retained to enable the company to see how many such requests then turned into bookings. Using these two sources, the telephone system and the bookings database, enabled the company to monitor its media selection. It could tell not only which sources generated the most enquiries and therefore could calculate a cost per brochure mailed, but could also work out a conversion ratio. Using this enabled them to discover that relatively cheap adverts in outlets like the *Sun* newspaper (a downmarket tabloid) generated a large number of brochure requests but relatively few bookings. By contrast, rather more expensive adverts in outlets like the *Guardian* (a quality broadsheet) generated relatively few brochure requests, but a far higher conversion rate. Thus the rate per booking was lower with the more expensive advertisement.

Source: Green 1992

will return. Workflow systems provide yet another example of systems which not only handle data but also create it.

HANDLING DATA: CONCLUSION

The experience at Country Holidays, coupled with the preceding discussion, should suggest some implications of data intensive applications for our information literate manager. One of the key attributes of such a manager was 'awareness of the range of sources available to them'. We have seen that such sources have expanded dramatically with ICT developments. Managers now have a far greater range of data to analyse, but this brings with it certain important considerations. We might suggest that the following are of particular importance:

- Data quality becomes a key issue for many managers: in a number of applications that we discussed, a major stumbling block to effective use has been the quality of data available. In particular, we have seen the importance of 'meta data', that is, data about data. In the Country Holidays example above, without an automatic form of tracking, in which a particular piece of data identifying source was attached to transaction data, the sort of analysis carried out could not have been effective.
- Asking the right questions: the mention of meta data suggests that we need to have thought in advance of data collection what features we need to record to enable subsequent analysis. The Country Holidays example suggests that such awareness resulted in the effective capture and transformation of data. However, the example that we reviewed of PDM suggests that such matters are not straightforward. The extensive use of data often reveals different levels

of organizational understanding. As D'Adderio suggests, the solution is not a technical one, but rather opportunities to understand different frames of meaning.

- Extensive data sources and integration: our information literate manager may well be faced with an abundance of data, but this requires integration if it is to be used effectively. The experience with data warehousing suggests that this is a difficult task, particularly with external data. Organizations need the means for debating data definitions that take them out of a technical realm. Managers also need to be aware of the capacity to capture data automatically with a view to correcting potential mistakes at source. Questions about data capture therefore become an important managerial concern – but they might often be 'technical' responsibilities by default.

- The ability to collect, store and interrogate extensive bodies of data raises important ethical questions. The ability to cross-reference such data and to sell it on for unexpected purposes raises important questions about privacy. Such considerations also apply to the use of internal performance data for monitoring purposes. This raises important questions of both policy and individual awareness.

Our discussion should also indicate some more general concerns that we can relate back to our earlier discussion about technology. They confirm the importance of considering the features of technology, as these have allowed us to distinguish between the capabilities of particular applications. In addition, as D'Adderio suggests, a narrative based solely on images of failure and resistance does not seem to account for the importance of many of these applications. However, it might be argued that we are only scratching the surface of the application of ICT in contemporary organizations. Many such applications deal not with the type of structured data that we have been reviewing here, but with rather more unstructured forms. In particular, there is now more of a focus on the 'communication' element of ICT. This is what we consider at more length in the next chapter.

SUMMARY

- Definitions of technology need to avoid either privileging technical forms (and so falling into the trap of technological determinism) or downplaying the constraints posed by the material properties of the technology.

- It can be useful to conceive of technology as having a number of levels and features. This gave us a working definition of ICT as 'technologies for the processing, storage and transmission of digital material, consisting of ensembles of hardware and software with distinctive feature sets allowing for the physical storage and logical representation of different forms of data'.

- While we can agree that it is how technology is used that is the most important aspect, this does not remove the need to be specific about the technology. Different combinations of features allow us to do different things with data and make others more difficult.

- ICT has enabled the automatic generation, collection and storage of much larger volumes of data and so has seen the generation of a range of systems dedicated to the analysis of data.

- The potential offered by such systems is conditioned by organizational factors such as data ownership and definition.

REVIEW QUESTIONS

1 What are Inmon's attributes of a data warehouse?

2 Explain the meaning of 'drill down' in the context of Executive Information Systems.

DISCUSSION QUESTIONS

1 Take the Country Holidays example which featured at the beginning of this chapter. What recommendations would you make to the company following your reading of this chapter?

2 If one feature of being information literate is 'knowledge of major current resources', how might this be affected by the systems we have covered in this chapter?

FURTHER READING

Humby, C., Hunt, T. and Phillips, T. (2003) *Scoring Points: How Tesco is Winning Customer Loyalty*. London, Kogan Page.

Rare example of extended treatment of the practical and strategic implications of intensive data analysis, based on insights of those who developed analysis systems for Tesco. Very readable account with some illuminating examples.

Hutchby, I. (2001) *Conversation and Technology: From the Telephone to the Internet*. Cambridge, Polity.

More to do with communication in the public sphere, but not only some implications for the study of communications in organizations but also some helpful pointers about the importance of the material properties of technology.

Latour, B. (2005) *Reassembling the Social: An Introduction to Actor–Network-Theory*. Oxford: Oxford University Press.

The latest version of Latour's actor–network theory. Always an interesting and entertaining writer, if sometimes infuriating.

Orlikowski, W. (2000) 'Using Technology and Constituting Structures: A Practice Lens for Studying Technology in Organizations', *Organization Science*, 11(4): 404–428.

A good summary of much of the rich work carried out by Orlikowski and her collaborators and stating her position about the nature of technology use in organizations.

REFERENCES

Ackroyd, S. (2002) *The Organization of Business: Applying Organizational Theory to Contemporary Change*. Oxford, Oxford University Press.

Allison, I. (1996) 'Executive Information Systems: An Evaluation of Current UK Practice', *International Journal of Information Management*, 16(1): 27–38.

Archer, M. (1995) *Realist Social Theory: The Morphogenetic Approach*. Cambridge, Cambridge University Press.

Ballard, M. (2004) 'IT projects – Piecing Together the ERP Jigsaw', *Retail Week*, October 1: 22.

Belcher, L. W. and Watson, H. J. (1993) 'Assessing the Value of Conoco's EIS', *MIS Quarterly*, 17(3): 239–253.

Benders, J., Batenburg, R. and Van der Blonk, H. (2006) 'Sticking to Standards; Technical and Other Isomorphic Pressures in Deploying ERP-Systems', *Information and Management*, 43(2): 194–203.

Beunza, D., Hardie, I. and MacKenzie, D. (2006) 'A Price is a Social Thing: Towards a Material Sociology of Arbitrage', *Organization Studies*, 27(5): 721–746.

Bolton, R. J. and Hand, D. J. (2002) 'Statistical Fraud Detection: A Review', *Statistical Science*, 17(3): 235–255.

Boudreau, M. and Robey, D. (2005) 'Enacting Integrated Information Technology', *Organization Science*, 16(1): 3–18.

Ciborra, C. and Patriotta, G. (1996) 'Groupware and Teamwork in New Product Development: The Case of a Consumer Goods Multinational', in C. Ciborra (ed.) *Groupware and Teamwork: Invisible Aid or Technical Hindrance?* Chichester, Wiley: 122–143.

Ciborra, C. (2002) *The Labyrinths of Information: Challenging the Wisdom of Systems*. Oxford, Oxford University Press.

Cottrell, N. and Rapley, K. (1991) 'Factors Critical to the Success of Executive Information Systems in British Airways', *European Journal of Information Systems*, 1(1): 65–71.

D'Adderio, L. (2004) *Inside the Virtual Product: How Organizations Create Knowledge Through Software*. Cheltenham, Edward Elgar.

Dahlbom, B., Hanseth, O. and Ljungberg, J. (2000) 'Conservative Success: Organization and Infrastructure Evolution at SKF', in C. Ciborra (ed.) *From Control to Drift*. Oxford, Oxford University Press: 87–104.

Davenport, T. (1998) 'Putting the Enterprise into the Enterprise System', *Harvard Business Review*, 76(4): 121–131.

Day, G. S. (2003) 'Creating a Superior Customer-Relating Capability', *MIT Sloan Management Review*, 44(3): 77–82.

Earl, M. (1994) 'Shorko Films SA', in C. Ciborra and T. Jelassi (eds) *Strategic Information Systems: A European Perspective*. Chichester, Wiley: 99–112.

Ennew, C., Watkins, T. and Wright, M. (1995) *Marketing Financial Services*. Oxford, Butterworth-Heinemann.

Finnegan, P. and Sammon, D. (2002) 'Fundamentals of Implementing Data Warehousing in Organizations', in S. Barnes (ed.) *Knowledge Management Systems: Theory and Practice*. London, Thomson Learning: 195–209.

Giddens, A. (1984) *The Constitution of Society: Outline of the Theory of Structuration*. Cambridge, Polity.

Green, P. A. (1992) 'Handling Direct Response', *Insights*, January: A79-A83.

Grint, K. and Woolgar, S. (1997) *The Machine at Work: Technology, Work and Organization*. Cambridge, Polity.

Guillen, M. (1994) *Models of Management: Work, Authority, and Organization in a Comparative Perspective*. Chicago, University of Chicago Press.

Hayes, N. and Walsham, G. (2000) 'Safe Enclaves, Political Enclaves and Knowledge Working', in C. Pritchard, R. Hull, M. Chumer and H. Willmott (eds) *Managing Knowledge*. Basingstoke, Macmillan: 69–87.

Houdeshei, G. and Watson, H. J. (1987) 'The Management Information and Decision Support (MIDS) System at Lockheed-Georgia', *MIS Quarterly*, 11(1): 126–139.

Humby, C., Hunt, T. and Phillips, T. (2003) *Scoring Points: How Tesco is Winning Customer Loyalty*. London, Kogan Page.

Hutchby, I. (2001) *Conversation and Technology: From the Telephone to the Internet*. Cambridge, Polity.

Inmon, W. (2001) 'Corporate Information Factory Overview', *Corporate Information Factory*, accessed 30 November 2006: www.inmoncif.com/library/cif/#articles.

97

Jasperson, J. S., Carter, P. E. and Zmud, R. W. (2005) 'A Comprehensive Conceptualization of Post-Adoptive Behaviors Associated with Information Technology Enabled Work Systems', *MIS Quarterly*, 29(3): 525–557.

Jones, M. (1999) 'Structuration Theory', in W. Currie and R. Galliers (eds) *Rethinking Management Information Systems*. Oxford, Oxford University Press: 103–135.

Jones, M., Orlikowski, W. and Munir, K. (2004) 'Structuration Theory and Information Systems: A Critical Reappraisal', in J. Mingers and L. Willcocks (eds) *Social Theory and Philosophy for Information Systems*. Chichester, Wiley: 297–328.

Kaplan, R. S. and Norton, D. (1993) 'Putting the Balanced Scorecard to Work', *Harvard Business Review*, 71(5): 134–149.

Kellog, K., Orlikowski, W. and Yates, J. (2006) 'Life in the Trading Zone: Structuring Coordination Across Boundaries in Postbureaucratic Organizations', *Organization Science*, 17(1): 22–44.

Latour, B. (1987) *Science in Action: How to Follow Scientists and Engineers Through Society*. Cambridge, MA, Harvard University Press.

Latour, B. (1993) *We Have Never Been Modern*. Hemel Hempstead, Harvester Wheatsheaf.

Latour, B. (1999) *Pandora's Hope: Essays on the Reality of Science Studies*. Cambridge, MA, Harvard University Press.

McKinlay, A. (2002) 'The Limits of Knowledge Management', *New Technology, Work and Employment*, 17(2): 76–88.

Mintzberg, H. (1973) *The Nature of Managerial Work*. London, Harper and Row.

Monteiro, E. and Hanseth, O. (1996) 'Social Shaping of Information Infrastructure: On Being Specific About the Technology', in Orlikowski, W. *et al.* (eds) *Information Technology and Changes in Organizational Work*. London, Chapman Hall: 325–343.

Mutch, A. (1993) 'Successful Use of Information Technology in a Small Tourism Enterprise: The Case of Country Holidays', *Journal of Strategic Information Systems*, 2(3): 264–276.

Mutch, A. (2002) 'Actors and Networks or Agents and Structures: A Critical Realist Critique of Actor–Network Theory', *Organization*, 9(3): 477–496.

Orlikowski, W. (1992) 'The Duality of Technology: Rethinking the Concept of Technology in Organizations', *Organization Science*, 3(3): 398–427.

Orlikowski, W. and Gash, D. (1994) 'Technological Frames: Making Sense of Information Technology in Organizations', *ACM Transactions on Information Systems*, 12(2): 174–207.

Orlikowski, W. and Yates, J. (1994) 'Genre Repertoire: The Structuring of Communicative Practices in Organizations', *Administrative Science Quarterly*, 39: 541–574.

Orlikowski, W. (2000) 'Using Technology and Constituting Structures: A Practice Lens for Studying Technology in Organizations', *Organization Science*, 11(4): 404–428.

Payne, A. and Frow, P. (2005) 'A Strategic Framework for Customer Relationship Management', *Journal of Marketing*, 69(4): 167–176.

Payton, F. C. and Zahay, D. (2003) 'Understanding Why Marketing Does Not Use the Corporate Data Warehouse for CRM Applications', *Journal of Database Marketing*, 10(4): 315–326.

Rockart, J. F. (1979) 'Chief Executives Define Their Own Data Needs', *Harvard Business Review*, 57(2): 81–92.

Scott-Morton M. (ed.) (1991) *The Corporation of the 1990s*. New York, Oxford University Press.

Thompson, J. (2006) 'MFI Considers Suing Over Supply Systems Dispute', *Retail Week*, June 30.

Trist, E. L. (1963) *Organizational Choice: Capabilities of Groups at the Coal Face Under Changing Technologies: The Loss, Rediscovery & Transformation of a Work Tradition*. London, Tavistock.

Walsham, G. (1997) 'Actor–Network Theory and IS Research: Current Status and Future Prospects', in A. S. Lee, J. Liebenau and J. I. DeGross (eds) (1997), *Information Systems and Qualitative Research*. London, Chapman & Hall: 466–480.

98

Walsham, G. (2001) 'Knowledge Management: The Benefits and Limitations of Computer Systems', *European Management Journal*, 19(6): 599–608.

Westerman, P. (2001) *Data Warehousing: Using the Wal-Mart Model*. San Francisco, Morgan Kaufmann.

Wheeler, F. P., Chang, S. H. and Thomas, R. J. (1993) 'Moving from an Executive Information System to Everyone's Information System: Lessons From a Case Study', *Journal of Information Technology*, 8(3): 177–183.

Whittington, R. (1992) 'Putting Giddens Into Action: Social Systems and Managerial Agency', *Journal of Management Studies*, 29(6): 693–712.

Whyte, J. (2005) 'Taking Time to Understand: Articulating Relationships Between Technologies and Organizations', www.mngt.waikato.ac.nz/ejrot/cmsconference/2005/proceedings/criticalrealism/Whyte.pdf, Cambridge: 4th Critical Management Studies Conference accessed 26 May 2006.

Yates, J. and Orlikowski, W. (1992) 'Genres of Organizational Communication: A Structurational Approach to Studying Communication and Media', *Academy of Management Review*, 17(2): 299–326.

Zuboff, S. (1988) *In the Age of the Smart Machine: The Future of Work and Power*. London, Heinemann.

Chapter 5

Technology 2: ICT and communication

INTRODUCTION

The applications we have reviewed so far have been those which deal with forms of structured data. They are in many senses the 'traditional' applications one associates with computers, ones to which ICT has been ideally suited. Yet there are many claims that most organizational knowledge resides in the form of unstructured data, notably various forms of document. At the same time, many applications have been developed which enable the manipulation of unstructured forms of information. These applications frequently have some impact on communication, so in this chapter our focus shifts towards the 'communication' part of ICT. Our discussion of information literacy suggested a relationship to systems in which information is *retrieved*. However, a key theme of this chapter is that the development of what we might term 'communicative competence', an approach which sees information as embedded in a web of relationships, might be the core component of what it takes to be information literate in work organizations. That is, the quality of working relations might be more important than the quality of technological tools. However, in order to understand this we need to be clear about the features and limitations of such tools. In order to set the scene for our discussion of some important applications in more detail, we begin by reviewing some theories about how ICT might impact on communication in organizations.

 This chapter will examine:

- some influential approaches to the impact of ICT on communication in organizations
- the impact of some important ICT applications on forms of unstructured information, with a particular emphasis on patterns of communication and sharing

THEORIES OF COMMUNICATION

Clearly, communication in organizations is a significant topic for debate and analysis in its own right. A very comprehensive overview of the issues is supplied by Jablin and Putnam's (2001) *New Handbook of Organizational Communication*, which contains detailed surveys of the literature. The point of this section is to review some of the more prominent approaches with a view to framing the discussion of the detailed applications which follow. Our starting point is with an influential perspective know variously as Media Richness Theory or Information Richness Theory – we will use MRT as a shorthand from now on as that was the formulation in the seminal work by Daft and Lengel (1986). Their ideas, particularly as developed with Trevino (Daft, Lengel and Trevino 1987), are set in the context of the conundrum that we examined in the last chapter – the lack of use by senior managers of information systems aimed directly at them. They argued that a closer examination of patterns of management communication might suggest why this was so. For them, an important consideration was the equivocality which surrounded tasks and the communication of information about them. That is, some tasks are relatively structured and unambiguous. The information which conveys the nature of this task can therefore also be fairly straightforward. Other tasks, by comparison, are inherently ambiguous and there are problems in conveying the complexity of such tasks. A second assumption was that particular forms of communication were inherently richer than others and more suited, therefore, to conveying equivocal information. Their dimension of richness addressed the following features:

- Feedback – the assumption is that the ability to feedback understanding of what has been communicated will lead to richer communication. Some communication channels allow for multiple forms of feedback, others for very little feedback as to whether a message has been received and understood.
- Multiple cues – richer forms of media possess a range and variety of cues – what we would often refer to as 'body language' being important among these.
- Language variety – some forms of language, such as numbers, lend themselves to greater precision. Others, notably natural language, enable the development of complex concepts.
- Personal focus – communication is wrapped up, argue Daft, Lengel and Trevino, in emotions. Feelings are not therefore an 'add on' but a central part of the communication process.

Using these assumptions, Daft, Lengel and Trevino (1987) produce a hierarchy of media richness, based on four types of channel. They were ordered by their capacity to deal with equivocal situations based on the attributes of richness that each possesses. *Face to face* communication, they argued, was the richest form of communication and hence the most appropriate to situations of high equivocality. This is because there are multiple cues which encourage high quality feedback. Understanding can be questioned and checked and the nature of the message reinforced not only by a range of gestures but also by the emotion with which it is invested. However, such communication is time consuming and may not be necessary for relatively unambiguous information, which might be conveyed effectively in numerical form in a standard report. Such *unaddressed documents*, that is, documents for general circulation without a named recipient, come at the opposite end of the spectrum, possessing little variety and no immediate feedback channel. In between these two types are *telephone calls* and *addressed documents*. The former has some of the immediacy of the face to face conversation, but lacks the visual channels for feedback and understanding. It is, however, richer than memos or letters, which are better suited to less equivocal tasks for which clear instructions can be issued. Daft, Lengel and Trevino (1987) went further and posited a link, based on some research with executives in a petrochemical company, between managerial performance and media selection. They argued that a group of managers who seemed to be more sensitive about matching the needs of the communication task with the channel were more likely to be in the group judged as high performing by their organization than managers whose media choice seemed somewhat random. This has been an influential perspective which is still widely cited (e.g. Hodgkinson and Sparrow 2002) but one which has been subject to some criticism.

Some of this criticism derives from the difficulty of applying MRT to new forms of media as we will see, but a deeper criticism is that the approach makes assumptions about the choices people make. These are that managers are in a position to exercise choice about the channels they use and that they are capable of making such choice. This is, in the eyes of some, to underplay the impact of the social setting in which communication takes place. Daft, Lengel and Trevino (1987) do explicitly state that they were unable to examine the impact of new media on the managers in their research, but an article by Lynn Markus (1994) did examine the impact of the then very new technology of email. She took an institutional approach to examine the impact of email in an organization. She found that despite email scoring as a 'lean' medium in terms of MRT it was widely used by managers in her research for equivocal tasks. Similar findings were reported by Robertson, Sorenson and Swan (2001) in their study of a scientific consultancy. Despite possessing tools which possessed richer features for communication, notably the type of groupware which we will examine in more detail below, managers continued to use email. Some of this usage relates to critical mass – people will prefer to use media which others use, given that this will give them more opportunities to get their message across. Also important are the general levels of expectation within the organization. But a further aspect of the setting in which managers communicate is provided by the interesting notion of communication genre.

Metaphor is extremely important in how people communicate and reason (Lakoff and Johnson 1980; Tsoukas 1993). It provides innovation by drawing on analogies from one aspect of life and applying them to another, often giving new ways of looking. However, such analogies can also be a powerful conservative force, as those who use, say, a new technology, assimilate to what they are familiar with. It is possible to suggest that we can find a number of examples of ICT-enabled applications whose successful adoption has owed much to their similarity to very familiar information tools. However, this very success can in turn limit use. So, for example, the word processor replicates many features of the typewriter which proceeded it as the main means of producing documents (Carroll and Mack 1995). The keyboard layout mimicked that of the typewriter and many of the features, such as tab stops, bear a resemblance to those familiar on the older technology. Such metaphors facilitated the widespread acceptance of word processing, but they could also mean that the more extended features were not applied – such as when a list was required it was re-typed, rather than using sets of data as input. This is because the technology is being assimilated to the familiar analogy of paper. Similar metaphorical framing can be found in other instances. The spreadsheet, for example, won widespread acceptance on the basis of its similarity to traditional analysis paper. However, without training in modelling techniques it can often be used as little more than a convenient calculator. In the

102

context of our focus on communication, the most powerful metaphor is that of the message which underlies the success of email. We are familiar with the notion of sending messages out, but rather less familiar with the notion of visiting locations to retrieve our information. As we will see, something like this might account for the excessive sending of large attachments and the lack of use of applications like groupware and intranets which offer considerable benefits.

Yates and Orlikowski (1992) develop this idea in an interesting way in their application of the notion of 'genres of organizational communication'. In a way which is rare in both the organizational theory and the information management literature, they take a historical approach, based in part on the stimulating work of Yates (1989) on the development of office technology at the turn of the twentieth century. Rather than assuming, as in MRT, that people make conscious choices about communication channels, they suggest particular ways of communicating become embedded in genres, such as reports and presentations, which then become taken for granted and structure the way in which people in organizations communicate. One particular genre which they examine in some depth is the development of the memo. They suggest that this became a dominant genre of communication and formed some of the taken for granted frames which could be applied to email usage. In a study of communication practices within a community developing new standards for a programming language they suggest that 'approaches that concentrate on the characteristics of new media may be less useful for certain purposes than those that focus on communicative practices' (Orlikowski and Yates 1994: 572). More recently, together with Kellog, they have suggested that the PowerPoint presentation has become a central genre enabling in their case study the fast production of work across specialist boundaries – but doing little to promote reflection and learning (Kellog, Orlikowski and Yates 2006). Rather than just supporting work practices such tools almost become ends in themselves. Their use becomes practically obligatory in order to demonstrate 'relevance' but in the process other elements of communicative value are lost.

One of the most powerful genres in organizations remains the report. Another is the form, used to gather information both internally and externally. These are just some examples of the types of documents in organizations and, following on from our considerations towards the end of the last chapter, this is where we start our examination of applications in a little more detail. In the rest of this chapter we look at:

- document management systems
- groupware
- intranets
- email
- knowledge management systems

before concluding by drawing out some key themes from our study of technology. As in the previous chapter, our focus is on the information implications, with other aspects dealt with in subsequent chapters. A complicating factor in our discussions is the blurring of the boundaries between these categories, with the same application capable of use in several categories. A notable example is the package Lotus Notes, widely discussed in the research literature for its part in knowledge sharing. It is a package which would generally be positioned as groupware, that is, software which enables collaborative working. However, it is used in many organizations, as we will see, simply as email with many users unaware of its other capabilities. These capabilities include the possibility of applications development to support activities like the workflow management that we discussed in the previous chapter. By the same token, companies can use applications on their intranets to emulate some of the capabilities of groupware packages. The categories I use are therefore for ease of discussion, although the blurring I have pointed to can have real consequences for which features are used and, often more importantly, not used in organizations.

ICT FOR COMMUNICATION AND SHARING

Document management systems

As we noted at the end of the previous chapter, many organizations, especially in sectors such as financial services, use workflow systems to coordinate the flow of tasks. These are often supported by document management systems, which take incoming documents, such as letters and claim forms, and scan them so that they can be allocated electronically. However, many other organizations also generate considerable volumes of documentation, documentation which can contain valuable information. For example, many companies prepare tender documents when bidding for new business. Such documents can contain valuable information about past practice, but the storing of such documents as paper makes access difficult and time consuming. However, just because such documents have been prepared electronically does not make finding and using them any easier. On the contrary, paper filing systems were well established and often under central control, with clear disciplines about retention. The creation of documents on personal computers with no conventions about file names and storage could mean that this valuable resource was scattered about an organization (Zantout and Marir 1999).

Two options present themselves: specialist document management software or software which can search unstructured documents. The first is particularly suited for those cases in which large bodies of standard documents are created and used. The second, particularly associated with the Cambridge, UK-based company Autonomy, is the searching, based on complex algorithms, of documents in a variety of forms to find common patterns. Such systems achieved public exposure in their use by New Labour in the 1997 general election in the UK. Their Excalibur system stored details of previous policy statements by their opponents and was used extremely effectively to rebut claims which were inconsistent with these statements. This demonstrates the value of archived material. Orna (2005) notes how this experience was then transferred to the Department of Health in a system called Comprehensive Information Portfolio which was used to brief ministers.

Table 5.1 Document Management Systems

Level	Features
Data	Documents of varying types
Software	Recording and searching of range of document types. Version control
Hardware	Document scanning and handling; client-server network

Groupware

Groupware can be broadly defined as software to support collaborate work – hence the often used acronym CSCW – Computer Supported Collaborative Work (Baecker *et al.*, 1995). Such systems are premised on the increasing importance of collaborative work in the contemporary world. The importance of teams at work, both as a means of organizing work and as a feature of social systems in organizations, is not, of course, a new one. Concern with group dynamics was a central feature, for example, of the Hawthorne experiments in the USA in the inter-war period. However, partly under the influence of movements like the quality of working life movement inspired by the Tavistock research which we reviewed in the last chapter, focus on ways in which group working can be enhanced and supported gained momentum from the 1960s. The power of ICT in overcoming considerations of time and space lie behind the enthusiastic espousal of concepts like the 'virtual team'. Such enthusiasm often reflects a rather uncritical view of the power of technology which we will challenge in this section. However, we have first to recognize again some difficulties of definition here. On the one hand, the broad term groupware can be used to encompass all the systems which could potentially help people work together. Email, for example, is one of the most significant tools in many organizations for enabling the sharing of work. However, such a broad focus means that we lose sight of what it is that tools for supporting collaborative work can give us that email cannot. On the other hand, some applications are very specific in their use. For example, some systems can be used to support activity when all the participants are present in the same location. An example of such systems is a Group Decision Support System, which includes features such as electronic voting (DeSanctis and Poole 1994). The use of such systems can mean that difficult decisions can be taken anonymously, overcoming some of the dynamics of power present in meetings, where participants may be wary of voicing their real opinions in public. However, this is a very specific and limited application; of more importance are systems which have broader reach, the key example of which is Lotus Notes.

The focus on Notes comes not just because it has been widely applied, but also because it has been widely researched. This gives us an extensive body of work to draw upon which is interesting in showing how organizational factors are crucial in the use of such applications for the sharing of information. However, such applications are often difficult to understand; one way of understanding the features which they offer is to compare them to email. A useful starting point here is with the metaphor of the message. Email works with the familiar metaphor of sending messages; the familiarity of the metaphor used enables us to relate a new application

Table 5.2 Groupware

Level	Features
Data	Unstructured as well as structured data; messaging and documents; shared temporal data (diaries and calendars)
Software	Discussion databases, email, user application development tools
Hardware	Client-server network with automated replication

to existing practices and so feel comfortable in its use. So we have address books and folders in which to store our mail. Of course, nothing forces us to store our messages in a structured fashion (or any fashion at all!). Similarly, just as we might reply to some correspondents without letting others involved in the correspondence know, so too we can choose who we include in our communication. Often we may choose to include some, through the cc option, who we wish to know about our involvement but equally we may choose to ignore others. So if an email is sent to, say, five participants, some may choose to copy everybody in to their reply, others to reply only to the sender. What this creates is a complex pattern of interactions. Now, this might not be crucial in the ordinary run of events, but if it becomes important to track the progress of a decision, then the complexity can be problematic.

Groupware such as Lotus Notes operates with an alternative metaphor, that of the document. This is where rather than sending a message out, users come in to work on a common project which is shared between them. In a paper based operation we might well circulate drafts which then are annotated with suggested changes or covered in Post-It notes. Applications like Notes enable this process to be recorded so that there is a trail for other participants to follow. It also possesses useful technical features which preserve the security of and access to information, but for our purposes the particular interest is in this ability to support collaborative work. In particular, it has been claimed that through user-controlled discussion forums it enables the type of informal information sharing that we have seen as being so important – and which Mintzberg (1994) seemed to dismiss as a role for ICT.

Despite these capabilities, it would appear that they are frequently not used. At the Norwegian state owned oil company StatOil, for example, the capacity of Lotus Notes to construct databases was little used, with most simply using the email capability (Monteiro and Hepso 2000). Where aspects were used to manage quality documentation, this was restricted to a very limited set of users. We have already noted that in the scientific consultancy examined by Robertson, Sorenson and Swan (2001) people preferred the use of email, despite the advanced facilities that would seem particularly relevant to this group of users. In part we can suggest this is because email is familiar and 'to hand'. In their study of the introduction of Lotus Notes in Unilever, Ciborra and Patriotta (1996) noted this preference for immediate and familiar methods of communication, such as the telephone, over what was perceived to be a more time consuming method. Of course, one might argue that these are transitory effects, related to

INFORMAL INFORMATION AND GROUPWARE

A marine insurer was dealing with a claim for a shipment of grain, ruined, it was claimed, by water damage at sea. The company had a network of agents across the globe, all using Lotus Notes to share reports. The person handling the claim came across a note recording a conversation between an agent and the ship's captain, in which the latter complained that the sacks the grain was carried in were splitting and sub-standard. This was something he had reported to the ship's owners before sailing, but his complaints had been ignored. This information helped in ruling the claim void, so saving the insurers a considerable sum of money.

Source: Dourado 1996

GROUPWARE, INNOVATION AND HIERARCHY AT UNILEVER

Unilever is a major consumer products company operating across the globe. In its dental care division, it wished to be able to develop products capable of sale worldwide and to draw in the full range of the organization to help in product development. Accordingly, it installed a Lotus Notes system for the design and development of new products. Its designers in Milan, Italy, would place their ideas on this database so that they could be viewed by a global audience, who could make their views known about suitability. However, one day a comment was placed by a director from the London head office. This made the designers realize that all their working ideas could be viewed by a global audience, including by those at a considerably higher level in the organizational hierarchy. The result was that they stopped using the database until access controls were placed on it. These controls segmented the database into 'above the line' and 'below the line' sections. Only the designers had full access to working ideas, with public access being limited to outline reports on progress. This, of course, prevented the free flow of ideas on work in progress which had been desired.

Source: Ciborra and Pattriota 1996

lack of familiarity and awareness. However, other factors appear to be important in explaining this relative lack of use.

Ciborra and Patriotta (1996) use a threefold distinction to analyse their case material: infrastructure, infostructure and infoculture. The infrastructure relates to the provision of the technology and means of accessing it, which was relatively unproblematic in this case (albeit that the telephone often seemed a more 'to hand' means of communication). The infostructure refers to the way in which what counts as information is defined in the organization, which recalls some of our earlier discussions about data definition. Of most importance for Ciborra and Patriotta in understanding this particular case was the notion of an 'infoculture', which covers levels of expectation about the use of information within the organization. An alternative perspective on the nature of infoculture can be seen in another examination of the use of Lotus Notes.

SALES REPRESENTATIVES AND INFORMATION SHARING

Compound UK was a UK-based pharmaceutical company selling into the National Health Service (NHS). Changes in the patterns of buying within the NHS meant that senior managers felt that they required more information about sales reps working practices and customer contacts. They used Lotus Notes for two purposes – as a contact recording system and as a discussion forum. The experience proved less than satisfactory for two reasons. The reps resented filling in the contact details, feeling that it was additional work of little value to them and distrusting it as a mechanism for monitoring their activities. The level of participation in the discussion databases was split. Some of the older and more experienced reps only participated in local discussion forums, thereby not contributing to company wide discussion. These discussions were dominated by the 'career reps', younger reps with an eye to career progression, who used the wider discussion forums as a way of getting themselves noticed.

Source: Hayes and Walsham 2000

Hayes and Walsham (2000) use a notion, drawn from the work of Goffman, of 'front' and 'back' regions. Front areas, like front of stage in a theatre, are areas for public display. Here the 'career reps' utilized the 'textualization' that Zuboff (1988) notes ICT offers to present themselves in the most favourable light. We see here that information sharing is not just about the reduction of uncertainty, but is part of the positioning of people in the organization. The more experienced reps, very cynical about such attempts, kept themselves to the back stage areas, in which they felt more comfortable about sharing information that was of value to them. As in the Unilever case, we can see that information sharing is not something which automatically follows from the implementation of a particular form of technology. Similar findings are also apparent in Orlikowski's (2000) work.

What is common to all these cases is the impact of the way in which work is structured in hierarchical organizations. As Zuboff suggests, such forms of structure come into conflict with the lateral communications enabled by applications such as groupware. Existing reward structures tend to be misaligned with the work practices suggested by aspects of the technology, something which also seems to be a feature of another widely encountered class of applications, Intranets.

LOTUS NOTES IN A MANAGEMENT CONSULTANCY

Alpha is a large multinational management consultancy, employing thousands of consultants across the world. Lotus Notes was implemented by an enthusiastic Chief Information Officer, who felt that its features were perfectly suited to the knowledge sharing which ought to increase organizational effectiveness. However, members of the organization reacted in very different ways. The technical staff responded enthusiastically to its use, designing their own databases and contributing to discussion groups. By contrast, the bulk of the consultants rejected its use. In large measure this was due to the 'up or out' promotion system which governed their work (and which did not apply to the technical staff). Being only as good as their last assignment, they saw little merit in sharing their knowledge, as it was this that would bring them better assignments and so secure their position. They also had little incentive to find time to learn about the features of the system, as there was strong emphasis on billing hours to clients – training was wasted time. There was a small group of more senior consultants who did use more of the features of the package to enhance their individual effectiveness. However, this use was far from the widespread knowledge sharing which was envisaged.

Source: Orlikowski 2000

Intranets

The development of a network infrastructure in many organizations enabling personal computers to communicate meant that it was a relatively simple step to deploy the same type of network protocols (the instructions which route messages and determine how items will be displayed) on internal networks as used on the Internet as a whole. This led to the rapid development of intranets, internal networks using the same browsers as used for Internet access but restricted to internal users. What this facilitated was the ability fairly readily to publish material which could be easily accessed by those across the organization with access to a web browser. This meant that many interface restrictions could be lifted. Studies of the managerial use of ICT indicated that a major problem was the need to learn several different interfaces for applications which were regularly used only on a casual basis (Gunton 1988). This could often mean that these applications were not used, as the time needing to be devoted to them was ill afforded by busy managers. The subsequent widespread use of web browsers from the late 1990s could give a familiar and relatively intuitive interface to applications held not only on personal computers but to the type of data intensive applications held on more specialized machines that we looked at in the last chapter.

Intranets are widely used for formal documents which need close version control but which change relatively little. Companies who send out paper copies of such documents not only incur substantial cost but also have problems with version control. If such documents are no longer sent out, but are updated on a website, then some of these problems are overcome. This reinforces some of the trends that we saw under our discussion of groupware but also introduces a new metaphor, that of publishing. This in turn raises some concerns to do with roles and skills.

The Web in general encourages considerable autonomy among those who publish material. It is possible to construct a website very easily with readily available tools (Scarbrough 2003). There is no control over content and considerable freedom in designing how a page looks. This might encourage the free expression of ideas, but within an organization this brings about problems. If a site is to be used by a wide variety of users, many of whom will be unfamiliar with the ideas which lie behind the structuring of content, then finding material can be extremely difficult. In addition, much content may be irrelevant, misleading or even damaging. This leads some to lay down strict guidelines which aim to provide a common 'look and feel' to websites (Greenberg 1998). The problem here is not just one of a constraint on creativity, but the imposition of delays on the process of creating content. If this has to be vetted by a central group, then this creates a bottleneck which can lead to intense frustration. However, without such control, the content of sites can very quickly become dated. It is very easy to

Table 5.3 *Intranets*

Level	Features
Data	Unstructured as well as structured data
Software	Standard web authoring and browsing tools
Hardware	Client-server network

create websites which are simply collections of static pages, often with content transferred from other systems. The challenge is to move from this to the integration of content from supporting systems on a dynamic basis. This, however, suggests new challenges for roles and skills which we return to in Chapter 8. One way of dealing with such challenges is through the creation of policies which lay down standards for the use of intranets, something which we cover in more detail in the next chapter.

One of the ways in which intranets tend to blur some of the distinctions which we raised earlier in this chapter is by being used for some of the functions for which other companies use packages like Lotus Notes. Another is the blurring of the distinction between being a container for content and being a mechanism for delivery of that content. That is, the material which appears on an intranet may have been produced specially for the purpose, with some of the problems of quality control which that poses. We will consider this more when we look at ratings systems under knowledge management. However, intranets may act as a carrier for material produced elsewhere and made available electronically. The distinction is clearer if you consider your own access to electronic copies of academic journals via the Internet. These continue to have printed versions and to be subject to traditional mechanisms of quality control, such as peer review. By contrast, much of the other material which you might come across has no such guarantees and we might argue that a key attribute of our information literate manager is the ability to distinguish between the two.

We have noted that a key feature of intranets is the use of a publishing metaphor, in which material does not leave the site unless selected by the user. This, as with groupware, can be contrasted to the messaging metaphor underlying electronic mail. The distinction has very practical considerations for organizations with the enormous volume of network traffic caused by the free use of facilities such as attachments to distribute information. Such attachments, often from very resource intensive applications such as presentation software, impose considerable loads on internal networks (Bradbury 2004). One response might be to charge for network usage, but this might prove unpopular among those who have come to depend on email and regard its use as 'free'. However, there are other implications beyond resource usage which we need to consider.

Email

We have noted the widespread acceptance of email for both internal and external communication, based on the familiarity of the messaging metaphor on which it is based. Email offers facilities

Table 5.4 *Email*

Level	Features
Data	Messages containing largely unstructured data; attachments for range of data
Software	Composition, forwarding and storing of messages; rules for treatment of messages
Hardware	Client-server network

for the transmission of messages in a variety of formats, with multiple copies and the capacity to store messages. In many ways these facilities have led to the breakdown of traditional methods of records management and to new norms of communicative competence. In particular, we can explore two aspects which relate to issues which we have discussed already: the blurring of the line between formal and informal information and the textualization of the workplace.

We examined the distinction between formal and informal information in Chapters 2 and 3. We saw that Mintzberg (1994), in particular, has a view of the impact of ICT on information use which tends to downplay the impact of systems such as email. Formal information has historically been associated with a set of genres, notably the memo and the report. Yates and Orlikowski (1992) trace the historical development of the memo and the conventions associated with it, showing that it is closely coupled to the forms of technology available for records storage. Thus the need to restrict a memo to one subject and to indicate this subject in a heading facilitated the storage of records in a vertical filing system. Email takes elements of this genre but mixes it with more informal modes of information sharing associated in particular with the telephone. Thus, there is often mixing of personal information in emails, as with the conventional practice in many telephone conversations of not starting with business matters immediately but inquiring after the respondent's well being (Hutchby 2001). This runs to a degree of informality of address and a tendency not to adhere to conventions such as naming the subject of the correspondence.

This blurring of the distinction between formality and informality can have consequences when combined with other features of the technology. The ability to respond immediately to messages, for example, removes the space for reflection which the physical production of a memo engenders. This, together with the removal of both conventions and the social cues one gets from other forms of communication (most notably with face to face communication, but also through cues such as tone of voice on the telephone) can lead to the phenomenon of 'flaming', the rapid escalation of disputes (Lea et al., 1992). However, the removal of such cues and the growing informality of communication do not only have negative consequences. The removal of visual indicators of gender and ethnicity which might lead to exclusion in face to face meetings can mean a greater degree of participation in decision making. This, of course, could tend to prolong the decision making process. There are no clear ways to bring discussions to a close. Indeed, the facility to be able to copy multiple recipients and the ability of these recipients to respond in different time frames mean that debates facilitated by email can continue for long periods. This is where organizations might wish to consider an etiquette for the use of email and whether alternative means of communication are appropriate.

To add to the complex blurring of the formal and informal that email brings about, we have to add their formal status as legal documents. In 1997 the Norwich Union insurance company in the UK had to pay damages of nearly half a million pounds to the Western Provident Association for untrue allegations circulated in internal emails (Bellos 1997). Subsequent high profile cases, such as the subpoenaing of internal emails from Microsoft in the US Department of Justice ongoing anti-trust investigations have confirmed this legal status. Increasingly strict regulatory requirements mean that emails need to be treated under the heading of records management, with provisions for access, retention and archiving. When one adds in concerns about the circulation of potentially offensive material, it is no surprise that organizations have taken steps to include emails in disciplinary procedures. The unfortunate side effect of this has been perhaps to downplay positive attempts to establish an appropriate etiquette for email usage. However,

SETTING LIMITS TO EMAIL

Greene King is a major regional brewer and owner of public houses in the UK. Its Pub Partners division is responsible for almost 1,200 tenanted pubs across the south of England. These are pubs run by independent business people who draw on the support of 29 Regional Managers (RM), who are expected to spend most of their time in the field assisting in business development. These RMs are supported by head office staff in a variety of functions and appropriate communication is central to the smooth running of the whole operation. However, the widespread use of email put extra pressures on the RMs, many of whom spent considerable time in the evenings after their busy working day answering emails, some of which were of questionable relevance. Following complaints, the managing director decided to remove email from RMs altogether for a six month period. This caused considerable upset originally, with support staff having to revert to alternative means of communication. However, at the end of the six months, 40 per cent of RMs were happy to continue without email. The remaining 60 per cent wanted to see it reintroduced but with controls over its use. Now, for example, emails sent to an RM on holiday will be greeted with the message that 'this person is on holiday and this email will be deleted'. This means that RMs returning from holiday are not faced with excessive numbers of messages – any vital messages can be diverted to the appropriate support person and re-sent. In addition, RMs have been supplied with tablet PCs which they use for development activities with tenants (thus doing away with paper plans) and they can use these at the wireless network equipped managed outlets that another division of the company runs, thereby picking up email during the day rather than in the evening. In this way the company is using a mix of policy and technology to aim for the most effective form of communication.

Source: interviews with Greene King Pub Partners 2006

it does also indicate to us another effect, that of the textualization of work. Zuboff (1988) referred to the way in which ICTs produce a trail of not only what work has been done but how it has been done, a trail which lays such work open to inspection. This characteristic is particularly evident in email and features such as the ease of copying organizational members into communications has led to the observation of the use of email for internal politics (Brown and Lightfoot 2002). That is, what counts is not what is said but who is observed to say it, often leading to those at nodes of communication becoming swamped with email traffic.

Knowledge management

If email blurs boundaries between types of communication, knowledge management straddles several of the applications we have been discussing. Consider the example in the box on p. 113. Baumard uses the details recounted here to call this a failure of a 'knowledge management system'. Of course, with our previous discussion of EIS, we might be in a position to question this. We might want first to draw attention to the fact that British Airways, too, employed an

INFORMATION OR KNOWLEDGE IN QANTAS

The Australian airline Qantas installed an Executive Information System, complete with touchscreens to handle, among other things, competitor profiles. However, after the initial enthusiasm utilization rates declined and the system was abandoned within six months. During this time, the airline had entered into collaborative arrangements with British Airways. On a visit to the latter's headquarters, members of the Qantas team had been amused to find hand drawn graphics in a comparative analysis of competitor performance.

Source: Baumard 1999

EIS, and, from the published evidence, rather successfully (Cottrell and Rapley 1991). Of course, we have also seen that EIS can often 'fail' to meet the needs of their target audience but in fact be more widely used. But our earlier discussion might indicate that we would never want to describe them as 'knowledge' management systems. They might be used as better ways into data and they might merit the term of handling information, but they were never designed to handle the 'softer' forms of knowledge which are Baumard's chief area of concern. He seems to have fallen into the trap of believing the rebadging which many vendors engaged in – what Tom Wilson (2002) calls 'search and replace' marketing, in which applications previously sold as data or information systems were renamed to match a new trend.

Does this mean that we should simply be cynical about such systems and their effectiveness? Certainly, this is the main theme of many accounts of such systems, but in the spirit of our earlier discussions we need to be a little more specific about what technologies we are talking about. In practice, systems badged as knowledge management have often relied on the type of systems we have discussed, such as Lotus Notes and intranets. The problems these have experienced in living up to some of the wilder fantasies of senior managers have been in part because of the failure of such managers to realize the social characteristics of the knowledge they are dealing with, but also in part because of exaggerated views of the capabilities of ICT, born in part out of the claims made for artificial intelligence. Accordingly we look at such claims in a little detail, before going on to consider the relation between systems claiming to handle knowledge and the types of social systems in which they have been inserted.

We have already seen in Chapter 2 the enthusiasm with which Simon and others approached the prospects for the application of computers to human decision making in the late 1950s. The enthusiasm was born out of a belief that advances in science would lead to an understanding of the human brain equivalent to our knowledge of computing processes: 'we are making good progress,' argued Simon (1977: 34), 'towards constructing psychological theories that are as successful as the theories we have in chemistry and biology.' This optimism has proved to be sadly unfounded and the experiments in artificial intelligence which followed have played their part in this disillusionment. Attempts to use a computational model of human intelligence have been stoutly resisted as impoverished models which underplay the role of emotion and feeling (Winograd and Flores 1986). This is an on-going debate with little sign of resolution, but in general the high hopes for artificial intelligence have foundered, to be replaced by more modest systems which use rules to mimic certain aspects of decision making. The hopes foundered on a number of rocks, the sharpest of which was the problem of what was termed 'knowledge elicitation'. The hope was that a new science of 'knowledge engineering' would see 'engineers' eliciting knowledge from experts and building this into systems which would deploy it. This met with two obstacles. As we saw in the example of the baker in the Matsushita case, many experts do not know why they do what they do, nor why it is successful. That is, they might be perfectly willing to share what they know, but they are unable to articulate vital parts of it. If we return to the distinction we drew earlier between tacit and implicit knowledge, the latter might be knowledge, built up over long periods of experience, which is available to share. However, availability does not mean willingness to share and many experts do not wish to share that which might preserve their position in the organization. We will return to the different propensity of experts to share their knowledge later, but such unwillingness certainly placed constraints on the effectiveness of the so-called 'expert systems' which came to be the most effective instantiation of artificial intelligence.

In practice, then, such systems came to be used in relatively restricted domains in which clear rules could be articulated. One further problem for the success of expert systems was that they would need to work in stable domains in which rules were predictable and could be formulated to cater for the vast majority of cases. If there was unpredictability or confounding factors then the systems would prove less effective. Thus, for example, in the medical domain the use of such systems tended to drift away from diagnosis, where it was hoped that they would make a major impact, and into use as teaching aids. In business operations they found an important role in handling large masses of data, in which the application of rules by humans might have been fairly simple on a case by case basis, but where the sheer volume of cases would defeat human endeavour. So, for example, they can be used to examine bodies of data acquired through supermarket scanning systems or to look for suspicious patterns of transactions in credit card data (Rangaswamy, Harlam and Lodish 1991). As such they have proved extremely successful, but this is a considerable distance from the original hopes for them. They continue to be developed for such cases with the application of techniques such as neural networks, where rule-based systems can amend their own rules based on the data which they encounter.

However, another restriction has been their interaction with work processes. Even in the successful cases noted above, patterns need to be reported out for further human action. Thus the interaction with work practices is important (see box 'Expert System Failure' on p. 115). A similar pattern seemed to occur in the use of an expert system in aero engine maintenance in Scandinavia. When the system was used to attempt to substitute for human judgement it led to a decrease in productivity, as engineers took its suggestions to the letter even when they sensed they were infeasible. When the system was reconfigured to act as a support for the engineer's fault finding it was far better received (Hirschheim and Klein 1989).

What this experience seems to indicate is that while the wilder claims for artificial intelligence seem unfounded, there does seem to be modest success in bounded areas of application. These areas are relatively stable, involve clear rules which can easily be elicited, and deal with large volumes of data which yield patterns of relationships which are not readily apparent to human decision makers. They also fit with working patterns and give something of value to those who use them, rather than demanding that they can change their working patterns to suit. These conclusions can also be related to efforts to build knowledge management systems using applications such as Lotus Notes and intranets. Here we need to balance accounts which place their emphasis on informal sharing of tacit knowledge, in which knowledge management systems

EXPERT SYSTEM FAILURE IN A COMPUTING COMPANY

CompuSys, a US computer company, developed an expert system named CONFIG which was designed to help sales reps produce accurate equipment configurations. The hardware the company sold was available in complex combinations to fit customer need and inaccurate configurations caused extensive amendments to orders. The system worked well technically but was not used. The interface was perceived as a problem and extensively remodelled, but the system was still not used. There were two reasons for this. One was that the production of high quality configurations brought no benefits to the reps. Further, producing high quality configurations took time, even with the system, and so got in the way of the selling activity by which the reps were measured. The system was not integrated with pricing information, which made the production of a quote much more time consuming.

Source: Markus and Keil 1994

SHARING TECHNICAL INFORMATION ACROSS THE WORLD: XEROX'S EUREKA

The photocopier company Xerox has developed a system called Eureka for sharing technical knowledge among photocopier engineers. This system has some 20,000 users across the world who use it to enter tips about how to solve problems with machines and to request assistance.

For example, in Brazil a customer had problems with a Xerox DocuColor 40 production colour copier/printer to the point where the technicians were going to replace the $40,000 machine. Using Eureka, the technicians in São Paolo discovered a tip from Canada that suggested replacing a 90-cent connector. The technicians replaced the connector and fixed the machine. That tip was sent back to manufacturing and the problem could be remedied at the source.

The system now contains nearly 50,000 tips. It began as an effort to develop an artificial intelligence application, but this was rapidly superseded by an approach focused on sharing of insights. This was based in turn on an ethnographic study of the way in which engineers swapped 'war stories' often in informal settings of interaction.

Source: Xerox PARC 2006; Bobrow and Whalen 2002; example Moore 1998

are seen as at best an irrelevance, at worst an obstacle, with those examples (see box above) where some degree of sharing facilitated by ICT seems to have been successful.

A similar example can be found in Siemens, the German electrical engineering company. A comparable system was particularly well used for an urgent request system, as well as for entering tips. Using this request system:

for insurance purposes an ICN [Information and Communications Network] project manager in South America tried to discover how dangerous it was to lay cables in the Amazon rainforest. He posted an urgent request asking for help from anyone with a similar project in a similar environment. A project manager in Senegal responded within several hours. Obtaining the right information before the cables went underground saved Siemens approximately US$1 million.

(Voelpel, Dous and Davenport 2005: 12)

This proved so useful that when the company went through some difficult economic conditions the rate of posting tips went down, but the level of requests for information went up. In part the success of such systems relates to the willingness of those in technical environments to share such tips. We saw this in the Alpha case where members of technical staff were enthusiastic in their use of Lotus Notes when others did not join in (Orlikowski 2000). In part this related to the nature of the information being shared and in part to the emphasis on visible technical expertise as a form of reputation. All of these systems depend on the recognition of the latter, although some also integrated reward systems (which we consider in more detail in Chapter 8). However, it is not a simple matter of all technical material lending itself to such sharing. In a Taiwanese chip fabrication plant, equipment engineers found a tips database useful, but field engineers did not use it (Hsiao, Tsiao and Lee 2006). The equipment engineers worked with linear problems in which a step by step problem solving technique could be applied, as opposed to the interactive complexity of the field engineers' work. What might suit the latter situation better, argue Hsiao *et al.*, is the translation of experience into scenarios. Of course, such a strategy would demand extra effort and if we turn to examples of failure then we can see this as a major problem.

We have seen in our discussion of groupware how the sales reps in a drug company did not want to record extra details of sales visits, in part because of the extra effort involved, effort which would bring the reps themselves little benefit (Hayes and Walsham 2000). A similar situation obtained in another two drug companies in which attempts at knowledge management have been attempted. In World Pharma a debriefing exercise 'lessons' became little more than a routine part of project completion (McKinlay 2002). A similar pattern was observed in Pharmco National where 'learning review reports' were routinely not completed. As well as involving extra work, they also required contextual detail in order to be understood, contextual material which was difficult to convey (Currie and Kerrin 2004). Importantly, in these stories of failure we move outside the ranks of technical specialism into the worlds of sales and marketing or product development, worlds in which not only is the form of knowledge more complex, but the forms of reward are such that there is incentive to hoard knowledge. We will revisit these questions of rewards in Chapter 8.

One further question which we will consider that emerges from this discussion is the impact of existing structures on the effectiveness of systems for knowledge sharing. We have already observed the impact of hierarchy on the use of groupware in Unilever (Ciborra and Patriotta 1996). For all the talk of flatter organizations and horizontal communication facilitated by ICT, McKinlay (2002: 85) observes 'the profound difficulty corporations experience in dislodging functional hierarchy as the central premise of their organizational design'. This is an issue to which we will return in Chapter 7. Finally, an issue which has an impact on our discussion of training in Chapter 8, and which impinges on our information literate manager, is that of the degree of technical awareness which managers need. For at several points during the examples we have presented technical issues stubbornly intrude. While our balance sheet of experience might draw more attention to questions of organizational structure and knowing and of

THE INFLUENCE OF PLACE ON COPIER USE

Jeanette Blomberg of Xerox's Palo Alto Research Centre carried out field observation of the use of two identical copiers. Both were undertaking similar volumes of work, but one was seen as being very dependable, the other was considered very undependable. The low dependability machine was on the fourth floor of a five storey building. The department responsible for maintaining the machine was located in the basement and only 15 per cent of key users were located close to the machine. This meant that there was little or no build up of shared expertise, with potential signs of failure going unreported and little sharing of knowledge about advanced features of the machine. By contrast, the highly dependable machine was located close to both support staff and to key users. This meant that problems could be spotted quickly and resolved and that users learned from each other how to carry out more advanced tasks without having to call on user support. The physical location of the machine and the layout of the office played a key role in determining whether a machine was dependable or not – not its technical features.

Source: Blomberg 1987

individual competence, technical matters refuse to fade into the background altogether. For example, in EBank questions of bandwidth constraints which had not been anticipated by the project team were a major constraint (Scarbrough 2003). Similarly, the knowledge management team in National Pharmco found themselves being more and more drawn into technical considerations when faced by poor design. For Currie and Kerrin (2004: 18) this means that 'those responsible for the development, design and implementation of the intranet became captured by the technology itself'. We might choose an alternative perspective, one which suggests that their initial lack of awareness meant that they were not prepared for these challenges. This suggests that while technical questions might not be the most important, they still remain salient ones. It would be fair to argue that in many of the cases which we have examined, the precise nature of these 'technical' issues remains unclear, as most accounts fail to be at all specific about the nature of the problems encountered (Clarke and Preece 2005).

INFORMATION AND PLACE

It is worth ending this chapter on a note which considers a very different form of 'technology', that of the technology which forms the built environment. Many of the developments which we have considered so far have been to do with the facilitation of communication which overcomes barriers of time and space. However, at the same time the influence of place on communication has become of more interest, especially in the design and construction of workplaces. In many respects this is due to the work which has been done, such as that on the photocopier technicians which informed the design of the Eureka system, which has explored the importance of place in sharing stories. Stories are often best exchanged in informal situations where people get together around a common focus which might be an important but mundane part of day to day activities, like the water cooler, the coffee machine or, indeed, the photocopier

117

(Cross and Parker 2004). For example, in the design of a new BMW research and engineering centre in Munich designers tried to locate shared facilities in such a way that unplanned encounters between staff from different functions might be facilitated (Aldersey-Williams 1996).

A key part of the learning from data that occurred in the Shorko example that we introduced in the last chapter was the grouping of monitors which recorded data on the state of processes in a central control room (Earl 1994). This brought operators together in such a way that they could discuss what data represented on the monitors could mean. This then enhanced the collective learning which in turn, as we will see, shifted the strategic direction of the company. Architects are now designing buildings round metaphors like the street, designed to be lined with cafés to facilitate causal encounters, such as the headquarters of British Airways and the Nationwide Building Society in the UK (Tannis and Duffy 1999). These examples should remind us that the layout of physical work remains important and that we should not overlook the impact of other technologies on communication, no matter how significant and embedded the use of ICT.

CONCLUSION

In the spirit of our injunction to be specific about technology, I have tried over the last two chapters to present something of the variety which lies behind the simple label of 'ICT'. Our focus has been on the impacts on data, information and knowledge, rather than on the operational details of the system. Such details are properly the province of specialists within organizations, but one conclusion might be that our information literate manager needs to be aware of the impact which these operational details can have on the types of information available to her. Without such awareness, she will not have a clear sense of what types of information might be available and in what ways technical constraints might prevent her using some of it to full effect. An awareness of such possibilities is also important for imagining whether it is possible to do things differently. Such considerations lead us to look at organizational strategy and its relation to both ICT and to information in the next chapter.

SUMMARY

- Communication in organizations is not just a matter of individual cognitive ability. It is also a matter of the expectations generated by the social setting. Communications media may be selected not because of their communicative efficiency but because of social expectations about what constitutes the right medium.

- Metaphor and genre are important in conditioning the ways in which people communicate. The familiar messaging metaphor of email may account for its popularity over systems which use alternative metaphors of documents and publishing.

- There has been considerable effort to develop applications which support forms of team working across functional boundaries, applications such as groupware and intranets. However, traditional boundaries of function and hierarchy remain important and exercise strong constraints on the effectiveness of such systems.

■ Systems designed for knowledge sharing seem to be most effective when dealing with technical forms of information in bounded domains when there is clear benefit to the participants in shared work processes. Systems which involve additional work which is perceived as unproductive are less well received, especially when these conflict with existing reward structures.

■ 'Technical' considerations remain important for our information literate manager, who needs to be aware of the range of possibilities opened up by ICT and of the constraints which technical features continue to impose on what is possible.

REVIEW QUESTIONS

1 Where would you place email on the hierarchy of media richness?

2 Distinguish between the features and uses of groupware and email.

DISCUSSION QUESTIONS

1 Review the 'case of the unopened envelope' that we discussed in Chapter 1. Using the hierarchy of media richness, how might you communicate the information concerned? How might the tools we discussed in this chapter be brought to bear to ensure more effective communication?

2 Is information literacy more a matter of establishing the appropriate relations than of being able to retrieve information? Use the discussion in Chapter 2 based on the work of Alistair Preston to form the basis for your conclusions.

CASE EXERCISE

Chevron and Amoco are two major oil companies which were each at the forefront of intranet design, but the two companies adopted very different approaches. In Chevron, the look and content of the intranet was tightly controlled, with a central team laying down strict guidelines. By contrast, Amoco adopted a more bottom up approach, with very few controls on content (Greenberg 1998).

What are the advantages and disadvantages of each approach?

FURTHER READING

C. Ciborra (ed.) (1996) *Groupware and Teamwork: Invisible Aid or Technical Hindrance?* Chichester, Wiley.
   Useful collection of articles which includes the Unilever case study discussed in this chapter.

C. Pritchard, R. Hull, M. Chumer, and Willmott, H. (eds) (2000) *Managing Knowledge*. Basingstoke, Macmillan.

>A somewhat uneven collection that brings a critical eye to bear on many aspects of knowledge management, including the use of groupware.

C. Ciborra (ed.) (2000) *From Control to Drift*. Oxford, Oxford University Press: 148–171.

>This collection of articles has much of relevance to the following chapter on strategy, but perhaps most of the interest comes from some of the detailed cases of applications in practice. Heavily influenced by actor–network theory and not always convincing in its application of this.

REFERENCES

Aldersey-Williams, H. (1996) 'Office Designers Lobby for the Corridors of Creativity', *Independent on Sunday (Inside Business)*, 5 May: 8.

Baecker, R. M., Grudin, J., Buxton, W. and Greenberg, S. (1995) 'Groupware and Computer Supported Cooperative Work', Introduction to Chapter 11 of R. M. Baecker, J. Grudin, W. Buxton and S. Greenberg, *Readings in Human-Computer Interaction: Toward the Year 2000*. San Francisco, Morgan-Kaufman: 742.

Baumard, P. (1999) *Tacit Knowledge in Organizations*. London, Sage.

Bellos, A. (1997) 'Insurance Company Pays Out £450,000 in E-Mail Libel Test Case by Business Rival', *The Guardian*, July 18: 5.

Blomberg, J. L. (1987) 'Social Interaction and Office Communication: Effects on User Evaluation of New Technologies', in R. Kraut (ed.) *Technology and the Transformation of White-Collar Work*, Hillsdale, NJ, Erlbaum: 195–210.

Bobrow, D. G. and Whalen, J. (2002) 'Community Knowledge Sharing in Practice: The Eureka Story', *Reflections*, 4(2): 47–59.

Bradbury, D. (2004) 'Can You Make Network Users Pay to Play?' *Computer Weekly*, September 28: 52.

Brown, S. and Lightfoot, G. (2002) 'Presence, Absence and Accountability: E-Mail and the Mediation of Organizational Memory', in S. Woolgar (ed.) *Virtual Society? Get Real!: The Social Science of Electronic Technologies*. Oxford, Oxford University Press: 209–229.

Carroll, J. and Mack, R. (1995) 'Learning to Use a Word Processor: By Doing, by Thinking and by Knowing', in R. M. Baecker, J. Grudin, W. Buxton and S. Greenberg (eds) *Readings in Human-Computer Interaction: Toward the Year 2000*. San Francisco: Morgan-Kaufman: 698–717.

Ciborra, C. and Patriotta, G. (1996) 'Groupware and Teamwork in New Product Development: The Case of a Consumer Goods Multinational', in C. Ciborra (ed.) *Groupware and Teamwork: Invisible Aid or Technical Hindrance?* Chichester, Wiley: 122–143.

Clarke, K. and Preece, D. (2005) 'Constructing and Using a Company Intranet: "It's a Very Cultural Thing"', *New Technology, Work and Employment*, 20(2): 150–165.

Cottrell, N. and Rapley, K. (1991) 'Factors Critical to the Success of Executive Information Systems in British Airways', *European Journal of Information Systems*, 1(1): 65–71.

Cross, R. and Parker, A. (2004) *The Hidden Power of Social Networks: Understanding How Work Really Gets Done in Organizations*. Cambridge MA, Harvard Business School Press.

Currie, G. and Kerrin, M. (2004) 'The Limits of a Technological Fix to Knowledge Management: Epistemological, Political and Cultural Issues in the Case of Intranet Implementation', *Management Learning*, 35(1): 9–29.

Daft, R. L. and Lengel, R. H. (1986) 'A Proposed Integration Among Organizational Information Requirements, Media Richness, and Structural Design', *Management Science*, 32(5), 191–233.

Daft, R. L., Lengel, R. H. and Trevino, L. K. (1987) 'Message Equivocality, Media Selection, and Manager Performance: Implications for Information Systems', *MIS Quarterly*, 11(3): 354–366.

DeSanctis, G. and Poole, M. S. (1994) 'Capturing the Complexity in Advanced Technology Use: Adaptive Structuration Theory', *Organization Science*, 5(2): 121–147.

Dourado, P. (1996) 'Hot Gossip', *Computing*, 24 October: 50.

Earl, M. (1994) 'Shorko Films SA', in C. Ciborra and T. Jelassi (eds) *Strategic Information Systems: A European Perspective*. Chichester, Wiley: 99–112.

Greenberg, R. (1998) 'He Says, She Says', *CIO Web Business Magazine*, www.cio.com/archive/webbusiness/080198_central.html.

Gunton, T. (1988) *End User Focus*. Hemel Hempstead, Prentice Hall.

Hayes, N. and Walsham, G. (2000) 'Safe Enclaves, Political Enclaves and Knowledge Working', in C. Pritchard, R. Hull, M. Chumer and Willmott, H. (Eds) *Managing Knowledge*. Basingstoke, Macmillan: 69–87.

Hirschheim, R. and Klein, H. H. (1989) 'Four Paradigms of Information Systems Development', *Communications of the ACM*, 32: 1199–1216.

Hodgkinson, G. P. and Sparrow, P. R. (2002) *The Competent Organization: A Psychological Analysis of the Strategic Management Process*. Buckingham, Open University Press.

Hsiao, R., Tsai, S. D. and Lee, C. (2006) 'The Problems of Embeddness: Knowledge Transfer, Coordination and Reuse in Information Systems', *Organization Studies*, 27(9): 1289–1318.

Hutchby, I. (2001) *Conversation and Technology: From the Telephone to the Internet*. Cambridge, Polity.

Jablin, F. M. and Putnam, L. L. (2001) *The New Handbook of Organizational Communication: Advances in Theory, Research and Methods*. Thousand Oaks, CA, Sage.

Kellog, K., Orlikowski, W. and Yates, J. (2006) 'Life in the Trading Zone: Structuring Coordination Across Boundaries in Postbureaucratic Organizations', *Organization Science*, 17(1): 22–44.

Lakoff, G. and Johnson, M. (1980) *Metaphors We Live By*. Chicago, University of Chicago Press.

Lea, M., O'Shea, T. and Fung P. S. (1992) '"Flaming" in Commuter Mediated Communication: Observations, Explanations, Implications', in M. Lea (ed.) *Contexts of Computer-Mediated Communication*. Hemel Hempstead, Harvester Wheatsheaf: 89–112.

Markus, M. L. (1994) 'Electronic Mail as the Medium of Managerial Choice', *Organization Science*, 5(4): 502–526.

Markus, M. L. and Keil, M. (1994) 'If We Build It, They Will Come: Designing Information Systems that People Want to Use', *Sloan Management Review*, 35(4): 11–25.

McKinlay, A. (2002) 'The Limits of Knowledge Management', *New Technology, Work and Employment*, 17(2): 76–88.

Mintzberg, H. (1994) 'Rounding Out the Manager's Job', *Sloan Management Review*, 36(1) 11–26.

Monteiro, E. and Hepso, V. (2000) 'Infrastructure Strategy Formation: Seize the Day at Statoil', in C. Ciborra (ed.) *From Control to Drift*. Oxford, Oxford University Press: 148–171.

Moore, C. (1998) 'Best Practices: Eureka! Xerox Discovers Way to Grow Community Knowledge . . . and Customer Satisfaction', *KMWorld* 7(1): www.kmworld.com/publications/magazine/index.cfm.

Orlikowski, W. and Yates, J. (1994) 'Genre Repertoire: The Structuring of Communicative Practices in Organizations', *Administrative Science Quarterly*, 39: 541–574.

Orlikowski, W. (2000) 'Using Technology and Constituting Structures: A Practice Lens for Studying Technology in Organizations', *Organization Science*, 11(4): 404–428.

Orna, E. (2005) *Making Knowledge Visible: Communicating Knowledge Through Information Products*. Aldershot, Gower.

Rangaswamy, A., Harlam, B. and Lodish, L. (1991) 'INFER: An Expert System for Automatic Analysis of Scanner Data', *International Journal of Research in Marketing*, 8: 29–40.

Robertson, M., Sorenson, C. and Swan, J. (2001) 'Survival of the Leanest: Intensive Knowledge Work and Groupware Adaptation', *Information Technology and People*, 14(4): 334–352.

Scarbrough, H. (2003) 'Knowledge Management, HRM and the Innovation Process', *International Journal of Manpower*, 24(5): 501–516.

Simon, H. (1977) *The New Science of Management Decision*. New Jersey, Prentice Hall.

Tannis, J. and Duffy, F. (1999) 'A Vision of the New Workplace Revisited', *Site Selection Online*, www.siteselection.com/sshighlites/0999/p805/ accessed 18 December 2006.

Tsoukas, H. (1993) 'Analogical Reasoning and Knowledge Generation in Organization Theory', *Organization Studies*, 14(3): 323–346.

Voelpel, S., Dous, M. and Davenport, T. (2005) 'Five Steps to Creating a Global Knowledge-Sharing System: Siemens' ShareNet', *Academy of Management Executive*, 19(2): 9–23.

Wilson, T. (2002) 'The Nonsense of "Knowledge Management"', *Information Research*, 8(10) [available at http://InformationR.net/ir/8-1/paper144.html] paper no. 144.

Winograd, T. and Flores, F. (1986) *Understanding Computers and Cognition: A New Foundation for Design*. Reading, Addison-Wesley.

Xerox PARC (2006) 'Eureka', Xerox PARC, www.parc.xerox.com/research/projects/commknowledge/eureka.html.

Yates, J. (1989) *Control Through Communication: The Rise of System in American Management*. Baltimore, The Johns Hopkins University Press.

Yates, J. and Orlikowski, W. (1992) 'Genres of Organizational Communication: A Structurational Approach to Studying Communication and Media', *Academy of Management Review*, 17(2): 299–326.

Zantout, H. and Marir, F. (1999) 'Document Management Systems from Current Capabilities towards Intelligent Information Retrieval: An Overview', *International Journal of Information Management*, 19(6): 471–484.

Zuboff, S. (1988) *In the Age of the Smart Machine: The Future of Work and Power*. London, Heinemann.

Chapter 6

Strategy, information and ICT

INTRODUCTION

There is a voluminous literature on organizational strategy and information is implicit in much of it. Take the thorny problem of defining 'strategic information systems'. Are these strategic because they support the strategic direction of the organization or because they themselves change the balance of strategic forces at play? Or is it that they provide information which is in itself the key strategic resource? Or are such systems only those which supply information to those responsible for taking the decisions? This chapter explores some of these issues, taking into account some of the implications of technology that we have explored already.

This chapter will examine:

- some of the most important positions in the strategy literature, with a particular focus on the impact of considerations of knowledge, information and data
- ways in which aspects of knowledge, information and data might be conceptualized in the context of strategy
- the debate over the impact of ICT on strategy, in particular the difficulty of aligning organizational strategy with ICT

VARIETIES OF STRATEGY

Strategy is to a greater or lesser degree concerned with purpose, orientation and direction. While some would argue, as we will see, that strategy is emergent rather than intended (and that the whole question of intentionality is a matter of considerable debate within organizational theory) it can be helpful to see strategy as in some sense concerned with what the organization is doing and why. This sense may well be the result of a process of dissension and debate rather than being in some sense the unified view of the organization, but strategy is concerned with deciding on the areas within which an organization operates. The extent to which such a strategy involves interaction with the world in which the organization is embedded is also a matter of debate. As we have seen, Daft and Weick (1984) suggest that some organizations actively make that world, rather than being passive analysers of it. However this operates, strategy as a subject is particularly concerned with the external face of organizations and how they translate into imperatives for internal activities. It is also concerned with aspects of the future, rather than of the past or present. In terms of information this means that we are often concerned with forecasts and visions, in which considerations of accuracy and completeness are called into question. Finally, it is important to point out that much of the strategy literature is as concerned with prescription as it is with analysis. That is, much of it seeks to advise organizational members on how to carry out strategy, often based on the presentation of a few exemplary cases rather than on the detailed examination of practice. We often lack clear detail on just how strategy is carried out in practice.

However, a number of clear themes stand out and it is these which we examine first in order to frame our discussions of knowledge, information and data. One starting point is to distinguish between two influential broad approaches, those which look at the positioning of organizations in a competitive environment and those which explore the resources available for an organization to carry out its strategic purpose. The first is particularly associated with the work of Michael Porter (2004). His work can be set in the context of a broader disciplinary setting of economics and a concern among American scholars in particular from the late 1950s on the conditioning role of market forces. Porter's work uses two primary analytical devices to suggest that there are a limited number of generic strategies which organizations can pursue. They can either compete on the basis of the price which they offer their goods at, seeking to be the lowest cost supplier, or they can seek to differentiate their products and services from those of others. In seeking to analyse the options available to an organization the first device is that of value chain analysis.

Within an organization Porter argues that there are certain activities, such as logistics and production, which add value to a product or service. Other activities, such as finance or human resources, are support for these activities rather than sources of value in their own right. The imperative for an organization is to ensure that it adds value by enhancing its value adding aspects and controlling its non-value adding support activities. It needs to do this because its internal value chain forms part of an industry value chain in which organizations only exist to the extent that they add value as products pass through them. Thus, an industry may have upstream raw material producers who add relatively little value to their products but whose place in the value chain is as a primary supplier. Their products are then transformed during the manufacturing process before entering the downstream part of the chain, in which wholesalers add value by their expertise in logistics and distribution. Retailers are the final realizers of the value which has been added during this chain. As we will see, analysis of the value chain is essential in determining the likely influence of information and ICT on the shape and nature of activities carried out within it. The second analytical device is concerned with the positioning of the organization in a competitive environment made up of five forces: competitors, suppliers, buyers, substitutes and barriers to entry. The analysis of each of these then suggests opportunities for positioning the organization and activities which need to be undertaken to strengthen those factors (notably barriers to entry) which protect the position of the organization and to weaken those (such as the power of suppliers) which threaten it.

In an influential article in 1985 Porter and Millar sought to explain how developments in ICT were reshaping the balance of forces. They relied in particular on the notion of 'information intensity'. This was a measure developed by Henderson which explored two dimensions: the amount of information in a particular product and the importance of information in the value chain in which that product appeared. Thus, they argued, some products have an intrinsically high information content, such as newspapers, whereas others, such as cement, have very little, if any, information content. However, products which have little information content may well appear in a value chain in which high amounts of information are transferred, such as in oil refining. The combination of these two dimensions allows for the positioning of organizations and suggests both the degree of impact information and ICT will have on their positioning and what they might do about it. One criticism of this approach is that it operates with a fairly crude view of information which sees it very much as a product. Thus many would argue that the information content of many newspapers is actually comparatively low, whereas there is much tacit knowledge that accompanies the creative use of cement. The focus on content here, rather than what is done in an active process, can lead to a rather misleading approach.

However, what Porter and Millar (1985) suggested was that by having an impact on the value chain both within organizations and, perhaps more crucially, in the value chain, ICT could affect the whole competitive position of organizations. This was, of course, in the days before the widespread use of the Internet for commercial transactions, but even at this stage, drawing on some of the examples which we explore in a little more detail below, Porter and Millar were able to argue that the balance of forces was considerably affected by the use of ICT and the information which it produces. The relative balance of these two forces is a matter of some debate, as we will see, but it can be useful to apply some of this thinking to a specific case which is one which affects all our lives, that of supermarkets.

SUPERMARKETS, INFORMATION AND STRATEGY

Supermarkets and data

The concentration of the retailing of groceries in the hands of a very limited number of large companies has caused considerable concern and debate in a number of countries. The process is probably most accelerated in the USA and UK, and the major focus of the following discussion is on two companies, Wal-Mart and Tesco, which figure as among the most successful in their respective markets and have growing international reach and influence. The comparison of the two companies immediately raises differences of style and operation, but the main focus here is on how ICT and the use of information has affected the balance of forces in the industries in which they operate. We need to be aware that there are other reasons for their success, and other causes for concern, that are not discussed in any detail here (Bevan 2005). In both cases application of planning restrictions and the ability to secure advantageous store locations seems of importance. Wal-Mart's labour policies have been subject to particular criticism in the USA (Lichtenstein 2006). Both are representatives of an industry which has also been criticized for distorting supplier relationships and having adverse impacts on food quality and the environment (Blythman 2005). These criticisms have, of course, been fiercely contested by the industry. However, our concern here is with exploring how information has an impact on strategy in order to illustrate the broader points that Porter and Millar (1985) are raising. We do this firstly through an examination of how the organizations' 'traditional' ICT applications, notably the data warehouses that we explored in Chapter 4, affect the balance of forces. We then bring the Web into the equation.

The threat of the web is a clear part of the consideration of potential substitutes for the supermarket as a means of shopping, so we will bracket this for now. Working our way clockwise round the model we arrive at 'buyers' and here we have our first point of comparison between our two main companies. Wal-Mart has made some experiment with customer loyalty cards, but its main focus is on supply and cost competition. By contrast, Tesco was an early adopter of a loyalty card programme which saw millions of customers issued with a plastic card, the Tesco Clubcard (Humby, Hunt and Phillips 2003). While this was used to promote loyalty to the store by providing rewards based on shopping levels, the key factor for its success for Tesco was in obtaining customer details and then tying these to purchasing history. As Tesco gained more such data it was able to carry out increasingly sophisticated and complex segmentation of its customer base. By doing this it was able to target offers and rewards at specific groups of customers. We have already seen the impact of this type of detailed analysis in response to price competition; another example was in the launch of the 'Finest' range. This was a premium range of grocery products, priced accordingly and targeted at Tesco's most affluent customers. The initial strategy was to launch the product only in certain stores where it was felt that groups of such customers were concentrated, but initial sales were disappointing. 'So', report Humby, Hunt and Phillips (2003: 160), 'Tesco removed the range, and re-merchandized it in shops where Clubcard identified the largest number of customers with a 'Finest' lifestyle, to create the sales impact it wanted'. While, as we will see, there can be arguments that in certain situations ICT gives buyers a wider range of information, and so more power, in this case the possession of detailed data about shopping patterns gives Tesco a particular advantage. Other retailers in the UK, notably Boots (a retailer with a particularly strong position in the over the counter drugs market), also introduced their own cards (Chaffey and Wood, 2004: 423–424). Others, such as the supermarket chain Sainsbury's, after starting their own card, sought to move into multi-supplier cards. Thus the Nectar loyalty card scheme links the customers of Sainsbury's with those of the motor fuel company BP, the department store Debenhams, the car supplier Ford, and a number of other providers. The question here is the degree of firm-specific data which is accessible (Humby, Hunt and Phillips 2003).

However, one clear argument is that the very existence of such banks of data, and the capability to make something of it, are key barriers to entry. We will discuss the question of capabilities later, as this becomes a core criticism of the positioning approach, but in both the case of Tesco and of Wal-Mart the existence of large bodies of data, acquired over many years, is not only a core part of their success but also a resource which is difficult to imitate. This is in large part because of the importance of time. Many shopping patterns only become clear with historical analysis, for which a reasonable run of data is required. The scale of the investment in ICT is also important here, but probably a diminishing asset. This is because advances in technology reduce the cost of ownership and make it feasible for storage and analysis to be carried out using much cheaper technology. For example, Westerman (2001) argues that when Wal-Mart was building its data warehouse, buying a very expensive specialist machine was its only option, but new entrants would not have this burden to bear. Indeed, Ciborra (2000) has argued that we tend to underestimate the extent to which the 'installed base' of the information infrastructure becomes something of a hindrance to change. What once gave competitive advantage can thus be something of a two-edged sword (Hopper 1990). However, the data themselves but, more significantly, the capacity to analyse them remain a key barrier to entry.

We have already seen that Wal-Mart's key strength is in its use of information to manage supplier relations and we have here to appreciate a difference in the 'business models' adopted with regard to suppliers on either side of the Atlantic. Tesco and other UK supermarkets maintain full control over the stocking of shelves in their stores based on their internal expertise in logistics. They use their data on stock levels to maintain and enhance what is on the shelves, but stocking decisions remain in their control. Wal-Mart also maintains control over its shelves, but does this by using the data it has on transactions to put pressure on its suppliers to keep those shelves filled. It allocates a certain amount of space to suppliers and places the responsibility on them to keep the shelves filled. If they fail to do so, using the extensive data it has on product performance, Wal-Mart will allocate space elsewhere. In both countries this has brought complaints that the balance of power has shifted too far towards the supermarkets, with the latter being able to use their extensive data to squeeze supplier margins. Of course, there are factors other than data analysis here, but such analysis remains at the heart of operations. Wal-Mart, for example, requires its major suppliers to use its Retail Link system to check on the status of shelves (Westerman 2001). Data can also be transferred from the retailer to the supplier in order to enable them to gain greater insight into customer buying patterns. In effect the supermarkets are doing direct market research, but based on what customers actually buy as opposed to their stated intentions, data which are of great value to suppliers. Of course, what this also does is place more control in the hands of the supermarkets and such control has been argued to be one of the reasons behind increasing concentration among suppliers, such as the merger in 2005 between Proctor & Gamble and Gillette.

Finally, we have noted that Wal-Mart and Tesco have different approaches to their operation of supermarkets. Wal-Mart tends to focus on cost and tight management of its relationships with suppliers; Tesco is more focused on customer understanding. However, in both cases the intensive use of data has been a key part of their success and it is one which is difficult for competitors to emulate. The upmarket UK supermarket, Waitrose, for example, was reputed to have said that '[t]rying to analyse all the data is madness' after it abandoned attempts to build a data warehouse (Humby, Hunt and Phillips 2003: 4). Another key competitor, Asda (now owned by Wal-Mart) argued that '[c]ustomers aren't fooled by marketing gimmicks . . . Shoppers' real loyalty only comes from offering the lowest prices on the right range of products' (Humby, Hunt and Phillips 2003: 9). However, these responses, suggest Humby, Hunt and Phillips, miss the importance of the understanding of the data and what is done with the results. This is something to which we return below, but we need also to consider the impact of the Web.

Supermarkets and the Web

At the peak of the 'dot.com' era Eric Clemons suggested that '[u]ltimately, online grocery shopping may come from companies over which retailers have no power, such as Internet service providers' (Clemons 2000: 131). This was a common suggestion when enthusiasm for the power of the Internet was at its height and one key argument was that the power of the Web would enable suppliers to bypass the middleman entirely and deal directly with customers – the so-called phenomenon of 'disintermediation'. The experience in grocery retailing is interesting in enabling us to be sceptical about such claims. In particular they suggest rather hidden elements about organizational operations that will lead us to challenge aspects of the positioning school. The argument in the case of grocery retailing, then, was that the advent of the Web would enable new entrants to the market based on their excellence in new channels of distribution resting on the information content of the products on offer. That is, if the only task is supplying customers with a range of goods to choose from then this can be done effectively using web technology to enable orders to be made and then fulfilled. Indeed, this marked something of the success of Web start ups like Amazon in the book market. However, some crucial differences were in operation here. One was the ratio between distribution costs and the value of the product. Many grocery products are fairly bulky and of low value, thus incurring distribution costs of a different order to those of books. In addition, books can be distributed utilizing a channel, the postal service, which is well established and non-proprietary. So the spread of the Web can offer the threat of substitutes to certain operations, but the supermarkets seem not only to have beaten off such threats but also to have used it to further cement their position.

In terms of buyers, the spread of the Web ought to make them relatively independent of existing suppliers. That is, the power of the Web to compare offerings between supermarkets means that they need exhibit no loyalty to them. However, this is to suggest that branding and loyalty play no part in supermarket shopping. This may be true for some customers, but, as we have seen, only a small minority of Tesco customers turned out to base their loyalty on price alone. Loyalty is a difficult construct to measure – after all, some shoppers may be loyal simply because they have little alternative given the continuing importance of distribution channels and physical location – but it does seem that some customers have reasons for shopping at a store that are more complex than simple price. Some of this is down to having the range of products on offer. For example, Safeway used its data warehouse to examine the impact of the withdrawal of a low selling type of cheese. While sales were low, those customers affected (and who complained) were disproportionately regular shoppers with high expenditure (Field 1998). Of importance when choosing where to shop was, among other things, the range of goods available. Indeed, Humby, Hunt and Phillips argue that one problem for Safeway in its use of the data from its warehouse was that they quickly identified that families with young children were a key customer segment. 'Unfortunately,' they argue, 'the company's strict inter-pretation of which customers it wanted to become most loyal tended to alienate the other customer segments' (Humby, Hunt and Phillips 2003: 83). Once again, we see that there is more behind the shopping experience than crude analysis of aggregate data indicates.

A further problem with a simple disintermediation model is that it ignored the importance of excellence in areas of logistics and distribution. This was seen early on in the application of web technology in UK supermarkets. As in the USA, the most popular initial model was of specialist distribution centres. Companies such as Sainsbury's built large warehouses optimized for picking orders. However, they reckoned without the problems of distribution, problems which Tesco solved by a store based system. What this did was to build on existing distribution channels, not only in physical terms but also in terms of knowledge about what worked. A tradition of expertise in filling customer orders via the replenishment of stores was put to good use in meeting demand from the new means of reaching customers. Once again, the key barrier to entry was not the IT systems or the physical stores (although these were of considerable importance, the latter being considerably underestimated by the more enthusiastic advocates of the Web) but the capacity to fill customer orders – which in turn could be seen to rest on both extensive knowledge of customers gleaned from historic data and an orientation towards customers.

We have seen how the supermarkets used their command over customer data to cement their position in the value chain. This could be extended using the Web to enable suppliers to access internal systems directly. This could tie them more closely in to the fortunes of the supermarkets. In some circumstances it does become possible for suppliers to bypass the intermediary, because of the data which they possess on operations. For example, airlines have been successful in many cases, especially those involving simple flights, in enabling direct booking of their services. The crucial distinction here might be that they themselves held the data on flight patterns. However, the complexity of the offerings in the leisure market in particular meant a continuing need for intermediaries, some of which were existing agencies, other new start ups. However, the experience has been that it has been highly difficult for these new intermediaries to operate profitably. As we will see when we examine some further examples of the impact of IT more generally on business strategy, this is because we have tended to underestimate the importance of existing capabilities. Competition in the supermarket section, therefore, has been affected by the advent of ICT, but the result has tended to be the strengthening of existing competitive positions based on broader factors, rather than the complete reconstruction of the industry. Table 6.1 summarizes our discussion. However, this discussion has indicated at a number of points some weaknesses with the positioning approach to strategy which suggests that a different approach might be illuminating. This is the resource based view (RBV) of strategy.

Table 6.1 *Information and the Internet in supermarket shopping*

	Information	Internet
Substitutes	Range of offerings makes substitutes difficult	Possible new entrants; strength of existing brands (implicit knowledge)
Buyers	Customer loyalty; additional data on preferences	Ability to compare offerings by customers; more targeted offerings
Barriers to entry	Banks of data; scale of ICT investment; capacity to analyse	Existing distribution channels; logistical capability
Suppliers	Information to control supplier performance	Direct access to sales data for partnership or control
Competitors	Better understanding of customer preferences or lower cost based on supplier control	Threat of new entrants but consolidation of existing players

KNOWLEDGE AS RESOURCE

One criticism of the positioning school is that it exhibits a form of market determinism. That is, its focus is on the structuring of a particular field of endeavour, without recognizing the extent to which organizations can alter the shape of this field by their actions. They can do this by developing a unique bundle of resources, particularly those which have been built up over time. It is these resources which then form the basis for sustainable competitive advantage. Many facets of performance, such as products, can be copied and so, while they may give a short term advantage, they cannot form the basis of sustainable success. Thus, attention shifts to these unique resources which are hard to imitate and knowledge proves here to be central. At a number of points during our discussion of the positioning school, we noted that the view of information seemed a rather impoverished one, equating it often to either a product or to the inevitable outcome of ICT. However, a resource based view gels much better with our previous discussion of knowledge as an implicit part of organizational functioning (resource based theorists will often use the term 'tacit', but based on our previous discussion we prefer to use 'implicit'). This is an approach which also emphasizes history, in that strategy is often constrained by the pattern of previous decisions. Thus, while an organization may be able to analyse its positioning in the market place, it might often lack the capabilities to do anything about it.

A second form of criticism emanating from this perspective is the emphasis on planning in the positioning school. Given the emphasis on analytical means of exploring the environment, the positioning approach is associated with the desire to plan the entire strategic process. This gave rise to immensely complex schemes of planning which Mintzberg (1994) mercilessly pulls apart in his *Rise and Fall of Strategic Planning*. This is not to argue that planning is not important, but that it is the consequence of creativity and innovation, not the cause of them. This approach therefore places the creative process, emerging from the historical formation of the organization at its heart. On this reading, the most important organizational activity may be to create the space for learning. This has led many to argue that rather than being intentional, strategy is best seen as emergent, a process in which luck and contingency play an important role. One classic example that is often given of strategy as emergence is the development of Post-It notes at the 3M company.

If we explore some of the classic cases of ICT-enabled strategic advantage we can see a combination of luck and the building on existing operational capacity. The most famous

CREATIVITY AND EMERGENT STRATEGY

The 3M company has an unwritten guideline, but one widely understood, that its researchers can spend up to 15 per cent of their time on unauthorized projects. This guidance emerged out of the success of Post-It notes, which emerged by accident from failed results of developing new adhesives. Despite the originator of the idea being unable to persuade his management that the idea should be taken further, he continued to work on the idea until it was accepted. The result was a major new line of business for the company.

Source: DeSimone 1995

example of the way in which ICT can affect strategy is that of American Airlines and its Sabre system (Wiseman 1985). This had its origins in the application of the newly developed computer systems in the 1950s to the process of booking airline seats, something facilitated by a chance meeting on a flight between executives of IBM and the airline. Commercial computing was fairly new and had been largely applied to payroll, but the standard parameters and high volumes of the seat booking process proved an ideal application. The capacity of American to solve its operational problems led to it also hosting the bookings of other airlines. Through placing terminals allowing access to the combined systems in travel agents offices the company invented the notion of the Central Reservation System (CRS). This was successful among travel agents as it cut down on the time needed to find vacant seats. It also gave considerable advantage to American as in early versions its flights were always rated as the first on the screen as a result of searches. As they were forced to amend this as a result of investigations by competition authorities, they came to develop the system in its own right. It spawned a number of imitators, but the success of the system prompted the observation by the then chairman Robert Crandall that if he had to choose he would sell the airline rather than the system (Pemberton, Stonehouse and Barber 2001).

A number of other well-cited systems share this origin in operational features. Another case which is often cited is that of American Hospital Supplies, which had its origins in a salesman observing the difficulties of hospitals ordering supplies (Henderson and Venkatraman 1993). The response was to supply a terminal for direct ordering, a response which was so successful that its spread gave the company significant market share. However, both these cases, as well as illustrating the role of chance, operations and the requirements imposed by external regulation, indicate how once successful systems can become problematic as technology changes (Hopper 1990). This is what Ciborra (2000) refers to as the legacy of the installed base. These once successful systems become locked into a particular form of technology which can be leap-frogged by new developments. The problem for the innovators is that they now have to pay heavy switching costs.

In such circumstances, and coupled with the success of some Internet ventures, some have questioned the importance of IT as a competitive factor. In a polemical article in *Harvard Business Review* in 2003, for example, Carr suggested that the continuing improvement in performance of IT, coupled with declining cost, eroded the advantage that applications of IT brought, given that organizations could quickly copy successful systems. More than this, many organizations were turning away from bespoke systems to implementing packaged software like ERP systems from SAP. In doing so, in the hope of emulating best practice, they were in fact removing the distinctive competitive edge that their processes might give them. Sustained competitive advantage from ICT was therefore a mirage. Such points are well made (although they have been made by others before, notably Hopper (1990)) but what they tend to ignore is that the important component is the integration of ICT into business operations. An interesting illustration of this is given by the comparison of the use of ICT by two US credit card companies (see box overleaf).

What the focus on ICT tends to neglect is the potential advantage which might be obtained from more intensive use of the data and information that organizations possess, often facilitated by ICT. That is, it is not the ICT itself that brings advantage but the use made of the information (Galliers and Newell 2004). The use of data has been rather neglected in such discussions, but recent work by Davenport (2006) has suggested that a number of companies (CapitalOne being one exemplar) are using what he terms 'analytics', that is, the intensive exploitation of bodies of data about customers and services as the central part of their competitive strategy.

131

ICT, INFORMATION AND CUSTOMERS IN THE CREDIT CARD INDUSTRY

CapitalOne is a recent entrant to the credit card business in the USA (with a successful business in the UK as well). The use of ICT-enabled data is at the heart of its business success, but this requires other factors, as Day (2003) illustrates in his comparison with a longer established issuer, First USA. Day argues that three factors need to be aligned – the orientation towards customers, the 'configuration' of the organization to support this orientation and the use and quality of information – in order to create a capability of customer relations. Without attention to all three, endeavours to build effective CRM systems will fail.

Day contrasts an orientation to customers at First USA, which does not distinguish between groups of customers except at the broadest level, with very detailed segmentation at CapitalOne. This segmentation is facilitated by the intensive use of customer data, much of it purchased from external suppliers like Experian. This data is used to seed customer specific models which pay close attention to risk profiles and adjust product offerings on that basis. Because of such models, CapitalOne are able to develop profitable business even in niche markets where the risk factors are traditionally considered too high. This orientation to customers and information is supported by reward structures which focus on the retention of profitable customers. Staff are organized in groups which centre on the development and marketing of particular products, with ICT expertise fully integrated into these groups.

Day argues that because of these approaches CapitalOne had a higher net interest income per cardholder ($43) than First USA ($26). Its profit margin, customer attrition rate and labour turnover were all also better than the mass market provider. This indicates for Day the value of a targeted approach to customers, but it is one which depends on the alignment of all three areas.

Source: Day 2003

One reason why such a focus might be emerging now is the effective deployment of the data warehousing systems that we reviewed in Chapter 4, but another is that such advantage often depends on the collection of data which allow the construction of time series. From such series, trends and relationships can be discerned which can be distinguished from merely contingent events. Davenport suggests that such strategies have a number of implications, not least for the type of skills that organizations require, and we will return to these in later chapters.

STRATEGY AS PROCESS AND PRACTICE

The CapitalOne experience and others like it have led to some suggesting that rather than viewing strategy through a lens of 'content', where what is important is the output (perhaps in the form of a strategic plan, perhaps in the form of a capability), we should instead be attending to the 'process' of strategy formation. This form of 'processual' thinking is in accord with a broader trend within organizational theory where Watson and Harris (1999), for example, have contrasted the merits of a 'processual-relational' approach to a 'systems-control' perspective. The latter is seen to be too static and to not pay attention to the way in which the process by which strategies are developed can be as important as the outcome itself. That is, strategies which are developed by a small strategic planning group without the wider involvement of others in the organization may fall down at the implementation stage, as there is no commitment to them by the rest of the organization. It is the quality of the formulation process that is crucial in this reading. We will see below that such an approach is an important part of the criticism of strategic planning for information systems. It directs our attention away from an image of strategy as involving a small group of people and suggests that we need to pay much more attention to involvement and implementation. The process of involvement may lead to strategies which are evolutionary in character, responding as they do to the increased pace of change. Indeed, the impact of the Internet has been to increase the emphasis on the evolution of strategy in a dynamic inter-relationship with changes in the relationships in which the organization is enmeshed. We will revisit some criticisms of this approach in the next chapter, but a further perspective, that of strategy as practice, has also emerged which seeks to distinguish itself from the process school.

What the strategy as practice approach seeks to draw our attention to is the prescriptive nature of much of the material on strategy (Whittington 2006). It tends to seek to lay down better ways of formulating strategy, rather than attending to the detailed practices whereby strategy is made. The strategy as practice school intends to direct our attention to the sites where strategy is made, whether this is through the detailed investigation of conversations at board level or though the operation of institutions like the strategy 'away day'. In such investigations, the impact of ICT may be not so much on the strategy of the organization but on the way that it is formulated. The ability to communicate across boundaries of time and space offer the prospect of involving more people in strategy formulation. The wider availability of data and the capacity to analyse these in more detail may allow for the improved modelling of projected outcomes. However, the strategy as practice approach, in trying to focus on how strategy is actually achieved, may also have the impact of re-focusing our attention on senior decision makers. There is a tendency in the strategy as process approach to place the main focus on emergent as opposed to intended strategies. This tends to downplay the extent to which, successful or not, strategy formulation and monitoring still tends to be the preserve of a small group of senior decision makers.

We have seen, therefore, that there are a number of ways of looking at strategy, all of which have considerations of information at their heart. However, the degree to which these have explicitly considered questions of knowledge, information and data explicitly has varied. In our next section, therefore, we turn to look at how some of the features that we have discussed, and in particular the generation of new forms of information, have been considered in the literature.

BRINGING INFORMATION IN

In this section we consider the following:

- information resource management in Michael Earl's discussion of IS strategy;
- the Information Orientation approach of Marchand and colleagues;

- the notion of strategy as 'data plus sense making' suggested by Galliers and Newell;
- links to human resource management strategies;
- the advocacy of information policies by Elizabeth Orna.

Michael Earl is somebody who has used the portmanteau term 'information strategy' to cover both the information systems strategy and something which he terms the 'information resource strategy'. His earlier work (Earl 1988), starting from the need to support business strategy, argued that an information strategy ought to consist of three elements, all inter-related but dealing with different aspects. These were strategies for information technology, information systems and information management. Based on the demands laid out by the business strategy, an organization would need to determine what technical means were needed to fulfil them. These requirements formed the basis for the IT strategy, which would address such questions as the type of IT to be used and the relationships to be developed with suppliers. For example, this might determine whether the organization would deal with one supplier for its full range of equipment (thereby trying to ensure inter-operability) or treat IT as a commodity to be bought off the shelf. (Here, the type of developments discussed by Carr (2003) tend to favour the latter approach, except perhaps in the case of highly specialist equipment like that used for data warehouses.) This element of strategy is closely linked to the question of IS strategy, but here key questions are those such as whether the organization will build its own systems or buy them 'off the shelf'. If the latter is the case, as it is for many organizations given developments in the quality and reliability of application software, the question then becomes the selection mechanisms to ensure that such applications work well together. Finally, Earl suggested that there need to be mechanisms to manage the overall process, what would now be termed mechanisms of IS governance. This Earl terms 'information management', although his formulation focuses on aspects such as the development and project management methodologies to be adopted. These aspects of Earl's original formulation are to the left of the dotted line in Figure 6.1.

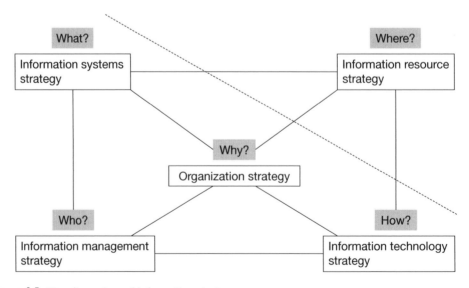

Figure 6.1 *Five dimensions of information strategy*

It will be clear that the original formulation had a dominant orientation on what the IS function itself has to do, as opposed to the imperatives for the rest of the organization. It said nothing about the links to other strategies and, most importantly, the central focus on what was being dealt with, namely information, was completely absent. (Similar things could also be said about other influential models of the time, such as the MIT framework.) As Earl himself later admitted:

> Now we can see that a fifth domain was missing – one we still find difficult to formalize but in which companies increasingly have objectives, principles and policies. This is the domain of information as a resource, or of information resource (IR) strategy.
>
> (Earl 2000: 20)

Of course such a move is subject to all the criticisms about information as a resource that we examined in Chapter 3. Earl himself has very little to say about what he takes information to be, apart from to recognize the complexities of the issues and to point to the importance of data. His inclusion of the IRM dimension has the merit of drawing explicit attention to the importance of information. A much more ambitious attempt is that provided by Marchand, Kettinger and Rollins (2001a, 2001b). The authors propose that they have isolated a series of measures which they term 'information orientation' which has a direct link to organizational performance. They go further to claim that, thanks to their research, 'For the first time, managers have a business metric, which is grounded in proven statistical and psychometric research techniques, to measure the levels of information capabilities in their company' (Marchand, Kettinger and Rollins 2001a: 10).

Information orientation consists of three linked capabilities. These are examined under the headings of information technology practices, information management practices and information behaviours and values. They point in particular to the neglect of information management practices: 'because improving information usage effectiveness was not a major focus of the human resources, operations, and control disciplines, it remained a side issue.' (Marchand, Kettinger and Rollins 2001b: 6). This seems an important point (if one perhaps not as innovative as they suggest) to which we will return, but what the authors claim goes beyond a simple suggestion that these are important areas. Rather, they claim to have found a measurable link between performance in these three areas and business performance. They claim that their work 'empirically shows the existence of IO as a new comprehensive measure of effective information use and then establishes a direct causal link between higher IO and higher business performance' (Marchand, Kettinger and Rollins 2001b: 14). This is clearly a strong claim, but when we examine the research in a little more detail some doubts creep in. What we have is a relationship between the perceptions of senior managers about information practices in their companies and the perceptions of the same people about business performance. While the authors argue that this means that the information practices cause the business performance, we could argue that if we were looking for causality it could go the other way, that is, because we are successful (in our perception) we must have successful information practices. Beyond pointing our attention to the consistency between senior managers' perceptions (which might be of interest in its own right if perhaps predictable) the research turns out to tell us little about the causal link between information practices and business performance. What the book is important in suggesting is that areas such as information management, drawn very differently from Earl's definition, and information cultures are worthy of further investigation.

A key suggestion here is that areas such as information usage have been neglected by functions such as human resource management. If we are seeking a more modest formulation of strategy which does not claim to have established metrics but which draws on some of the material about data which we have presented already and has consequences for HR policy, then we can examine the interesting, if rather under-developed suggestions by Galliers and Newell (2004) that we conceive of strategy as 'data plus sense making'. Galliers and Newell point to the increasing importance of data in organizations, although their treatment of this aspect of their equation is rather slight (but could be bolstered by the examples given in Davenport 2006). Given their audience (in a book about images of strategy) their focus is more on the sense making dimension. That is, such an approach places more emphasis on the abilities of organizational members to use information in a creative fashion, rather than simply on the ability to access it. Our problem here is that HR policies are rarely developed with an understanding of information practices in mind. A very rare example of a discussion of these issues in the HR literature comes with the examination of knowledge management strategies adopted in Scottish law firms by Hunter, Beaumont and Lee (2002). In the five firms they examined all the knowledge management approaches were based on combinations of IT and readily articulated information. What they also found was that companies in their recruitment strategies were relying to a greater extent on formal credentials. This, they argued, tended to underplay the tacit learning that occurred during a master-apprenticeship model of learning. Their conclusion was that:

> the application of tacit knowledge, and its conversion into explicit form, are significant influences on competitiveness, and that these will be more likely to develop through human process management. If this is so, and the traditional nurturing of process through culture is weakening, the implication is more, not less, attention needs to be paid to the management of process and the social context. In our law firms, so far, the pursuit of technology solutions and the business drive seem to have obscured this need.
>
> (Hunter, Beaumont and Lee 2002: 17)

This neglect of the crucial area of information practices also forms a powerful theme in the work of Elizabeth Orna on information policies.

Information policies: the missing link?

Orna's (1990, 2005) work has been developed in the context of her disciplinary background in Library and Information Science (LIS). When she talks of 'information professionals' she means those trained as librarians and employed in a variety of capacities to manage information; the skills they have of classification, cataloguing and indexing are those developed by LIS education. Her concern is that these skills are under-estimated and ignored in organizations, with those possessing them having a marginal role. Her vehicle for bringing them to the centre of organizational life is variously termed an 'information policy' or an 'information strategy'. It is quite clear that when she uses the latter term she is thinking of something very distinct from strategies concerned with IS or IT. She points to the way in which both business and IS strategies make assumptions about what is done with information that fail to address central aspects of information handling. For example, in one of the organizations examined, she observed:

> a lack of appreciation within the company of the importance of the work done by the staff who actually analysed the data. It was regarded as a clerical job, demanding primarily keyboard skills. It was not realized that the 'highlighting' part of the job (marking up the data sources, selecting items for input to the computer system, and deciding on the terms to be used for them) was actually a quite high level indexing job, of a kind done in other contexts by people with professional training. Nor were the other implications of being a totally information-based firm – the need for high standards of quality control, and for detailed and efficient records-management procedures, for example – fully understood.
>
> (Orna 1990: 284)

When this is coupled with the way in which information is distributed across an organization it means that key decisions might be taken on faulty or missing information. The aim of an information policy is to make an organization aware of the information it has and then lay down some ground rules for its use. For example, one of the key features of databases that we examined in Chapter 4 is that they can make information widely available across departmental and functional boundaries. In the words of Walker and Zinsli, in their account of the implementation and use of a database in Coors' Shenandoah brewery:

> by permitting free access to the information, there is the opportunity for people throughout the organisation to provide different perspectives on problems facing the business that might otherwise be confined to one segment of the organisation.
>
> (Walker and Zinsli 1993: 41)

However, if access is blocked by the assumptions in the information policy then these benefits will never be realized. For it is perhaps possible to claim that in this area organizations have 'information policies' even if they are not known by that name. This can be seen in the common assumption that one has to prove a 'need to know' before gaining access to information. This enables those who own information to act as gatekeepers simply based on their control of access. Davenport (1994) suggests that a widespread attitude among US firms of secrecy, with, for example, prohibitions on the comparison of salary levels, knocks on to broader assumptions about the availability of information. Orna would suggest that these presumptions need to be stood on their heads and that an explicit policy governing access needs to be promulgated. While recognizing that some information is quite properly restricted in access (not least by regulation) this would seek to open up what ought to be shared. In the words of a set of guidelines for drawing up information policies in higher education, 'any information that should be available for sharing (and most will be) is well defined and appropriately accessible' (JISC 1995). Some guidelines based on commercial practice are given in the box overleaf.

These seem sensible suggestions and information policy is a valuable vehicle for getting these issues discussed. Davenport (1994), for example, draws our attention to the importance of data definitions in organizations and the need for a process for determining these. This is

GUIDANCE ON INFORMATION USE

In a discussion of activities in the UK retailer Marks & Spencer to reduce the volume of paperwork, Birkby (1993) describes some interesting guidelines which, while not given the formal heading of 'information policy', suggest some facets of such a policy. These guidelines included the following:

- Justify information or scrap it: in many organizations information continues to be produced for historical reasons, long after the initial conditions in which it was used have passed. This guidance suggests an active policy of reflection on the purpose of particular information.
- Do not legislate for exceptions: in many cases information is kept 'just in case'. Often this is because of the management style adopted. That is, if instant answers to questions are demanded, then staff will keep everything 'just in case'. This 'information hoarding' can then get in the way of the information that is needed to complete the job in hand.
- Trust staff to interpret broad guidelines: this suggestion is aimed at the behaviour of senior managers, as their actions may cause junior staff to operate at too great a level of detail.
- Use sensible approximations: in many cases it would appear that people demand information which is too detailed for the task in hand. This guideline suggests that it is acceptable from an organizational perspective to use the information that is appropriate to the task at hand.

Source: Birkby 1993

often, by default, the IT department in designing databases, but this might be precisely the wrong place. Once such decisions are taken they can have profound organizational consequences. In an electronic products distributor, for example, Orna (2005) finds that decisions about 'taxonomy', that is, the codes which are used to describe products, are crucial to the ability to display goods in web catalogues. They have learned that information now needs to be kept at a much finer level of detail than for print catalogues, with Product Managers being responsible for 'providing the appropriate taxonomy codification, and managing such digital assets as images and pdf data sheets relating to the products' (Orna 2005: 93). She argues that this is a rare example of an organization taking the consequences of 'information products' seriously across its range of activities. It is noticeable that this is also a rare private sector example; most of her examples are from local government and, in particular, the arts world (Hall 1994). In the higher education experience in the UK, the push for all institutions receiving public funding to have an information policy in place appears to have fizzled out, as we explore further in Chapter 10.

In many cases this is because regulatory pressures have overtaken events. In many public sector organizations moves to ensure accessibility of information under Freedom of Information legislation has led to requirements to be clearer about the ownership of information. In private sector companies the equivalent would be the impact of the Sarbannes-Oxley legislation.

Introduced for all companies listed on US stock exchanges, this imposes a personal duty on directors for the accuracy of internal controls. Such controls now apply not only to accounting data but also to many other records which support financial performance reporting, including emails. Other regulatory measures also have the effect of making records management a more pressing concern. On top of this, concerns about information security and the use of email and Internet facilities have also given rise to codes of conduct. The problem is that such codes all have a disciplinary intent, driving out the developmental aspects of information polices as initially conceived. The focus shifts away from guidance on how particular tools might be used to restrictions on their use. Such restrictions are, of course, important, but only to preserve an organization's position, not to enhance it. So Orna reports, for example, that the Department of Trade and Industry, a UK government department, has in its information strategy:

> a welcome emphasis on the structure of communications, i.e. understanding how people need to be communicated with on particular topics, for example what should go on the intranet, what should be sent as email, and what requires print on paper.
>
> (Orna 2005: 90)

Another area which might be addressed by an information policy but which might be overshadowed by compliance concerns is that of information ethics. We have noted in Chapter 4 that the collection of large volumes of data raise important concerns about privacy. Many such questions are tackled by data protection legislation which is beyond the scope of this text, but it would be dangerous to consider that all the questions are solved by external legislation. In an extensive consideration of information ethics, Mason, Mason and Culnan (1995: 214) suggest that 'organizations should have policies and procedures for controlling their information practices. These policies should encompass the entire information life cycle and address issues such as property, privacy, accuracy and quality, access, burden and gatekeeping'. Such policies then frame the consideration of individual responsibilities which we cover in Chapter 8.

However, one suspects that such considerations are rare and that the marginal place of information professionals (in Orna's terms) will continue to mean that the consideration of information practices remains one which falls between a number of strategies (Herring 1991). We might also suggest that lying behind advocacy of information polices is a unitary view of organizations which neglects consideration of power. For example, Orna argues that the advantage of having an information policy is that it:

> provides the basis for objective decision-making on resources for information activities, and on the management of information, because it is integrated within the framework of corporate objectives and priorities.
>
> (Orna 1990: 21)

However, we have already seen that we could question several parts of such a statement, notably the status of 'objective' decision making and the idea that we can identify a single set of corporate objectives. Like much of the literature emanating from LIS (Choo (1998) is another good example), the interesting ideas are developed largely in isolation from work in organization studies, work which indicates the divided, conflictual and power-ridden nature of organizations. Orna, for example, is enthusiastic about the work of Marchand and his colleagues, seeing support

139

in its focus on information practices for her perspective and not recognizing the flaws we have pointed out. However, Orna does also make positive reference to the work of Ciborra (2002) and his critique of systems driven approaches to information systems strategy. It is to this critique that we turn next.

IS STRATEGY: THE MYTH OF ALIGNMENT?

Much of our discussion has focused on the informational consequences of organization strategy and the rather neglected area of information practices. While ICT has figured in our discussions, we have deliberately inverted the normal order of discussion, as the focus often drifts away from information and towards technological developments. However, such developments are important and give us an insight into the complexities of ICT and its impact on strategy. The key question to be addressed here is the way in which ICT is not only a support for the achievement of organizational strategy; it can also profoundly reshape that strategy. This is the difference from a traditional model of strategy formulation, in which the key direction of the organization is decided first and then resources are mobilized accordingly. The pace and nature of technological development means that new forms of technology can emerge which can completely derail existing strategies and can suggest new ones. Much of the literature on IS strategy is concerned with models of how to do detailed information systems planning and evaluation. That is not the focus of our discussion, as such detail can be found elsewhere (Currie 1995; Ward and Peppard 2002; Robson 2005; Clarke 2006). Rather, the concern here is with more fundamental debates over the nature of the 'alignment' of IS strategy with organizational strategy.

Some of the issues involved are illustrated in the debate over the impact of the Internet on existing practices. At the height of the dot.com boom there were many suggestions that traditional approaches to business were now obsolete, replaced by the Internet which would bring in completely new 'business models' (Magretta 2002). Porter (2001) expressed his exasperation with such thinking, arguing that many of the impressions emerging from initial implementation were misleading. The Internet was changing the structure of competition, but in a way which made strategy more rather than less important. The challenge was for organizations to recognize how structures had been changed, most notably by giving customers wider access to information by which to make comparisons. This not only applies to private sector organizations; clients of health and education providers in the public sector are now far more able to get ranked information to enable them to compare provision (albeit that such information might be a little misleading in its reduction of complex reality to numerical indicators). What Porter was anxious to stress was the way in which the Internet could complement existing lines of business. Porter's critics, by contrast, suggest that he remains too wedded to a model of the vertically integrated corporation and place their stress on the development of partnerships (Tappscott 2001). This is the world of the 'hollow corporation', that is, of the company which possesses few resources of its own but uses the power of digital communications to construct a network. It is the network that delivers the product or service, not a single firm. We will return to this debate over organizational structure in the next chapter, because the evidence is far from clear that large corporations are disappearing, but the debate indicates the complexity of ICT-enabled possibilities.

Of course, as we have seen, ICT is far more than the Internet and the challenges of responding to the opportunities it brings have been recognized for some time. Building on some of the case studies that we have already touched upon, such as American Airlines, and profoundly affected by the contemporary focus on Business Process Re-engineering (which we consider a little more in the next chapter), Venkatraman suggested in 1991 his model of IT-enabled business transformation (Figure 6.2).

One problem that Venkatraman draws our attention to here is that a focus on ICT as support for organizational strategy leads to the automation of existing practices, which might promote short term efficiency and which can be seen as 'strategic' relative to past practices, but which rarely produces long term benefit. For many organizations this resulted in the creation of localized 'silos' of information, with the next stage being an attempt to integrate these better. Venkatraman's (1994) suggestion is that the increasing commoditization of ICT would make any success here also relatively easy to copy. While his own account tends to make little of information, tending to use the term IT, he pointed to the possibility of using IT to radically redraw organizational processes, something we will touch upon in the next chapter. Suffice it to say for the present that the experience of such initiatives rather casts some doubt on the efficacy of such moves, largely because they underplayed the implicit aspects of knowing that have proved so important in our discussions so far.

These were changes that could occur within the organization; others, more radical in their impact, lay outside organizational boundaries. The shift from competing as an independent entity to a focus on networks lay in the suggestion that strategic advantage could come from the ability to redefine and create such networks. Finally, the ultimate prize would be to do what American Airlines and others had done, to use the power of ICT to completely redefine the scope of the business which the organization and its collaborators were engaged in. The challenge then for strategists was to place themselves at the appropriate level on the model and consider what potential there might be to move from another. Viewing strategy in this way tends to cast some doubt on the models of strategic alignment that had been proposed and which are discussed below, but Venkatraman argues that we still need some measure of

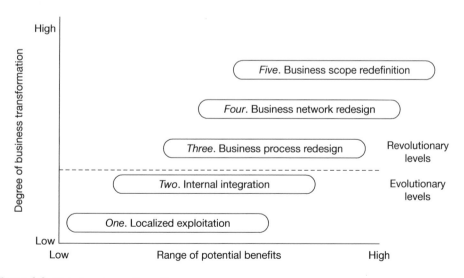

Figure 6.2 *IT-induced reconfiguration*

alignment between the strategies we choose and the structures which these entail. However, he suggests that in a knowledge economy this might have to be more concerned with networks than discrete entities, something we return to in the next chapter (Venkatraman and Subramaniam 2002: 474).

This means that there is still value in exploring the ideas about strategic alignment that were proposed by Henderson and Venkatraman in 1993, albeit with the caveat that these assume a focus on the individual organization which models of transformation might suggest is a little narrow. That is, a challenge for business alignment might be to take in not only internal arrangements but also those that pertain between members of a network. The first point perhaps to notice here is the place of publication – the *IBM Systems Journal*. This perhaps explains the focus which is entirely on IT with nothing on the strategic use of information. They argue that not only has IT strategy to be aligned with organizational strategy, but that each strategy also has an internal dimension. That is, it has consequences for the internal processes and systems which are required to implement it. This then gives a two by two matrix which, say the authors, can then be navigated in a number of directions, each of which has different consequences for organizations. These different approaches are:

a) Strategy execution (Figure 6.3): the traditional top down route in which decisions about organizational strategy are taken without any strategic IT input. The IT consequences are simply those which flow from the need to support internal processes which themselves have been shaped by the strategy.

b) Technology transformation (Figure 6.4): this is where the strategy depends on changes in technology which place the focus on aligning technology infrastructures.

c) Competitive potential (Figure 6.5): this is where the organizational strategy is informed by strategic thinking about the potential of IT to generate new means of doing business.

d) Service level (Figure 6.6): in this process the vision is that IT can improve internal processes . by changing the accompanying IT infrastructure.

As with much of the literature we have been examining, these proposals are based on a remarkably small set of examples and are entirely prescriptive in tone. They do suggest,

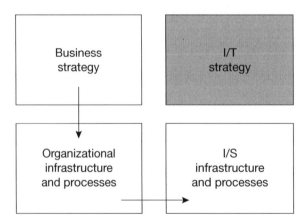

Figure 6.3 *Strategic alignment – strategy execution*

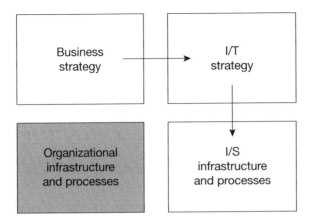

Figure 6.4 *Strategic alignment – technology transformation*

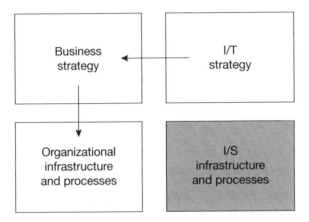

Figure 6.5 *Strategic alignment – competitive potential*

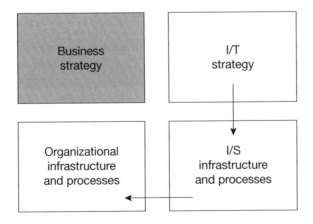

Figure 6.6 *Strategic alignment – service level*

however, the importance of process, that is, that the ideas are suggested as exemplifying possibilities for organizations to follow, not detailed prescriptions.

Drawing on critiques such as that by Ciborra, which we consider below, Peppard and Ward (2004) suggest that the implication is that organizations need to build an information systems capability. Recognizing that any advantage from any particular application of ICT is likely to be short lived, they suggest instead that organizations needs to build a capability for implementing and realizing the benefits from a series of applications. They draw a distinction, drawing on resource based views of strategy, between:

- resources – those factors under the control of an organization, like data or systems;
- competences – the skills to do with the control and exploitation of resources;
- capabilities – bundles of competences and the articulations between them.

One important observation they make is that an effective IS capability is a *distributed* one. That is, not all of such a capability is under the control of an IS function. However, the competences they suggest do still seem to have a strong IS flavour and they are relatively silent on how such competences would be articulated. We will look at some relational mechanisms in Chapter 8 when we look at roles and responsibilities. Something of the IS leaning flavour of their suggestions can be seen if we examine the most 'business' focused of their competences, those bundled under the heading of 'exploitation'. These are:

- benefits planning;
- benefits delivery;
- managing change.

This is where we might expect something on how the information might be used, where consideration of information literacy might be of relevance, but they are silent on this point. This seems like an area that is ripe for development.

However, this is where authors like Ciborra (2002) question the whole focus of this approach. They argue that it reflects an obsession with control and neatness, which is not appropriate for a fast-changing world. Such models, they would argue, are the product of large bureaucratic organizations. We can see from our discussions already that such models tend to downplay the degree to which strategies are emergent from operations and are dependent to some degree on chance. This leads Ciborra to suggest an alternative perspective based on emergence and creativity. The important practical consideration here is not to produce more and more complex strategies but to attend to the means by which an organization can adapt to changing circumstances. He argues that:

> If we draw the full consequences of imagining an economy filled by ephemeral, knowledge-based organizations, able to move, disassemble, and reconfigure themselves to meet customer demands and technological innovations . . . we need to shift gears, and drop the language of planning, controlling, and measuring through which organizations, teams, and projects have been managed so far.
>
> (Ciborra 2002: 103)

This approach is rather lacking in concrete examples, but we can see some of the consequences if we reflect back (Chapter 5) on the genre analysis that Kellog, Orlikowski and Yates (2006) produce of the use of PowerPoint presentations to span boundaries of expertise in a web advertising company. While the combination and recombination of elements proved an effective means of communication and enabled projects to be completed, it did so in a way which closed off the space for reflection. What Ciborra terms 'bricolage' (that is, the combination of elements that are found to hand and in chance combinations) may therefore conceal the constraints on action supplied by the competitive environment in which organizations operate. We might, therefore, question the somewhat breathless emphasis on ephemeral organizations. Organizations, as we will see in the next chapter, are proving remarkably durable. Accordingly, we end this consideration of strategy with an alternative metaphor which might help you think of a combination of relative autonomy and central discipline.

CONCLUSION: MILITARY METAPHOR AND STRATEGY

A common opposition in writing on organizations is between metaphors of organizations based on military models and those based on looser structures such as networks. On this analogy, military organization is about hierarchy, strict discipline, and a command and control mode of management. This is often associated with traditional bureaucratic organizations and compared to more fluid forms of organizing. However, this contrast can be misleading on two counts. One is that many modern organizations (and we will review some in the next chapter) are far from being ephemeral and yet seem to be able to combine a degree of change and innovation coupled with fairly strong central direction. The second is that not all military operations work this way.

In discussions about differences in strategy and structure in the UK brewing industry, the former chairman of Whitbread, Sir Charles Tidbury, used a comparison between the Guards regiment and the Rifle Brigade to make this point (Mutch 2006). The Guards represent the traditional model of military organization, in which orders flow from a central command and are followed to the letter, regardless of consequences. Tidbury used this analogy to explain the actions of large companies in the industry who carried out the same operation in a uniform fashion across their range of activities (such as enforcing rigid brand standards across all outlets). Whitbread, as a smaller player, would never, he argued, be able to compete on these terms, Rather, he argued, drawing on the analogy of the Rifle Brigades, they would have to think round problems. The Rifle Brigades were light infantry units with a focus on a degree of autonomy within an enduring focus on central control and discipline. However, solders and officers shared the same training and soldiers were expected to pick up control if anything happened to officers. Decisions were to be based on the needs of the situation within the overall strategy determined centrally. The glue binding this all together was a strong focus on regimental history and identity.

The analogy of the Rifle Brigades seems more akin to many contemporary organizations, with their emphasis on the integrating power of culture but the persistence of central control and direction, than looser models. We will explore this question of organizational structure in more detail in the next chapter, but the deployment of alternative models can restore the importance of planning and control, not now in a central place but as essential supports to the

145

realization of strategic visions. A reappraisal of the value of military metaphor can also direct our attention to the central place of power and culture in our considerations, issues to which we return in Chapter 9. For now, however, we will seek to draw out some themes from our discussion of strategy.

SUMMARY

- The positioning school of strategy tends to place its emphasis on the impact of ICT and more explicit forms of information; the resource based approach seems better able to cope with more embedded, implicit forms of knowledge.

- A processual view of strategy makes sense of the way in which many applications with strategic impact have tended to emerge and suggests a need to focus on practices which will allow for learning from information.

- Questions of how information is used tend to be neglected in discussions of strategy formulation. This is particularly the case with the intensive analysis of data. Such examples throw up concerns about the availability of appropriate skills which tend to fall between considerations of business, IS and human resource strategies. The development of information policies is one way of securing more attention for these issues.

- A challenge for IT strategies is aligning the potential of IT with the more general business strategy, particularly given the pace of technological change. However, building a capability of dealing with such issues might be more productive than formal mechanisms. Such capabilities need to include means of better using the information which is produced, but this tends to be neglected. Our focus on information literacy might be a valuable corrective.

REVIEW QUESTIONS

1 What are the four routes to strategic alignment?

2 What are the levels of IT-enabled organizational change?

3 What aspects of 'information strategy' does Earl draw our attention to?

DISCUSSION QUESTIONS

1 How might an organization build a 'distributed capability' in the use of information, based on an understanding of information literacy and tacit forms of knowing?

2 What factors might feature in an information policy for an organization with which you are familiar?

CASE EXERCISE

Country Holidays, whose use of data we reviewed in Chapter 4, was founded in the 1980s by the son of a dairy farmer, Philip Green. Pressure on profit margins in farming meant that many farmers were seeking to diversify. One potential source of income lay in the conversion of redundant farm buildings into holiday cottages. However, channels of information were rather limited, requiring potential customers to carry out extensive information searches among disparate sources. Country Holidays sought to become a key intermediary, holding data on available cottages and making this available to potential customers (and making money by the commission it charged to owners). The market for holiday cottages was also a rather limited one. Green sought to expand the market for holiday cottages, aiming at a middle class market in which there was increasing demand for second holidays. He was an early adopter of computing technology, seeking to use it to manage large volumes of data and enable telephone booking. The combination of data from the telephone system and the booking system enabled more targeted marketing. The company rapidly became the dominant agency in the UK, expanding both by acquisition and by growth into other countries. It was able to use its data systems to facilitate Web searching and booking. The company underwent a number of changes of ownership before becoming part of the Cendant travel group.

Apply the categories in Table 6.1 to the Country Holidays case. What opportunities and threats can you see under each category?

FURTHER READING

Clarke, S. (2006) *Information Systems Strategic Management: An Integrated Approach*. London, Routledge.

In a companion volume in this series, Clarke explores strategic questions in much more depth than is possible here, with a particular focus on aligning human and technological aspects of information systems.

Orna, E. (2005) *Making Knowledge Visible: Communicating Knowledge Through Information Products*. Aldershot, Gower.

In a very distinctive approach which draws mainly on the discipline of library and information science, but also has a strong focus on information design, Orna supplies an information-centred perspective which is a welcome corrective to more technological focuses.

REFERENCES

Bevan, J. (2005) *Trolley Wars: The Battle of the Supermarkets*. London, Profile.

Birkby, K. (1993) 'The Business Review of Information and Paperwork', *Business Change & Re-engineering*, 1(1): 16–21.

Blythman, J. (2005) *Shopped: The Shocking Power of British Supermarkets*. London, HarperPerennial.

Carr, N. (2003) 'IT Doesn't Matter', *Harvard Business Review*, 81(5): 41–48.

Chaffey, D. and Wood, S. (2004) *Business Information Management: Improving Business Performance Using Information Systems*. Harlow, FT Prentice Hall.

Checkland, P. and Holwell, S. (1998) *Information, Systems and Information Systems: Making Sense of the Field*. Chichester, Wiley.

Choo, C. W. (1998) *The Knowing Organization: How Organizations Use Information to Construct Meaning, Create Knowledge and Make Decisions*. New York, Oxford University Press.

Ciborra, C. U. and Associates (2000) *From Control to Drift: The Dynamics of Corporate Information Infrastructures*. Oxford, Oxford University Press.

Ciborra, C. (2002) *The Labyrinths of Information: Challenging the Wisdom of Systems*. Oxford: Oxford University Press.

Clarke, S. (2006) *Information Systems Strategic Management: An Integrated Approach*. London, Routledge.

Clegg, S. R. (1990) *Modern Organizations: Organization Studies in the Post-Modern World*. London, Sage.

Clemons, E. (2000) 'When Should You Bypass the Middleman?', in T. Davenport and D. Marchand (eds) *Mastering Information Management*. London, FT Management: 127–132.

Currie, W. (1995) *Management Strategy for IT: An International Perspective*. London, Pitman.

Daft, R. L. and Weick, K. E. (1984) 'Toward a Model of Organizations as Interpretation Systems', *Academy of Management Review*, 9(2): 284–295.

Davenport, T. (1994) 'Saving IT's Soul: Human-Centred Information Management', *Harvard Business Review* 72(2): 119–131.

Davenport, T. (2006) 'Competing on Analytics', *Harvard Business Review*, 84(1): 99–107.

Day, G. S. (2003) 'Creating a Superior Customer-Relating Capability', *MIT Sloan Management Review*, 44(3): 77–82.

DeSimone, L. D. (1995) 'How Can Big Companies Keep the Entrepreneurial Spirit Alive?' *Harvard Business Review*, 73(6): 187–190.

Earl, M. J. (1988) *Information Management: The Strategic Dimension*. Oxford, The Clarendon Press.

Earl, M. (2000) 'Every Business is an Information Business', in T. Davenport and D. Marchand (eds) *Mastering Information Management*. London: FT Management: 19–21.

Field, C. (1998) 'Let Your Data Do the Work', *Computer Weekly*, 24 September: 40.

Galliers, B. and Newell, S. (2004) 'Strategy as Data Plus Sense-making', in S. Cummings and D. Wilson (eds) *Images of Strategy*. Oxford, Blackwell: 164–196.

Hall, H. (1994) 'Information Strategy and Manufacturing Industry – Case Studies in the Scottish Textile Industry', *International Journal of Information Management*, 14, 281–294.

Henderson, J. C. and Venkatraman, N. (1993) 'Strategic Alignment: Leveraging Information Technology for Transforming Organizations', *IBM Systems Journal*, 32(1): 472–484.

Herring, J. E. (1991) 'Information Management – the Convergence of Professions', *International Journal of Information Management*, 11(2): 144–155.

Hopper, M. (1990) 'Rattling SABRE – New Ways to Compete on Information', *Harvard Business Review*, 68(3): 118–126.

Humby, C., Hunt, T. and Phillips, T. (2003) *Scoring Points: How Tesco Is Winning Customer Loyalty*. London, Kogan Page.

Hunter, L., Beaumont, P. and Lee, M. (2002) 'Knowledge Management Practice in Scottish Law Firms', *Human Resource Management Journal*, 12(2): 4–21.

JISC, (1995) Guidelines for Developing an Information Strategy, Joint Information Systems Council, www.webarchive.org.uk/pan/13734/20060324/www.jisc.ac.uk/indexd367.html.

Kellog, K., Orlikowski, W. and Yates, J. (2006) 'Life in the Trading Zone: Structuring Coordination Across Boundaries in Postbureaucratic Organizations', *Organization Science*, 17(1): 22–44.

Lichtenstein, N. (2006) *Wal-Mart: The Face of Twenty-First-Century Capitalism*. New York, The New Press.

Magretta, J. (2002) 'Why Business Models Matter', *Harvard Business Review*, 80(5): 3–8.

148

Marchand, D. A., Kettinger, W. J and Rollins, J. D. (2001) *Information Orientation.* Oxford, Oxford University Press.

Marchand, D. A., Kettinger, W. J and Rollins, J. D. (2001) *Making the Invisible Visible: How Companies Win with the Right Information, People and IT.* Chichester, Wiley.

Mason, R., Mason, F. and Culnan, M. (1995) *Ethics of Information Management.* Thousand Oaks, CA, Sage.

Mintzberg, H. (1994) *The Rise and Fall of Strategic Planning.* Hemel Hempstead, Prentice Hall.

Mutch, A. (2006) 'Military Metaphor and Organization Theory: Time for a Re-Examination?', *Organization,* 13(6), 2006, 751–769.

Orna, E. (1990) *Practical Information Policies.* Aldershot, Gower.

Orna, E. (2005) *Making Knowledge Visible: Communicating Knowledge Through Information Products.* Aldershot, Gower.

Pemberton, J. D., Stonehouse, G. H. and Barber, C. E. (2001) 'Competing with CRS-generated Information in the Airline Industry', *Journal of Strategic Information Systems,* 10(1): 59–76.

Peppard, J. and Ward, J. (2004) 'Beyond Strategic Information Systems: Towards an IS Capability', *Journal of Strategic Information Systems,* 13: 167–194.

Porter, M. (2004) *Competitive Advantage.* London, Free Press.

Porter, M. (2001) 'Strategy and the Internet', *Harvard Business Review,* 79(3): 62–78.

Porter, M. E. and Millar, V. E. (1985) 'How Information Gives You Competitive Advantage', *Harvard Business Review,* 63(4): 149–160.

Robson, W. (2005) *Strategic Management and Information Systems.* Harlow, Pearson.

Tappscott, D. (2001) 'Rethinking Strategy in a Networked World (Or Why Michael Porter is Wrong about the Internet)', *Strategy+Business,* Third quarter www.strategy-business.com/press/16635507/19911.

Venkatraman, N. (1991) 'IT-Induced Business Reconfiguration' in M. Scott-Morton (ed.) *The Corporation of the 1990s.* Oxford: Oxford University Press: 122–158.

Venkatraman, N. (1994) 'IT-enabled Business Transformation: From Automation to Business Scope Redefinition', *Sloan Management Review,* 35(2): 73–87.

Venkatraman, N. and Subramaniam, M. (2002) 'Theorizing the Future of Strategy: Questions for Shaping Strategy Research in the Knowledge Economy', in A. Pettigrew, H. Thomas and R. Whittington (eds) *Handbook of Strategy and Management.* London, Sage: 461–474.

Walker, K. B. and Zinsli, T. (1993) 'The Coors Shenandoah Experience', *Management Accounting (US),* March: 37–41.

Ward, J. and Peppard, J. (2002) *Strategic Planning for Information Systems.* Chichester, Wiley.

Watson, T. and Harris, P. (1999) *The Emergent Manager.* London, Sage.

Westerman, P. (2001) *Data Warehousing: Using the Wal-Mart Model.* San Francisco, Morgan Kaufmann.

Whittington, R. (2006) 'Completing the Practice Turn in Strategy Research', *Organization Studies,* 27(5): 613–634.

Wiseman, C. (1985) *Strategy and Computers: Information Systems as Competitive Weapons.* Homewood, IL, Dow Jones–Irwin.

Chapter 7

Structure and information

INTRODUCTION

'For a long time,' argues Richard Whittington (2002: 113) in a recent overview, 'the study of corporate structure has seemed rather old-fashioned.' The 1960s and early 1970s were a time when considerable attention was paid to the way in which large organizations were structured, to debates such as that over the proper degree of centralization or decentralization of decision making, to spans of control, to the division between line and staff. However, thanks to a number of causes (one of which was the perception about the changes ICT would bring), rather less attention has been paid to these questions in more recent years. Rather, the default assumption has been that such questions themselves would fade away alongside the large corporations which spawned them, as companies became smaller and flatter, with their boundaries blurred. For there are two related aspects to the consideration of structure. One is an internal focus, in which the key questions are the way in which organizations are structured both vertically and horizontally. The second is the external one, as many of the assumptions about internal structuring flow from a conception of an organization as a legal and practical entity with clear boundaries. Such clear cut boundaries, both internal and external, have been challenged by many contemporary writers and the aim of this chapter is to review such debates, with a particular focus on our concerns with knowledge, information and data.

In such a review, we will become conscious of a number of factors. One is that these are enduring debates where we can discern a number of reasons for change and debate. This is not just a simple story in which ICT shapes organizational form. Another is that much of the debate is indeed about ICT but that such a focus obscures what we have noted at many points of our discussion so far, the embedded and implicit nature of many forms of knowing in organizations. This will become a common refrain, as we temper the claims for radical change with an appreciation of the limits that are imposed by such embedding. Another point which will crop up in a number of places but is worth making at the outset is that often the claims we make are based on rather shaky evidence, which might also cause us to retain a degree of scepticism about some of the wilder claims. In particular, we need to recognize that there are often contradictory tendencies at work.

THE DEATH OF THE MIDDLE MANAGER?

This chapter will examine:

- changes in the vertical structuring of organizations, with a particular focus on claims that middle managers will disappear with developments in ICT
- changes in the horizontal structuring of organizations under the pressure of such initiatives as Business Process Re-engineering, which claim to abolish traditional functional boundaries
- the growing importance of project-based forms of operation, contrasting the implications for knowing with those suggested by a focus on communities of practice
- claims that organizations will become 'hollowed out', replaced by networks of inter-related small organizations linked by ICT and flows of information

As Haeckel and Nolan acknowledge, this is a stable and simple business model with high labour turnover in the branches. Mrs Fields Cookies experienced a number of problems when they sought to expand overseas, as their models were based on the assumed behaviours of US store managers. However, further examples can be drawn from other comparable product markets. Barbara Garson (1998: 146), for example, argues that the measuring of data in McDonald's creates an 'information grid' where 'dozens of vectors cutting vertically, horizontally and diagonally across a small work area result in a grid bisected so many ways that each person has only the tiniest space within which he can manoeuvre'. Her concern was with local store managers, but such systems also have implications for those in the middle, those who would traditionally form the link between local operations and head office. For example, Ramtin argues that:

> Managerial control over social production will become highly centralized as almost all intermediary supervisory layers will be removed, their functions to a very large extent incorporated into technological systems.
>
> (Ramtin 1991: 89)

DOING WITHOUT MANAGERS?

Mrs Fields Cookies has branches across the USA, both directly owned and franchized, selling cookies. It uses a system developed in-house to monitor the sales of each branch and to issue instructions on an hourly basis to store managers about which types of cookies to bake and many other decisions. The coordination work that in many such chains would be carried out by area and regional managers is handled by the computer, with rules built into a database and adjusted by head office staff. Using the analogy of modern airplanes which can only be flown by computer because their design is so sensitive, Haeckel and Norton describe this as 'managing by wire'.

Source: Haeckel and Nolan 1993

In this section we examine some of the evidence for contentions that middle managers will disappear as a consequence of the shift to flatter organizations.

One of our concerns at the beginning must be the difficulties of definition, which mean that the evidence against which to judge these debates is difficult to assess. In the discussion above I have assumed that middle managers are the area managers who form the link between the local management and those in head office. This is certainly a common pattern in many retail operations, but in some accounts these would be junior managers. That is, from the perspective of the local unit these are in the middle, but head office might regard them as at the bottom of the managerial hierarchy, with local store 'managers' being considered more in the category of team leaders. By contrast, from the perspective of the head office of a multi-divisional, multinational organization, the heads of divisions might be the 'middle', a level which would appear as the very top to those in a local retail unit (Whittington and Mayer 2000). We can conclude from this that the term middle management is a relational one which only makes sense in a particular context. This makes it very difficult to draw broad conclusions about their status.

Predictions about the demise of the middle manager have a long pedigree. We have already seen the distinction that Simon drew between programmed and unprogrammed decisions. On the basis of this distinction he argued that 'We are gradually acquiring the technological means, through these techniques, to automate all management decisions, nonprogrammed as well as programmed.' (Simon 1977: 30). His argument was that the reduction in middle managers that this would inevitably bring would be conditioned by economic rather than technological factors. Underpinning such assertions was a particular model of information and the way in which managers used it. This was nicely summarised by Drucker when he described many middle managers as 'relays' – 'human boosters for the faint, unfocused signals that pass for communication in the traditional pre-information organization' (Drucker 1988: 46). On the basis of such an analysis he predicted that in twenty years' time organizations would have both far fewer levels of managers and smaller numbers of managers.

In this, Drucker was echoing predictions which had been made in the 1950s by Leavitt and Whisler (1958). Their article in *Harvard Business Review* in 1958 predicted that by the 1980s computing technology would shrink the number of middle managers, leading to a greater degree of centralization. Reviewing their predictions thirty years later, Applegate, Cash and Mills (1988) argued that, particularly in the context of waves of downsizing, their predictions were fairly accurate. Their account was particularly dependent on the impact of systems such as executive information systems. They suggested that the combined power of such systems and newly emerging personal computers would allow a combination of centralized direction and local decision making in what they called the 'cluster organization'. In particular, they suggested that techniques such as neural networks would make a substantial contribution to decision making. The changes would, they suggested, bring greater autonomy and satisfaction to those closer to operations. This rather rosy view could be countered by considering the impact on the discarded middle managers. For Scarborough and Burrell (1996) this was a gloomy one indeed, with managers facing a process of proletarianization. We can question the evidence base of such predictions but before we do so it is worth revisiting some of the material we covered in previous chapters about the systems which lie at the heart of these arguments. These can be considered under three headings: the pressure from above in systems such as EIS; the pressures from below arising from, for example, workflow management; and the claims about artificial intelligence.

EIS are at the centre of claims that senior managers will be able to by-pass middle managers altogether and use systems which access operational data directly. We can see the potential of such systems in examples such as Mrs Fields Cookies, but our previous discussions should give us pause for thought on a number of grounds. One is that such systems depend on the quality of the supporting data systems. Many operations can be automatically recorded and monitored, but often this depends on a simple business model being in place. More complex products and services lead to much greater difficulty in collecting data. The experience with data warehouses indicates that many organizations simply do not possess data of the required quality that they can depend upon. The second point that we focused on was the way in which such systems are not used by senior managers because they do not fit the way in which they work. Rather, they prefer to have information supplied to them – often by people in positions which we might term 'middle management'. So the evidence we have that suggests that many such systems fail to meet expectations or, if they are successful, work because they are used by lower levels of management, does not tend to support the thesis presented above.

The other pressure comes from below, as information systems such as workflow management are used to carry out the coordination functions previously carried out by managers, often with a degree of job enrichment for operational staff. Such systems lie behind the claims that '[t]he jobs of many middle managers involve employee oversight, data gathering, report generation, and general coordination – all functions that, to a greater or lesser extent, can be performed with computerised networks and fewer people' (Kraut 1987: 27). However, while we have seen that such systems do have impacts on managerial work, this is usually at a lower level – what we would often term front line management. Here it is feasible that some tasks, such as coordination, can now be performed by rules inscribed into software, while certain levels of decision making are now carried out at the team level, with operational team management being carried out by team leaders. However, this still requires that the rules are created and maintained, tasks often carried out at the middle management level.

The remaining concern with the claims made is to do with artificial intelligence. An over-estimation of the nature and impact of developments here rests in turn on a failure to appreciate the implicit and embedded nature of much knowing in organizations. We have seen that in practice the success of artificial intelligence techniques has come in bounded applications with rules which are fairly easy to elicit and represent. If managerial work resembles these conditions, such as with credit scoring, then perhaps they will be replaced. But if much managerial work involves complex processes of interpretation and translation, as we argued when we looked at managerial work, then it is perhaps little surprise that there are powerful counter-arguments to those presented above.

Such arguments rest above all on the contention that managerial work, notably that at middle management level, is not disappearing but changing. In this perspective, it would certainly be the case that those elements of work which simply involved the transmission of material would indeed be threatened. However, if we accept the argument that much knowing in organizations is implicit, then middle managers are well placed to assist in the process of understanding and mobilizing such forms of knowing. So Nonaka and Takeuchi argue that:

> Middle managers play a key role in the knowledge-creation process. They synthesise the tacit knowledge of both front-line employees and senior executives, make it explicit, and incorporate it into new products and technologies.
>
> (Nonaka and Takeuchi 1995: 16)

The continued importance placed on middle managers by Japanese companies is contrasted to the downsizing that occurred in many US companies in which it was often found that substantial amounts of experiential knowledge had left with the departing middle managers.

This continuing importance of the middle manager is supported by some of the limited evidence that we have. One interesting indicator at a national level is that the number of those reporting themselves in occupational censuses as having managerial titles continues to increase. For example, Wilson and Thompson (2006) point to the steadily increasing numbers of managers reported in the UK census, with significant increases in the proportion of managers in the workforce. Of course, these are self-reported figures which, as they note, could be caused by 'terminological drift' – as when, for example, the post traditionally known on the UK railways by the title of 'conductor' or 'guard' is renamed 'train manager'. However, even here this can represent real changes in the scope of responsibilities. This broad evidence of the continuing health of the category of manager is reinforced by other evidence. For example, Storey, Mabey and Thomson report, based on a survey of 904 UK companies, that 'less than one-third of the respondents had fewer management tiers than they had 10 years ago, while a quarter had actually added more levels' (Storey, Mabey and Thomson 1997: 29).

Where we do find IT having an impact the crucial relationship seems to be with the related changes in the clerical workforce. For example, the introduction of electronic point of sale

MIDDLE MANAGERS AND EXPERIENTIAL KNOWLEDGE

In 1996 the Union Pacific Railroad (UP) took over the Southern Pacific Railroad (SP). The latter had endured years of under-investment and much of its physical plant was in poor condition. One particular problem area was with a classification yard (a site where trains are spilt and reassembled for further transit) in Houston, Texas: Englewood. This was well known to SP managers, who knew that they had to keep trains moving through the yard or face severe congestion. However, UP was known at the time for a strong belief in its own operating practices and abilities. Many of the SP managers departed and UP proceeded to enforce its own procedures. These overlooked the constraints that Englewood imposed and the yard became full of traffic. The result was severe congestion that slowed down access to the important chemicals plants in Houston and began to spread across the USA as limits on working time meant that trains were abandoned in sidings, thus causing further congestion. The resulting service problems took a year to remedy and brought detailed oversight from Federal regulatory bodies, something which the industry as a whole was anxious to avoid. The experience suggests that successful operations often require a good deal more expertise than is evident on the surface.

Source: Burke 1998

(EPOS) terminals into public houses run by the UK brewer Bass saw reductions in 'large numbers of stock-takers, input account clerks and other office workers' (Baker, Wild and Sussmann 1998: 20). This has led to a reduction in the number of managerial layers, but it is not clear that this means less managers. Indeed, the trend within public house management has been an example of the way in which capitalism sucks ever increasing numbers of previously self-employed traders, in this case publicans, into the ranks of management. Further, ICT, and EPOS is a good example, has the potential to create vast amounts of data to fuel the interpretative effort. In this process human interpretation, rather than artificial intelligence, has been central. Attempts, for example, to harness computers to the analysis of scanner data have only had marginal success, and this is restricted to performing the initial analysis in the production of data for human consideration (Bayer and Harter 1991; Rangaswamy, Harlam and Lodish 1991). These considerations suggest that the impacts of ICT on the ranks of management might be rather more complex than the suggestions made above. Indeed, organizations which have used ICT to remove layers of management have sometimes had to replace those layers in recognition of the demands for interpretation which have accompanied them (Boddy and Gunson 1996). In a study of the National Health Service in the UK which explicitly addresses the impact on middle managers, Currie and Procter (2002) report that middle managers do indeed feel that ICT has enlarged the scope of their role, with a particular focus on their interpretation of information for senior managers.

They also note that 'any increase or reduction in the number of middle managers appears not to be directly caused by MIS/IT. This is tied up with government policy more generally' (Currie and Proctor 2002: 115). This echoes Davenport's observations that:

> in working with several hundred companies over the past fifteen years, I've never encountered one that reorganised, flattened itself, or embarked on cultural change because of the availability of information technology. In fact, I don't believe organizational designers are comfortable enough with information technology to make it a major part of their grand schemes.
>
> (Davenport 1997: 180)

We have to be careful not to posit a causal mechanism because of the simple correlation of organizational change involving middle managers on the one hand and the presence of ICT applications on the other. Shifts in the composition of management may be related to other trends. For example, the Brazilian entrepreneur Ricardo Semler (1989) has argued trenchantly, in an account which if anything downplays the use of ICT, for an approach of 'managing without managers'. His argument, expanded upon in a subsequent popular book (Semler 1994), is that top down styles of management with detailed planning and control systems are counter productive and that much more can be achieved by devolving decision making down to the workforce. In practice, as Semler himself notes, this is not entirely to do without managers, but rather it is to redefine their role and the decisions they get involved in. However, his example suggests that it is far from the case that the sole or most important reason for changes in managerial role is the use of ICT. This draws our attention to the variety of factors which may lie behind shifts in managerial work. In assessing such claims, however, as well as stressing the importance of interpretation, we may well wish to note that authority relations remain important. That is, for all the talk of self-directed teams, some sense of central direction remains important (Gantman 2005). What may well have shifted, as we have seen in our discussion of groupware, is the collaborative nature of much managerial work. We will explore this a little further in considering a shift towards teams and a project style of working. However, we first need to consider another challenge to divisions within organizations, that of Business Process Re-engineering.

CHALLENGING FUNCTIONS: BPR

The work of those who have looked at changes in administrative work at the turn of the twentieth century have demonstrated that claims that we live in an 'information age' are a little overstated (Beninger 1986; Yates 1989). The application of tools like the typewriter and techniques like vertical filing systems engendered an earlier 'information age', one which made possible the building of large industrial corporations. The issuing of standard instructions through the elaborate hierarchy of managers and supervisors was one way in which the achievements of firms like Ford were made possible. However, these massive organizations also depended on the emergence of functional forms of organization, forms of organization which have proved to be remarkably enduring (Chandler 1962). Such forms of organization involve the grouping together of particular specialists, such as accountants or engineers, in departments. Such groupings enable information to be brought to the specialists, something which in times of paper based information was the most efficient form of utilizing specialist resources. However, while this is effective for discrete problems which do not involve other specialists, those problems which crossed functional boundaries posed challenges.

These were two fold. From the point of view of those outside the organization, such as customers, the internal form of organization was immaterial. However, functional forms of organization could mean that there was no overview of where a particular piece of information was at any one time. Hence customers and others could be passed from one department to another, engendering frustration. The second was the delays that passing information from one function to another caused. Each function possessed its own hierarchy, with information often only being allowed to be passed on at the appropriate level. This meant delays as information moved up and down hierarchies. As organizations strove to become more integrated and functions became more dependent on each other, then this clearly became a barrier. These divisions between functions, although only virtual in character, took on the characteristics of physical divisions, with terms like 'functional silos of information' being used. This was reinforced by the early application of computing technology. This tended to be applied to discrete problems of automation. Thus, say, a billing system would be purchased to invoice customers while another separate system was built to order supplies. Such systems would be designed to meet the needs of the individual function, and often did so satisfactorily, but they would be unable to communicate with each other. They often ran on different machines or possessed completely different data structures. This meant that they effectively inscribed existing functional structures in software, making change difficult. We have already seen that the removal of such barriers was one of the claims made for the introduction of databases.

Databases, and the challenge which they posed to traditional forms of organization, were one of the impetuses behind the movement known as Business Process Re-engineering. The other, and arguably the more important, was the shock given to, in particular, American big business by Japanese competition. The large industrial corporations, such as Ford and General

Motors, which consolidated their position in the 1950s, saw many years of market dominance threatened by Japanese competition. This drew analysts to look at many aspects of Japanese organization, including their means of performance measurement and information use (Johnson and Kaplan 1991). A common theme in this examination was that of Japanese emphasis on process design. That is, where the Anglo-American approach might have been to seek to automate existing processes, thus rendering ineffective processes a little more efficient, the Japanese approach was seen as one which first established the most effective process to use and then applied automation as required. The use of 'Just in Time' stock systems, where items were not built to be stockpiled but made just when the next part of the process required them, was one important example. The simplicity of the information systems employed here, using visual symbols hoisted above a workstation to indicate when new items were needed, was seen to be a dramatic contrast to the ever more elaborate computer systems favoured by the management science paradigm.

The Mazda and Ford example is one of the most widely cited in the literature arguing for a fundamental shift in the way in which business processes are redesigned. It combines the two essential elements: the example of Japanese approaches and the power of computing technology. This combination was used to argue for a revolutionary approach. It was no longer good enough to automate existing practices; the goal had to be radical redesign along process lines. In the somewhat feverish words of the *Harvard Business Review* article, which drew attention to the whole movement, the call was 'reengineering work: don't automate, obliterate' (Hammer 1990). This became a wildly popular message, with the subsequent book (Hammer and Champy 1993) selling millions of copies and many consultancies offering their services to help corporations redesign their processes. It would be inevitable, therefore, that functions would be swept away in a new focus on process.

LOOKING AGAIN AT PURCHASING PROCESSES

Ford in the USA employed 500 clerks to run their accounts payable function. This involved the issuing of a purchase order to a supplier and the subsequent matching up of a goods received note to the supplier's invoice. If up to 14 data items matched on the three documents then the payment could be released. This caused a good deal of work in tracking missing documents. Ford were exploring the possibility of implementing a more efficient computer system which would reduce the number of people involved by approximately 100, when managers visited Mazda of Japan, a company in which Ford had recently taken a minority equity stake. They found that Mazda's purchasing department employed five clerks and that the volume of work was not 100 times less! They were able to do this because Mazda paid for goods on receipt. This required an excellent system for booking goods in, one which could be trusted by both parties. This meant that clerks could then spend their time chasing exceptions. Ford drew on this example to remove the need for suppliers to send invoices, as payment was automatically triggered when an electronic purchase order was matched by the goods scanned electronically on receipt, thus reducing the administrative work involved.

Source: Hammer 1990

As we have seen, Business Process Re-engineering had a considerable impact on ideas about the alignment of ICT with business strategy but doubts began to creep in about both the manner and the consequences of its application. In practice it came to be associated with a wave of downsizing in which large numbers of employees, and particularly managers, left many large organizations. In the process, as well as the human costs, organizations began to realize that with their departing managers went much of the knowledge that they had accumulated over the years. Once again, we can see that much of the conception of information that lay behind BPR was an objectivist one which equated it with data. If we look again at the Ford example then we can see that at its heart lay new means of capturing and recording data which enabled better storage and manipulation. However, this was to ignore some of the arguments that had been presented by authors such as Zuboff which had stressed the value of the knowledge which could be gleaned from the new systems (Taylor 1995).

The realization of this potential required both the active participation of employees and their capacity to be able to handle the new information, neither of which figured particularly strongly in BPR. In part this was because ideas which had been developed in academia which had stressed involvement and empowerment became simplified in their repackaging (Mumford 1994). BPR then became little more than another management fad, with a particular association with ICT. For example, it became particularly associated with the implementation of ERP systems, which, as we have seen, demanded that business processes were reorganized to meet the needs of the system (Boudreau and Robey 2005). This meant that there was frequent lack of success, with resistance founded on the ways in which such systems did not take account of the less explicit forms of organizing and knowledge. What such implementation efforts often revealed were differences in functional information which had not been evident until attempts were made to cross previous boundaries.

For example, we have seen that organizations using Product Data Management systems seek to cross previous boundaries between, for example, design and production to give one unified record of work. In D'Adderio's detailed investigation of one such system it was found that, despite the data being the same, it was interpreted in different fashions, something which she attributed to different disciplinary backgrounds. Her conclusion was that '[r]ather than promoting inter-functional co-ordination and collaboration, the new configuration has emphasized a clash in function-specific languages, cultures and knowledge bases that, until that point, had only been latent' (D'Adderio 2004: 120). Once again, we are drawn back to the importance of local systems of meaning creation, often implicitly held, which undermine the dreams of smooth information transfer (Stinchcombe 1990). D'Adderio suggests that what is needed is greater attention to promoting understanding of these differences, something which suggests that functions have proved rather more resistant to change than the advocates of BPR imagined.

We also need to add important questions of identity to our discussion. That is, functions are more than simple bundles of information. Rather, the way in which information is perceived and used is also a matter of identification with particular ways of being which are not simply interchangeable. That is, the views of, say, an accountant have been shaped by years of experience and professional socialization so that information is seen, typically, as structured data amenable to processing in a fashion very distinct to, say, the views of somebody in marketing or human resources. What might be important about the implementation of databases is not the disappearance or harmonization of such differences but, as we noted in our discussion of the Coors Shenandoah example, the ability to draw on them while having a common and unified set of data. What this review of the experience of BPR should indicate is the continuing importance of boundaries, both vertical and horizontal, to the use of information. One response to such boundaries has been the increasing focus on the value of project work.

PROJECTS, TEAMS AND INFORMATION

Of course, a project style of working has long been familiar in many industries, such as construction or civil engineering, where a specific task has to be completed within a specified timeframe. What distinguishes such organizations is that the project is the central focus of attention, with project managers monitoring the activities of diverse groups of specialists. A broader change has been in the employment of such project teams within more functionally organized companies, those in which project teams are employed to cross those functional boundaries but not to remove them. Such team working has been the outcome of initiatives such as Total Quality Management, with their emphasis on the need to deal with the causes of organizational problems rather than the symptoms. They also relate to the recognition that modern organizations are often tightly inter-linked and so it is not possible to tackle concerns simply within the boundaries of particular functions. Project teams can also be distinguished from other forms of work teams in that they are often of a temporary nature, assembled to meet the needs of a specific concern and then disbanded. Increasingly, they may cross not only functional but also organizational boundaries, as we will see in the next section. In this regard, their formation has been assisted by ICT in a number of ways. We have noted the way that tools are now available that are designed to support collaborative work regardless of differences in time and space. In addition, there are specialist project management tools that are designed to support the monitoring of complex projects.

However, the existence of such tools does not necessarily mean that knowledge is shared either within or between project teams. In particular, studies of projects in practice have indicated that learning generated within projects is often not shared within the larger organization (Bresnen, Goussevskaia and Swan 2004; Scarbrough *et al.* 2004). One key issue here is the composition and durability of project teams. If teams are regularly formed and disbanded, then any learning is quickly dissipated. If teams are kept together, and especially if they share a degree of physical proximity, then they can often learn a good deal about how to run projects effectively. The challenge then is to spread this learning to the rest of the organization. Of course, project teams are groups which are deliberately formed by an organization for a particular purpose. These boundaries to knowledge sharing can be reinforced if we consider more informal groupings, such as those we have already touched on in our discussion of functional identities. These groupings have achieved considerable importance in the literature on organizational learning under the heading of 'communities of practice'. We have noted at a number of points that much knowing in organizations is implicit. That is, it is embedded in particular contexts and is generated through experiential learning. It can be difficult to share, simply because it rests on many unarticulated background assumptions, assumptions which are shared through the identities generated through practice. It is the focus on practice which distinguishes this approach, as groups based on practice can cut across formal boundaries in organizations.

The approach emerged from work on learners who were able to produce a competent performance in some settings, often work based, but not in others, especially not in those associated with formal education (Rogoff and Lave 1984). This sent Lave and Wenger (1991) back to the literature on forms of apprenticeship learning and led to their development of the linked notions of communities of practice and 'legitimate peripheral participation'. The latter refers to the way in which apprentices start on the periphery of work practices, but their participation is legitimated by traditional norms. As they learn, they gradually move to the centre of what it means to be an expert in that particular practice. Such forms of learning rely more on informal and experiential forms of learning than on formal bodies of theory. Importantly, the learning is as much about how to be a member of the community as on how to perform particular tasks. Learning, that is, flows from identity. Communities of practice are those groups, then, which emerge around a focus on a shared practice, in which learning about that practice is tightly bound up with becoming an accepted member of the group.

This work has proved extremely influential. A key part of the design of the Eureka system at Rank Xerox, for example, was based on the ethnographic investigation of how the community of practice of copier technicians learned (Bobrow and Whalen 2002). This indicated that they learned not from manuals but from swapping stories and that they would benefit from ICT which reinforced this form of learning and drew on, in particular, the importance of reputation. What the work suggests is that occupational groupings can develop a particularly strong body of ways of making sense of their world, ways which can cut across organizational boundaries (Orr 1996; 2006). When the formal systems in Qantas broke down under external pressures, argues Baumard (1999), organizational members retreated to their communities of practice. Such communities are particularly strong because they involve the identities of their members, who see themselves primarily as identified with the practice, not with the organization. Thus we get the debates over classifications, debates which are invested with assumptions about the values which lie behind the occupational grouping. These ideas might be particularly strong in more technical areas, where a common focus, and in particular the common language supplied by the technology, unites specialists in a way which much vaguer talk about corporate missions cannot.

The community of practice approach has been extremely influential, although subject to a number of critiques. A key part of the original conceptualization was of the importance of time in the learning process. Learning to become a member of a community involves a long journey from the margins to the centre. This conceptualization also stresses the importance of co-presence. It is noticeable among the photocopier technicians, for example, that it was the swapping of war stories in social settings that was important in the transfer of ways of knowing. However, the application of the term 'community of practice' to user groups organized using discussion boards over the Internet by software houses seems to lose any sense of these key attributes (Hildreth and Kimble 2004). This in turn raises important questions about the whole notion of 'community' which relate to our concerns about the 'myth of cultural integration'. Raymond Williams (1976) pointed out that 'community' was one of the few words which had only positive connotations. It is widely used to cover very diverse groups such as the 'academic community' or 'the Asian community' which are in truth riven by differences. In these senses the rhetorical appeal is too small, closed groups such as those found in rural areas where there is an assumption of harmony and common purpose. Closer examination often finds these assumptions wanting, but there is a clear 'halo' effect where the desired attributes are carried over to the target grouping. This can deflect our attention away from tensions and conflicts within the group, tensions which can exist at different levels of ways of knowing (Mutch 2003).

A further observation might be that if we examine the type of apprenticeships which Lave and Wenger (1991) founded their observations on then we would note that their sites of investigation – Yucatec midwives, Vai and Gola tailors, US Naval quartermasters, meat cutters, and non-drinking alcoholics – are at some distance from the forms of work practice found in many contemporary organizations, especially from project forms of organization. This does not render their insights invalid, but it does suggest the need for further investigation. One consequence of that further investigation is that we raise the problem of sharing between communities of practice. The focus on implicit knowledge generated through shared experience is extremely useful in understanding the phenomenon of 'sticky' knowledge, that is, the difficulty of transferring knowledge from its place of generation to others in the same organization (von Hippel 1994). This is based on the language and assumptions used within the communities which might not be available to those outside. However, the widespread use of temporary project teams has led Lindkvist (2005) to argue for the use of the term 'collectivity of knowledge' in which he stresses the lack of time to develop shared language and understanding, suggesting the importance of more abstract forms of understanding. In particular, the question of common knowledge becomes important in considering how some of these barriers to knowledge sharing can be overcome.

One useful focus is that supplied by Carlile (2004) in his consideration of knowledge boundaries. Carlile suggests that increasing conditions of difference and dependence in knowledge are brought about by novelty. That is, novel situations emphasize the extent to which different groupings have different conceptions of similar terms. They also lay bare the extent to which one group depends on another for elements of its own knowledge. Carlile draws on the interplay between different groups in the process of automobile design to illustrate these relationships. For example, the design of external styling and engine capacity are mutually interdependent – a larger engine size brings greater power but requires a larger compartment to contain it, thus impinging on styling decisions. Groups can manage these inter-dependencies in stable conditions but their extent is often revealed by new challenges. Carlile suggests that an examination of situations of increasing novelty indicates a number of different learning boundaries, each with different implications.

The *syntactic* boundary refers to the situation where terms need to be defined in order that they are understood. This involves the supply of a common lexicon in order to understand terms and is related to the widely used information processing model, where knowledge sharing is simply a matter of transferring from one party to another, often using ICT. This is the model which underpins much work on knowledge management and it may be sufficient in some circumstances, but these basic situations are the least important ones in contexts of innovation. Such situations reveal other boundaries, the first of which is that to do with meanings or what Carlile terms a *semantic* boundary. That is, the literature on communities of practice and other material has indicated that knowledge sharing is not a simple matter of transfer but rather involves *translation*. This involves considerable effort to surface background assumptions, which are the more powerful for being taken for granted. Carlile suggests that much of the literature on communities of practice has underestimated this problem. Hedlund (1994) also suggests that in its focus on skills, skills built up over time and taken for granted, the communities of practice literature underplays the importance of cognition. In other words, part of the common knowledge that is important in overcoming syntactic boundaries remains a necessary but not sufficient part of overcoming semantic boundaries. However, Carlile suggests that the community of practice literature also underplays the degree of political difference between groups. There is a further boundary involved, which he terms the *pragmatic* boundary. That is, knowledge sharing is not simply a matter of better use of language and improved conversations between groups, for knowledge is also something which is a valuable resource for those groups and is not to be given away lightly.

One means of generating common knowledge to enable sharing across these boundaries is through the notion of boundary objects (Star 1989). These are seen as means of translation across different bodies of knowledge. For example, in Carlile's context of automobile design, the traditional boundary object was the clay model. This was produced during the prototyping process and used to form a basis for debates over the dependencies between different design engineering groups. However, the clay model in itself represented the power relations between the groups, reflecting the historical dominance of the styling group. The emergence of new groups such as climate control and safety, reflecting changes in perceived demands, meant that the clay model no longer played an adequate role. However, attempts to introduce an ICT-based 3D model only partly succeeded. This was because the new boundary object raised questions about the power relations on the pragmatic boundary that had been implicit in the clay model. Carlile suggests that any model of knowledge boundaries has to recognize this dimension and how it builds on the previous levels of knowing.

Such an approach returns us to questions of authority and power, questions which we look at in a little more detail in Chapter 9. Such questions indicate why it is that there is a persistent tension between prescriptions based on the need for access, transparency and reflection to enable knowledge sharing and the use of hierarchical devices to control and monitor organizational action. The former cluster are increasingly required for competitive success, but they run up against, in many cases, adherence to forms of organization which in their turn are a response to the perceived needs of the world in which those organizations operate. Organizations, that is, are not entirely free to choose their internal arrangements. However, there are many arguments that the external world is also changing, in particular that, in large part thanks to the enabling features of ICT, we are in a 'network age' in which the previously firm legal boundaries of the organization are blurred by new forms of organization, forms which in turn reflect a shift away from hierarchy towards more diffuse centres of authority (Castells 2000). It is to a consideration of some of these external facets of structure that we turn next.

TOWARDS THE NETWORK AGE?

We need to set contemporary developments in the form and nature of work organizations in the context of historical developments. There has always been a movement between those activities which are carried out within the boundaries of the organization and those conducted by external parties. Much of early economic activity in the Industrial Revolution in the UK, for example, was carried out in 'clusters', with organizations relying on others for the provision of specialized services (Wilson and Thomson 2006). It was later that we saw the growth of the vertically integrated organization, giant corporations which brought more and more activities within their internal control, often because the vagaries of the market threatened the smooth running of their core activities. We need to set contemporary developments in historical context in case we exaggerate their novelty and impact. There are three broad developments that are particularly relevant to our focus on information and knowledge: outsourcing, cooperative projects and the 'knowledge intensive firm'.

Outsourcing is the contracting out of services to external providers. It was given a great fillip by the shift in strategic thinking towards resource based perspectives, with their focus on 'core competences' (Hamel and Prahalad 1994). This suggested that firms should 'stick to the knitting', that is, focus on the activities in which they had distinctive capability and let others do routine activities. What is of importance here is the definition of what constitutes 'routine'. Organizations have long contracted out basic services like cleaning and security, but more contemporary developments have seen activities like information systems and accounting, activities which might traditionally be seen as more integrated with core business, considered as candidates for outsourcing (Lacity and Willcocks 2001). Such a move has been affected in part by the growth of external providers with the capability to supply these services, but also by developments in ICT. The reduction of barriers in time and space has meant that activities, especially those dependent on ICT, can be performed in locations other than those where the main activities are carried out.

So, for example, intensive data input and back office services can be performed in lower cost developing economies where there is a sufficient level of education in the workforce without the differences in location impinging on core activities. This has been taken further in areas like software development, where the ability to transfer work at the end of the working day across time zones means that it is possible to have 24 hour production. This mimics the existence of 24 hour trading in financial markets, facilitated by easy data transfer. Areas in which activities can be easily represented in computer manipulable data are particularly amenable to this form of outsourcing. The transfer of activities both out of the company concerned and outwith geographical boundaries is known as 'off shoring' and has been the cause of dramatic economic growth in economies such as India. It parallels for many service industries the trend towards basic manufacturing being carried out in China and other lower cost economies. We should note that this capacity is not dependent on the Internet, although it has been facilitated in particular by growing ease of communication using Internet protocols. Many applications of ICT are in this sense somewhat hidden from view; what the Internet does is tend to make them more visible and more accessible to smaller organizations.

Outsourcing is part of the trend towards what some have termed the 'hollowed out corporation'. This is where the core organization retains control of the key financial, marketing and design capabilities and contracts out most other activities to a network of supplier organizations. What ICT offers is the ability to more tightly coordinate supply chains, securing effective control over them without necessarily having to bring functions in house. Such control is not only the preserve of the small design led organization. Using its analysis of sales data, for example, Wal-Mart is able to dictate terms to its suppliers. This is reinforced by its increasing insistence that key suppliers use their Retail Link system to access the data themselves, making them responsible for the replenishing of shelves (Lichtenstein 2006). In this way the access which large retailers have to customer choices as recorded in their sales systems gives them considerable control over their suppliers.

This desire to integrate suppliers more closely – either, in more positive terms, as long term partners or, in negative terms, to make them more dependent – meets something of a contradiction when we examine the impact of the Internet. Here the suggestion is that new intermediaries such as business auction houses will lead to new models of procurement, in which firms select the lowest cost suppliers based on bidding at open auctions facilitated by the Internet, which gives access to a much greater range of potential suppliers. However, this again is predicated on the ability to specify requirements exactly in a way which leads to interchangeable supply, something which is likely to apply to only basic products. What is less spectacular and visible, but possibly more enduring in its impacts, is the ability of organizations to cooperate in forms of alliance facilitated by ICT. What ICT allows is for information to travel rather than the experts, meaning that joint alliances do not have to be physical, legal entities (Goldman 1994). What all these developments tend to do is to blur the edges of organizations. Often, members of supplier organizations work alongside members of the 'host' organization, making it difficult to see who belongs to which body.

A key part of the rise of these chains of cooperating organizations has been the development of what has been termed the 'knowledge intensive firm' (KIF) (Alvesson 2004). The KIF is an organization which specializes in the provision of services based on unique knowledge. The precursors of such firms were advertising agencies and market research bureaux. But they are particularly associated with the ascendancy of the management consultancy. The spread of the consultancy has in part been based on the shift to forms of production based on specialized knowledge, knowledge which is often the product of basic research in areas such as biotechnology. The mediating force here, often as a spin out from basic research team, is the consultancy which seeks to commercialize such knowledge. The KIF is distinguished by the employment of a highly qualified expert workforce, whose expertise makes them highly mobile in both geographical and employment terms. This then requires a different management style, one which relies on factors other than either money or control as motivational factors.

Thus the KIF possesses features which place them at the extreme end of the developments towards flatter organizations that we reviewed above. One concern, however, is that it is possible to exaggerate the differences. Too great a focus on the KIF might lead us to ignore the embedded knowledge that is vital to even the simplest form of operation. This knowledge might not be expressed in the more formal terms of the KIF, but, as we have seen, knowledge embedded in practice is vital to operations, even when it becomes invisible by being taken for granted. KIFs form an important part of a shift towards constellations of organizations. However, the tendency of such firms to cluster in patterns which are reminiscent of the early Industrial Revolution suggests some limitations of an analysis which focuses only on the transfer of computer generated information, important though this is.

One of the key forms of explanation of the balance between the internalization and externalization of activities has been transaction cost economics (Wilson and Thompson 2006). This school of thought seeks to explain why organizations seek to manage activities in terms of the state of markets. If markets can supply services at lower cost than they can be handled internally, then organizations should externalize them. However, such a perspective tends to neglect the nature of knowledge, reducing it to a matter of information (Hedlund 1994). That is, in cases where knowledge can be reduced to information and a common syntax exists, then in Carlile's (2004) terms this is a transfer problem which is amenable to externalization. However, as we have seen, a common language is necessary but not sufficient for it neglects the implicit nature of much knowledge, tightly bound up as it is in practices. Transaction cost economics also ignores the question of legitimacy. That is, as we will explore in more detail in Chapter 10, organizations not only seek to operate effectively, they also seek to operate in ways which are considered as legitimate in their context. This means that they may operate in ways which are economically irrational, but which fit the prevailing expectations of their particular context.

In the case of track maintenance (see box below), the knowledge that was lost when the work was outsourced was not just about how the work should be undertaken, but how much it cost. This type of knowledge was only to be acquired by actually carrying out the work. While specifications could be laid down in detail, it was the accompanying knowledge which was particularly valuable. It is this knowledge which is of particular importance when outsourced work is integrated into activities. What organizations have often found is that they require new capabilities in relationship management when they outsource complex activities (Lacity and Willcocks 2001). Contracts by themselves cannot specify the full details of such a relationship and are a last resort. Again, what such contracts tend to reveal is how much has been taken for granted. These forms of implicit knowledge, and their embedding in personal relationships of co-presence, are also to be found in the clustering of many forms of organization in particular locations. The high technology clusters of Silicon Valley in California or Cambridge in the UK are mirrored by similar biotechnology clusters, for example in Boston (Owen-Smith and Powell 2004). Granovetter's (1985) work on networks expresses this in terms of 'strong' and 'weak' ties. Strong ties are those based on personal relationships. Weak ties, typically expressed in formal contracts and patents, work effectively when the information to be transferred is easily renderable in objective forms. However, more complex knowledge which requires translation and transformation to move from one context to another, works best with ties of trust and personal relationship.

CONCLUSION

Shifts towards a network form of organization are not necessarily completely novel and might be exaggerated (Thompson 2004). We have seen in this chapter that large organizations

OUTSOURCING AND KNOWING

When the railways in the UK were privatized, the maintenance and engineering work was outsourced by the new company in charge of the physical network, Railtrack. This was in the belief that specialized engineering and construction firms could bring their expertise to bear and so lower costs. In fact, spiralling track engineering costs were one of the contributory causes to the collapse of the company. The replacement organization, Network Rail, decided to bring one contract back in house in order to get better knowledge about maintenance costs. This decision led to further contracts being taken back in house.

Source: Caulkin 2003

structured on the basis of functional hierarchy, such as Wal-Mart, remain of considerable importance. Such firms have always had their clusters of suppliers and their use of information in many ways enables them to exercise still tighter control over them. We need to remember this when considering more optimistic views of chains of small, flexible, flat knowledge intensive organizations. Part of the problem here is the downplaying at a number of levels of the embedded nature of knowing in all organizations and its confusion with knowledge reduced to information manipulable by ICT. What we can point to is a tension which runs through much of this discussion. This is between the dependence on forms of embedded knowledge to bring about improvements in operations and the control which ICT offers. The exercise of that control seems to offer benefits in measurement and monitoring, but its exercise neglects those strong ties of trust and reflexivity which seem vital to the mobilization of implicit forms of knowledge.

These structural consequences of, and constraints on, information use are one important part of our understanding of the changing importance of knowledge and information in organizations. However, at a number of points we have noted the implications for individual roles and responsibilities. These are explored in greater detail in the next chapter.

SUMMARY

- Despite predictions of the demise of middle managers thanks to direct access by senior managers to data via ICT, their survival points to the importance of their role of interpretation. While their place as agents of information transmission has been diminished, tools such as groupware have encouraged greater lateral communication.

- The structuring of organizations by functional specialism remains important, despite attempts to remove such boundaries by techniques such as Business Process Re-engineering. Databases enable greater cross-functional working, but processes of identity formation which are closely linked to knowledge formation mean that functional forms of organization are widely retained.

- Project working is a means for organizations to overcome functional barriers, although effective knowledge sharing depends on a stock of common knowledge. There is a difference between relatively temporary project teams and more enduring communities of practice. The latter encourage deep forms of learning but present barriers to sharing, because of the assumptions which are embedded in the forms of knowing and identity generated.

- While there are some shifts in the networks of organizations which constitute particular sectors, with ICT facilitating outsourcing and collaborative environments, the large hierarchically organized corporation remains of considerable significance. This poses a contradiction for knowledge use. The conditions which encourage wider knowledge sharing seem to come into conflict with competitive imperatives, despite success in that competition increasingly being seen to rest on the effective use of knowledge.

REVIEW QUESTIONS

1 What are the three barriers that Carlile identifies and how do they operate?

2 How might we distinguish a community of practice from a project team?

DISCUSSION QUESTIONS

1 Based on our earlier discussion of the nature of managerial work are reductions in the numbers of middle managers likely to be due to ICT or are other factors involved?

2 If tacit knowledge is a central part of knowing in organizations, what problems do trends towards outsourcing and the blurring of organizational boundaries pose?

3 Why does Business Process Re-engineering run counter to what we know about the nature of managerial work?

CASE EXERCISE

In 1995, the UK utility company British Gas, faced with increasing private sector competition, announced radical changes to the organization of its servicing function. Rather than having engineers allocated by managers, the company shifted to an ICT-facilitated system, in which engineers were allocated by a job scheduling system based on details taken in a call centre. The engineers were given laptops which they used to record their arrival and departure from a job. Based on this data about availability, plus data stored on the system about skills and on stores (which were scanned into the engineer's van), the system could allocate a call to the next appropriate engineer. This removed the coordination activity previously carried out by support staff (often workload managers) and increased the ratio of field to support staff from one to six to one to thirty. (Source: Hobby 1995).

1 What implications does this case have for middle managers?

2 Is it better to categorize the managers here as 'junior' or 'front line'?

3 What might the implications be for knowledge sharing among engineers?

FURTHER READING

Cross, R. and Parker, A. (2004) *The Hidden Power of Social Networks: Understanding How Work Really Gets Done in Organizations*. Cambridge MA, Harvard Business School Press.

Very accessible account of the practice and value of social network analysis, which indicates the importance of informal networks in sharing information across formal boundaries.

Lave, J. and Wenger, E. (1991) *Situated Learning: Legitimate Peripheral Participation*. Cambridge, Cambridge University Press.

Influential short work which crystallized much of the interest in communities of practice.

Orr, J. (1996) *Talking About Machines: An Ethnography of a Modern Job*. Ithaca, NY, Cornell University Press.

Widely cited account which starts from the lived experience of photocopier technicians to build a rich picture of information sharing in practice.

Wenger, E. (1999) *Communities of Practice: Learning, Meaning and Identity*. Cambridge, Cambridge University Press.

Ambitious attempt to create a social theory of learning based on the earlier work with Lave. Not always successful when measured against some of the core tenets of social theory, but an interesting attempt to bring learning to centre stage.

REFERENCES

Alvesson, M. (2004) *Knowledge Work and Knowledge-Intensive Firms*. Oxford, Oxford University Press.

Applegate, L. M., Cash, J. and Mills, D. Q. (1988) 'Information Technology and Tomorrow's Manager', *Harvard Business Review*, 66(6): 128–136.

Baker, M., Wild, M. and Sussman, S. (1998) 'Introducing EPOS in Bass Taverns: A Report of the Case and an Exploration of some of the Issues', *International Journal of Contemporary Hospitality Management*, 10(1): 16–23.

Baumard, P. (1999) *Tacit Knowledge in Organizations*. London, Sage.

Bayer, J. and Harter, R. (1991) '"Miner", "Manager", and "Researcher": Three Modes of Analysis of Scanner Data', *International Journal of Research in Marketing*, 8: 17–27.

Beninger, J. R. (1986) *The Control Revolution: Technological and Economic Origins of the Information Society*. Cambridge, MA, Harvard University Press.

Bobrow, D. G. and Whalen, J. (2002) 'Community Knowledge Sharing in Practice: The Eureka Story', *Reflections*, 4(2): 47–59.

Boddy, D. and Gunson, N. (1996) *Organizations in the Network Age*. London, Routledge.

Boudreau, M. and Robey, D. (2005) 'Enacting Integrated Information Technology', *Organization Science*, 16(1): 3–18.

Bresnen, M., Goussevskaia, A. and Swan, J. (2004) 'Embedding New Management Knowledge in Project-Based Organizations', *Organization Studies*, 25(9): 1535–1556.

Burke, J. (1998) 'UP's $1.4 Billion Decongestant', *Railway Age*, 199(6): 34–36.

Carlile, P. (2004) 'Transferring, Translating and Transforming: An Integrative Framework for Managing Knowledge Across Boundaries', *Organization Science*, 15(5): 555–568.

Castells, M. (2000) *The Rise of the Network Society*. Oxford, Blackwell.

Caulkin, S. (2003) 'In-house and Back on Track', *The Observer*, 30 November.

Chandler, A. (1962) *Strategy and Structure: Chapters in the History of the Industrial Enterprise*. Cambridge, MA, MIT Press.

Currie, G. and Procter, S. (2002) 'Impact of MIS/IT Upon Middle Managers: Some Evidence from the NHS', *New Technology, Work and Employment*, 17(2): 102–118.

Davenport, T. with Prusak, L. (1997) *Information Ecology: Mastering the Information and Knowledge Environment*. New York, Oxford University Press.

D'Adderio, L. (2004) *Inside the Virtual Product: How Organizations Create Knowledge Through Software*. Cheltenham, Edward Elgar.

Drucker, P. (1988) 'The Coming of the New Organization', *Harvard Business Review*, 66(1): 45–53.

Gantman, E. (2005) *Capitalism, Social Privilege and Managerial Ideologies*. Aldershot, Ashgate.

Garson, B. (1988) *The Electronic Sweatshop: How Computers Are Transforming the Office of the Future into the Factory of the Past*. New York, Simon and Schuster.

Goldman, S. R. (1994) 'Co-operating to Compete: From Alliances to Virtual Companies', *CMA Magazine*, 68(2): 13–17.

Granovetter, M. (1985) 'Economic Action and Social Structure: The Problem of Embeddedness', *American Journal of Sociology*, 91(3): 481–510.

Haeckel, S. H. and Nolan, R. L. (1993) 'Managing by Wire', *Harvard Business Review*, 71(5): 122–132.

Hamel, G. and Prahalad, C. K. (1994) *Competing for the Future*. Boston MA, Harvard Business School Press.

Hammer, M. (1990) 'Reengineering Work: Don't Automate, Obliterate', *Harvard Business Review*, 68(4): 104–112.

Hammer, M. and Champy, J. (1993) *Re-engineering the Corporation: A Manifesto for Business Revolution*. London, Brealey.

Hedlund, G. (1994) 'A Model of Knowledge Management and the N-Form Corporation', *Strategic Management Journal*, 15: 73–90.

Hildreth, P. and Kimble, C. (2004) *Knowledge Networks: Innovation Through Communities of Practice*. Hershey, PA, Idea Group.

Hobby, J. (1995) 'Survival of the fitters', *Computer Weekly*, 12 October, 52.

Johnson, H. T. and Kaplan, R. S. (1991) *Relevance Lost: The Rise and Fall of Management Accounting*. Cambridge MA, Harvard Business School.

Kraut, R. R. (1987) *Technology and the Transformation of White-Collar Work*. New Jersey, Lawrence Erlbaum Associates.

Lacity, M. and Willcocks, L. (2001) *Global Information Technology Outsourcing: In Search of Business Advantage*. Chichester, Wiley.

Lave, J. and Wenger, E. (1991) *Situated Learning: Legitimate Peripheral Participation*. Cambridge, Cambridge University Press.

Leavitt, H. and Whisler, T. (1958) 'Management in the 1980s', *Harvard Business Review*, 36(6), 41–48.

Lichtenstein, N. (2006) *Wal-Mart: The Face of Twenty-First-Century Capitalism*. New York, The New Press.

Lindkvist, L. (2005) 'Knowledge Communities and Knowledge Collectivities: A Typology of Knowledge Work in Groups', *Journal of Management Studies*, 42(6): 1189–1210.

Mumford, E. (1994) 'New Treatments or Old Remedies: Is Business Process Reengineering Really Socio-Technical Design?', *Journal of Strategic Information Systems*, 3(4): 313–326.

Mutch, A. (2003) 'Communities of Practice and Habitus: A Critique', *Organization Studies*, 24(3): 383–401.

Nonaka, I. and Takeuchi, H. (1995) *The Knowledge-Creating Company: How Japanese Companies Create the Dynamics of Innovation*. New York, Oxford University Press.

Orr, J. (1996) *Talking About Machines: An Ethnography of a Modern Job*. Ithaca, NY, Cornell University Press.

Orr. J. (2006) 'Ten Years of Talking About Machines', *Organization Studies*, 27(12): 1805–1820.

Owen-Smith, J. and Powell, W. W. (2004) 'Knowledge Networks as Channels and Conduits: The Effects of Spillovers in the Boston Biotechnology Community', *Organization Science*, 15(1): 5–21.

Ramtin, R. (1991) *Capitalism and Automation*. London, Pluto.

Rangaswamy, A., Harlam, B. and Lodish, L. (1991) 'INFER: An Expert System for Automatic Analysis of Scanner Data', *International Journal of Research in Marketing*, 8: 29–40.

Rogoff, B. and Lave, J. (1984) *Everyday Cognition: Its Development in Social Context.* Cambridge, MA, Harvard.

Scarbrough, H. and Burrell, G. (1996) 'The Axeman Cometh: The Changing Roles and Knowledges of Middle Management', in S. Clegg and G. Palmer (eds) *The Politics of Management Knowledge,* London, Sage: 173–189.

Scarbrough, H., Swan, J., Laurent, S., Bresnen, M., Edelman, L. and Newell S. (2004) 'Project-based Learning and the Role of Learning Boundaries', *Organization Studies,* 25(9): 1579–1600.

Semler, R. (1989) 'Managing Without Managers', *Harvard Business Review,* 67(5): 76–84.

Semler, R. (1994) *Maverick: The Success Story Behind the World's Most Unusual Workplace.* London, Arrow.

Simon, H. (1977) *The New Science of Management Decision.* New Jersey, Prentice Hall.

Star, S. L. (1989) 'The Structure of Ill-Structured Problems: Boundary Objects and Heterogeneous Distributed Problem Solving', in M. Huhns and L. Gasser (eds) *Readings in Distributed Artificial Intelligence.* Menlo Park CA, Morgan Kaufman.

Stinchcombe, A. (1990) *Information and Organizations.* Berkeley, University of California.

Storey, J., Mabey, C. and Thomson, A. (1997) 'What a Difference a Decade Makes', *People Management,* 12 June: 28–30.

Taylor, J. (1995) 'Don't Obliterate, Informate! BPR for the Information Age', *New Technology, Work and Employment,* 10(2): 82–88.

Thompson, G. F. (2004) 'Getting to Know the Knowledge Economy: ICTs, Networks and Governance', *Economy and Society,* 33(4): 562–581.

Von Hippel, E. (1994) '"Sticky Information" and the Locus of Problem Solving: Implications for Innovation', *Management Science,* 40(4): 429–439.

Whittington, R. and Mayer, M. (2000) *The European Corporation: Strategy, Structure and Social Science,* Oxford, Oxford University Press.

Whittington, R. (2002) 'Corporate Structure: From Policy to Practice', in A. Pettigrew, H. Thomas and R. Whittington (eds) *Handbook of Strategy and Management,* London, Sage: 113–138.

Williams, R. (1976) *Keywords: A Vocabulary of Culture and Society.* London, Fontana.

Wilson, J. F. and Thomson, A. (2006) *The Making of Modern Management: British Management in Historical Perspective.* Oxford, Oxford University Press.

Yates, J. (1989) *Control Through Communication: The Rise of System in American Management.* Baltimore, The Johns Hopkins University Press.

Chapter 8

Roles, responsibilities and change

INTRODUCTION

We have seen how structural factors can have a powerful influence on the use of information in organizations. However, there are also considerations at a more individual level. There is a relationship between the level of individual abilities and the social setting in which they are exercised which means that we need to pay equal attention to both. Once again, paying a little more attention to the ways in which our information literate manager might become aware of and competent in the types of information that we have explored reveals that this is another area which is often neglected because it falls between a number of specialist areas. We will return in this chapter again, in particular, to the concerns about the lack of attention to these issues within Human Resource Management that we discussed in our chapter on policies and strategies.

 This chapter will examine:

- the implications for training of the applications we have discussed, with a particular focus on the problems of application specific training. We will consider in particular the areas of data analysis and communicative competence
- changes in roles and responsibilities attendant on the applications we have discussed, such as the emergence of the 'power user'. The implications for reward structures of such roles and of knowledge sharing more generally are considered
- the nature of recruitment and selection if organizations are to become more knowledge based. In their assumption that educational credentials bring with them some of the competences we have discussed earlier, employers may be neglecting the importance of socialization into ways of knowing in their organizations
- the ways in which organizational change in areas involving the applications we have discussed either parallels or departs from established models of organizational change. In particular, we will return to our discussion of management to look at managerial resistance to change involving threats to their information base

APPLICATION SPECIFIC TRAINING: THE LESSONS FROM END-USER COMPUTING

The late 1980s saw the emergence of interest in 'end-user computing'. This was the type of computing where people used packages such as spreadsheets and databases to build applications which came to be of some significance in the running of areas of the organization (Nelson 1989). Particular concerns arose when those other than the original builder of the system became dependent on its use, something which often became significant when that person had moved on to other things. It was then that substantial problems could emerge, problems which were often attributed to the nature of the training which the developer had received. Table 8.1 summarizes a number of factors isolated by Naomi Karten (1991) that were associated with too great a focus on application specific training. She argued that:

> Because most end-user training focuses on software features and functions, it does not adequately prepare employees to use computers to solve business problems and address business needs. Although this product-oriented training helps users master the mechanics of software, it can also lead to their taking a narrow view of the application development process, resulting in negative consequences for these users and the IS groups that support them.
>
> (Karten 1991: 75)

Some of the concerns which Karten expresses, such as the inefficient use of staff time and becoming too dependent on particular people, can be better dealt with in our next section on roles, but we can illustrate some of the problems that arise from too narrow a focus in training on the features of a particular application by looking at experience with spreadsheets. Widespread use is made of spreadsheets for not only financial applications but also a wide range of other applications where operations can be expressed in numerical form (Kreie *et al.* 2000; McGill and Klobas 2005; Saran 2006). Along with such widespread use comes a significant level of error (Kreie *et al.* 2000). There are multiple causes of such errors, but one significant cause is the failure to regard the use of spreadsheets as a form of modelling. That is, their features are so easy to use that applications tend to be developed with a minimum of prior

Table 8.1 *Negative consequences of application specific training*

Consequence
Access to more data than needed
Inefficient use of staff time
Key resource dependent
Poor back up and documentation
Reports based on wrong data
Multiple, contradictory systems
Inflexible and situation specific models
Unaware of resource consequences

Source: Adapted from Karten, 1991

172

design activity. Such models tend to grow organically, to be inflexible in changing situations and to be relatively undocumented.

One key problem area is the prevalent practice of putting direct values into formulae. Good model design practice is to separate out variables and to refer to these indirectly, so that when the assumptions underlying a model are changed the spreadsheet can be easily and transparently changed. So, for example, an inflation rate should be specified as a variable held outside of the formula that uses it. However, many spreadsheet users (up to 47 per cent in one sample) write values directly into formulae (Kreie *et al.* 2000: 149). The problems that this can cause are compounded when users simply assume that changes they make are reflected in results, assumptions that can result in considerable financial loss for some organizations. What we are pointing to here is the need for a level of abstraction, with a divorce between the logical world of variables and the material form of the spreadsheet. This form of understanding is often not communicated in training on the specific features of spreadsheets, with trainers assuming that this will be dealt with elsewhere. But we have already seen that managers are often poor at knowing what data are available.

The consequence, then, is that spreadsheets multiply, often using slightly different sets of data to produce results which purport to be about the same activity but which give contradictory results. If these systems then draw on other systems which go beyond departmental boundaries, then the consequences can be considerable, not least for other users. The example we explored at the head of Chapter 4, where a relatively unsophisticated writer of a database query launched a poorly written request which slowed down all the other users in Country Holidays, is one example of the results of a lack of awareness of the connections between immediate actions and resource usage. Simply learning about product features is insufficient.

The distinction we might draw in terms of training, following Karten (1991), is between:

- application specific training: training which explains the particular features of a standalone application;
- information management: training which seeks to explain what might be done with the information an application can produce;
- information strategy: how to get benefit from the information derived, with a particular focus on the potential for doing differently.

The latter two areas might, in the light of our discussion of information literacy, be seen as the two most important, but they are also, as we will see, the most neglected. We will consider the information management issues in two clusters, clusters which broadly relate to Chapters 4 and 5 on technology. These consider the training implications of intensive data analysis and of the need for communicative competence. We will see that some of these demands cannot be necessarily met by training that emphasizes product features, in particular if we consider that they require what we will term 'practical reasoning'. This leads us into our discussion of roles and rewards.

Training for data analysis

The example of Shorko in the box overleaf illustrates some wider concerns about the use of extensive data sets. This is that, as we saw in Chapter 2, human beings are fairly poor

TRAINING FOR DATA AT SHORKO

As we saw in Chapter 4, Shorko Films manufactured plastic packaging film in France. It moved to a process control system, which replaced manually operated valves with computer controls and produced a mass of data. In order to operate the new plant, process operators not only learned the operating practicalities, but also attended courses at a local college in mathematics and basic physics. The learning derived from the new data available allowed the company to move into new niche markets for specialist packaging materials.

Source: Earl 1994

statisticians. We tend to draw relations when none exist and to take action based on what is vivid and memorable, rather than what is representative. Accordingly, there is a need for particular skills in the analysis of large bodies of data, skills which go beyond familiarity with the application. The problem is expressed by McKean as follows:

> Mathematics is a functional aspect of information mastery. Math is the key to unlocking the meanings of information. Many firms found that such mathematical and statistical skills were conspicuously absent in their firm. Firms found that they just could not hire people with good mathematical or statistical skills to create value from their information. The skills of mathematicians and statisticians had to be acclimated to the information environment.
>
> (McKean 1999: 115)

Davenport (2006) has pointed out that some educational systems might not produce the required number of people with the requisite skills to enable companies to compete on the basis of intensive analysis of data. One suggestion is that such work is performed by those who have had such training, by 'offshoring' the work to countries such as India. However, as we have seen, there are problems associated with such a strategy when we move beyond basic analysis to work which requires a close understanding of the context. This suggests that such work needs the involvement of functional specialists who understand the context of the data, but the conundrum here is that while the skills are needed, they are very difficult to impart to those who have been recruited for a very different purpose. At British Telecom, for example:

> Staff used to relying on intuition, aggregated data or market research to define their targets have to learn to mine this information out of the database. To help move staff to the new style of working, BT has setup a structured training course which employees must go through before being authorised to use the system.
>
> (Lamb 1997)

By contrast, those who have the required skills may not necessarily have the ability to relate these to business priorities. Their interest might be more in the technical elegance of their solutions. When Tesco developed its data warehouse, it used a specialist agency to analyse the data and construct categories based on their technical expertise (Humby, Hunt and Phillips 2003). This enabled them to access people who were not only good statisticians but also creative in their application of their knowledge to the sort of business questions which Tesco wished to pose.

This is, then, a very specialist form of training, but the intensive use of data also suggests that those with less direct contact with the data need to have broader awareness. We saw in Chapter 2 that data gathered in one place in the Bank of Scotland were not suitable for use elsewhere and that changes had to be made to responsibilities for data quality. One further implication was that 'training in data awareness is now part of our core competencies for all staff and makes a huge difference to data quality' (Goodwin 1999). One aspect of such training might be the awareness that data has systemic implications. This realization keys into some of the concerns expressed by Senge (1990) that managers reacted to problems at hand without considering the broader implications of their actions. The concern he expressed was that the increasing inter-connection of aspects of organizational life meant that the consequences of such local decisions could have rapid consequences at times and places not envisaged by the managers taking the decisions. Accordingly, he suggested, managers needed to be more exposed to systemic modes of thought (something we return to below in considering the notion of 'practical reasoning') – that such modes of thought see the interconnections between local instances and the broader picture of which they form a part, recognizing that local actions might have implications at a distance.

Communicative competence

If we recall the use of Lotus Notes by Unilever that we examined in Chapter 5, then you will remember that one of the consequences of an intervention by a senior manager was that access to the system was split into an 'above the line' and a 'below the line' section. The above the

DATA AND ITS IMPACT IN WAL-MART

Westerman in his account of data warehousing at the US retailer Wal-Mart gives the following vivid example of the ways in which actions which make sense at the local level then create data which can be confusing out of context:

> some stores in Louisiana were selling lawn tractors at half price, but they were selling twice as many as were shipped. Actually, the problem was that the POS system was not able to manage the special tax situation in Louisiana. In Louisiana, lawn tractors are considered farm equipment and are taxed at half the normal rate. The store managers, to quickly solve this problem, placed two bar codes at half the retail price on the mowers. One bar code was taxed at a full rate while the other was not taxed. This gave the consumer the proper tax rate of half the normal tax, quickly solving the customer problem, but it confused the calculations of accurate inventory figures at the home office.

Source: Westerman 2001: 44. Reproduced by permission of Elsevier

line section was populated with formal reports on progress by the design teams. This required them to write reports in business English. This posed local challenges for designers based in Italy recruited for their design rather than linguistic competence, but it raises more general points. As Ciborra and Patriotta (1996: 137) point out, this means that 'everything has to be laid out in a clean and structured form because the audience can be vast and hierarchically important'. The increasing pace of globalization means that such audiences may have very different background assumptions from those which are held at the local site. The 'textualization' of work means that this form of competence in written communication becomes more significant and opens many organizational members up to concerns that their abilities will be judged against demanding standards. Thus, while there was a higher rate of posting of 'knowledge objects' to the Siemens ShareNet system in China than in the USA, most of these postings were by more senior managers, something which the authors attribute to concern about loss of face if communicative competence was found to be lacking (Voelpel, Dous and Davenport 2005). By contrast, there was resistance to posting in English at all by those in the German head office.

These concerns, raised by the use of groupware and intranets for knowledge sharing, can be generalized to the much wider use of email. We noted in Chapter 5 that such systems blurred the distinction between formal and informal communication. The etiquette for constructing emails remains fluid and emergent, based in part on existing genres (Hutchby 2001). However, training in this area is often stronger on features such as the sending of messages than on other disciplines which might aid communication. Thus, in a small scale study, Burgess, Jackson and Edwards (2005) note that improvements in the use of email (as ranked by recipients) followed from some training in giving emails appropriate subject headings. These enabled recipients more quickly to determine whether the messages were relevant to them. Attention to matters like this, as well as to routines for filing messages, might be of considerable help in coping with the overload that email potentially brings. However, they also raise questions about the nature of the communication within the message. Such questions are also raised by the widespread use of applications such as intranets.

These questions are above all to do with the importance of context. One of the reasons why intranets are less than successful is because information requires some context if it is to be meaningful and supplying this context means communication from the perspective of the intended audience. Frequently this audience is not known; even where it is, as we saw in Chapter 2, we frequently make assumptions about its needs rather than investigating them. This is all too common in the design of intranet sites, where more attention is paid to the tools for creating content than the content itself. Orna (2005) raises a very important area of competence here, that of information design. She notes in one organization which produced both paper and web-based product catalogues that:

> web technology demands much smaller data elements than the modules created for pages of printed catalogue – for example all parameters for tables are stored in a 'global product database' . . . which had to be created as a bespoke product from scratch.

> (Orna 2005: 98)

So, as well as creating product specific content at a much lower level than before, this had to be detached from the rules which created the final product. This then involves a much more abstract reasoning process, one in which the final product is the combination of items which are not materially created until the moment of production. One approach to this problem is to use content management systems, in which the 'look and feel' of an application is handled by the ICT-based system and content is produced according to laid down guidelines by nominated persons. This removes one problem with many intranets, that of poor visual design on the part of those who have had no training in this area, but Orna notes that the processes in the organization she examined were 'in some ways more cumbersome than the traditional one of negotiations with supplier, paper processing, filling in a Word template keyed in from various sources, and passing to the publishing department, because no suitable content management system is yet available' (Orna 2005: 98). Similarly, at Siemens the experience is that '. . . global editors still have to do content management manually. . . . Maintaining consistent terminology and overall quality within a global knowledge-sharing system is an extensive task' (Voelpel, Dous and Davenport 2005: 19).

One important issue here is the persistent recourse to technological solutions to solve problems posed by technology, rather than engaging in forms of training which might be more effective. So, for example, we have rules for handling email traffic rather than consideration of policy issues which might shape the traffic at source. This is not to dismiss technological solutions entirely, but to suggest that an exclusive focus might be misguided. In our previous discussions we have observed how in so many cases information and knowledge are embedded in webs of social relations. A powerful way of looking at management, we saw, was one which focused on management as negotiation achieved through conversations. The focus, therefore, might be on ways of achieving better conversations, whether face to face or electronically mediated. This might involve, for example, training in forms of working in teams, drawing on models of effective team building. Such training exists but in an interesting account Coulson-Thomas and Drew (1996) contrasted the efforts organizations thought were important in helping to foster teamwork against those in which they were engaged. Training of the type we have discussed was rated as the most important (over the implementation of groupware, the upgrading of networks or the changing of processes) but the picture was reversed when looking at what companies had actually done. Such training now sank to the bottom, being used by 22 per cent of the sample (as against the 54 per cent which thought it was important) while the figures for the other factors were all in the 30 per cent range. In other words, it is perhaps easier for organizations to invest in 'hard' options – buying a system or installing a network – than it is to commit to 'softer' actions.

Information ethics

We have noted at a number of points that the increasing ability to collect, store and analyse large volumes of data raise important ethical concerns (Mason, Mason and Culnan 1995). These can be summarized under two headings: external and internal. An increasing number of organizations collect large bodies of data about customers and their actions. Supermarkets deploying customer loyalty cards not only collect data about transactions but using address data can often cross reference this to build up a picture of particular buying habits. This raises the spectre of being able to identify individuals and their behaviour in great detail. In practice it would appear that such organizations tend to analyse their data at a much higher level. The fantasy (or spectre, depending on your position) of 'one to one' marketing seems in practical terms some way off. In addition, customer data receives some protection from data protection legislation which requires the establishment of and compliance with policies which give informed consent to the use of data. Of course such data still need to be kept secure. Part of such security rests with access controls to prevent external intrusion, but in practice many of the threats to security come from inside organizations. However, one could argue that the real ethical concerns are with the use of detailed customer transactions to put pressure on suppliers to cut margins and speed up deliveries. Here there is less regulatory protection and more reliance on the adherence of employees to voluntary codes established by organizations.

In internal terms, as we will see in Chapter 9, the ethical questions are raised by the use of data for monitoring purposes. This takes a number of forms, from the monitoring in real time of call centre effectiveness to the construction of league tables of performance. Of course, discussing such concerns under the heading of individual awareness is problematic for two reasons. One is that it is a corporate responsibility to adhere to regulatory structures and to formulate policies effectively. The second, and perhaps more important, is that to pose these questions as simple matters of individual awareness is to ignore the power differentials that we cover in Chapter 9. Individual employees, as we know from cases such as that of Enron, are often put under pressure to carry out unethical practices, such as the shredding or manipulation of vital information. However, it still remains the case that individual employees need to be aware of their responsibilities under both legislation and organizational codes of conduct. The problem is that this is often put in terms of compliance instead of in positive terms.

'Practical reasoning'

At several points in the discussion above we have pointed to aspects of more abstract thinking, a need to go beyond the local and the material to understand the place of data, information or knowledge in a wider context. We note this in connection with the construction of spreadsheets, databases or Web pages, where system developers will draw a distinction between the logical and the physical. That is, the most important product from an information system – a report, say, where several items are brought together – will only 'exist' on screen or paper when certain routines are brought into play. Beyond this, we note that there are aspects of business which are 'systemic'. That is, what happens in one part of the organization has knock on effects in other parts, often at times or in places which are not self-evident to those carrying out the original action. Thus the actions of branch staff in creating customer accounts in the Bank of Scotland (as covered in Chapter 3) had consequences, ones which they could not foresee until they were brought to their attention, for the marketing staff who later wished to rely on them for an altogether different purpose. Patriotta (2003), for example, notes the need for systemic inference skills in a heavily automated car manufacturing plant in Italy. In such a setting '[t]he task of the operators involves making sense of the data provided by machines and using them in a purposeful way. Accordingly, knowledge of the machinery, method, and inferential capabilities are very important' (Patriotta 2003: 129).

Such demands echo the paper mill workers of Zuboff's (1988) much earlier study, many of whom found it difficult to shift from a tactile world to one of abstract data. As we have seen, Zuboff argued that in order to take full advantage of the 'informating' properties of the systems she examined there was a need for what she termed 'intellective skills'. Similarly, in the chemical and nuclear plants studied by Carroll (1998) there was a need, often uncomfortable in practice, to go beyond the existing boundaries of practice in seeking to understand data. A study by Moss-Jones (1990: 153) of five manufacturing plants found that '[t]raditional, practical skills are disappearing; new conceptual skills related to information management and to operating in more creative, flexible, less routinized ways are developing'. These skills are very distinct from those bundled under the heading of IT skills. They more nearly approach the elements of critical thinking which Bruce (1997) isolated as one face of information literacy. It may be, however, that rather than training for such skills, organizations use their recruitment processes and, in particular, educational credentials as a way of acquiring them. These processes will, therefore, be considered in more detail after we have examined some potential changes in roles.

CHANGING ROLES

In addressing the need for more attention to what she terms 'information products' in the context of our discussion of content provision, Orna argues that one response:

> is a clear statement in job descriptions that the holders of specified information content are responsible for providing it for given information products, and that they should interact with named job holders in this connection. Their need for support in this aspect of the job should be recognized (e.g. by training in managing information, help from technology tools in transforming new knowledge into information), and the organization's information resources should include details of the authoritative sources who should provide content on specific topics.
>
> (Orna 2005: 93)

This suggestion is a useful introduction to a focus on the changing roles suggested by the applications in Chapters 4 and 5. In particular our focus will be on the notion of the 'power user', often found in conjunction with applications like data warehouses and on jobs reinventing notions of 'editors' and 'librarians' in conjunction with knowledge management systems.

'Power users'

The notion of the 'power user' often crops up in discussions of data warehousing, but it is also significant in other technically complex applications. The early incarnation of this role is to be met in the shape of the 'end user' who we met earlier. In Karten's (1991) discussion one of the dangers of user-produced systems is that they become 'key resource dependent'. That is, they are often developed by enthusiasts whose job is not formally that of systems development but rather something like 'market analyst' or 'management accountant'. These people can develop often quite complex systems using standard desk top tools such as spreadsheets or databases. The problem with these (aside from questions of the suitability of the design and the efficiency of the application) arises when the developer leaves, often without having formally documented their efforts. This then exposes the organization to considerable risk as there is nobody present to take over the application and maintain it.

The power users in the data warehousing literature are not necessarily systems designers; rather they are those who can interrogate the system and produce the necessary results, often for their departmental colleagues. What is important about data warehousing is that it is based on complex data models which are not always intuitive (unlike, say, spreadsheets or intranet applications). Access to data is therefore frequently mediated by technical specialists, which raises issues of specialist language. The emergent role of power user relates to those users located in user departments who have become expert in accessing the application and can either access data for other users or provide them with immediate support. Payton and Zahay (2003) note that as a result there was a tendency for these experts to become over-worked. Massa and Testa (2005) report the emergence of such power users in two of their three cases, but in only one of these cases was the role formalized. McKean notes the difficulty of finding the combination of analysis skills and database knowledge, while Cooper *et al.* note that either 'traditional' analysts found the IT skills too difficult to acquire or that those who did possess the required combination of skills were difficult to retain (McKean 1999: 116; Cooper *et al.* 2000).

As with the 'end users' there are two feasible responses. One is to ban all such efforts and to shift responsibility firmly within a technical function. However, this is to ignore the importance of having those within a business function who understand and can translate the needs of applications to best effect. The other response is, as Orna suggests, building tasks and responsibilities into job descriptions and providing the appropriate resources and training. This is an emerging area in which there are considerable debates within organizations about the appropriate location for such specialists.

THE RE-EMERGENCE OF THE LIBRARIAN?

If we examine our earlier discussions of applications broadly under the heading of knowledge sharing we will see a number of implications for new roles in organizations – or rather, roles which appear in new guises seeming to have much in common with the traditional capabilities associated with librarians. These capabilities would include skills in the classification and categorization of material, skills which make the subsequent retrieval of material more effective. The paradox is that as librarians appear to be becoming more marginal in the affairs of many organizations, many of their skills appear to be in much demand. We have already noted the existence of global editors in the Siemens ShareNet system, whose job is to edit content, making sure it meets certain quality thresholds (Voelpel, Dous and Davenport 2005). The management consultancy Price Waterhouse has a role of 'knowledge concierge' in charge of about 25 Lotus Notes databases whose role is 'constantly purging, adding and reordering information such that any consultant in the firm can tap another's knowledge by accessing the Notes database' (Halper 1997: 12). At Buckman Laboratories forum specialists 'make sure questions get answered and don't die on the vine or rot on the bulletin board' (Halper 1997: 12). The suggestion at a Taiwanese chip fabrication plant is that people are needed to construct narratives which help the understanding of knowledge in context (Hsiao, Tsai and Lee 2006). All these examples suggest that knowledge sharing is not simply a matter of using ICT in a passive sense, but involves active intervention in shaping and maintaining material. These roles suggest a combination of the skills of publishing and librarianship. From librarianship come skills in the classification of material, from publishing those in the editing of material.

It is perhaps not surprising then that such trends have occasioned some debate among the ranks of librarians. The dominant argument is the need for those who staff such corporate libraries as remain in existence to take a more proactive approach than they have done in the past (Owens, Wilson and Abell 1996). Case studies appear to indicate that many of their traditional roles are being occupied by others in areas such as marketing or public relations, despite these staff perhaps not possessing the necessary skills. One company was 'using the same staff who ran the data processing department to organize the information management function. They admitted that some of the staff found it difficult to come to terms with information management concepts' (Owens, Wilson and Abell 1996: 36). This meant that the focus shifted to efficient storage and retrieval, rather than the quality of the information provided. However, what this work seems to suggest is that the need is to disperse information specialists into business areas, where they will become as involved in internal as well as external information provision (Skelton and Abell 2001). In an observation which chimes with several themes we have pursued so far, Melanie Goody suggests that:

> Increasingly, data now go straight to the end user . . . Users often do not know where information is coming from, making it very difficult to interpret or evaluate. This is where the information profession must play its role in the process – in interpretation and evaluation. Everyone is becoming more IT literate; we should help in the process of making users more *information* literate.
>
> (in Owens, Wilson and Abell 1996: 165)

Spanning boundaries: the hybrid manager?

The focus of this book is on the use of data, information and knowledge rather than on the application of ICT. However, one area of debate is worthy of review despite its being more concerned with the latter. This is the debate over the ways in which the boundaries between those functions concerned with the provision and maintenance of ICT-based systems and those in business areas should be spanned. The relevance of this debate is in the blurring that we have already noted between roles but the persistence of functional divisions in organizations. As we have seen, the latter persist because they are efficient in the use of resources and, more importantly, chime with the construction of identities within organizations. However, they also pose barriers to the flow of information. Given, as we have seen, the increasing importance of a range of ICT-based applications in providing this information, then means of improving this provision are needed.

Part of the impetus behind the hybrid manager movement was the desire on the part of ICT professionals to preserve and enhance their organizational position. We have seen something similar with librarians, but many working in ICT saw more opportunity to stress their centrality to businesses dependent on the technology they supported and so to move into positions of influence. Some took seriously the shifts identified by librarians in seeking to position themselves as the information specialists in the organization. As part of this move some influential figures, such as Colin Palmer, former deputy managing director of Thomson Travel (a company which achieved considerable success with an early booking system for travel agents), suggested that organizations needed to work towards the creation of hybrid managers, defined as:

181

People with strong technical skills and adequate business knowledge, or vice-versa . . . hybrids are people with technical skills able to work in user areas doing a line or functional job, but adept at developing and implementing IT application ideas.

(Earl and Skyrme 1992: 170)

There are a number of aspects of this definition that need further discussion. One was that this was not seen as a particular role but as a set of capabilities. However, that set of capabilities raised questions about how they mapped on to existing roles in organizations. In part some of the problem lies with the level of management that we are discussing. Much of the early discussion was closely related to the debate about the desirability of having information systems (IS) representation at board level (Palmer 1990). Accordingly, the hybrid debate became one about the competences required by senior managers. However, lower down the organization the same debates existed. On the IS side there were roles such as project management where the concern was whether managers with considerable technical skills could obtain the inter-personal skills and the business knowledge that were perceived to be required. From the business side there were the 'power users' who we have already examined, who might require advanced technical skills (such as a facility with relational database querying for data warehouses) which were not catered for under existing training schemes or role descriptions. In practice, the debate at this level has cohered round the notion of 'relationship managers', who translate between business and technical functions (Coughlan, Lycett and Macredie 2005).

However, this to some extent simply leaves open the question of the nature of 'technical skills'. For what counts as a 'technical' skill to some (some as the querying of databases) is for others an aspect of end-user computing. Much of the debate around hybrid management seemed to founder on this question, with some seeing it as the dilution of specialist skills (Currie and Glover 1999). What this tended to lead to was a marginalization of the questions raised by our focus on information literacy, where the questions of how the information might be used tended to be overlooked. In addition, another problem thrown up by the debate was the sheer range of attributes and competences that were felt to characterize a successful hybrid. These suggested that perhaps an approach which focused on the development of these capabilities across a team might be a more realistic approach. In many ways, this debate echoes a much longer debate, that is, the debate over whether managers should be seen as generalists or specialists. Work on management practices across countries has indicated substantial differences in how the role is perceived. In a comparison of managers in Germany and the UK, for example, Ganter and Walgenbach (2002) note that in Germany managers are technical specialists whose authority is based on their knowledge, related in turn to an institutional context which places heavy stress on technical education. By contrast, management in the UK is seen as being about the leadership of people. In such a setting, managers are recruited on the basis of character traits rather than knowledge. However, such institutionalized concepts of management may require questioning given the broader use of information that we have examined, so we turn next to questions of recruitment and reward.

RECRUITMENT, REWARD AND CAREERS

In his review of the impact of knowledge management on human resource management (HRM), Harry Scarbrough (2003) suggests that it raises questions about what organizations look for when they select people for jobs with a high knowledge content, how they reward them for sharing that knowledge, and how the careers structure impacts on the use of knowledge. We have already seen some of the problems that knowledge use poses for organizations. On the one hand is the blurring of roles, on the other the embedding of the skills that people need to use information effectively in their day to day activity. If we accept that such information use is embedded in a web of relationships, in which relationship building and communicative competence are important skills, then the elucidation of just what skills are required becomes even more difficult. It is far easier to recruit against technical skills and competencies and so information skills become hidden in the process.

This is perhaps one of the reasons why information literacy poses a challenge to work organizations. Its definition remains unclear, especially when it shades into attributes such as critical thinking. As a consequence, educational credentials are used as a surrogate. That is, it is assumed that the necessary skills and attributes have been acquired during education, especially during higher education. As we have seen, information literacy is built into the requirements of graduates in one major educational provider, Australia, and it remains an important focus of concern in debates in higher education in many countries. However, the degree to which such debates and initiatives have met with success is open to some question. The nature of graduate recruitment and the extent to which the perceived attributes line up with those required is, as we have seen, the subject of some debate (Brown and Hesketh 2004). However, if we approach this from the perspective of the organization then we get a sense of some of the problems with this approach.

As we saw in Chapter 6, Hunter, Beaumont and Lee (2002) studied five Scottish law firms with a view to determining their approach to knowledge management. In nearly all cases (one firm was a partial exception) such initiatives were heavily ICT-based and neglected the tacit knowledge accumulated in the firms. Such tacit knowledge, the authors argued, was accumulated through experience coloured by a socialization pattern akin to a master-apprenticeship pattern, in which new recruits learned how to think like a lawyer. However, the firms were increasingly relying on educational credentials and formal training in their recruitment process and the degree of on the job training and socialization appeared to be diminishing. In such circumstances, the authors argued, 'the implication is more, not less, attention needs to be paid to the management of process and the social context' (Hunter, Beaumont and Lee 2002: 17).

Another consideration is the way, once recruited, people use and share information, a consideration which has come to the fore in the examples of ICT-facilitated knowledge sharing that we have already come across. We noted that in some of the cases of relative failure that in part there was resistance to doing additional work which brought no measurable benefits to those supplying the information. By contrast, in the Xerox Eureka system, in the Siemens ShareNet system and in the Taiwanese chip fabrication plant, incentives were put in place to encourage engineers to share their tips for improvement. Such rewards might be set at relatively modest levels, but if accumulated would provide a significant reward. Siemens, for example, operated a points system in which accumulated points could be exchanged for products such as mobile phones (Voelpel, Dous and Davenport 2005). However, such systems might not have the desired effect. In one Taiwanese plant which operated a similar system to that examined by Hsiao, Tsai and Lee it was found that:

Most engineers submitted tips by cut-and-paste knowledge appropriated from Internet sources. To ensure they could receive the reward, engineers also colluded to produce

183

hyperlinks to each other's tips, and accessed one another's tips to demonstrate a high retrieval rate. This not only wasted the company's resources invested in the system (containing mostly cut-and-paste tips), but also reduced engineers' energy in carrying out repair tasks.

(Hsiao, Tsai and Lee 2006: 1314)

In Siemens, it was discovered that in some parts of the world, such as India, points were traded, meaning again that people were 'tending to share their knowledge without reference to business needs and . . . neglecting their actual jobs'. But what was also found in Siemens, as in Xerox, was that many valued the recognition that the points brought rather than the material rewards they reaped. 'Despite accumulating large numbers of shares,' report Voelpel, Dous and Davenport (2005: 16) '. . . few users ever converted them into prizes. ShareNet managers speculated that the knowledge had become its own reward and users did not want to relinquish the status of a high share total by redeeming it.' All of these examples report the need to maintain processes for editing and monitoring the quality of the tips supplied and for encouraging systems based on recognition and reputation, such as having tips rated by users and basing recognition on the results.

Other areas also have implications for reward systems. For example, we have noted at several points the Bank of Scotland example, in which data quality at branch level becomes crucial for use 'downstream' in marketing activities. Here, one solution to the problem of data quality was to make part of the branch manager's bonus conditional on achieving an acceptable level of performance in an audit of data quality (Amos 1997). Of course, what is being done here is to individualize responsibility for the quality of data; when we examine more complex cases of knowledge sharing, then the problem is that this happens in a web of relationships in which it is difficult to disentangle individual effort. Certainly, the traditional bonus schemes operated in sales environments are a positive disincentive to sharing customer knowledge, as Currie and Kerrin (2004) point out.

Another disincentive that we have observed operated in the use of Lotus Notes by the management consultancy Alpha (Orlikowski 2000). Here a career structure for consultants that operated on an 'up or out' basis, in which decisions on promotion were based on performance in the most recent project, and in which knowledge about what constituted success would assist in securing lucrative future contracts, meant that there was no incentive to share any of that knowledge. In addition, this organization operated a charging regime in which consultants' time was billed to clients and the aim was to minimize non-billable time. Even if there was some interest in learning how to use the new system, finding time was difficult; the few consultants who pursued this route did so only to improve individual efficiency, not to contribute to wider sharing. By contrast, technical staff and senior partners did not face such pressures and so were willing to share what they had. Once again, we see the need to place both the sharing of knowledge and the technological means advanced for its achievement in the broader organizational context. This is also important when we come to look at information and change.

INFORMATION, RESISTANCE AND CHANGE

There is extensive material looking at how processes of change in organizations should be carried out (Burnes 2004). Such material suggests processes of unfreezing current attitudes to make people receptive to change and then involving them to carry through the change. In many ways, therefore, it has that focus on the process that we have already encountered in other contexts. That is, the focus is not so much just on the nature of the change itself but on the way in which it is carried out. Much of this material, and the problems which have been encountered, also apply to change involving information, but in this section I want to explore some specific facets. In particular, we need to consider whether ICT-related change is in any way different from other forms of organizational change. For example, Markus (2004) suggests that what she terms 'technochange' requires a different approach, one which is a blend of technical and business perspectives. The concern might be that in such a process, as we have already seen in many other contexts, the focus on information itself gets lost. Accordingly, while I will be drawing on models drawn from experience with ICT-based systems, I will try to bring out some of the information consequences, consequences which might not seem obvious at first glance. This is particularly important in the context of managers and their use of information. As Zuboff observes:

> The shifting grounds of knowledge invite managers to recognize the emergent demands for intellective skills and develop a learning environment in which such skills can develop. That very recognition contains a threat to managerial authority, which depends in part on control over the organization's knowledge base.
>
> (Zuboff 1988: 391)

In order to explore these issues, I will draw upon an overview of the literature related to resistance to information systems change provided by Hirschheim and Newman (1988) (Table 8.2).

The overall conclusion that Hirschheim and Newman drew was that:

> The development and implementation of computer-based information systems is a type of major organisational change. Only those development strategies which view such change in terms of social and political processes are likely to prove satisfactory.
>
> (Hirschheim and Newman 1988: 406)

Table 8.2 *Causes of resistance to information systems change*

Causes of resistance to information systems change
Innate conservatism
Lack of felt need
Uncertainty
Lack of involvement
Redistribution of resources
Operational invalidity
Lack of management support
Poor technical quality
Personal characteristics of the designer

Source: Extracted from Hirschheim and Newman 1988

This is important when so many such projects start from a technical perspective and so fail to make the changes which are envisaged. For example, in the Alpha case (Orlikowski 2000) the Chief Information Officer responsible for the implementation of Lotus Notes did so in the belief that the application would engender knowledge sharing. This belief was based on the basis of the properties of the technology, failing to appreciate the organizational factors which, as we have seen, would lead to lack of use. In the Norwegian oil company Statoil the same package was introduced as a replacement for an email system and this is how it remained (Monteiro and Hepso 2000).

In some ways we can see that the term 'resistance' is not entirely applicable to such cases. Rather, the problems here were either with a lack of fit to existing processes or of a lack of awareness of possibilities. Markus (2004) compares two implementations of a data warehouse. In one case, which was led by IS and related to a desire to cut costs by producing standard reports more effectively, this is what was achieved but no more. That is, the system met with no 'resistance' and was effective within the parameters set, but these were considerably below realizing the potential which we discussed in Chapter 4. By contrast, another project engaged marketing managers at the outset and worked actively to change their use of information. As Markus records, this entailed 'a painstaking process of one-on-one coaching by which he introduced the marketeers to linear regression (without ever calling it that!) and changed the culture of the marketing organization' (Markus 2004: 6). So, much depends on the expectations set for the systems at the outset. Another feature is the extent to which changes in the use of information can be expected at the early stages of implementation. One problem with our studies of systems implementation, as Jasperson, Carter and Zmud (2005) point out, is that they tend to concentrate on the early stages. In many cases this gives us a distorted picture, as it takes time for such systems to be accepted and for new working practices to be accepted. It might be that were we to examine such systems at a later date we might find that significant changes in information use had occurred. These general points should make us cautious in our approach to the evidence, especially when such evidence tends to focus on resistance and failure.

What Hirschheim and Newman (1988) isolate is a cluster of factors which speak to the need for involvement and communication. In traditional systems development processes such involvement was often limited, but contemporary methods such as prototyping and rapid application development allow for a greater degree of user involvement. In such systems, software tools are used to provide rapid models of what a system might look like. These are particularly useful in web development, where interactive design is more feasible. However, such developments only raise questions about who ought to be involved. This is particularly important when it comes to considerations of information use. We have already seen that managers, when asked, often find it difficult to specify in advance what information they require. It can be that if those chosen to represent a department or function are too distant from questions of information use that they are either stuck in existing models of use or that they are simply unaware of what those models are. Markus (2004) notes a particular problem here on the more significant projects, where users who join project teams as experts rapidly become identified with the project rather than their area of work and so become distanced from their former colleagues. Power users are seen as one way of tapping into user concerns, but their very competence can be misleading if designers mistake it for the average (Sherman 2005). However, they can be powerful advocates for a new system.

This takes us back to our earlier concerns about training. The problem with a lot of training is that it fails to address local concerns. That is, it is often presented using generic problems (and solutions) which fail to engage with problems as they present themselves in a work context (Spender 1998). This is why in practice much training is on the job training. The problem with such training, of course, is that the very things which make it effective – its integration with the familiar and its immediate addressing of the task in hand – can make it limiting and, at worst, simply lead to the reproduction of bad habits. It is in this situation that a properly trained 'power user' can be important. What we would want, however, is for such initial training to consider the questions we considered under training for information management, in order that awareness can be spread of the impact of new systems on the type of information available.

If involvement and participation can shape the acceptance of a system and perhaps build awareness of what can be done with information, a central part of failure may not be at this level but with what Hirschheim and Newman term 'redistribution of resources'. The resources which they have in mind in particular are power and authority and this is where we return to the observation of Zuboff about the threat to managerial authority. The popular image of resistance in the context of technological change is that of shopfloor resistance, notably in cases such as printers in the newspaper industry and dockers faced with containerization. However, these very visible and 'spectacular' examples can be profoundly misleading. When it comes to resistance then it can be middle managers who are the main contenders.

The example of telephone managers in the UK indicates some of the reasons why managers might resist change. Such resistance is given more power because it might not have to be active resistance to block change. By virtue of their position their simple unwillingness to participate may be a much more powerful weapon. We have seen that many data warehousing projects founder on the rock of data ownership. This can be where a manager has a certain legitimacy

MANAGING TELEPHONE EXCHANGES

A major technological change in telephone exchanges occurred when manual exchanges were replaced by automatic versions. In the older exchanges moving parts came into contact with each other to form circuits which enabled the connection of lines. In such exchanges fault finding was a matter of observation, not just by eye but also by ear, as a skilled technician could find faults by listening to the contacts as they connected. Managers in such exchanges tended to have been promoted from the ranks of technicians and were able to find faults in the same fashion. Their authority, therefore, derived in large part from their technical expertise. In an automatic exchange, by contrast, fault finding was done in a more abstract fashion, involving the logical tracing of events and the removal of parts for correction elsewhere. While technicians received training in such fault finding, this was not the same for their managers. They were now expected to manage several exchanges in a way which focused more on the development of staff. This was difficult for more experienced managers to adapt to, especially when such considerations were not taken into account when devising new working practices.

Source: Clark *et al.*, 1988

on the basis of access to data and they fail to carry out the necessary actions to make that data more widely available. Zuboff noted that the same managers who were advocates for systems which made shopfloor activity more visible resisted the application of the same logic to their own positions. A manager she spoke to commented:

> They want to have access to real-time data from the mills. But as plant manager, I do not want to be second-guessed. I don't want them breathing down my neck or wasting their time on the nitty-gritty from the shop floor. Right now, I have some flexibility in terms of deciding what data they see, when they see it, and how it is presented. I lose control over that, it is an important piece of my job over which I will have less control.
>
> (Zuboff 1988: 339)

As we saw in several examples of knowledge management systems, refusal to carry out additional tasks of loading material on to such systems can mean that they fail to reach critical mass. In WorldDrug, there were no procedures or sanctions to ensure that project managers posted lessons on the central database (McKinlay 2002). Given that many found the practice either irrelevant or threatening, they chose to ignore it. We noted in the previous chapter that middle managers seem set to retain an important role in organizations, even if the nature of that role has changed. The power to hold up such initiatives seems, therefore, unlikely to disappear, even if this is only a passive refusal to do those things which are necessary for success. As we have already noted, managers are also employees, with a need to preserve their own position. This reinforces the observation of Hirschheim and Newman that organizational change is a political matter, in which thought needs to extend beyond technical considerations.

Our local authority example below illustrates some of the more 'technical' concerns that Hirschheim and Newman isolated. In many cases, information is not used from such systems because it does not fit the working patterns of those for whom it is intended. Such considerations are particularly important for that increasing part of the workforce that is mobile for a significant part of their working day. Again, much of this may not be resistance so much as a desire for

AVAILABILITY AND EXAMPLE IN ICT-ENABLED CHANGE

When I was involved in teaching a group of employees (ranging from the chief executive to his secretary) at an English local authority some interesting observations were made about a newly introduced email system. One housing manager worked in a neighbourhood 'one stop shop', where the priority during opening hours was on using information and ICT to solve client problems. This meant that the two available terminals were used for access to housing information systems, with the manager being restricted to certain times of the day to access her email. As she was unable to work round such a restricted timetable, she made no effective use of email. Another junior manager reported that he and colleagues made relatively little use of email because their perception was that the chief executive and senior managers failed to use it. While the chief executive felt that his job didn't require the use of email, he was prepared (following some discussion!) to concede that his actions had a symbolic impact.

information which is 'to-hand'. As we have seen in numerous examples, the need is to fit the technology to working practices, rather than the other way round. Our local authority example also reinforces the symbolic as well as the material influence of senior managers. If we take this observation and extend it to questions of information and knowledge, then the symbolic importance of the appointment at senior levels of Chief Knowledge Officers in some organizations might be important in stressing the commitment of an organization to taking knowledge seriously (Davenport 1996). However, as we saw with the case of the renaming of executive information systems, it is easy to change the name of a role without changing the substance of what is involved. Many organizations contain a role of Chief Information Officer when the content of the role is really about the management of ICT. Such labelling simply risks cynicism and confusion. In addition, much of the concern with the role of a Chief Knowledge Officer seems in practice to be based on an 'objectified' notion of knowledge, with a particular focus on the protection of intellectual property rights (IPR) through the enforcement of patents and copyright. Such concerns are of course of vital importance to many organizations, but they do tend to rather over-shadow the more relational forms of knowledge that we have examined.

The final two categories that Hirschheim and Newman suggests, poor technical quality and the personal characteristics of the designer, are lower down their list and less relevant to our focus on information. However, we have noted how, for example, poor response times because of unanticipated problems with network bandwidth had an adverse impact on the use of intranets in EBank (Scarbrough 2003). What is important here are user expectations and definitions of what 'response time' might be, rather than any universal technical definition. In a data warehousing context, users might be prepared to wait for several hours for the results of a query, provided that this is predictable and they can build it in to work schedules (Westerman 2001). By contrast, delays measured in seconds can induce frustration in those using intranets and lead to the seeking of alternative channels. The personal characteristics of designers are not our concern here except in so far as they have a bearing on the quality of relationships between technical specialists and business users and, in particular, on views of information. There is some evidence that cognitive styles of ICT managers and general managers do not diverge to any statistically significant extent (Wilcoxson and Chatham 2006), but what might be of more importance than individual style might be the views of the nature of information engendered by taken for granted functional working practices. The regular and routine demands for precision in dealing with the data formats required by ICT systems can generate an image of information as structured data that is at odds with the relational view embedded in more general organizational use. This might be a considerable limitation on the use of relationship managers with a focus on information whose background is in ICT.

CONCLUSIONS

What we can observe in looking at information and organizational change is that it remains, as we have noted at various other points, rather overshadowed by other considerations. In particular, the focus of many organizational change efforts is on concrete actions, whether these are the installation of a new system or a change to a business process. The assumed benefit of such a change is often improvements in the use of information, broadly defined, but the success factors are on the completion of the concrete action. In addition, responsibility for the realization of the information benefits is often vague. Thus, in an ICT project, those in technical functions might reasonably claim that the realization of benefits is a matter for general management; however, general management may not have considered the information issues, especially if their training has focused on application specific aspects of the project. In addition project evaluation is often not undertaken and, if it is, it might occur at too early a point for the significant changes in information use to be detectable. These observations suggest a number of factors which might be worthy of attention, in addition to more general prescriptions about handling organizational change.

We might suggest that at an early stage specific elements for information use need to be written into project proposals, together with realistic provision for their evaluation. This might mean that such evaluations take place over a rather more extended time than is usual. Of course, there are considerable problems with the measurement of such effects, but this might require a different approach to their estimation and investigation. Our focus on senior management commitment suggests that any project sponsor needs to be particularly aware of the potential impact on information, which returns us to Karten's point about the desirability of training in information strategy. It also suggests that Orna's formulation of the distinction between an information policy and an information systems strategy needs reinforcing. The starting point here ought to be with the information, rather than the means of its provision.

Drawing on our brief review of the debate over the hybrid manager, we can note that this has moved on to suggest the need for an overall governance structure which specifies the relationship between the organization and its ICT support (Coughlan, Lycett and Macredie 2005). The problem here is ensuring that questions of information use are taken as central, rather than defaulting to technical specialists. Key components of such a governance structure are steering committees and relationship managers. Steering committees ought to be forums for the clarification of the sort of issues about data definition that we have already encountered. It is here that representation from information specialists might be particularly valuable. Orna (2005), for example, points to the importance of an ongoing working group in establishing a successful information policy at Essex County Council.

The other key component might be the relationship manager, somebody who translates the different languages of organizational and technical specialists. In 1994 Thomas Davenport suggested (in an Internet article which now seems to have disappeared!) that IT academics and practitioners 'should know more than anyone else about what information is needed by a business, whether it fits well on a computer or not. We should know how people like their information and how they use it.' This, however, meets with the competition of those information specialists seeking a broader role in organizations (Oppenheim 1997). This does seem to be an important role, but one whose shape is emergent and by no means settled. We return, therefore, to the questions about the nature of training and roles. More focus on the information management dimension of roles and on training in aspects which cannot be covered in application specific training seems to be of considerable importance. However, to talk of such matters in the abstract is to neglect important considerations of power and culture which have cropped up at a number of points; we explore these in a little more detail in the next chapter.

SUMMARY

- Training in information often neglects the aspects of information literacy that we have identified, with a focus on application specific training. Such a focus neglects effective use of information.

- A number of changes to roles can be identified, which suggest that approaches to recruitment and reward need to be revisited. However, such processes often place more emphasis on formal credentials than the socialization into roles and ways of knowing that are suggested as important by a more practice based focus.

- Information, broadly defined, is often difficult to disentangle in processes of organizational change. However, attitudes to that change, especially on the part of middle managers, can often be shaped by the importance of information in their roles and the threats which change poses to their control of it.

- In considering how information might be made more visible, we return to the importance of embedding such considerations in the policies of the organization and in the roles and structures which it adopts.

REVIEW QUESTIONS

1 What are the negative consequences of application-specific training?

2 What are the key features of resistance to ICT-facilitated organizational change?

DISCUSSION QUESTIONS

1 Take a role with which you are familiar (such as market analyst) and consider what you would add to a job description to take into account information responsibilities. Distinguish between competences required to handle data, information and knowledge and those concerned with ICT.

2 Returning to the Country Holidays example, apply the three levels of training (strategic, information management and application specific): what would you expect to be covered in each?

FURTHER READING

Clark, J., McLoughlin, I., Rose, H. and King, R. (1988) *The Process of Technological Change: New Technology and Social Choice in the Workplace.* Cambridge, Cambridge University Press.

191

While this book is about engineering systems (specifically the shift from analogue to electronic telephone exchanges) it has much of value about broader technological change. In some places it parallels Zuboff's focus on the impact of technology on information, although this is not treated at the same length.

Senge, P. M. (1990) *The Fifth Discipline: The Art and Practice of the Learning Organization*. New York, Doubleday.

Very influential book which argues for the need for a systems perspective as a key discipline for contemporary managers. The particular interpretation of systems thinking is a contested one, but much of the argument relates to the points made in this chapter about practical reasoning.

REFERENCES

Amos, S. (1997) 'Bank Boosts Sales Through Profiling', *Computer Weekly*, 13 November: 8.

Brown, P. and Hesketh, A. (2004) *The Mismanagement of Talent: Employability and Jobs in the Knowledge Economy*. Oxford, Oxford University Press.

Bruce, C. (1997) *Seven Faces of Information Literacy*. Adelaide, AUSLIB Press.

Burgess, A., Jackson, T. and Edwards, J. (2005) 'Email Training Significantly Reduces Email Defects', *International Journal of Information Management*, 25: 71–83.

Burnes, B. (2004) *Managing Change: A Strategic Approach To Organisational Dynamics*. Harlow, Financial Times Prentice Hall.

Carroll, J. (1998) 'Organizational Learning Activities in High-Hazard Industries: The Logics Underlying Self-Analysis', *Journal of Management Studies*, 35(6): 699–717.

Ciborra, C. and Patriotta, G. (1996) 'Groupware and Teamwork in New Product Development: The Case of a Consumer Goods Multinational', in C. Ciborra (ed.) *Groupware and Teamwork: Invisible Aid or Technical Hindrance?*, Chichester, Wiley: 122–143.

Clark, J., McLoughlin, I., Rose, H. and King, R. (1988) *The Process of Technological Change: New Technology and Social Choice in the Workplace*. Cambridge, Cambridge University Press.

Cooper, B. L., Watson, H. J., Wixom, B. H. and Goodhue, D. L. (2000) 'Data Warehousing Supports Corporate Strategy at First American Corporation', *MIS Quarterly*, 24(4): 547–567.

Coughlan, J., Lycett, M. and Macredie, R. (2005) 'Understanding the Business-IT Relationship', *International Journal of Information Management*, 25(4): 303–319.

Coulson-Thomas, C. and Drew, S. (1996) 'Transformation Through Teamwork: The Path to the New Organisation', *Management Decision*, 34(1), 7–17.

Currie, W. and Glover, I. (1999) 'Hybrid Managers: An Example of Tunnel Vision and Regression in Management Research', in W. Currie and R. Galliers (eds) *Rethinking Management Information Systems*. Oxford, Oxford University Press: 417–443.

Currie, G. and Kerrin, M. (2004) 'The Limits of a Technological Fix to Knowledge Management: Epistemological, Political and Cultural Issues in the Case of Intranet Implementation', *Management Learning*, 35(1): 9–29.

Davenport, T. (1996) 'Knowledge Roles: The CKO and Beyond', *CIO Magazine*, April 1. www.cio.com /archive/040196_davenport.html [accessed 14 November 2006].

Davenport, T. (2006) 'Competing on Analytics', *Harvard Business Review*, 84(1): 99–107.

Earl, M. J. and Skyrme, D. J. (1992) 'Hybrid Managers – What Do We Know About Them?' *Journal of Information Systems*, 2: 169–187.

Earl, M. (1994) 'Shorko Films SA', in C. Ciborra and T. Jelassi (eds) *Strategic Information Systems: A European Perspective*. Chichester, Wiley: 99–112.

Ganter, H. and Walgenbach, P. (2002) 'Middle Managers: Differences Between Britain and Germany', in M. Geppert, D. Matten and K. Williams (eds) *Challenges for European Management in a Global Context*. Basingstoke, Palgrave Macmillan: 165–188.

Goodwin, C. (1999) 'Ignorance Isn't Always Bliss', *Computing*, 24 June: 43–48.

Halper, M. (1997) 'Everyone in the Knowledge Pool', *Computing Global Innovators*, December 11: 8–9, 12–13.

Hirscheim, R. and Newman, M. (1988) 'Information Systems and User Resistance: Theory and Practice', *Computer Journal*, 31(5) 398–408.

Hsiao, R., Tsai, S. D. and Lee, C. (2006) 'The Problems of Embeddness: Knowledge Transfer, Coordination and Reuse in Information Systems', *Organization Studies*, 27(9): 1289–1318.

Humby, C., Hunt, T. and Phillips, T. (2003) *Scoring Points: How Tesco Is Winning Customer Loyalty.* London, Kogan Page.

Hunter, L., Beaumont, P. and Lee, M. (2002) 'Knowledge Management Practice in Scottish Law Firms', *Human Resource Management Journal*, 12(2): 4–21.

Hutchby, I. (2001) *Conversation and Technology: From the Telephone to the Internet.* Cambridge, Polity.

Jasperson, J. S., Carter, P. E. and Zmud, R. W. (2005) 'A Comprehensive Conceptualization of Post-Adoptive Behaviors Associated with Information Technology Enabled Work Systems', *MIS Quarterly*, 29(3): 525–557.

Karten, N. (1991) 'Integrating IS Disciplines into End-User Training', *Journal of Information Systems Management*, Winter: 75–78.

Kreie, J., Cronan, T., Pendley, J. and Renwick, J. (2000) 'Applications Development by End-Users: Can Quality be Improved?', *Decision Support Systems*, 29: 143–152.

Lamb, J. (1997) 'Target Practice', *Computing*, 13 February: 36.

McGill, T. and Klobas, J. (2005) 'The Role of Spreadsheet Knowledge in User-Developed Application Success', *Decision Support Systems*, 39: 355–369.

McKean, J. (1999) *Information Masters: Secrets of the Customer Race.* Chichester, Wiley.

McKinlay, A. (2002) 'The Limits of Knowledge Management', *New Technology, Work and Employment*, 17(2): 76–88.

Markus, M. L. (2004) 'Technochange Management: Using IT to Drive Organizational Change', *Journal of Information Technology*, 19: 3–19.

Mason, R., Mason, F. and Culnan, M. (1995) *Ethics of Information Management*, Thousand Oaks, CA, Sage.

Massa, S. and Testa, S. (2005) 'Data Warehouse-in-Practice: Exploring the Function of Expectations in Organizational Outcomes', *Information & Management*, 42: 709–718.

Monteiro, E. and Hepso, V. (2000) 'Infrastructure Strategy Formation: Seize the Day at Statoil', in C. Ciborra (ed.) *From Control to Drift*, Oxford, Oxford University Press: 148–171.

Moss-Jones, J. (1990) *Automating Managers – The Implications of Information Technology for Managers.* London, Pinter.

Nelson, R. R. (1989) *End-user Computing: Concepts, Issues and Applications.* New York, Wiley.

Oppenheim, C. (1997) 'Managers' Use and Handling of Information', *International Journal of Information Management*, 17(4): 239–248.

Orlikowski, W. (2000) 'Using Technology and Constituting Structures: A Practice Lens for Studying Technology in Organizations', *Organization Science*, 11(4): 404–428.

Orna, E. (2005) *Making Knowledge Visible: Communicating Knowledge Through Information Products.* Aldershot, Gower.

Owens, I., Wilson, T. and Abell, A. (1996) *Information and Business Performance: A Study of Information Systems and Services in High Performing Companies.* London, Bowker-Saur.

Palmer, C. (1990) '"Hybrids" – a Critical Force in the Application of Information Technology in the Nineties', *Journal of Information Technology*, 5: 232–235.

Patriotta, G. (2003) *Organizational Knowledge in the Making: How Firms Create, Use and Institutonalize Knowledge.* Oxford, Oxford University Press.

Payton, F. C. and Zahay, D. (2003) 'Understanding Why Marketing Does Not Use the Corporate Data Warehouse for CRM Applications', *Journal of Database Marketing*, 10(4): 315–326.

Saran, C. (2006) 'Tesco Drops Spreadsheets for Retail Planning', *Computer Weekly*, 28 February: 6.

Scarbrough, H. (2003) 'Knowledge Management, HRM and the Innovation Process', *International Journal of Manpower*, 24(5): 501–516.

Senge, P. M. (1990) *The Fifth Discipline: The Art and Practice of the Learning Organization.* New York, Doubleday.

Sherman, R. (2005) 'Couples Therapy for IT and Business Users (Business Intelligence Goes Back to the Future Part II)', Athena Solutions, www.athena-solutions.com/bi-brief/aug05-issue20.html [acessed 13 November 2006].

Skelton, V. and Abell, A. (2001) *Developing Skills for the Information Services Workforce in the Knowledge Economy.* London, Library and Information Commission Research Report 122.

Spender, J. (1998) 'The Dynamics of Individual and Organizational Knowledge', in C. Eden and J.-C Spender (eds) *Managerial and Organizational Cognition: Theory, Methods and Research.* London, Sage: 13–39.

Voelpel, S., Dous, M. and Davenport, T. (2005) 'Five Steps to Creating a Global Knowledge-Sharing System: Siemens' ShareNet', *Academy of Management Executive*, 19(2): 9–23.

Westerman, P. (2001) *Data Warehousing: Using the Wal-Mart Model.* San Francisco, Morgan Kaufmann.

Wilcoxson, L. and Chatham, R. (2006) 'Testing the Accuracy of the IT Stereotype: Profiling IT Managers' Personality and Behavioural Characteristics', *Information & Management*, 43(6): 697–705.

Zuboff, S. (1988) *In the Age of the Smart Machine: The Future of Work and Power.* London, Heinemann.

Part Three

Power, culture and the institutional formation of information

CHAPTER SUMMARY

KEY QUESTIONS

Chapter 9 Power, culture and information

- How does power affect the use of information in organizations?
- How is information used to monitor and control activities, and what impact does this have on learning?
- What is organizational culture and how does it affect the use of information?
- What is the impact of national culture on conceptions of information and knowledge?

Chapter 10 Institutions and information

- Why do institutionalist perspectives offer a useful way of looking at information use?
- What are the distinctions between institutionalist approaches and why do they matter?
- Can ideas drawn from critical realism help overcome some of the weaknesses in institutionalist approaches and how?
- In what ways can critical realism help us understand better some of the issues we have been tackling?

Chapter 9

Power, culture and information

INTRODUCTION

Remember in Chapter 1 the observation from a manager that information use in his department:

> . . . arises from a strong need for control and to invite comments from the department's more junior staff, let alone customers, would be high risk as it might lead to a challenge, which would not be welcome, of the status quo.
>
> (Mutch 1999: 327)

He attributed this to 'strong cultural influences', but we might also wish to observe that there is power at work here. The two topics of power and culture that we examine in this chapter are strongly intertwined and have been a shadowy presence in our discussions so far. We saw, for example, the suggestion by Ciborra and Patriotta (1996) in their investigation of groupware use that we needed to pay attention to what they termed the 'infoculture'. We also saw the way in which hierarchical position had a powerful impact on patterns of information use, even when it was not used in an overtly controlling or authoritarian sense. It can be difficult, then, to disentangle the impact of the two, but we will look at each in turn in this chapter.

It is important to do this because these are areas which are not always given their due weight in much of the mainstream literature. If we return to the MIT model, for example, culture is viewed as an emergent property of the relationship between roles and responsibilities, organization structure and management processes, but this is not strongly related to the broader debate in the organizational literature. In part this is due to an enduring technological focus. Starting with the technology often means that effects of culture and power are mistakenly attributed to the technology in a modified form of technological determinism. However, it is also the case that in several of the traditions we have examined that management tends to be viewed as a technical matter, somewhat divorced from the broader positioning of the organization. A similar criticism could also be made of much of the literature on information use (e.g. Choo 1998), where techniques of information retrieval and storage are discussed without reference to the ways in which organizations can be the site of conflicts, conflicts which often revolve around the use of information. Sometimes this situation is remedied by treating such examples of conflict as matters of 'culture' (Davenport 1997), but questions of power are an ever-present feature of human relationships.

This chapter will examine:

- theories of power as they can be applied to the use of information in organizations. In particular, we consider the use of information for monitoring and control, as well as the role information plays in inter-functional conflict.
- ideas of information cultures at organizational and national levels, with a particular focus on the way in which ideas about information are embedded in wider systems of knowing

THEORIES OF POWER AND INFORMATION

A good starting point for our consideration of power is with Zuboff's work. The theme of challenges to managerial authority runs throughout her account. It is this challenge that she suggests will be a prime reason why organizations fail to achieve the benefits of the potential of ICT to 'informate' activities. She observes that the 'intellective' skills which need to be applied to make the most of the information that ICT can offer are a challenge to that part of managerial authority which rests on their control over what it is to know in the organization (Zuboff 1988: 391). Several of these themes crop up in our discussion below. However, Zuboff's account draws heavily on the work of Michel Foucault, a social theorist whose work on power has been both extremely influential and very contentious (McKinlay and Starkey 1998). It does so in a rather one-sided way, one which places all its emphasis on authority and control and does not accommodate what some see as a more positive conceptualization of power as an enabling force. Moreover, it tends to the view of power as based on possession of resources, an approach which is often rejected in favour of a more relational approach. Accordingly, we need to consider some of these ideas about power in a little more detail before looking at some more concrete examples.

The 'classical' view of power, both in academic and lay views, is that of power as something which a person or group of persons possesses which enables them to get their way. This is a 'zero sum' view, in which the fact of possession means that others are without. The theme which runs throughout Zuboff's account is that of the structuring of organizations along traditional hierarchical lines with a 'command and control' style of operation. Emerging out of the mass production systems of the inter-war years, these are organizations in which power takes two forms, authoritative and allocational. The exercise of authoritative power depends on the legitimacy accorded to a particular position. Such a concept of power lay at the heart over struggles with trade unions over 'the right to manage' (Edwards 1980). This was often a view which saw conflict in very stark terms and also depended on attitudes to authority held in society more generally.

With the development of both more complex organizations and of changing attitudes towards authority more generally, such conceptions of power in the workplace came under challenge. At their heart often lay conceptions about the level of knowledge held by shopfloor workers, workers who under the conditions of Taylorism and Fordism were required to do as they were told rather than act on their own initiative. However, this use of 'direct control' was always a feature of particular contexts, as it underplayed the degree of implicit knowledge which workers brought to their jobs. Given the shifts in the changing nature of work, which was to seek to draw more on this knowledge, and given changing attitudes to authority, many organizations shifted to a position of 'responsible autonomy'. This move was the forerunner of terms like 'empowerment', which sought to give more control, although still within clear lines determined from above, over the completion of tasks.

The focus of this line of research has been in particular on the interface between managers and shopfloor workers. However, in other parts of the organization, control of the allocation of resources is another important form of power. This is one which remains significant even as innovations in running organizations such as 'management by objectives' were introduced. Under such schemes the detail of how managers were to achieve particular targets was left to them, but control was exercised through mechanisms such as budgetary systems. Of course such systems are above all about information and they have been developed in the direction of increasing detail in incarnations such as the 'balanced scorecard' and 'performance management' that we examined in Chapter 4. ICT is often at the heart of such systems, enabling senior managers to get direct access to operational data. We have, however, already noted some limitations to this approach and we will look at these in more detail when we consider the use of information for monitoring managerial performance.

These restrictions on 'classical' forms of power as a resource are compounded by other forms of resource which can also form the basis of power. As Giddens (1990) notes, a key feature of modernity is our dependence on 'expert systems' in a variety of forms (not in this context any form of artificial intelligence, but the combination of human practice, skills and knowledge). We have seen the shift towards the embedding of knowledge into products and services, making many organizations dependent on the experts who they employ to produce it. Such experts are often an increasing part of an organization's workforce and they possess particular forms of power (Scarbrough 1996). One is the ability to move easily as their skills are in demand. Many experts also often have a primary loyalty to external organizations, such as the professional bodies that accredit their knowledge and demand that they keep it up to date. Their membership of such bodies gives them a resource to draw upon to resist organizational pressures. They may, for example, be committed to a code of ethics which they can present as a reason for not carrying out activities. This makes such experts particularly difficult to manage, especially when they are in possession of an esoteric body of knowledge which they are able to use as a shield to cover their activities. This is possibly most clearly illustrated in financial services organizations, where increasingly complex products such as derivatives are based on complex mathematical models which are only understood by a select group (Mackenzie 2003). This lack of understanding was a contributory cause of the collapse of Barings Bank in the wake of the fraudulent activities of the 'rogue trader', Nick Leeson (Greener 2006). However, in this case it could be argued that it was not so much the possession of expertise as the use of information to conceal activities which was the key resource.

Accordingly, we can also view information as a key resource in battles for organizational position. We can distinguish here between use and possession of information. Some positions are based on expertise in the use of particular forms of information. However, many more, and particularly managerial positions, are based on the possession of the information. One of Zuboff's paper mill workers observed that:

Managers need to believe that hourly people are dumb. They come out of school and have to show that they are smarter than the people who have been working here for so long. They can't share information with us, because only by holding onto knowledge that we don't have can they maintain their superiority and their ability to order us around.

(Zuboff 1988: 264)

Many managers thus occupy positions as 'gatekeepers', in which their position gives them control over access rights to information (Pettigrew 1972). As we saw in our discussions of information policy, a key issue is that of access to information. The default position in many organizations of needing to prove a 'need to know' before getting access to information reinforces the power of such gatekeepers. In many organizations this position is challenged by the widespread access to data provided by applications such as databases and ERP systems. As Walker and Zinsli (1993: 41) observe of a database implemented in Coors Shenandoah brewery: 'the system helps to minimize the bureaucracy that usually develops to accumulate and protect information based on functional interests.' However, we have also noted that such efforts often stumble at the hurdle of data ownership. It has often been traditional to lodge, frequently by default, ownership of data at the point of creation. This reinforces the need for policy statements which make it clear that such ownership resides in the broader organization. However, such considerations do reinforce the importance of control over access to information as a central part of power in organizations.

As we have seen, aspects of data, information and knowledge lie at the heart of the use of power in organizations. They are not only shaped by that power but also contribute to its maintenance. However, this focus on power as the possession of resources has been challenged by a number of accounts, most powerfully by Foucault. Rather than seeing power as something to be possessed, Foucault sees it as fundamental to human existence and implicated in every activity. It is thus a relational activity whose impact cannot be escaped. Foucault (1991) used examples drawn from the history of institutions such as prisons and asylums to develop his argument, examples drawn upon most notably in the image of the Panopticon.

This image is extensively used in discussions about information and surveillance. For example, it forms a central part of Zuboff's discussion. However, for Foucault what is important is the self-discipline which such systems induce in inmates. Rather than having to use coercion, power is much more effective if it is exercised by people from within. Whether this is a matter

DEVELOPING THE PANOPTICON

British prison reformers in the early nineteenth century, most notably the Utilitarian philosopher Jeremy Bentham (who sought to provide the greatest happiness for the greatest number – hence the focus on utility), wanted to change the basis of prison discipline. A key part of their suggestions was the design of the physical space. They came up with a 'hub and spoke' design in which long straight wings radiated off a central hub. Prisoners would be visible from the observation points provided in the central hub at all times but would not know when they were being watched. This design was dubbed the Panopticon, for the all seeing vision this afforded.

Source: Zuboff 1988

of belief or a matter of the knowledge that one can be observed is of little importance; what is important is the effect. But Foucault goes further than this, generalizing from the examples of prisons and asylums to a general picture of power in modernity which involves regimes of knowledge/power. Central to these are the notion of 'discourse' (Foucault 1972). Discourse does not refer here to simple linguistic forms, but to the rules, often embedded in language and taken for granted, which determine what can be said and thought. These are not something which is actively chosen by knowing subjects, but rather something which *constitutes* those subjects. We are all, on this account, born into discourses which determine what we think and do. We may have the illusion of free choice, but this is an illusion as there is no escape from the totalizing power of the discourse.

It can be seen immediately that this is a very powerful account of power and one with knowledge at its heart. Its merit is in seeing power as something which is central to social life. This can also mean that power is not simply coercion, but is central to getting things done. Power can be, on this account, an enabling force and one which is relational in character. It is not something which is simply possessed by a group of people as they too are constituted by the discourse. However, it has, not surprisingly, its critics. Giddens (1984), while welcoming the broader view of power, argues that there are problems in generalizing from total institutions such as prisons and asylums. The problem is that as far as possible the 'outside' is excluded from such settings, but it cannot help obtruding into other forms of organization. This gives different resources on which to draw and the possibility of escape from the totalizing gaze. A key argument about Foucault's ideas has been over the possibility of resistance. The formulation of discourse as so all enveloping seems to rule out the possibility of resistance and yet, as we will see, this is an ever present possibility. The focus on the self-discipline that Foucault draws attention to is an important one, but does not allow for the possibility of change and competing discourses. The problem is that discourse seems to come from a space outside of social relations. If we relax these assumptions then the important points about forms of classification as means of power become significant.

This control over what it is that can be known is part of an alternative perspective, that provided by Steven Lukes (1974). For Lukes, there are three dimensions to power. Two of these dimensions relate to those which can be seen, whether in decision making or in agenda setting. That is, the clearest form of power is that which is exercised directly, as in commands to do or not do something. However, such forms of direct control are often not as effective as mechanisms such as being able to control how decisions are taken, by setting agendas or limiting discussion. The most powerful dimension, however, is that which operates, as it were, behind the scenes and simply rules out certain options as available for selection. This form of power is most effective because it operates through taken for granted practices. The sociologist Basil Bernstein attempted to develop this further in the context of education through his notions of classification and framing (Bernstein 1990). Classifications are the rules by which items are given definitions and so allocated places and priorities. He suggested that classifications are linked to power in that they rule in certain procedures and rule out others. If certain items never appear as a priority, then they were never seen a matter for debate. In turn, if the same social group who controlled the rules of classification also retained control over how those rules were transmitted in education, he argued, this would give to some rules of recognition that helped them understand the logic of the situation they were involved in and so produce an appropriate performance. As well as developing rules of classification, he suggested, societies also developed processes of framing, which were to do with the ways in which, through the education process, people came to the ability to produce a competent performance. Thus we need both rules of recognition, which govern what is appropriate in a situation, and rules of realization, which govern the performance we will produce. Those in the strongest position, therefore, were those who could both see the needs of the context and produce the appropriate performance. (For an application of these ideas in the context of management education, see Mutch 2002.) This accounts for those situations where more is required than formal knowledge. Gee notes that:

> Autodidacts [that is, the self taught] are precisely people who, while often extremely knowledgeable, trained themselves and thus were trained outside of a process of group practice and socialization. They are almost never accepted as insiders, as members of the club (profession, group).
>
> (Gee 1996: 140)

We might note here connections with the communities of practice literature, with its emphasis that learning is a matter of developing a particular identity, of learning how one acts as a member of a community. While this is presented in that literature as an inclusive practice, particular forms of identity are a form of power which rule some out. Our discussion, therefore, suggests that an important dimension of power as it relates to knowledge is to do with how what counts as knowledge is decided. Having raised some questions about power in more abstract terms, we can now look at some concrete examples, starting with the use of information for surveillance.

INFORMATION AND SURVEILLANCE: CALL CENTRES

The call centre, a workplace dependent on the use of the telephone to conduct business, has rapidly become a key part of contemporary organizations. A call centre uses a combination of telephony and ICT, reliant on the way in which digitalization has caused both forms of technology to converge, to route calls to the appropriate person. Call centres can take a variety of forms and deal with a range of tasks, and be more or less scripted in their approach to those tasks, but at their heart lies the potential to use data acquired during the course of work to monitor and control that work. Thus the systems employed can record and report how many calls are waiting, how fast they are answered and how long they take to deal with. This data can then be displayed in real time and used as a mechanism for monitoring and disciplining the workforce. Not only is the individual agent aware that they can be monitored at any time, but they also do not know when this might happen. They are therefore subject to the discipline of an electronic panopticon. Such disciplines can also be applied to other forms of ICT-enabled work, such as those which use workflow management systems. Here the status of any particular job can be ascertained and the amount of work at hand can be ascertained. Such data can be used to monitor performance. Other employees can be monitored on the number of keystrokes for data input clerks or the volume of goods processed for supermarket checkout operators. However, it is call centres which have caught the imagination, not least of academics, who have generated a considerable debate over the extent and effectiveness of monitoring and of

EXAMPLES OF MONITORING IN CALL CENTRES

Case M
Strike rate (40% calls converted to loans)
Wrap time (clerical work on transactions – 4% permitted)
Idle time (10% permitted)

Case T
90% calls answered within 10 seconds
Average call four minutes
Quality of interaction against 18 criteria: e.g. opening and closing, pace, pitch, emphasis, rapport

Case E
13–14 calls per hour, calls 250–270 seconds
Quality of calls against 25 criteria: e.g. welcome, find out, interpersonal skills and understanding, solution, rapport, closing the call and overall summary

Source: Bain *et al.*, 2002

the possibility of resistance. Some examples of the range and nature of ways in which workers in call centres can be monitored by targets are given by Bain *et al.* (2002), who point out that increasing efforts are being made to introduce targets in more qualitative areas.

The argument that call centres represent the perfection of an electronic panopticon was made by Fernie and Metcalf in 1998. 'In call centres,' they write, 'the agents are constantly visible and the supervisor's power has indeed been "rendered perfect" – via the computer monitoring screen – and therefore its "actual use unnecessary"' (Fernie and Metcalf 1998: 9). This argument has been subjected to scathing critique by Taylor and Bain (2000) on the grounds of both its evidence and its conceptualization of the notion of the panopticon. They suggest that while agents are indeed monitored in considerable detail, ethnographic work suggests that spaces for resistance still exist. As well as drawing attention to traditional forms of resistance such as trade unions they also point to other forms such as humour as means of resistance (Taylor and Bain 2003). In particular, they point to the difficulties which organizations face in monitoring the sheer range of data available to them. Of course, one argument is that the organization does not have to do this if they can rely on the public use of targets and the internalization of work discipline to do it for them. However, Taylor and Bain suggest that knowledgeable agents could find ways round this. Of importance here is the variety in the type and nature of call centres. A key problem for management is reconciling quantity and quality. That is, a focus on meeting quantifiable targets such as duration of call could damage the more qualitative aspects of the encounter. While many call centres attempt to develop targets for the quality of calls these are much harder to achieve and the temptation is always to revert to the quantitative measures (Bain *et al.*, 2002). This draws our attention to the influence of different product markets and sectors in influencing the type of information used and its amenability to surveillance, something which we can also see in the case of the monitoring of managers.

SURVEILLANCE THROUGH THE 'INFORMATION GRID'

We have noted at a number of points the increasing use of ICT to construct performance data. As we saw in Chapter 7, Barbara Garson (1988) refers to this as an 'information grid' in which so many measurements are taken and monitored through information systems that the manager has little room to manoeuvre. She notes in particular the examples of fast food restaurants, where managerial performance is measured in so many ways that mangers have very little discretion in what they do. We also saw that in the US company, Mrs Fields Cookies, ICT-enabled systems saw rules which in other companies might be enforced by local managers being built into software. Such software enabled the detailed monitoring of operations, as well as the supply of instructions on operations to branch managers (Haeckel and Nolan 1993). The case of Mrs Fields Cookies shows us what is technically possible. However, it also indicates that even in simple product markets, where a limited range of fairly straightforward products are being sold, such detailed information control meets with problems. Haeckel and Nolan note in particular that when Mrs Fields Cookies moved outside the boundaries of the USA they found some difficulty in applying their operational model. The model was based on assumptions about the way in which managers would respond which was based on conditions in the USA which did not apply elsewhere.

This is still more the case with more complex problems requiring a highly skilled managerial and professional workforce. So we have already seen that Executive Information Systems allow in theory senior managers to monitor the progress of managers in great detail based on direct access to operational data. The British industrialist John Harvey-Jones was an enthusiastic exponent of such systems in his time as chief executive of the chemicals company ICI. However, his clear warning was that senior managers should not use the power that such information gave them to intervene. 'The ability to see a continuously updated view of the battlefield,' he argued, 'makes it extraordinarily difficult to let people alone so that they can get on with the job in hand' (Harvey-Jones 1993: 107). The problem was, he continued, that such intervention (as we have seen in the Unilever case) would mean that managers would stop taking risks. In doing so, they would cease to learn how to function autonomously and so a source of new ideas would disappear. We have noted McKinlay's findings that attempts to build a new knowledge/power regime based on knowledge management foundered in the global pharmaceutical company he examined. As well as the lack of sanctions over failure to update the various systems, McKinlay argues that such control ultimately founders on the need to have a creative and thoughtful workforce: 'The cost of developing more searching forms of surveillance for KM would be to endanger the very reflexivity it sought to increase' (McKinlay 2002: 86).

However, despite these restrictions, we should note that in a Foucauldian sense what is important is the impact that the existence of such systems has on the willingness of participants to accept the parameters that they set. In a world of performance league tables, if managers come to adhere to the targets set as a matter of internal discipline – if they come to accept the logic of such systems as natural – then the information grid will have succeeded in imposing its dimensions on action. We have noted the resources of resistance which shopfloor workers may possess. Managers and professionals may have their expert power with which to carve out space for themselves. Paradoxically, those most affected by the performance regime might be those senior executives who impose it in the hope of monitoring their subordinates. Keith Negus (1999) notes the pressure on senior managers in the recording industry who are now faced with regular monitoring of sales and market share and are expected to explain changes. In an industry characterized by considerable uncertainty and subjects to the vagaries of fashion, this simply increases levels of anxiety.

MANAGERS, AGENCY AND INFORMATION

There is, however, a danger in our casting information as simply something used by senior managers to seek control. A number of writers have suggested that we need to be reminded that managers are also employees and that this can have an impact on their actions as they struggle to retain their positions (Willmott 1998; Currie and Kerrin 2004). However, an approach based on a simple opposition between capital and labour can only take us so far, as it fails to take account of the contradictory position of managers. This is not only that they are responsible themselves for often managing the efforts of others, but also that they need to preserve their own positions as against other managers. You may recall the ideas of Peter Armstrong (1986) about managers as agents which we reviewed in Chapter 2. Briefly, his argument is that with the increasing divorce between ownership and control (that is, as owners no longer directly manage operations themselves, but entrust them to salaried managers) then managers compete to be seen as the most trustworthy agents.

His historical examples are those of the struggles between engineers and accountants at the beginning of the twentieth century, but we can see the emergence of other groups, notably marketing, with claims to best represent the interests of the ultimate owners (Fligstein 1990). In such struggles, the classification of information becomes important. If a group can impose its definition of the key terms such as what constitutes a 'customer' on the organization, then it also imposes its values as well. The concerns with data definitions that we observed in an earlier chapter are thus not just a 'technical' matter but ones with material consequences. This is taken further with the increasing power of ICT to gather more and more data. Thus Negus argues that in the recording industry customer knowledge:

> informs intra-departmental rivalry to the extent that knowledge of what consumers are doing – and legitimating that knowledge through 'hard' information and verifiable data rather than 'hunches' or 'intuition' – is deployed in struggles for influence and position within the organization.
>
> (Negus 1999: 59)

Such considerations lie behind the shift in many marketing departments from an attitude based on intuition to one seeking more data, explaining why many data warehousing initiatives have sponsorship from marketing. However, such attempts run up against not just the barriers of capability and training that we examined in the last chapter but also against what we could term an 'occupational culture'. That is, there is a set of taken for granted ideas which inform approaches to knowledge which are often resistant to the idea that this can be based on detailed data analysis. This might mean that recruits into the occupation lack the aptitude and skills for such analysis on entry and that their subsequent socialization into the 'community of practice' fails to emphasize it. This means that we need to consider questions about the nature of culture and its relationship to power in some further detail.

CULTURE AND INFORMATION

Culture is a difficult word to define and one whose meaning has undergone many shifts over time. Traditionally it was associated with artistic endeavour, especially with the production of 'high' culture such as classical music and painting. However, the dramatic growth of mass popular culture since the Second World War forced attention to the full range of imaginative endeavour, so democratizing the concept. Culture also has a broader meaning, reinforced by these shifts, of the way in which we make sense of our existence. Culture is, therefore, centrally concerned with ideas and meaning. Our human existence is something which needs constant interpretation and that interpretation is often undertaken not as an act of conscious reflection but using taken for granted standards of judgement. Culture is therefore concerned with how these taken for granted meanings are produced and reproduced and how they differ across particular groups. Watson defines it for organizations as:

> The set of meanings and values shared by members of an organisation that defines the appropriate ways for people to think and behave with regard to the organisation.
>
> (Watson 2003: 83)

This sense of culture has been applied to explanations of how organizations work since, in particular, the startling success of the book *In Search of Excellence* by Tom Peters and Robert Waterman (1982). This is not the place to review the many criticisms which have been made of this book and the nature of its evidence, but the impact was to make organizational culture a widespread term of explanation, not only in academic circles but also (and probably more importantly) in organizational ones as well.

It is clear that from our earlier discussions of the ways in which data and information are profoundly shaped by systems of knowing in organizations that culture has a central relation to our concerns. We can consider this at a number of levels. We have noted in the previous section that some would argue for a sense of occupational culture. Our discussion of the notion of communities of practice in Chapter 7 indicates that knowing can be as much a matter of identity and of becoming to be a member of a particular grouping over time as of formal knowledge. This suggests a reason for the persistence of functional identity in the face of movements like Business Process Re-engineering. The concept of culture has been most developed at the level of organizations and here we can consider the extent to which it overlaps with conceptions of power. An important dimension which has gained in significance as globalization brings questions of national difference within organizational boundaries is that of national culture. At all of these levels, which we will consider in more detail in turn, runs the problem of what Archer (1996) terms the 'myth of cultural integration'. This is that culture, as a taken for granted set of meanings, is by nature a homogeneous category, one which reconciles many of the conflicts we have already observed. In exploring aspects of information and culture we will need to be particularly focused on the extent to which culture is in fact composed of competing sets of ideas. We will also want to see it in relation to practice, for discussions are often conducted at an abstract level which makes culture into a semi-mystical quantity. A focus on the links with both power and practice will mean that we raise some concerns about the usefulness of some approaches to culture which we can explore in more detail in the following chapter.

ORGANIZATIONAL CULTURES OF KNOWING

Clear occupational identities can be one reason why organizations struggle to develop a common approach to ways of knowing. We saw earlier the work of Sackmann (1991), which suggests considerable differences in ways of knowing within an organization which she attributed to strong occupational cultures. In particular, the type of knowing found in corporate mission statements seemed particularly ineffective, with use restricted in practice to those who created them. This does not mean, however, that there have not been concerted efforts to engineer loyalty to such missions. Catherine Casey (1995), for example, outlines in considerable detail the attempts of one organization to win over the 'hearts and minds' of employees. The problem here, of course, is that such efforts assume that a 'culture' is something that an organization *has*, rather than something that it *is*. That is, we have seen in communities of practice how assumptions are built into practices which are then taken for granted. This suggests, as Patriotta (2003) argues, that we need to examine more closely how forms of knowing are institutionalized into practices.

He suggests, in an account which we will explore in more detail in the next chapter, that a crucial part of how ways of knowing become taken for granted in organizations is the way in which they are 'black boxed' into artefacts such as blueprints and reports. The form of these has been determined by particular ways of knowing but it then becomes available as a 'natural' way of guiding the knowing of others. This then often becomes taken as 'culture' and is described in rather general and abstract terms. It is only, argues Negus (1992), by taking specific examples and working them through that we can get beyond such generalizations. In looking at how recording artists are selected for development, for example, Artist and Repertoire (A&R) staff might start with generalizations like 'gut instinct' or 'intuition', but closer probing indicates a clear set of criteria. In his example, these criteria were press attention, a focused set of songs, live performance ability and personality in the voice. Such 'working theory, or practical knowledge, of recording industry staff is most clearly articulated in discussions about specific examples, rather than in generalisations' (Negus 1992: 51). The danger of such generalizations is that they produce assumptions about shared meanings which reside at the level of individual cognitions, rather than emerging from shared practices. It is not necessary for everybody in the organization to share the same sets of ideas or beliefs for them to produce common output. The achievement is the result of the articulation of shared practices which contain assumptions about the world which direct activity.

Once again, the concern is with the integrating force of ideas, with culture seen as a unifying factor. This can tend to blur the connections with power. For example, Andrew Brown and Ken Starkey (1994) consider the case of a manufacturer of sugar confectionary. 'Candy's' 'strategic focus' as the authors term it (what we might express as their 'dominant logic') was as a focused operator producing a very narrow range of products with a lack of willingness to move outside this group of products, let alone outside this sector of the industry. It was not, they argue, an 'information conscious' business. They employed no information professionals and the circulation of material was poor. This created, they argued, a culture which favoured ad-hoc communication because of a stress on informality and interpersonal contact. However, there were also examples of the manipulation of information in order to preserve position:

> The deliberate construction of reports by subsidiaries so as to fail deliberately to reveal a clear picture of their activities had a detectable cultural basis. Such actions reflected a lack of confidence on the part of subsidiaries (especially subsidiary 1) in the holdings board's intentions. This low level of confidence had its origins in the restructuring of the company which had effectively disempowered subsidiary 1.
>
> (Brown and Starkey 1994: 821)

However, it is here where we run up against the limitation of cultural explanations. This seems to be more a question of the use of information as a resource in a power struggle. We might also want to relate the overall finding of the authors to the positioning of the company against the assumptions that Daft and Weick (1984) suggest shape interpretation systems. Their conclusion is that:

> If one had to single out one particular aspect of Candy's culture as particularly powerful, one might concentrate upon its tendency to introspection, indicated, for example, by the company's concern with its own internally produced detailed reports on its own plans and performance rather than data concerning the industry and the market. Products therefore tended to be manufactured without regard for the existing and likely future state of the market. The company had very little sense of, or concern for, as a cultural trait, sources of information outside the organization.
>
> (Brown and Starkey 1994: 824)

This seems to have much in common with those organizations that Daft and Weick characterized as engaging in 'conditioned viewing' in which there is passive reliance on largely internal sources of information. The trouble about viewing this as a 'cultural trait' is that this gives us little sense of where such traits come from. As well as examining questions of power and practice as potential sources, we might also turn our attention to the broader environment in which organizations operate and it is here that considerations of national culture come into play.

NATIONAL CULTURES OF INFORMATION

If outlining the nature and place of organizational culture is contentious and difficult, this is even more the case for national cultures. Not only do we run the risk of falling into convenient stereotypes, but we encounter the myth of cultural integration at source, for the use of the term culture in anthropology tended to assume a homogenous entity. If such a usage has been challenged for the rather small scale and isolated groups which were the focus of much early anthropology, how much more is it the case for much larger societies with the divisions of labour consequent on industrial development? You may be aware of the work of Geert Hofstede who has explored what he terms the 'collective programming of the mind' (Hofstede 2001). Based on a large data set covering IBM employees in over 70 countries he suggested that he could identify four cultural dimensions: individualism; masculinity; power distance; and uncertainty avoidance. (A subsequent fifth dimension – long term orientation – was later added.) This approach has been heavily criticized on a number of grounds, including the representativeness of the respondents (McSweeney 2002). In particular, there is concern that the approach assumes homogeneity on the basis of a particular set of people when we are aware that there can be bitter debates within countries about some of the dimensions covered. So we need to be cautious in approaching this subject, lest we confuse particular groups and their views, often the dominant ones in a particular society, for the whole. However, there does seem to be some evidence that points to the importance of very different taken for granted approaches in different regions of the world. The box below gives one example.

The primary reason why the project failed, argues Walsham (2001) (drawing on work done with Sahay), was that the concept of using a map to represent spatial data was not a taken for granted one in India. Rather, place had different and more personal and spiritual connotations. Place was, therefore, conceptualized in terms of personal rather than collective correlates. In addition, the high social distance fostered by the caste system led to a situation where those mapping and developing the system felt no responsibility for implementation. The system was simply delivered to those in the field with little or no explanation about how it might be used. The combination of these two cultural factors meant that the system was not used.

Walsham points to the way in which a large number of systems are developed in countries, particularly the USA, where taken for granted assumptions about some fundamental aspects of existence are written into them. For example, systems like Lotus Notes assume a culture of individualism in which knowledge is the possession of an individual rather than a group and so amenable to 'sharing' in a person to person fashion. One can extend this to suggest that many such systems, especially those based around the extensive use of data for monitoring and control also share assumptions about what motivates better performance. These assumptions are to do with an individualist approach and one which moreover places considerable emphasis on those elements which can be measured.

Some have argued that the USA came to develop a 'culture of organization' emerging out of the Protestantism of the early settlers (Hall 1984). In particular, the emphasis on detailed record keeping and accountability that characterized denominations such as Presbyterianism provided a powerful steer to subsequent practices. In generalizing this across a country with many immigrants and few founding myths, the emphasis came to be on establishing sets of

SPATIAL ASSUMPTIONS: GIS IN INDIA

The World Bank instituted a development project to apply a Geographical Information System (GIS) to the utilization of waste lands in India. The assumption was that before moving to plans to use wastelands for agricultural purposes it was necessary to know their extent and distribution. GIS are systems which are used to plot spatial data, enabling data sets cross-referenced by similar locational data to be combined. They are much used in store and outlet location planning by retail and leisure services operators, as they enable them to combine demographic data with transport details so enabling them to locate the best location to serve a particular target audience. However, the project was a failure in India, with no working systems in operation at the end of the five year project.

Source: Walsham 2001

rules according to which data can be produced. In addition to the prestige which adhered to science because of its material benefits, it could be seen that forms of investigation which produced data according to clearly defined techniques were held to be superior. Thus the focus in many US corporations on intensive data analysis is mirrored by the investigation of the same corporations by researchers dependent on sophisticated statistical techniques which place their emphasis on the quality of the technique rather than the data. The difference between this and other approaches can be seen in the rules-based approach to financial data which is employed by US regulatory authorities and which runs counter to the principles-based approach favoured by international standards. This approach to data runs deep in US approaches; it was part of the widely discredited application of business methods involving detailed quantification to the conduct of the Vietnam war (Garson 1988).

It does seem possible, therefore, to derive ways in which systems of knowing in organizations are shaped by taken for granted assumptions at national level, assumptions which are often written into software or codified in regulations. However, it can sometimes be difficult to determine just which of these factors come into play and perhaps because of this the concept of culture is stretched too far. Walsham (2001), for example, gives the example of a production control system, COPICS, which was unsuccessful in an Egyptian car plant. He attributes this failure to the assumptions that lay behind the system, in particular those to do with the role of the supervisor. The system was developed around the assumption of granting a considerable degree of autonomy to the workforce, an assumption which was not shared by the Egyptian supervisors who wished to maintain decision making authority for themselves. This could be seen to relate to wider attitudes towards power and authority in society. However, Walsham also points to other factors, such as a shortage of materials (many of which had to be imported), fluctuations in lead times (where the system assumed consistency) and government imposed changes, which seem to escape the bounds of what we would normally term 'culture'. They suggest that a focus on culture needs to be complemented by attention to what we would traditionally term 'political economy'. Ways in which we might achieve this are considered in the next chapter.

CONCLUSION

To conclude this chapter, let me suggest a way in which we can recognize the place of culture and its relation to broader features of national development without resorting to ideas about national unity and with due sensitivity to those issues of power and political economy which we have touched upon. In outlining the features of the business organization in the UK, Richard Whitley (2000: 55) points to the influence of a 'pervasive and long-established cultural norm of individualism'. He draws upon historical work to make this point, but this is work about *English* developments. While for many outside the country the equation of Britain with England is commonplace and unproblematic, this is to ignore the contributions of the other constituent parts – Scotland, Wales and Northern Ireland. If we take a comparative historical approach to the formation of individualism (Mutch 2006), we can see that there is a clash between the individual practices fostered by the organizational practices associated with the dominant religious practice in England, that of Anglicanism, and more collective practices fostered by the Presbyterianism of Scotland.

In this way a culture of individualism is not a monolithic whole but rather the unstable and shifting product of the clash between and reconciliation of different sets of ideas. These ideas are often not just developed as sets of abstract ideas but are contained in taken for granted practices which, in this case, then go on to influence ideas about appropriate forms of managing. In turn, then, we may get different perspectives on the use of information. In the case of the UK, a Scottish practice of detailed record keeping and accountability based ultimately on particular forms of religious belief can be contrasted with a more relational approach in England. Thus we can identify distinctive cultural patterns, but only by the detailed examination of their emergence over time. The approach adopted in this form of analysis is an 'institutional' one in which the focus is on taken for granted practices over time. We have caught glimpses of such an approach throughout this chapter; in the following chapter we take this approach a little further to look at ways in which we can broaden the analysis to take full account of the factors impinging on organizations and their ways of knowing.

SUMMARY

- Information, broadly defined, is central to power in organizations, but the source of that power might be as much to do with the rules about what constitutes information as about information as a resource.

- Information generated by ICT-enabled systems can and is widely used for purposes of monitoring and control. In non-managerial occupations this is likely to be by the direct setting and monitoring of targets, whereas in managerial positions this is likely to be exercised more indirectly through performance measurement systems. However, such monitoring conflicts with demands for reflexivity and creativity that are seen to be key elements of advantage in a knowledge economy.

- The rules about what counts as information are also carried in cultural norms at occupational, organizational and national levels. These norms are often carried in the taken for granted practices and artefacts which shape the use of information.

- While culture is an important consideration, it is important to recognize it as one factor in the complex system that the organization represents and in which it is embedded.

REVIEW QUESTIONS

1 In the context of the earlier discussion about 'dominant logic' does culture need to be shared in organizations?

2 What do you understand by the institutionalization of meaning in practices and artefacts?

DISCUSSION QUESTION

1 In the British Gas example given in Chapter 7 one of the arguments advanced for the system of engineers booking in and out of jobs via laptops was that it 'provides much more management visibility of the engineers'. What are the dangers of such visibility for both engineers and their managers?

REFERENCES

Archer, M. (1996) *Culture and Agency: The Place of Culture in Social Theory*. Cambridge, Cambridge University Press.

Armstrong, P. (1986) 'Management Control Strategies and Inter-Professional Competition: The Cases of Accountancy and Personnel Management', in D. Knights and H. Willmott (eds) *Managing the Labour Process*. Aldershot, Gower: 19–43.

Bain, P., Watson, A., Mulvey, G., Taylor P. and Gall G. (2002) 'Taylorism, Targets and the Quantity-Quality Dichotomy in Call Centres', *New Technology, Work and Employment*, 17(3): 154–169.

Bernstein, B. (1990) *The Structuring of Pedagogic Discourse Volume 4: Class, Codes and Control*. London, Routledge.

Brown, A. D. and Starkey, K. (1994) 'The Effect of Organizational Culture on Communication and Information', *Journal of Management Studies*, 31(6): 807–828.

Casey, C. (1995) *Work, Self And Society: After Industrialism*. London, Routledge.

Choo, C. W. (1998) *The Knowing Organization: How Organizations Use Information to Construct Meaning, Create Knowledge and Make Decisions*. New York, Oxford University Press.

Ciborra, C. and Patriotta, G. (1996) 'Groupware and Teamwork in New Product Development: The Case of a Consumer Goods Multinational', in C. Ciborra (ed.) *Groupware and Teamwork: Invisible Aid or Technical Hindrance?*, Chichester, Wiley: 122–143.

Currie, G. and Kerrin, M. (2004) 'The Limits of a Technological Fix to Knowledge Management: Epistemological, Political and Cultural Issues in the Case of Intranet Implementation', *Management Learning*, 35(1): 9–29.

Daft, R. L. and Weick, K. E. (1984) 'Toward a Model of Organizations as Interpretation Systems', *Academy of Management Review*, 9(2): 284–295.

Davenport, T. with Prusak, L. (1997) *Information Ecology: Mastering the Information and Knowledge Environment*. New York, Oxford University Press.

Edwards, R. (1980) *Contested Terrain: The Transformation of the Workplace in the Twentieth Century*. London, Heinemann.

Fernie, S. and Metcalf, D. (1998) *(Not) Hanging on the Telephone: Payment Systems in the New Sweatshops*. London, Centre for Economic Performance.

Fligstein, N. (1990) *The Transformation of Corporate Control*. Cambridge, MA, Harvard University Press.

Foucault, M. (1972) *The Archaeology of Knowledge*. London, Tavistock.

Foucault, M. (1991) *Discipline and Punish: The Birth of the Prison*. London, Penguin.

Garson, B. (1988) *The Electronic Sweatshop: How Computers are Transforming the Office of the Future into the Factory of the Past*. New York, Simon and Schuster.

Gee, J. (1996) *Social Lingusitics and Literacies*. London, Taylor and Francis.

Giddens, A. (1984) *The Constitution of Society: Outline of the Theory of Structuration*. Cambridge, Polity.

Giddens, A. (1990) *The Consequences of Modernity*. Cambridge, Polity.

Greener, I. (2006) 'Nick Leeson and the Collapse of Barings Bank: Socio-Technical Networks and the 'Rogue Trader', *Organization*, 13(3): 421–441.

Haeckel, S. H. and Nolan, R. L. (1993) 'Managing by Wire', *Harvard Business Review*, 71(5): 122–132.

Hall, P. D. (1984) *The Organization of American Culture, 1700–1900: Private Institutions, Elites and the Origins of American Nationality*. New York, New York University Press.

Harvey-Jones, J. (1993) *Managing to Survive*. London, Heinemann.

Hofstede, G. (2001) *Culture's Consequences: Comparing Values, Behaviours, Institutions and Organizations Across Nations*. London, Sage.

Lukes, S. (1974) *Power: A Radical View*. London, Macmillan.

Mackenzie, D. (2003) 'Long-Term Capital Management and the Sociology of Arbitrage', *Economy and Society*, 32(3): 349–380.

McKinlay, A. (2002) 'The Limits of Knowledge Management', *New Technology, Work and Employment*, 17(2): 76–88.

McKinlay, A. and Starkey, K. (1998) *Foucault, Management and Organization Theory: From Panopticon to Technologies of Self*. London, Sage.

McSweeney, B. (2002) 'Hofstede's Model of National Cultural Differences and their Consequences: A Triumph of Faith – a Failure of Analysis', *Human Relations*, 55: 89–118.

Mutch A. (1999) 'Critical Realism, Managers and Information', *British Journal of Management*, 10: 323–333.

Mutch, A. (2002) 'Applying the Ideas of Bernstein to In-Company Education', *Management Learning*, 33(2): 181–196.

Mutch, A. (2006) 'The Institutional Shaping of Management: In the Tracks of English Individualism', *Management & Organization History*, 1(3): 251–271.

Negus, K. (1992) *Producing Pop: Culture and Conflict in the Popular Music Industry*. London, Arnold.

Negus, K. (1999) *Music Genres and Corporate Cultures: Strategy and Creativity in the Music Business*. London, Routledge.

Patriotta, G. (2003) *Organizational Knowledge in the Making: How Firms Create, Use and Institutonalize Knowledge*. Oxford, Oxford University Press.

Peters, T. and Waterman, R. (1982) *In Search of Excellence*. London, Harper and Row.

Pettigrew, A. (1972) 'Information Control as a Power Resource', *Sociology*, 6: 187–204.

Sackmann, S. (1991) *Cultural Knowledge in Organizations: Exploring the Collective Mind*. Newbury Park, CA, Sage.

Scarbrough, H. (1996) *The Management of Expertise*. Basingstoke, Macmillan.

Taylor, P. and Bain, P. (2000) 'Working in the Call Centre: Entrapped by an Electronic Panopticon?', *New Technology, Work and Employment*, 15(1): 2–18.

Taylor, P. and Bain, P. (2003) '"Subterranean Worksick Blues": Humour as Subversion in Two Call Centres', *Organization Studies*, 24(9): 1487–1509.

Walker, K. B. and Zinsli, T. (1993) 'The Coors Shenandoah Experience', *Management Accounting* (US), March: 37–41.

Walsham, G. (2001) *Making a World of Difference: IT in a Global Context*. Oxford, Oxford University Press.

Watson, T. (2003) *Sociology, Work and Industry*. London, Routledge.

Whitley, R. (2000) *Divergent Capitalisms: The Social Structuring and Change of Business Systems*. Oxford, Oxford University Press.

Willmott, H. C. (1998) 'Rethinking Management and Managerial Work: Capitalism, Control and Subjectivity', *Human Relations*, 50(11): 1329–1359.

Zuboff, S. (1988) *In the Age of the Smart Machine: The Future of Work and Power*. London, Heinemann.

Chapter 10

Institutions and information

INTRODUCTION

We have already noted in the previous chapter that explanations of why organizations view information in a particular way have to take into account more than internal factors. Those approaches termed 'institutionalist' are an influential way of explaining the relationship between the inside of organizations and the context in which they operate. Consider the following example. 'Lean manufacturing systems' (that is, systems which devolve considerable autonomy to shopfloor workers) that are successful in Germany do not work in the equivalent American manufacturing plants, even those where the technological base and the nature of the processes are similar. Freil (2005) argues that the differences are attributable to institutional factors, specifically the nature of labour laws and training systems. US labour laws encourage the use of temporary workers, whereas this is much more difficult in Germany. The consequence is that many temporary workers in the US plants are functionally illiterate, that is, unable to interpret the technical instructions on which lean processes depend. However, Freil argues that the problems are not only attributable to the nature of the workforce, but that workforce skills can be linked to broader training systems. The German focus on apprenticeships means that it was feasible to change training to emphasize problem solving and team working – just some of the skills that we observed were important in our earlier chapters. Freil concludes that:

> The nature of the countries' training systems seems to be the critical factor. If companies find it difficult to hire and retain workers with broad-based and analytical skills, lean production would prove difficult even if all other institutions were favorable.
>
> (Freil 2005: 57)

This is an example of an institutionalist approach. You will note that Freil does not invoke cultural factors to explain the differences between the two countries, although institutionalist approaches can accommodate this. However, there are differences in institutionalist approaches which include such fundamental matters as the nature of institutions themselves! Accordingly, this chapter looks at two particular approaches, the comparative business systems perspective and 'new institutionalism', with a view to seeing how they can help us understand how the context in which organizations operate can influence their views of information.

This chapter will examine:

- the comparative business systems approach, with a focus on the notion of institutional logics and how these might influence the dominant logic within an organization
- the new institutionalist approach, with an examination of how it might be applied to the adoption or otherwise of information policies
- a way of tying the two approaches together using the resources of critical realism

WHAT IS AN INSTITUTION?

The term 'institution' is one of the most frequently used but least commonly agreed upon terms in domains of inquiry spanning sociology and economics (Jary and Jary 2000). In institutional economics and in most sociological approaches the term is used for supra-organizational systems of regulation and meaning (Rowlinson 1997). While institutions might be manifest in organizational form, such as when the law is enforced through courts and police forces, they tend to be concerned with broader considerations than those of a particular organization. So Seo and Creed, for example, suggest that 'the major institutions of con-temporary Western society' might be considered as 'a capitalist market, the nuclear family, the bureaucratic state, liberal democracy, and Judeo-Christian religious traditions' (Seo and Creed 2002: 228). However, as we will see, in the tradition within which they write there is a persistent interchange of the terms institution and organization. For institutional economics this will not do. Institutions arise because they fill the gaps left by market forces. They regulate the markets which enable organizations to operate (Hall and Soskice 2001).

This sense of institutions being part of a hierarchy in which the affairs of organizations are in some degree conditioned by broader forces is also common to much sociology, although it would not share the functionalist assumptions of the use within economics. (By 'functionalist' is meant the idea that institutions emerge because they fulfil a function that is needed for markets to operate smoothly, but that markets by themselves will not supply. This might be need for trust, for example, which might be supplied by institutions like the family or religion. However, such a view either restricts the view of institutions to only those which smooth the path of commerce or fails to acknowledge that institutions like religion, although their effects might be helpful for commerce, come into being for entirely different reasons.) So, for example, Margaret Archer notes that in the case of India 'the entire matrix of . . . institutions was internally related, and interconnecting lines could be drawn between caste/religion/kinship/economy/polity/law and education' (Archer 1995: 219). She does not provide a clear definition of institution and organization in her work, but scattered references indicate that she clearly favours a distinction between the two. In *Culture and Agency*, for example, she argues that 'there is no ready fund of analytical terms for designating the components of the cultural realm corresponding to those which delineate parts of the structural domain (roles, organizations, institutions, systems, etc.)' (Archer 1996: 1). So for the purpose of this discussion I will be adhering to this usage of the term, that is, of institutions as being supra-organizational, but I need first to contrast it to a very different use in another influential body of work that we will be covering.

215

The approach known as 'new institutionalism' that we look at in more detail later has developed within organizational sociology and has a particular focus on the process of institutionalization. That is, it is concerned to explore how certain practices come to be taken for granted. We will see that this has useful lessons for us in considering the use of information, but it brings with it a problem. This is that the definition of institution expands to cover organizations and routines within them. This promiscuous intermixing of organization and institution is seen as its sharpest in Tolbert and Zucker's (1999) use of the term 'institution' for routines within organizations. Thus, for Tolbert and Zucker, the following are examples that have passed through particular stages and so have a greater chance of survival than 'those in the pre-institutionalized stage': 'team-based production, quality circles, gain-sharing compensation plans, internal consultants, sensitivity training programs for management, managers of work/family policy, and employee assistance programs' (Tolbert and Zucker 1999: 177). Why does it matter that they apply the term 'institution' to this range of phenomena? It matters because of the problem of change. That is, different social phenomena can change at different paces. Routines can be the subject of internal debate within organizations and, while some are remarkably durable, the ability to change them can be within the control of those working in the organization. By contrast, the types of institutions that Seo and Creed refer to are rather more durable. Such institutions then form the taken for granted context in which organizations and their members operate. In drawing on work from this tradition, therefore, it needs to be born in mind that it 'should be treated more as a general orientation than as a fully developed theory, because there is a significant lack of agreement among its adherents as to its precise specification' (Abercrombie, Hill and Turner 2000: 181). I will be using it not because I agree with the looser definition of an institution, but because it seems to offer some useful ways of considering the process of institutionalization.

INSTITUTIONAL SYSTEMS AND LOGICS

As we have noted, the idea that organizations do not operate in a vacuum but rather one which is conditioned by a particular complex of institutions is a widespread one. I wish to concentrate here in particular on an approach known as the comparative-business-systems perspective, in particular as summarized in the work of Richard Whitley (2000). I want to relate this to work on institutional logics which suggests the way in which institutional complexes shape the logics with which organizations operate. The comparative business systems approach seems particularly valuable because it does not share the functionalist assumptions of similar approaches developed within economics. It seeks to show that economic logics themselves, that is, what counts as economic success, are themselves socially constituted, shaped by the constellation of institutions which has developed over time. Such constellations are durable and resistant to change because they are inter-dependent. We have already noted the relationship between labour laws and training systems in the comparison of the USA and Germany. Such interlocking relationships can influence both the material and the ideational resources available for organizations to draw upon. These relationships tend to grow up within national boundaries. So Whitley argues that in the case of Britain, in an example we have already touched upon:

> The peculiarities of the prevalent business system in Britain, for example, cannot be
> adequately understood without taking into account the combined consequences of the

interconnected pre-industrial state and financial systems, their links with the development of the training 'system' and organization of labour markets, and the pervasive and long-established cultural norm of individualism.

(Whitley 2000: 55)

Whitley suggests that on the basis of a combination between the degree of coordination based on ownership and the extent of integration based on non-ownership we could identify six ideal types of business system (Table 10.1).

It will be noted that these types of system tend to map onto national boundaries because of the importance of broader institutional features in both fostering and supporting these types of system. So the development of legal systems which support ownership structures based on sophisticated financial instruments will tend to encourage compartmentalized business systems. There is therefore a 'fit' between broader institutional characteristics and business systems which, because of the importance of the state in developing and maintaining forms of regulation, often means that business systems are found in particular locations.

We can use these suggestions to explore the impact on information by looking in a little more detail at the case of Japan. We have noted that Nonaka and Takeuchi (1995) identified a particular pattern of knowledge creation in their examination of the process of innovation. This argued that, in contrast to US firms, Japanese companies saw knowledge as more embedded in practices of organizing. It was feasible, they argued, to access this tacit knowledge, but only if the right conditions are created within the organization. This example has been widely used to argue that rather than focus on the creation of complex ICT-based systems to foster knowledge sharing, systems which rely on misguided assumptions about the nature of knowledge, more attention needs to be paid to fostering the conditions for sharing knowledge.

We have seen these at a number of points in our discussion. They involve, for example, developing and encouraging communities of practice and providing the appropriate settings

Table 10.1 Characteristics of national business systems

Business system	Characteristics	Example
Fragmented	Small owner controlled in direct short term competition and relationships	Small firms in Hong Kong shifting rapidly between unconnected activities
Coordinated industrial district	Inter-connections between small firms with employee flexibility	Italian industrial districts
Compartmentalized	Large firms with dispersed ownership coordinated through markets; low commitment and collaboration	Anglo-American corporations
State organized	State guided economic development of large private companies	South Korea
Collaborative	Alliances between firms within sectors and high degree of trust of skilled workers	Continental Europe
Highly coordinated	Alliances across sectors with networks coordinating a wide range of activities	Japan

Source: Extracted from Whitley 2000

to encourage and enhance informal information sharing. However, what one notes on returning to the examples given by Nonaka and Takeuchi (1995) is the extent to which they are embedded in a particular institutional context. For example, a key recommendation is that of 'redundancy' of information. That is, while it might be seen as a useful goal to ensure that people in an organization know just what they need to know in order to perform their tasks and no more (the classic Taylorist position), Nonaka and Takeuchi argue that overlapping information is essential to knowledge sharing. This is because it gives people the background information to make sense of what might otherwise be seen as specialist knowledge.

One way of building in such redundancy 'is through a "strategic rotation" of personnel, especially between vastly different areas of technology or functions such as R&D and marketing' (Nonaka and Takeuchi 1995: 81). However, such a suggestion is dependent on a range of institutional conditions. While such rotation is a familiar Japanese practice, it depends on both the structure of business organizations (with alliances giving opportunities for such rotation) and the broader systems of secure employment and high commitment. Similarly, Nonaka and Takeuchi cite the chief executive of Canon as stating that 'I made sure that the younger people have ample opportunity to voice their opinion. For example, I have them say whatever is on their mind for 30 minutes every morning during the *chorei* [morning gathering], write it up as a memo, and distribute topics before noon' (Nonaka and Takeuchi 1995: 150). Apart from the *chorei* being a very specific form of practice which might not translate to other contexts, it again makes large assumptions about the institutional background which produces those willing to participate in such events.

Nonaka and Takeuchi (1995) relate such willingness to what we might term cultural factors, notably language and philosophy. They suggest that the ambiguity of the Japanese language, in which meaning is not conveyed through a grammatical code but through aspects of context, renders speakers particularly attuned to tacit knowledge. Further, the lack of a tradition of philosophical inquiry means that 'the Japanese have a tendency to stay in their own world of experience without appealing to any abstract or metaphysical theory in order to determine the relationship between human thought and nature' (Nonaka and Takeuchi 1995: 29). Aspects of their own recommendations, such as the following, seem to contradict this perspective:

> To create knowledge, business organizations should foster their employees' commitment by formulating an organizational intention and proposing it to them. Top or middle managers can draw organizational attention to the importance of commitment to fundamental values by addressing such fundamental questions as *"What is truth?"*, *"What is human being?"* or *"What is life?"*
>
> (Nonaka and Takeuchi 1995: 75)

More significantly, what is noticeable in their account is the way in which they abstract from some of the institutional characteristics which Whitley draws our attention to. Thus, an account of the business system which fosters such approaches to knowledge might also draw upon a tradition of state coordination of economic activity which can be traced back to the initial response to the forcible opening up of Japanese markets by the US Navy in the mid-nineteenth century (Clegg 1990). This fostered a tradition of intensive borrowing from other economies and a willingness to engage in incremental improvement (Hedlund 1994). More recently would be the wholesale reorganization of Japanese business following the Second

World War (and the attendant suppression of independent trade unionism). This created the climate for the broad business alliances and certain distinctive labour practices. It also fostered attachment to a process of customer led process improvement, with the aim of quality enhancement processes being the relentless improvement of working practices.

This institutional background lies behind the success of knowledge sharing for innovation. However, these are innovations of a particular type. While much of the focus in the literature on knowledge management in organizations has been on creating the conditions for the better exploitation of tacit knowledge (with broad acceptance of Nonaka and Takeuchi's perspective of this, despite the critique of Tsoukas (2003)), a recent account suggests that the value of the approach within which tacit knowledge is embedded can itself be questioned. Collinson and Wilson (2006) track attempts at two Japanese companies, Sumitomo Chemical and Nippon Steel, to shift direction. Both are heavily dependent on basic products and domestic markets, both of which are under pressure. However, the routines which brought success in stable markets, based on incremental and customer-led process improvement, have led, argue the authors, to a degree of inertia when faced by changing conditions.

They contrast this to the formal ties which the UK chemicals company ICI has with a range of universities which enabled it to make a successful move out of bulk chemicals and into more specialist areas. An institutionalist approach would therefore suggest that we need to look at a range of conditions in considering the context which form particular organizational ways of knowing. We might note here, for example, if we return to the US context, that these institutional factors affect not only organizational training systems. In advocating a shift to a much more data-focused strategy, Davenport (2006) acknowledges the shortages of those with the right balance of skills, especially mathematical and statistical skills, to be able to implement such strategies. The nature of the institutions of education may be a fetter on such a strategy – or they may suggest new organizational forms, such as the outsourcing of such work to economies such as India where the focus of much of the education system is on a more fact-based and didactic approach.

However, we can take this further to suggest that the appeal of data driven approaches derives in large part from the institutional logics (Friedland and Alford 1991) available to actors. That is, institutions are complemented by bodies of ideas which seek to explain their relevant domain. These ideas then become available either because they complement existing institutions or because they are drawn upon by those who wish to change those institutions. Thus, Stewart Clegg (1990) develops the notion of 'modes of rationality'. These are sets of ideas which suggest what are appropriate practices for organizations to follow. These are constructed, he argues, out of 'to-hand' materials which have been shaped by local custom and practice. Such practice may well emanate from domains other than the economic and be all the more powerful for that. Thus we have already alluded to the notion of a 'culture of organization' in the USA. We could trace this back to early practices of Protestant religion and in turn to the type of Presbyterian practices that we explored in the previous chapter. Such practices then formed taken for granted resources which shaped an approach which was deepened by the prestige accorded to scientific modes of inquiry. Developed through the focus on cognitive psychology this placed a premium on a particular style of decision making which stressed formal rationality and hard evidence over emotion, feeling and intuition. The actual practice of decision making might diverge from this idea, and that divergence might, as we have seen, contribute to considerable anxiety, but this mode of rationality became the yardstick against which

219

organizations were judged. This approach owes something to the type of institutionalist approach we have already explored, but also borrows considerably from the 'new institutionalism' in organization theory, so we take a closer look at this next.

NEW INSTITUTIONALISM

The development of what is known as the new institutionalism arose in the late 1970s as a response to what was seen as the impoverished nature of much organizational analysis. Relating to some of the trends we have already reviewed, this seemed to operate with a 'rational choice' view of individuals and organizations derived from economics. That is, agents choose courses of action based on their weighing up of the economic consequences. In so far as organizations were considered, this was as units which simply responded to economic stimuli. So arguments such as that presented by Chandler (1962), with organizational structure following strategy, were seen to be a form of market determinism which did not allow for variation in response. To this type of approach new institutionalist thought counter posed the problem of legitimacy. That is, it was argued that organizations needed not only to respond to economic imperatives, but also to do so in such a way that their actions were recognized as legitimate ones. We have noted that economic imperatives are in themselves socially constructed, although this insight was rather underplayed in the early days of the formulation of the approach. There are differences of emphasis in new institutionalism, a good overview of which is presented in Scott (2001). However, for the current discussion I wish to focus on ideas about 'isomorphism' derived from the work of DiMaggio and Powell (1991), work which represents some of the most influential from this school of thought. Isomorphism is a term in this context derived from ecology which describes the way that organisms in a similar environment come to exhibit similar features.

DiMaggio and Powell argued that there were four forms of isomorphism. They did recognize the existence of competitive pressures, although these have tended to be underplayed in subsequent accounts. So it is clear that in some circumstances organizations adopt practices because they are a matter of economic survival. Such responses are the stuff of classical economics, but new institutionalism suggests that their operation is relatively limited and likely to be moderated by broader social and cultural considerations. For these reasons, thinkers in this tradition focused more on the problem of legitimacy in looking for causes of similarity. For many organizations the easiest way to ensure legitimacy in their practices was by copying what was done elsewhere. DiMaggio and Powell termed this 'mimetic isomorphism', and it

---

FOUR TYPES OF ISOMORPHISM

- Competitive
- Mimetic
- Normative
- Coercive

Source: DiMaggio and Powell 1991

helps explain, they argued, why many organizations come to adopt the same practices. They do so because once set by an influential organization in their field, the safest approach is simply to copy. Such responses are encouraged by practices like benchmarking and by the spread of agencies such as consultancies. It is important to note that such practices are adopted because they are perceived to be legitimate, not because of their fit with organizational circumstances. We have already noted the extent to which organizations respond to fashion just in the same way that people do. The spread of knowledge management initiatives could be argued to be profoundly affected by this desire to appear to be doing what seemed to be good practice.

However, there are other reasons which might influence organizational behaviour, even if the senior managers do not wish to pursue it. One important force in contemporary society which stands to some extent outside organizations, although in a symbiotic relationship with them, is that of professional bodies. DiMaggio and Powell refer to this as 'normative iso-morphism'. While individual professionals might be marginalized within their own organizations, when they come together they can pursue an agenda which might reflect their perceptions of their own interests as an occupational group and use this to influence their status within their host organization. Thus, for example, initiatives on diversity management have tended to be developed at the level of the professional organization. These promulgate practices and write them into codes of practice which individual professionals are then bearers of when they return to their organization. The reason for adopting common practices is then not 'because everybody else is' but because 'this is the industry standard and we must not appear out of line'. Much of the attention in empirical work inspired by new institutionalism has been carried out in the public sector where such pressures are particularly strong (DiMaggio 1988).

Not only has such a focus tended to obscure competitive pressures as a source of change but it has also reduced the attention paid to the final category, 'coercive isomorphism' (Mizruchi and Fein 1991). This is where organizations are forced by a more powerful actor into choosing a course of action which they might not otherwise have chosen. This might be, for example, a particularly powerful customer who insists that suppliers all adopt the same information system. We have seen this argument in the context of supermarkets, which are able to use their control over the information which they derive from their point of sales systems to structure negotiations with their suppliers. Coercion may also operate in public sector bodies where funding is tied to the adoption of specific practices. One of these practices with a profound impact on the use of information within organizations is the insistence on performance data. The construction of league tables from such data then becomes a way of conditioning the practices an organization adopts, often under the label of 'best practice'. The problem is, of course, that what is best practice in one context often does not translate to a different context. This is an interesting set of ideas, although not without its critics. However, before considering these criticisms we will apply the concepts to something we have already touched upon, the implementation of information policies.

INFORMATION STRATEGIES IN HIGHER EDUCATION: AN INSTITUTIONALIST ANALYSIS OF THE UK EXPERIENCE

In 1994 the Joint Information Systems Committee (JISC), the body responsible for the provision of the ICT network which links higher education establishments in the UK, published some guidance on information strategies (JISC 1995). It sought to ensure that each HE organization developed such a strategy, with incentives through funding and suggested guidelines for such strategies. These clearly reflected the arguments of those, such as Orna (1990), who had been arguing for policies which took into account broader practices. For example, the guidance suggested that:

- any information that should be available for sharing (and most will be) is well defined and appropriately accessible (allowing for necessary safeguards);
- the quality of information is fit for its purpose (e.g. accuracy, currency, consistency, completeness – but only as far as necessary);
- all staff know, and exercise, their responsibilities towards information;
- there is a mechanism by which priorities are clearly identified and then acted upon.

(JISC 1995)

We can see in these themes the influence of those concerned with information literacy and the broader establishment of policies to encourage this. We could suggest that there were therefore elements of both coercive and normative isomorphism in the initial suggestions. Coercive because there was a requirement for each establishment to formulate its own strategy in line with the guidelines and normative because this reflected the agenda of those within higher education who had a concern with a broader definition of information than that which was associated with ICT. The idea of an information strategy as conceived in the guidelines was first raised in the Follett Report which reviewed the provision of libraries for the funding councils in 1993. This report had argued that 'each institution should fundamentally reassess the way it plans and provides for the information needs of those working within it, and the place of the library in meeting these needs' (Joint Funding Council 1993). The result was that the first recommendation of the report was that an information strategy should be drawn up. The tying of this recommendation to funding mechanisms in the subsequent work by JISC brought an element of coercion into the process, given the funding pressures that operated in the sector more generally – that is, many organizations would feel that they could not afford to pass up potential funding and so would feel constrained to implement the strategy. One commentary on the process argued that 'some [establishments] admitted quite candidly that their information strategies had been "made up" simply to keep the funding council quiet' (MacColl 1996).

However, such a response points to some problems with notions of isomorphism as a simple response to external pressures. One response could be that practices were adopted in a superficial form of adherence but that they had no fundamental impact on activities. Another facet was that such policy guidelines needed interpretation in the local context. Here a crucial factor was the position of those given the strategy to implement. The same commentator cited above suggested that 'Others had completed the exercise quickly, often as a trigger for the convergence of library and computing services' (McColl 1996). While the thrust behind the original proposal was one which put information firmly above information technology, it might be the person in charge of ICT who was tasked with developing the local strategy. This in turn related to the ambiguity of the terms used (Allen and Wilson 1996). We have already noted the way in which the term 'information strategy' in practice can often be translated as 'information *technology* strategy'. This degree of ambiguity gives scope for the ideas outlined in the original proposal to diverge at local level, especially if librarians locally have a marginal position in the organization. The consequence is that after an initial burst of enthusiasm there seems to be little trace of the original initiative. Of course, some of this is because of changing priorities, but in this case the type of organizational constraints that Orna and others tend not to consider seem to have been influential in preventing the adoption of information policies. What an institutionalist perspective might suggest is that ideas themselves, no matter how persuasive, will not win the day without bearers in the shape of those with sufficient organizational weight to get them implemented. In the case of HE one could argue that competitive pressures were unlikely to produce information strategies. Without organizational coalitions with sufficient interest in getting them in place, both coercive and normative pressures fell short. This might explain why it is so difficult to find information strategies elsewhere. Hazel Hall (1994), in one of the very few accounts to look at information strategies in manufacturing industry, although admittedly with a small sample, found no evidence of an information strategy in the textile companies she investigated.

LIMITATIONS OF AN INSTITUTIONALIST APPROACH

Of course, what this account suggests is that pressures towards isomorphism can be resisted. This links to a key criticism that had already been raised within the new institutionalist tradition, that it downplays the role of agency in change (DiMaggio 1988). That is, it often tends to take counts of the number of organizations adopting a particular practice as evidence of implementation. As we have seen, this ignores the ways in which practices can be translated so that outward conformance conceals local customization. It also tends to fall into the trap of viewing the organization as the unit of analysis, which ignores the way in which organizations come to adopt practices. In some cases this is as the result of struggles within the organization, with practices, such as more intensive data analysis, championed by particular groups, such as marketing. Such processes mean that while organizations might adopt what appears to be a similar outlook which conditions their ways of knowing, the content may be very different.

For example, there is evidence of a trend towards the adoption of a retailing orientation among brewing companies in the UK in the period from 1950 to 1990 (Mutch 2006). The dominant orientation, the logic according to which companies had organized their affairs, had been a production one in which companies saw themselves as brewers. If they owned public houses (bars), which most did, these were seen as distribution outlets for the products of the brewery. In such an environment knowledge about customers was relatively unimportant; what was needed above all was technical information about the production of beer. Thus in 1962 Colonel Whitbread, chairman of the family company, could declare that:

> Advertising agencies continually talk about market research. The ultimate consumer panel is the mass of the British public and I often wonder whether market research, particularly in our Industry where taste counts so much, really discovers what the people want.
>
> (Whitbread 1962: 8)

However, there were changing trends in consumption, with the growth of alternative leisure activities such as the widespread adoption of television, which caused companies to change orientation. Over a forty year period there was a shift towards a retailing orientation among the major companies which dominated the industry. By the end of the period all of them paid at least lip service to the notion that customer need, as expressed in the nature of the public house, was the most important factor and that production should take second place. However, this was not just a simple reaction to economic pressures; the process went much further and much faster in some companies rather than others. It was Whitbread which adopted practices in line with the new logic, practices which involved finding out about customer requirements, rather than some of the other companies. In part, again, this was due to economic position. Companies like Bass and Allied Breweries with strong market share in heavy industrial areas were much slower to respond than Whitbread with its heavily rural and suburban estate. However, Whitbread's more open attitude to change seemed to be conditioned by its own historical development which made it more receptive to innovation.

The consequence was that while all the major companies might appear to have retailing logics, in practice companies like Allied and Bass continued to be dominated by the production based logic of the brewery. This meant that their adoption of retailing practices was half-hearted and characterized by a rigid approach which made them less successful (Preece, Steven and Steven 1999). If we look inside the organizations, there was a conflict about the right way to approach the market which was dominated in some companies by established positions which proved hard to shake. The suggestions of DiMaggio and Powell about pressures towards iso-morphism are important ones, but only if we allow that they are subject to interpretation by competing groups in organizations.

This, then, gives us some insight into the process for the formation of dominant logics. This form of logic then feeds into the routines which condition day to day operations. It is the stress on the taken for granted nature of these routines which is such an important part of the new institutionalist project. If we reject the labelling of such routines as institutions (because of the confusion with the definition which we gave earlier and the problems which such confusion gives us when looking at process of change) then what we can focus on is the process of institutionalization, that is, how particular ways of knowing come to be embedded in taken for granted routines.

This is the focus which Patriotta (2003) adopts in looking at ways of knowing in Italian car manufacturing plants. He shows how practices adopted in the creation of a new plant carry forward into the subsequent routines. This accords with a further insight of institutionalist thought, that organizational practices often carry the mark of their inception (Stinchcombe 1965). At the beginning of operations a range of approaches is feasible, but gradually some come to be dominant and taken for granted. Once in place, as in our brewing example, these become hard to shake off.

Knowing is thus solidified into particular practices and artefacts. Patriotta (2003: 175) argues that 'sense making in organizations relies on the presence of black boxes which can be seen as embodiments of organizational knowledge and constitute a pre-condition for the utilization of that knowledge'. These 'black boxes', which we have explored in the context of 'boundary objects' in Chapter 7, range from artefacts, such as computers, to reports and blueprints. Patriotta suggests that it is only by examining situations of breakdown that we can reveal the assumptions inherent in such 'black boxes' and so trace the way in which knowledge comes to be represented in them. This is in accord with the approach we have observed Negus (1992) taking in teasing out the practical knowledge held by his A&R managers. Just as with the injunction to be specific about technology, we need to be more specific about organizational knowledge by exploring how it comes to be institutionalized in particular routines and artefacts.

An institutionalist approach, therefore, enables us to combine aspects of the inside and the outside of the organization in suggesting what information will count as valuable. However, we have noted that critics of institutionalist approaches suggest that it lacks an adequate theory of agency. As we have seen all through our discussions, the relationship between agency, that is, people taking action whether as individuals or collectively, and the contexts in which they find themselves is a central one in looking at how information is used. There are some approaches which would solve this tension by privileging one side of it, as in those accounts which stress the autonomous power of technology. We have seen how notions of technological determinism need to be rejected, but there are other approaches which equally tend to downplay the wider context in favour of a focus on what individuals do. For example, studies of information use often feature a detailed focus on patterns of search and retrieval which often tends to abstract from the organizational conditions which shape those patterns. Still, other approaches, such as actor–network theory, dissolve the relationship entirely by arguing that it is an irrelevance as the focus should be on networks of actors, whether these be human or artefacts. However, an alternative approach is that developed using the resources of critical realism. Such an approach has underpinned my approach at several points during my discussion and I wish to conclude this chapter by outlining this perspective in a little more detail.

CRITICAL REALISM, MORPHOGENESIS AND INFORMATION

Critical realism is a body of ideas derived from work in the philosophy of science (Collier 1994). It rejects both the logic of positivism, which claims that our knowledge of the world is simply a reflection of that world, and the logic of post-modernism, which claims that that world is unknowable and that all we can be concerned with are representations. From a critical realist perspective what we often call 'reality' is simply the world of sense impressions. This is what we might term 'common sense' realism, which takes the appearance of things for their actuality. Critical realism distinguishes between these surface impressions, which it terms the 'empirical' and what it terms the 'actual' – what we can determine on closer examination. The actual might be termed 'scientific realism' as this is what is often discovered when we adopt styles of investigation which go beyond surface impressions. However, for critical realists what constitutes the 'real' are the mechanisms which produce the actual. These are those mechanisms which, within a given range of conditions, produce particular effects.

This approach was developed in investigations of the natural world, whereas the social world is a little more complex. It is more complex as what we study is the product of human actions and humans can choose to change what they do. The nature of the interpretations which human actors make of their work can therefore be causal in changing or reproducing it, so they are also crucial parts of our investigations (Sayer 1992, 2000). A further consideration is the notion that reality, that is, the causal mechanisms which produce the world, is both stratified and emergent. It is stratified in that phenomena exist at a number of levels. Thus memory emerges from the biological constitution of the brain, which is in turn dependent on particular chemical and physical process (Rose 1993). However, memory cannot be reduced to such material properties. Investigations have found that it cannot be isolated to particular areas of the brain, but has self organizing properties – it constitutes a system in its own right, emergent from but not reducible to the material constitution of the brain. These ideas have been adopted by social scientists to argue for ways of approaching the agency-structure debate that we have seen lies at the heart of information use in organizations.

These ideas have had some application to the world of organization theory but they remain to be developed. A leading thinker in the development of these ideas at the level of social systems is Margaret Archer and the rest of this account draws heavily on her work. Her work is detailed and complex, so what follows can only be a summary, in which I try to show how her ideas might be applied to the study of information in organizations. Archer's (1995) starting point is that, consistent with the tradition of critical realism, we hold agency and structure apart to explore their inter-relationship over time. While it is clear that social reality is constructed by people, that there is no society without people, the majority of people involved in such construction are not those here present. That is, the actions of people in the past create the structures within which present actors have to operate. These structures have emergent properties of their own which make change an emergent process over time. In most cases, argues Archer, we elaborate on the structures which we find ourselves surrounded by, changing them in detail but confirming their essential properties. This is why it is important that we are clear in our definitions, as while routines in organizations might change relatively quickly, organizations themselves can be more resistant to change. In turn, the key institutions are much more durable – or change comes through more radical transformations, which by their nature are rare. Archer suggests that we examine processes of change which arise through the interplay of agency and structure by examining what she terms 'morphogenetic' cycles. The 'morpho' part of this term refers to change, the 'genetic' to the way in which such change is dependent on human agents deriving from the intended and unintended consequences of their actions. She uses the following diagram to illustrate this argument.

Her suggestion is that all action (starting at T^2) takes place in conditions which are objective in that they stand outside the actions of those taking part in the social interaction. This stresses the importance of history, not only in examining a successive round of cycles of interaction, but also in shaping the structural conditioning which begins at T^1. The setting of this point is a matter of analytical convenience, but in Archer's approach is much more than the brief sketching of context which one encounters in much organizational theory. Her work on educational systems, for example, encompasses a 700 year period (Archer 1979). In examining the dominant logics pertaining in the brewing industry, I suggest that one can find traces of

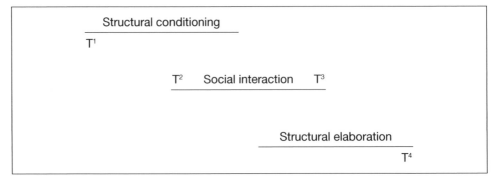

Figure 10.1 *The morphogenetic cycle*

the all important initial conditions in the mid-nineteenth century for some brewers (Mutch 2006). All social interaction results in some elaboration of the starting conditions, whether this is change or, more likely, the reproduction of existing conditions. In order to view episodes of information use using this lens, we need also to take into account the importance of interpretation when examining systems in the social, as opposed to the natural, world. This leads us to a focus on the systems of knowing that shape such interpretation.

Archer's (1996) suggestion here is that just as social structures emerge from social interaction but have a durability which outlasts any particular episode of interaction, so too do bodies of ideas. Her approach to culture is therefore to conceive of it as consisting of bodies of ideas standing in logical relation to each other. Just as with structures, so these logical relationships between ideas can guide and shape social action by providing logics of situated action. Culture is not a homogeneous body of ideas but contains conflicts and tensions within it at the level of logic. Such conflicts can either slumber ignored for years when they are not recognized and when there is no group to seize upon them, or they can form a resource for contending social groups. She suggests, therefore, that, drawing on the work of the philosopher Karl Popper (1979), there are bodies of 'objective knowledge'. This is not 'objective' in the sense of being value free but in being detached from the groups and individuals who created them. They then continue as a resource to be drawn upon and elaborated. This is clearly a very different perspective from an exclusive focus on tacit knowledge in that it suggests that bodies of ideas, which may well have been generalized from experience but now stand apart from it, are also important in shaping what draws our attention. In the next section we see how a focus on bodies of ideas standing in logical relations of contradiction and complementarity to each other can be usefully related to our focus on dominant logics at the level of the organization.

INFORMATION AND MORPHOGENESIS

If we then consider the process of organizational information use, we can firstly recognize how it is conditioned by the structural and cultural contexts in which it is carried out. The structural considerations that we have considered above relate to matters such as the nature of educational and training systems. These have considerable influence of the types of skills and aptitudes which are brought to bear on problems of information use. At the same time, there are bodies of knowledge about the way in which information should be used and, indeed, what it consists of, which are important resources to be drawn upon. For example, the work of Polanyi has proved of particular importance in shaping notions of tacit knowledge, despite the fact that it was created in response to different conditions. In persisting in the library of human knowledge it forms resources to be drawn upon in very different circumstances. The work of Popper, by contrast, has tended to be ignored in these debates, although it provides something of a counterpoint to Polanyi. However, it has not been seized upon by groups, such as academics and management consultants, with a social position which enables it to be mobilized. These resources exist at the broader level of societies and are conditioned by particular national histories, meaning that images of information differ from society to society. While the forces of globalization tend to favour some images over others, notably those associated with American corporations (and hence a global focus on performance management), such ideas are contested. In particular, the influence of durable patterns of thought such as those embodied in religious systems have a shaping influence on economic activity and perhaps need to be taken more into account.

At the level of the organization, these broader influences become contextualized in dominant logics which shape what counts as information in organizations. While drawing on broader resources, these logics are also the product of contending interpretations associated with groupings within the organization, of which the strongest remain functional or occupational groups. Such groups use contending ideas about information to seek to consolidate their own position in organizations. In doing so, a particularly powerful way is if they can inscribe their values into the ICT-enabled systems which the organization uses. Such inscription often occurs at the level of the rules, especially those to do with data definition, which form the basis of such systems. Definitions which accord with what is perceived as the 'natural' form of such technologies are particularly powerful. The technology does not in this sense determine such information use, but it suggests particular logics, reinforced by broader images, which are difficult to resist. These factors then form the taken for granted conditions in which organizational members use information. Such conditions are particularly powerful when built into regularly used artefacts, such as reports and blueprints, which suggest ways of using information which seem 'obvious' and 'natural'. As such, their limitations are only revealed in conditions of breakdown, when the taken for granted aspects of practical knowledge are revealed.

Information use, however, is not just a passive matter determined by organizational culture and technology. Rather, the participants in such information use bring with them ideas about information which are partly shaped by the broader institutional and cultural factors which we have alluded to and partly by other non-social factors. As we have seen, the type of educational experience that actors have been through not only gives them particular skills, but also orientations towards the world which are expressed at the level of identity. One does not have these orientations, one *is* them. As Bernstein (1996) indicated, the rules of what he termed 'recognition' and 'realization' are shaped by educational and social experience. Much of our focus is on realization skills, that is, on how to accomplish a competent performance in a particular context. However, how do we recognize what is appropriate in a particular context? It is the latter question which is bound up with questions of identity construction. Examination of the formation of communities of practice tends to reinforce this perspective, but it also fails to take account of the differential power resources that actors can draw upon. Archer also suggests that as well as these social shapings, we also have to recognize those factors which derive from the actor's encounters with the world as an embodied being. These draw our attention to the cognitive limitations which bear upon us all, as well as new sources of innovation drawn from encounters with the world. While such encounters need to be conveyed in linguistic terms, they offer the possibilities of new sources of metaphor and so potentially new approaches. This latter point means that we need to consider why it is that some people may respond very differently to the same 'objective' circumstances.

Information use, therefore, is in part a matter of shaping by factors at the level of both the organization and the society in which the organization operates. While organizations might operate with a dominant logic, this is not the only source of logic to condition organization use. Actors draw upon their individual and collective experience to form patterns of information use. However, while all actors might find themselves in the same context, not all respond in innovative ways. Many accept existing routines and practices and so organizations, and patterns of information use, come to be reproduced. This is the dominant condition, but in some cases actors respond differently. In part this is because of their position in the setting, what Callinicos (2006) terms their 'structural capacities'. Often change comes about from the margins, where actors have enough access to resources to be able to effect change but not so much that they are tied to existing patterns of use (Battilana 2006). Their particular position in the organization might both suggest new ways of acting and provide them with resources to enable those new ways. However, just because actors find themselves with such structural capacities does not mean that they will either recognize them or seek to use them. Archer suggests that this is at root a matter of reflexivity. While reflexivity, that is the monitoring of our condition and responding to it, is in some measure a part of being human, it differs, she argues, thanks to the way in which such monitoring is conducted. Drawing on a rich variety of thought she suggests that we carry out such monitoring through an internal conversation in which we evaluate our concerns (Archer 2003).

We have already noted that some see the essence of management as being the conduct of successful conversations. This stress on the importance of the reflexive monitoring of conduct through conversation is here brought inside persons, drawing on rich bodies of inquiry such as US pragmatism. In another influential view of agency which has many parallels with that outlined here, Emirbayer and Mische (1998: 974) also suggest that such conversations are central to the exercise of agency: 'we ground this capacity for human agency,' they write, 'in the structures and processes of the human self, conceived of as an internal conversation possessing analytic autonomy vis-à-vis transpersonal interactions.' However, this conversation, Archer argues, takes very different forms and so leads to different forms of reflexivity. For some (the majority in her exploratory study) the internal conversation needs to be completed in the context of others. Concerns, that is, have to be verbalized and shared with others in order for resolution to be obtained. This group are the 'conversational reflexives' and their engagement with the world is characterized by measures to maintain continuity of context. In this they will tend to avoid contact with structures or work 'with the grain'. We can imagine that their use of information is likely to be dominated by that gained through their network of relationships, with a focus on that which is familiar and trusted.

By contrast, the 'autonomous reflexive' completes their own internal conversation in relative (and these terms are all relative) isolation from the concerns of others. We can suggest that their use of information may be analytical in style and lend itself in particular to the dictates of performance management, with a focus on the 'objectivity' of information. This has the potential to bring them into conflict with and seek to change the structures which surround them. This desire for change is shared to some extent by the third category, that of the 'meta reflexive'. The meta reflexive uses the internal conversation not only to monitor personal projects but also to reflect upon the process of reflection itself. Thus, the meta reflexive more closely approaches the critical reasoning face of information literacy suggested by Bruce (1997). This does not necessarily lead to broader change, however, so much as to the dissatisfaction of the person with the nature of the world and their efforts in it. The final category is that of the 'fractured reflexive', the person who, for some reason, never acquires the ability to conduct a satisfactory internal conversation. These are society's victims, never able to achieve their personal projects and remaining in the position of what Archer would term 'primary agents', that is, with their life chances determined to a significant degree by their involuntary positioning.

Information use in organizations, on this account, is conditioned by the relationship between the context in which actors find themselves and the interpretations which they bring to bear on that context. The context itself contains resources which shape and condition those interpretations. Of particular importance here are sets of logics operating at both societal and organizational levels. These often suggest, in a taken for granted manner, the appropriate information to use. They are particularly powerful when built into organizational routines, especially when such routines are built into the artefacts which are used to complete them. Thus reports and other documents shape what is accepted as information in the organization, even if in many cases they are inadequate and recourse is had to more informal means of provision. Performance measurement systems facilitated by ICT are particularly important in this regard, inscribing a logic of what is felt to be appropriate in routines of measurement and reporting. That such systems often present an impoverished view of the reality they purport to represent does not negate the influence that they have.

However, such routines, systems and artefacts might shape the nature of information use, but they do not determine it. Those who shape action in organizations come from a variety of backgrounds and bring with them resources which might be used to counter dominant patterns. However, our analysis above might suggest that most are content to reproduce existing logics and routines, not merely because they are what is taken for granted and seen to be what has worked in the past, but also because their form of engagement with the world leads them to seek to work with, rather than against, existing arrangements. However, Tsoukas (2004) notes that new forms of information can disrupt this cosy arrangement by suggesting new alternatives. We can suggest that it will be the autonomous reflexives who seize on such information and use it as part of their endeavours to effect strategic change. Meanwhile, there are others who will challenge the very basis of such information, seeking to broaden the basis of the critical evaluation of information. However, such critics are likely to be rather marginal in organizations. The degree to which the innovative use of information by both autonomous and meta reflexives changes existing patterns is likely to rest in turn on their positioning within the social field. While activity at the margins is often a source of novelty, it needs to be supported by the structural capacity to effect change. As we have seen with librarians, the interesting ideas associated with notions like information policies often run into the sand as they lack the organizational power to embed their ideas in new organizational routines.

CONCLUSION

In this chapter I have outlined some ideas which tackle areas which tend to be neglected in consideration of information use in organizations. We started with an account which stressed the need for particular sets of skills if organizational arrangements were to work successfully, but which related these skills to broader factors, in this case educational and training systems. Much of what we read about information use in organizations assumes that such skills will be widely available and focuses its attention on organizational practices. Other bodies of work, notably those emanating from the discipline of library and information science, place their emphasis on the attainment of individual skill levels. However, what we have seen in this chapter is that what we need to do is to combine both perspectives and examine the interplay between the two. In so doing, we need to spread our analysis beyond the boundaries of the organization to examine broader contextual factors. This then enables us to incorporate some of the considerations that we discussed in the previous chapter. However, we now need to relate what we have discussed to our opening focus on information literacy. How does this concept fare when set against all that we have learned about information use in the contemporary organization? That is the task of the concluding chapter.

SUMMARY

■ The comparative business systems perspective suggests a number of durable sets of relationships between key institutions, such as the law and education, which shape the context in which organizations operate. While such complexes, often related to nation states, might be cut across by trends such as globalization, they remain remarkably strong in shaping information use.

■ New institutionalism suggests why it is that organizations come to adopt similar practices. It suggests the importance of taken for granted practices and gets us to look in particular at processes of institutionalization, that is how particular logics come to be embedded in routines, artefacts and systems. However, it is a perspective which is better at explaining continuity than change.

■ In this account I have stressed institutions as supra-organizational social practices, complemented by bodies of ideas, which condition what organizations do by setting standards of legitimacy that in turn are powerful influences on what counts as information within organizations.

■ Ideas drawn from critical realism, notably the work of Margaret Archer, suggest ways in which we can maintain a focus on the relationship between agency and structure. In particular, Archer's ideas on the nature of reflexivity are valuable resources in suggesting why some may use information in novel ways. However, they need further development. Some of these areas for development include:

  – The relationship of technology to agency and structure
  – The influence of ICT-facilitated information on patterns of reflexivity

REVIEW QUESTIONS

1 What are the types of isomorphism suggested by Powell and DiMaggio?

2 How does Whitley suggest that we can distinguish between business systems?

3 What are the three phases of Archer's morphogenetic approach?

DISCUSSION QUESTIONS

1 A key feature of the Shorko case was the data about processes that it accumulated as a result of installing a process control system. What aspects of the organization's institutional context might have a bearing on its ability to make use of this data?

2 What factors at the founding of an organization might influence its subsequent use of information?

FURTHER READING

Patriotta, G. (2003) *Organizational Knowledge in the Making: How Firms Create, Use and Institutionalize Knowledge*. Oxford, Oxford University Press.

Based on work in Fiat car manufacturing plants in Italy, both existing and greenfield, it argues for the need to look at the processes whereby knowledge comes to be institutionalized in artefacts such as reports and blueprints.

Scott, W. R. (2001) *Institutions and Organizations*. London, Sage.

An accessible introduction to and overview of new instititutuionalist ideas.

Whitley, R. (2000) *Divergent Capitalisms: The Social Structuring and Change of Business Systems*. Oxford, Oxford University Press.

A comprehensive account of the comparative business systems perspective.

REFERENCES

Abercrombie, N., Hill, S. and Turner, B. (2000) *Penguin Dictionary of Sociology*. 4th Edition. Harmondsworth, Penguin.

Allen, D. and Wilson, T. (1996) 'Information Strategies in Higher Education Institutions', *International Journal of Information Management*, 16(4): 239–251.

Archer, M. (1979) *Social Origins of Educational Systems*. London, Sage.

Archer, M. (1995) *Realist Social Theory: The Morphogenetic Approach*. Cambridge, Cambridge University Press.

Archer, M. (1996) *Culture and Agency: The Place of Culture in Social Theory*. Cambridge, Cambridge University Press.

Archer, M. (2003) *Structure Agency and the Internal Conversation*. Cambridge, Cambridge University Press.

Battilana, J. (2006) 'Agency and Institutions: The Enabling Role of Individuals' Social Position', *Organization*, 13(5): 653–676.

Bernstein, B. (1996) *Pedagogy, Symbolic Control and Identity: Theory, Research, Critique*. London, Taylor & Francis.

Bruce, C. (1997) *Seven Faces of Information Literacy*. Adelaide, AUSLIB Press.

Callinicos A. (2006) *The Resources of Critique*. Cambridge, Polity.

Chandler A. (1962) *Strategy and Structure: Chapters in the History of the Industrial Enterprise*. Cambridge, MA, MIT Press.

Clegg, S. R. (1990) *Modern Organizations: Organization Studies in the Post-Modern World*. London, Sage.

Collier A. (1994) *Critical Realism: An Introduction to the Philosophy of Roy Bhaskar*. London, Verso.

Collinson, S. and Wilson, D. (2006) 'Inertia in Japanese Organizations: Knowledge Management Routines and Failure to Innovate', *Organization Studies*, 27(9): 1359–1388.

Davenport, T. (2006) 'Competing on Analytics', *Harvard Business Review*, 84(1): 99–107.

DiMaggio, P. (1988) 'Interest and Agency in Institutional Theory', in L. Zucker (ed.) *Institutional Patterns and Organizations: Culture and Environment*. Cambridge, MA, Ballinger: 3–19.

DiMaggio, P. and Powell, W. (1991) 'The Iron Cage Revisted: Institutional Isomorphism and Collective Rationality in Organization Fields', in W. Powell and P. DiMaggio (eds) *The New Institutionalism in Organizational Analysis*. Chicago, University of Chicago: 63–82.

Emirbayer, M. and Mische, A. (1998) 'What is Agency?', *American Journal of Sociology*, 103(4): 962–1023.

Freil, D. (2005) 'Transferring a Lean Production Concept from Germany to the United States: The Impact of Labor Laws and Training Systems', *Academy of Management Executive*, 19(2): 50–58.

Friedland, R. and Alford, R. (1991) 'Bringing Society Back In: Symbols, Practices and Institutional Contradictions', in W. Powell and P. DiMaggio (eds) *The New Institutionalism in Organizational Analysis*. Chicago, University of Chicago Press: 232–266.

Hall, H. (1994) 'Information Strategy and Manufacturing Industry – Case Studies in the Scottish Textile Industry', *International Journal of Information Management*, 14, 281–294.

Hall, P. and Soskice, D. (2001) *Varieties of Capitalism: The Institutional Foundations of Comparative Advantage*. Oxford, Oxford University Press.

Hedlund, G. (1994) 'A Model of Knowledge Management and the N-Form Corporation', *Strategic Management Journal*, 15: 73–90.

Jary, D. and Jary, J. (2000) *Collins Dictionary of Sociology*. 3rd Edition Glasgow, Collins.

JISC (1995) *Guidelines for Developing an Information Strategy*. Joint Information Systems Council, www.webarchive.org.uk/pan/13734/20060324/www.jisc.ac.uk/indexd367.html [accessed 6 March 2007].

Joint Funding Council (1993) *Libraries Review Group Report (The Follett Report)*. Bristol, HEFCE. Available at www.ukoln.ac.uk/services/papers/follett/report/ [accessed 6 March 2007].

MacColl, J. (1996) 'Information Strategies Get Down to Business', Ariadne, 8, available at www.aridne.ac.uk/issue6/cover.

Mizruchi, M. S. and Fein, L. C. (1999) 'The Social Construction of Organizational Knowledge: A Study of the Uses of Coercive, Mimetic and Normative Isomorphism', *Administrative Science Quarterly*, 44: 653–683.

Mutch, A. (2006) *Strategic and Organizational Change: From Production to Retailing in UK Brewing 1950–1990*. London, Routledge.

Negus, K. (1992) *Producing Pop: Culture and Conflict in the Popular Music Industry*. London, Arnold.

Nonaka, I. and Takeuchi, H. (1995) *The Knowledge-Creating Company: How Japanese Companies Create the Dynamics of Innovation*. New York, Oxford University Press.

Orna, E. (1990) *Practical Information Policies*. Aldershot, Gower.

Patriotta, G. (2003) *Organizational Knowledge in the Making: How Firms Create, Use and Institutonalize Knowledge*. Oxford, Oxford University Press.

Popper, K. (1979) *Objective Knowledge: An Evolutionary Approach*. Oxford, Clarendon Press.

Preece, D., Steven, G. and Steven, V. (1999) *Work, Change and Competition: Managing for Bass*. London, Routledge.

Rose, S. (1993) *The Making of Memory: From Molecules to Mind*. London, Bantam.

Rowlinson, M. (1997) *Organisations and Institutions*. Basingstoke, Macmillan.

Sayer, A. (1992) *Method in Social Science: A Realist Approach*. London, Routledge.

Sayer, A. (2000) *Realism and Social Science*. London, Sage.

Scott, W. R. (2001) *Institutions and Organizations*. London, Sage.

Seo, M. and Creed, D. (2002) 'Institutional Contradictions, Praxis and Institutional Change: A Dialectical Perspective', *Academy of Management Review*, 27(2): 222–247.

Stinchcombe, A. (1965) 'Social Structure and Organizations', in J. March (ed.) *Handbook of Organizations*. Chicago, Rand McNally: 142–193.

Tolbert, P. S., and Zucker, L. G. (1999) 'The Institutionalization of Institutional Theory', in S. Clegg and C. Hardy (eds) *Studying Organization*. London, Sage: 169–184.

Tsoukas, H. (2003) 'Do We Really Understand Tacit Knowledge?' in M. Easterby-Smith and M. Lyles (eds) *The Blackwell Handbook Of Organizational Learning and Knowledge Management*. Oxford, Blackwell: 410–427.

Tsoukas, H. (2004) *Complex Knowledge: Studies in Organizational Epistemology*. Oxford, Oxford University Press.

Whitbread (1962) *Annual Report and Accounts*. London, Whitbread.

Whitley, R. (2000) *Divergent Capitalisms: The Social Structuring and Change of Business Systems*. Oxford, Oxford University Press.

Part Four

Conclusion

CHAPTER SUMMARY

KEY QUESTIONS

Chapter 11 The limits and potential of information literacy

- How useful is information literacy in examining information use in the workplace? Does it need refinement or extension and, if so, in what ways?
- How can we best address the questions of reflexivity which our discussion has raised?
- What are the impacts of broader structures on such reflexivity?
- Are there dangers in the widespread focus on tacit forms of knowing and how might we address these?

The limits and potential of information literacy

INTRODUCTION

We have now considered a wide variety of material with a bearing on the ways in which data, information and knowledge can be used in work organizations. In this concluding chapter I want to return to our initial focus on information literacy and see how useful this now seems. I will seek to develop an argument about information literacy and, through this, about the place of knowledge and knowing in contemporary organizations. In particular, having presented considerable detail about the impact of ICT I want now, as it were, to put it in its place. That is, I seek to weave consideration of ICT applications into the discussion rather than isolating it as a factor in its own right. I will do this so that we can maintain a focus on information, broadly defined, a focus which I will argue is often lost in many treatments. In some places I will be suggesting what managers might do, in others arguing that we need further research, but above all I hope to further stimulate your thinking in the area. In particular, I am concerned to address a question which has been with us throughout our discussions, that is, the relationship between individual skills, attitudes and knowledge and the logics, resources and constraints supplied by the contexts in which they are exercised.

This chapter will examine:

- the nature and value of information literacy in the context of work organizations, with particular focus on three dimensions: communicative competence, definitional work and awareness of context
- the limits of reflexivity, both as exercised by actors and as embedded in organizational practice
- the constraints imposed by structures, with particular emphasis on organizational hierarchy, on ICT and inscription, and on organizational and national culture

INFORMATION LITERACY AT WORK: A BALANCE SHEET

▶ **Chapter 8**

One observation that can be made about much of the material about knowledge management in work organizations is that it rests on assumptions about levels of individual capacity, assumptions which are often untested. That is, whether it is calling for a greater use of ICT in order to codify forms of knowing or whether it is resisting such calls in a defence of more experiential forms of knowing, the assumptions are often that those who engage in such practices (or who are being called upon to engage in them) have the capacity to so engage. In many cases, the result of these assumptions lying unpacked is that there is a default position of assumed competence leaving the field open for a mistaken emphasis on ICT skills. We have seen that such skills are important, but that unreflective focus on ICT skills and ICT skills alone can lead to considerable problems. This means that using the concept of information literacy can be a valuable corrective. Under this heading we can also encompass the focus on information policies, as this seeks to generalize from an individual to an organizational level. Using the twin lenses of information literacy and policy we can correct a tendency to focus on technical questions.

▶ **Preface**

These linked concepts force our attention back to questions which are often either taken for granted or fall between the cracks of disciplinary boundaries. That is, both in our work organizations and in our study of them, we tend to divide the world up into functional areas such as marketing or accounting, the better to either control or study them. These are understandable and indeed necessary moves, but in the process a focus on information tends to get lost, or becomes somebody else's concern. As we are either not clear about who that somebody else might be, or that somebody else (as in the case of librarians) occupies a somewhat marginal position, the questions that information raises are not addressed.

Information literacy is a useful way to correct this omission, but we have seen from our discussions that we may need some further refining to make the concept really work for us in the world of work as opposed to the world of education.

Let us remind ourselves of a useful definition drawn from higher education. In Chapter 1 we saw that the definition used in Australia was that an information literate graduate would possess:

- knowledge of major current resources;
- ability to frame researchable questions;
- ability to locate, evaluate, manage and use information in a range of contexts;
- ability to retrieve information using a variety of media;
- ability to decode information in a variety of forms;
- critical evaluation of information.

▶ **Chapter 1**

What we can suggest, based on our explorations of a range of work-based uses of information, is that we need to extend or modify this definition in three areas. However, before doing so it is important that we qualify our discussion in two ways. One is that there is a danger of over-extending the concept, of trying to make it do too much work. In particular, one might note the extension of the concept in the minds of some of Bruce's (1997) respondents so that it becomes closely aligned with critical thinking. The relationship of the skills subsumed under the heading of information literacy to some aspects of critical thinking is clearly of considerable importance, but there is a danger that we lose some of the specific skills if we cast the net too wide.

Thus, the discussion of the extensive use of data supplied by applications such as data warehousing drew our attention to the need for a range of skills of data analysis. Clearly, such skills need to be deployed in a relationship with ways of knowing, but they can be regarded as capable of separation for the purpose of examining this inter-relation. We will meet a similar relationship in discussing the notion of communicative competence below. However, the argument here is that there is value in not seeking to include everything under the rubric of information literacy. The second and related qualification is that information literacy needs to be seen as a concept in relation to other conceptual schemes. One criticism that we have encountered is that it fails to deal with questions of organizational power and culture. However, this is not to argue that the concept needs to be either discarded or radically amended. Rather it is to argue that it needs to be brought into relationship with other bodies of work which do treat such questions seriously. I have tried to do this in Chapters 9 and 10 and the considerations covered there continue to apply. With these qualifications in place, I wish to suggest that we need

▶ **Chapter 4**
Data warehouses

Chapter 8
Analysis skills

to extend the definition given above in three dimensions, which I label communicative competence, data definition and awareness of context.

The importance of communicative competence has to be related to our discussions about the nature of data, information and knowledge in organizations. We saw that what is often termed knowledge in views which place their emphasis on the power and potential of ICT can often be better described in Orna's (2005) terms as 'information products'. If we accept this definition, then we place our prime emphasis on the importance of systems of knowing in creating both information and data. This might be seen as contrary to many discussions of information literacy, which place more emphasis on the retrieval of pre-defined elements. The danger here is assuming that such elements mean the same to different audiences. By contrast, we have seen at a number of points that information requires active work of interpretation. The same information in the context of different ways of knowing can be seen and received in very different ways. The focus on much work on information literacy is on skills of retrieval, rather than on what is done with the information once retrieved. However, if we accept a focus on ways of knowing, then how such information is communicated becomes of vital importance.

We have seen that ICT offers a bewildering variety of communication options. Such options can deal with a wide variety of information types, most notably with increasingly unstructured forms of information. In these developments the visual becomes particularly important, so widening the range of skills of interpretation that we might wish to deploy. A key challenge is simply being aware of the range of communications options available and their suitability. It is here that we encountered the debate over media richness. On one side we had those who argued that a core competence of managers ought to be the ability to select and use the most appropriate communication mechanism. On the other are those who suggest that managers do not in practice engage in such selection processes but rather use those mechanisms which are to hand and which are congruent with the dominant orientations in the contexts in which they work. The matter is further complicated by the way in which certain applications, notably email, blur the boundaries, mixing elements of formal and informal means of communication in the same medium.

One way of seeking to reconcile these two positions is to suggest that here questions of organizational policy can be brought to bear. That is, the process of formulating a policy on forms of organizational communication which goes beyond technological features to suggest guidance on what might be appropriate can ensure that such choices are debated rather than being taken for granted. However, such policy considerations still rest on a level of individual awareness about how different media might be used.

240

It is here that training which goes beyond application specific features might be of particular value.

► **Chapter 8**

Of course, we are in danger here of again extending the definition of information literacy too far. We observed in particular that much information sharing is embedded in sets of relationships. We might be tempted to argue that a core part of being information literate is an awareness of the importance of relationships in the workplace and means of fostering them. However, we would then be in danger of losing the specific focus on information, so perhaps it is better to regard this as a key point of articulation between two sets of skills, both of which need to be fostered. Of course, in fostering such an articulation we have seen that place can be an important part of the construction of such relationships. It is here that the process of policy making could usefully focus on the nature of place as not just a complement to digital forms of sharing but as a crucial dimension in its own right. We need to note that there is a remarkable lack of research, with assumptions being made about the appropriate form of place, such as open plan offices, for information sharing which might be invalid in practice. This is another part of that missing debate which we have observed on a number of occasions. However, foregrounding communicative competence as a key part of information literacy in the workplace and bringing this into policy discussions is one way of crossing the boundaries that we have highlighted.

Another way of crossing such boundaries is a focus on definitions. We have noted that in the higher education sphere in which information literacy has been developed there is a tendency for such definitional questions to be in large part given by the context. While a crucial part of formulating and answering questions is an active consideration of questions of definition, in many cases such work has already been carried out. That is, students study particular disciplines, which have their own boundaries and concepts. In turn, the questions which are posed are often largely framed by the existing disciplinary specialists. While the aim might be to get students to formulate their own questions and to challenge definitions, this often occurs at the end of a long process. In the workplace the boundaries are in a sense both more fixed and less clear. They are less clear in that organizational problems do not present as neatly bounded but are complex messes. However, such messes are often reduced artificially to ones which can be handled within the boundaries of firmly defined functional areas. Within such functional areas definitions are often taken for granted, formed by the accretion of practices over many years. Such taken for granted practices are reinforced by the way in which occupational identities are formed.

► **Chapter 3**

Definitions are not therefore an abstract matter but bound up with what it takes to be a competent actor in the particular community of practice.

► **Chapter 7**

We have seen that the same term used in different functional areas can have completely different meanings, making information sharing difficult.

Such questions of definition are raised in stark form by ICT-enabled systems which seek to break down existing boundaries.

▶ **Chapter 4**
PDM

We have noted that in some cases ICT has compounded the solidity of local definitions by building them into isolated systems. Such systems then reinforce the boundaries between functions. When new systems are introduced which attempt to break down the 'silos' of information so created we find that they raise questions of data quality which at their heart are to do with competing definitions. The systemic nature of contemporary business, facilitated in particular by ICT systems which make data instantly available across a range of functions simply bring out differences in definitions more starkly. This suggests that a particularly important dimension of information literacy at work is the ability to work with and resolve competing definitions. Of course, this is not a matter of just individual skills and awareness, but importantly opportunities for organizational debate. Again, this is an area which can be addressed by information policy. While it would not be feasible or desirable to define every single item of data in use, those which cross internal boundaries are worthy of focus. It is here that a policy could lay down mechanisms for engendering and resolving debates about key items of data. However, we have also noted that this raises important questions of ownership and in their turn of power.

▶ **Chapter 9**

It is such questions that form part of the final dimension, that of awareness of context. While we have seen that power is an inescapable part of any social relationship, we would want to draw a distinction between the exercise of that power in educational and work settings. The relationship between student and tutor is an unequal one, but generally there are practices which ensure a more balanced relationship. In particular, information used by students is not likely in most circumstances to invoke the negative aspects of an unequal relationship. By contrast, the use of information in work settings is shot through with considerations of power. For example, we have noted how at the heart of debates about the ownership of data lie concerns about challenges to expertise, legitimacy and authority. Such concerns are often at their sharpest when they involve middle managers whose traditional basis of authority is being questioned by widespread access to the information. The challenge to the role of gatekeeper can bring about the mobilization of passive forms of resistance which, thanks to their structural position, are as effective as more outright challenge. The exercise of power is not just a negative matter, however. We have seen how data can be an ally in inter-managerial struggles for status and position. The recent conversion of marketing managers to data driven strategies, for example, can be related to an awareness that the use of such data gives them a powerful edge over those with other forms of data to deploy.

Awareness of context is not, however, just a matter of power, although an awareness of the ways in which information might be used seems a hidden dimension of what it takes to use information effectively, that is, not covered by more technical definitions of information literacy. In a more positive light, an awareness of the systemic nature of information use and impact in contemporary business seems to be an important dimension which needs further development. We have noted that managers often adopt an action orientation, being keen to be seen as taking decisions regardless of their long term impact. However, the systemic nature of organizations linked by ICT which undercuts previous barriers of time and space means that such decision making is ineffective. Now the demand is for information which enables managers to take into account the broader consequences of their decisions. Of course, the radical unpredictability of human affairs means that solutions are not to be found in ever increasing volumes of data. This might be comforting in its volume, but may be unlikely to offer any greater insights. Part of the solution here is to return to our discussion about the formulation of questions, but another part is in the generation of different alternatives. Such alternatives are offered by forms of strategic planning which eschew detailed forecasts in favour of the construction of scenarios (Beck 1984). Such scenarios draw on a more narrative based approach to kindle the imagination and, in the light of a more reflective awareness of what the future might hold, to adjust present actions to be better prepared.

▶ **Chapter 8**
'Practical reasoning'

Context also relates to questions of culture. As we have seen, this is a tricky term, often confused either with the exercise of power or with other forms of practice. However, the growth of global business is making clashes between different taken for granted ways of thinking become clearer. We have tried to cast such questions in the form of logics, logics which suggest particular forms of information. There are different terms in the literature for such logics. But they are powerful shapers of what counts as information in a particular circumstance. An industry recipe, for example, can suggest a commonly used measure, such as the percentage that wages form of sales in licensed retailing, that then becomes 'natural' and 'obvious' – even if it is no such thing. The ability to recognize the logics that are in operation and to be able to envisage alternative logics might be an important attribute of the information literate manager. However, such speculations raise the important issue of reflexivity.

▶ **Chapter 9**

REFLEXIVITY AND INFORMATION

All that has been said above carries considerable implications for the nature of reflexivity. In suggesting that managers can make choices about the communication mechanisms that they use, that they should address questions of the definition of basic terms and that they should be conscious of forms of power and culture at operation, we are assuming that such activities are possible both for all the actors involved and in the contexts in which they find themselves. However, what we have noted at a number of points are the limits posed to such reflexivity, both in the nature of the actors themselves and in the organizations in which they find themselves. If we consider the level of persons first, this requires us to take seriously the embodied nature of human cognition. This is a consideration often referred to but rarely taken into account. However, the insights of cognitive psychology would suggest that there are a number of limits to such embodied cognition. We have seen that human beings are poor intuitive statisticians, tending to assess probabilities on the basis of memorable but atypical incidents and neglecting the more representative events. In particular, and of considerable relevance to our present discussion, is the notion of metacognition. This notion, often to be found in courses about learning how to learn, refers to 'thinking about thinking', that is the conscious monitoring of forms of thought and from that attempts to change the patterns of such thought in more effective ways. However, there is some doubt about the ability to perform such metacognitive activity. Such limitations do rather cast some doubt on the efficacy of some suggestions in the knowledge management literature which depend on the widespread availability of the capacity for metacognition. For example, Garvey and Williamson (2002: 16) suggest that 'meta-cognitive capacity is a quality of individual human minds and something that can be nurtured to become a feature of the ways in which organizations of many different kinds can function'. More work is needed to test whether this assertion can be sustained, but it should be clear from the previous discussion that this contention seems a rather optimistic one. The response might be not to design practices as if such capabilities were widely available, but rather to design them in such a way that they both cater for difference and seek to encourage moves towards metacognition.

What the literature on cognition seems to suggest is the importance of conceptual schema in the light of certain limitations which are a property of embodied humans. That is, we do not remember disconnected facts but linked bodies of ideas, symbols and concepts. We can connect such schema to the emphasis on sets of logics to be found in Archer's (1996) work. However, it is worth again emphasizing her more nuanced discussion of reflexivity which also suggests, in a sociological rather than a psychological frame of reference, that we need to draw finer distinctions

► Chapter 10

► Chapter 2

► Chapter 10

between types of reflexivity. In the previous chapter we saw her suggestions about types of reflexivity and the ways in which these might map on to patterns of information use. This is a set of connections which needs further investigation, as does the nature of the reflexivity which she posits. In particular, are these forms of reflexivity durable dispositions to act which remain substantially the same in different contexts, or are they forms which tend to be 'triggered' by particular contexts, so that particular forms of reflexivity become engendered by the circumstances? Some support for the latter is given by the literature on situated learning, which suggests that forms of cognition are not simply transferable but become available in particular contexts. However, the thrust of Archer's (2003) work seems to be that modes of reflexivity are formed at an early stage of development and, while they are subject to change given the nature of social development, are powerfully resistant to change. Such questions remain to be investigated in more detail, but they should at least suggest some limitations to reflexivity.

If we carry these ideas over into the literature on knowledge management then recognition of the limits of cognition suggests a need to design organizational practices in such a way that they prompt reflection to the maximum extent possible. Thus, at a number of points Tsoukas (2004) seems to suggest that reflexivity in the strongest sense is an intrinsic property of human activity, but that this needs particular organizational circumstances in which to flower. He suggests that:

> Knowledge management then is primarily the dynamic process of turning an unreflective practice into a reflective one by elucidating the rules guiding the activities of the practice, by helping give a particular shape to collective understandings and by facilitating the emergence of heuristic knowledge.
>
> (Tsoukas 2004: 137–138)

We see here a focus on elucidating the rules which underlie the taken for granted use of information. Others might suggest similar mechanisms, if not in these terms. For example, one of Senge's (1990) responses to the problem of equipping managers with systemic knowledge which would overcome limited timeframes was by engaging in 'microworlds', simulations of business activities which would alert participants to different perspectives. Similarly, we can see that scenario planning might generate new ways of envisaging the world. We noted that in their analysis of fault finding in complex social settings, Hsiao, Tsai and Lee (2006) suggested the construction of stories which embodied experiences as a means of sharing knowledge. However, as Tsoukas (2004: 194) observes, 'in some organizations reflexivity is more encouraged and, therefore, more likely to be encountered than in others . . . In other words, reflexivity requires certain conditions for it to flourish'. This means we have to recognize what the barriers are to the establishment of the sort of practices which might engender reflexivity.

STRUCTURES AND INFORMATION

▶ **Chapter 7**

We have noted at a number of points the remarkable persistence of functional hierarchy as a way of structuring formal organizations. Despite a focus on the flattening of hierarchies and on alternative mechanisms, such as the network, the large hierarchically organized firm remains a key, if not growing, part of the economic landscape. This has an important impact on the use of information that we have already started to note when we suggested that to be information literate was to recognize what could and could not be done with information in particular contexts. We noted, for example, the way in which the intervention of a senior manager in electronic discussions in Unilever had a considerable impact on the future conduct of those discussions, even though the intention was benign. That is, setting aside considerations of unequal power, the actions of senior managers, by simple virtue of their position, can have a powerful modelling effect. We would want to draw the distinction that Argyris and Schon (1974) make between espoused theories and theories in use at this point. The espoused theory is the official story; the theory in use is what is actually done. In the case of information, we can suggest that it is the theory in use, that is, the actual observed and reported practice, which is most influential. So in the formulation of guidelines on the use of information

▶ **Chapter 6**

at Marks & Spencer a key consideration was to reduce paper work by establishing expectations that staff could be trusted to follow guidelines, that they should not keep information 'just in case' and that they should use sensible approximations in their work. However, all these injunctions relied on the practice of senior managers. If their theory in use was to demand immediate responses in considerable detail to specific questions, then the guidance, however sensible, would not be followed, as staff reacted to the demands in practice rather than the ideals espoused.

▶ **Chapter 4**
EIS

Chapter 9
Monitoring

Of course, the impact can be somewhat more direct than these rather more benign examples. Senior managers feel themselves accountable for results in a way which supports the seductive potential for data to be used as a control mechanism. This is particularly so when ICT offers the possibility of organizing such data in a way which suggests immediate access to performance data. We may be aware that such data might be unreliable (although the reliability is being improved over time) and that they offer only a partial view of complex reality, but the ability to 'see' organizational performance at any time is an attractive one. The impact in turn on information use is that the needs of the performance measurement system become paramount. Managers manage the system, rather than the situations on which it is supposed to be a partial window. This then conflicts with the demands for greater reflexivity in the use of information. While we have seen that there are debates about the value of terms such as 'tacit' knowledge, there is extensive evidence that much of what is valuable in work organizations is embedded in informal relations. It is developed through experience and shared through the telling of stories. We might debate the extent to which such forms of knowing can be formalized, but what seems clear is that they sit uncomfortably with the performance measurement systems which are so central to the management of large global corporations. A key tension is therefore between the forms of knowing which seem increasingly important for competitive success and the measures which are demanded as indicators of that success by other stakeholders. Of particular importance here is the conflict between the often short term objectives of key stakeholders, notably the suppliers of financial resources, and the longer term needs of knowledge generation. What we are coming to know about effective forms of knowing in organizations has to be set against the demands of the contexts in which those organizations must operate.

Many of those demands are inscribed in ICT in a way which further limits room for manoeuvre. Much current writing on ICT in the workplace would emphasize the flexibility of such technological forms, in particular to avoid charges of technological determinism. We have seen that many forms of ICT do indeed offer such flexibility, but we have to be careful not to elevate ideal properties above the practical and concrete use of ICT in the workplace. Not only do ICT applications come with particular ways of operating which seem 'natural' (and which can be difficult, given the practical constraints of time and expertise, to customize, even if that is a theoretical option) but the systems which are built on them are more enduring in their impact. One is thinking in particular of the data structures which are built. We have been clear that data are selected on the basis of bodies of knowledge, but once so selected and stored in electronic form, they can be powerful barriers to change. This requires us to appreciate the enormous volumes of data collected by the users of applications such as data warehouses. Such data are collected in order to be used to establish trends and patterns, but that use depends on a large volume of data stored against consistent definitions. This sheer volume then tends to cement in place existing definitions, which then colour further information use. We have to be clear that this is not a theoretical but a practical barrier, especially given the time needed should alternative views be required. The various forms of ICT that we have examined, be they hardware, software or data structures, impose structural constraints of their own on patterns of activity.

▶ **Chapter 4**

One further consideration flows from our exploration of the insights of the new institutionalists in the last chapter. We have noted above the competitive pressures, actual or perceived, which might shape the actions of senior managers. However, new institutionalism suggests the importance of legitimacy in such actions. That is, such managers are constrained to appear to act in ways which are considered appropriate. These may vary from time to time, but they emphasize that senior managers are just as prey to the whims of fashion as others. Indeed, it could be argued that faced with conditions of increasing complexity that the promise of certainty can be found in the ranks of the increasing volume of offers of help proffered by consultancies and support agencies. These might suggest particular forms of action, chief among which in recent years has been knowledge management. The flavour of these varies from consultancy to consultancy, but these in turn are embedded in cultural contexts which favour particular forms of knowing. The focus on performance measurement, with an emphasis on 'hard' facts, for example, seems to be a particular feature of the US context, but one which has widespread influence. The forms of debate over knowledge within organizations may owe as much to the prevailing ideas about what is appropriate, mediated through consultancy and the perceptions of senior managers, as to what might be considered to fit the needs of the organization. In particular, there is the potential for conflict here between ways of knowing as embedded in communities of knowing at the base of organizations and the prescriptions emanating from above. It is here that some suggest, such

as Nonaka and Takeuchi (1995), is the enduring value of middle managers. This enduring value, however, depends on their skills of mediation and interpretation. In particular, this requires that they meet the demands for performance data from above while continuing to shield and develop the capacity for knowing that develops from experience. What we have identified is a series of tensions that shape what counts as data, information and knowledge in organizations. We conclude in the next section by considering some ways in which we might explore these tensions further.

CONCLUSION

We have seen throughout this book that a particular feature of the investigation of knowledge in contemporary work organizations had been the focus on the tacit and the experiential. This has been developed against both conceptions of knowledge as consisting of bodies of formal abstract knowledge and ideas that knowledge can be reduced to information which can be manipulated by computer systems. This focus has been a welcome one, as it has corrected previous distortions and it has valued the work carried out in previously anonymous sites. This perspective has placed its emphasis on knowing as doing, intimately bound up with the formation and maintenance of identity. In this fashion, it has sought to rescue elements of creativity and ingenuity and give value to seemingly mundane everyday practices. However, such a focus is not without its dangers. One of the objections to the notion of 'community' is that while we value the notion of community for its sense of inclusion, such social settings can also be sites of unthinking and unreflective practice, in which those who do not conform to community norms are ostracized. Such communities can become inward looking and unresponsive to change. What can often be crucial are the links between such communities, in which boundary spanners, both in the form of people and objects can be of particular importance.

A key link lies in the abstraction of the knowledge created, in order to share its insights and debate its significance. Patriotta (2003: 166) cites Ginzburg to this effect: 'The force behind this knowledge resided in its concreteness, but so did its limitation – the inability to make use of the powerful and terrible weapon of abstraction.' This tension between concreteness and abstraction is not one which can be dissolved by simply studying more and more examples of concrete knowledge or by demonizing abstraction as formal knowledge. Rather, this speaks to a key question raised by our focus on information literacy and its links to critical thinking – the need to encourage reflexivity about forms of knowing. While Wenger (1999) may have put this tension in terms of a contrast between participation, that is experiential learning, and reification, that is rendering that learning in concrete form, in routines, reports and blueprints, he does seem to be getting at the importance of maintaining both. That is, a key relationship to be explored is that between knowing in practice and systems of knowing. The danger of too great a focus on learning in practice is that we lose the broader connections both in space and over time to the contexts in which such practice takes place. A key part of such contexts are the enduring bodies of knowledge which escape their conditions of production and become resources for us all.

Another concern about the focus on tacit and experiential forms of knowing is that it has tended to downplay the importance of data in organizations. This need not be the case, as the intensive and extensive analysis of large bodies of data has become a key part of the practice of many important groups in contemporary organizations. However, we know very little about such practices. Rather, our attention has been on other forms of knowing, selected one might suggest, in part because of their very diffuse nature which lends them to detailed investigation. The study of how copier technicians, for example, make sense of the fault finding process and share their knowledge is clearly an important one, not only for copier companies but for those interested in the practical application of knowledge sharing more generally. However, to demonstrate that knowledge about faults can only partially be captured in procedure manuals cannot then be generalized to all other forms of knowing in contemporary organizations.

Given the development of large retail organizations, for example, knowing the customer in the sense that a small shopkeeper knew the purchasing habits of her local customers is clearly impossible. It might be argued that forms of knowing generated from large bodies of data are impoverished by comparison, but they are being carried out on a large scale and, it would seem, with some success. It can be accepted that such forms of analysis may in turn be being carried out by communities of practice with their own embedded forms of knowing, but such forms of knowing may by their nature have more links with formal bodies of knowledge, such as statistical forms of knowing. It is likely that they generate questions about more abstract questions of data definition and modelling. We have also noted that they may involve multiple communities of knowing stretching across organizational boundaries. These linkages require further investigation, investigation which might suggest a more balanced perspective on knowing, placing as much emphasis on abstraction as on concreteness.

This increased focus on data analysis in organizations has also been founded on the development of particular forms of ICT, forms which are very different in their application and properties from those generally investigated in work on knowing in organizations. Here, if covered at all, the focus has been on flexible forms of technology. This supports the focus on emergent forms of knowing, but also reflects a very crude view of ICT. This associates ICT with the application of systems such as artificial intelligence. It can be conceded that there is much fantasy about the application and potential of such systems, but to leave the matter at that is to underplay the importance of other applications of ICT. We have seen that these can be very varied in character. One of the reasons for spending a good proportion of this book on elucidating the consequences for information of such variety has been to counter the rather vague approach often adopted. This has seen the paradoxical impact of the greatest research effort being devoted to those applications which, while clearly interesting and important, are among the least used (at least in terms of their promise) in organizations. At the same time we lack research which goes beyond the technical on applications of major impact such as data warehouses. The attention we paid to such systems followed the injunction, derived from those working with actor–network theory, to be specific about technology. It is hoped that some of the coverage in this book will suggest ways in which such investigations can be carried out. For those within organizations it is hoped that this will raise awareness of the potential that ICT brings for altering information use in a range of ways. A key part of what it means to be information literate is to be aware of such systems, but through such awareness to keep them in their place. That is, better awareness of the specifics of ICT can enable the focus to remain on why they are being used.

Finally, one of the issues which our consideration has raised (and one of the reasons why ICT cannot be left to ICT managers) is the way in which information is a missing dimension in many organizational debates. The focus on knowledge management is a welcome one as it raises the possibility of debating such issues, even if it does tend to neglect the key elements we have outlined above. However, the question of ICT awareness raises this missing dimension in stark form, for along with lack of awareness of the difference between applications of ICT often goes lack of attention to the information consequences. These are often held by default to be the responsibility of the function responsible for implementing and maintaining ICT use, but this is mistaken if we take a perspective of information and knowing being embedded in practice. It follows from such a perspective that those best placed to consider issues of information are those with deep familiarity with the practice. The practices of ICT managers relate to forms of knowing which place emphasis, as they have to, on logical forms of abstraction and precise definitions. These then colour the view of what constitutes knowing, making such managers the worst placed to influence knowing in the broader organization, even if they were in a position to do such influencing. The problem in most organizations is that those best placed to offer support through their own training are the most marginal in terms of organization position. While librarians as a professional grouping may aspire to greater influence, their organizational position often seems tenuous. Other groupings, such as HR, seem not to have the necessary awareness and so the position of influence is taken by other groups, such as public relations or marketing. One of the key steps which might be usefully taken is to bring information to centre stage as a matter for organizational debate.

The notion of an information policy seems one vehicle for doing this, although all too often it appears, both in the literature and in practice, to be subsumed under the rubric of an IT strategy. The problem once again is that attention shifts to the nature of the technology. Such technology plays a vital role in delivering services and enabling the use of information but, as we have seen, can readily be copied. What remains distinctive about organizations is what they know about their world and how they come to know it. Such forms of knowing are deeply rooted in experience. This is not just the experience of current members of the organization but is also the product of the historical development of the organization. These legacies from the past may in some cases be forces for conservativism, but they can also be powerful and unique resources. Whether they can be deployed effectively depends on the one hand on the complex relationships between different levels in the organization and on the other nature of the organization and the broader context in which it operates.

SUMMARY

■ Information literacy has been a useful concept to work with in our review of the managerial use of information, but it needs extension and refinement in three areas: communicative competence, focus on definitions and awareness of context.

■ An examination of knowledge and information in contemporary organizations suggests the importance of reflexivity. These modes of reflexivity are profoundly shaped by the structures within which they are exercised.

■ Much of the literature we have reviewed has a strong emphasis on tacit forms of knowing and on knowing in practice. This is valuable, but runs the risk of downplaying the importance of more enduing and abstract bodies of knowledge. The challenge is to examine the interplay between the two.

FURTHER READING

Much of this chapter has drawn upon the work of Margaret Archer, as has the book as a whole. This is a rich, complex and sophisticated body of work which is not for the faint-hearted! The main works relied on here have been:

Archer, M. (1995) *Realist Social Theory: The Morphogenetic Approach*. Cambridge, Cambridge University Press.

> The opening statement of Archer's broad approach, laying out ideas which are developed in greater detail in subsequent work.

Archer, M. (1996) *Culture and Agency: The Place of Culture in Social Theory*. Cambridge, Cambridge University Press.

> Archer's application of her ideas to the realm of culture which works at a high level of abstraction but suggests an alternative to what she terms the 'myth of cultural integration'.

Archer, M. (2003) *Structure, Agency and the Internal Conversation*. Cambridge, Cambridge University Press.

> Archer's more recent work has been concerned with questions of human agency and reflexivity, balancing the earlier focus on the context in which such agency operates.

REFERENCES

Archer, M. (1996) *Culture and Agency: The Place of Culture in Social Theory*. Cambridge, Cambridge University Press.

Archer, M. (2003) *Structure, Agency and the Internal Conversation*. Cambridge, Cambridge University Press.

Argyris, C. and Schon, D. (1974) *Theory in Practice: Increasing Professional Effectiveness*. London, Jossey-Bass.

Beck, P. (1984) 'Debate Over Alternative Scenarios Replaces Forecasts at Shell UK', *Journal of Business Forecasting*, Spring, 2–6.

Bruce, C. (1997) *Seven Faces of Information Literacy*. Adelaide, AUSLIB Press.

Garvey, B. and Williamson, B. (2002) *Beyond Knowledge Management: Dialogue, Creativity and the Corporate Curriculum*. Harlow, Pearson.

Hsiao, R., Tsai, S. D. and Lee, C. (2006) 'The Problems of Embeddness: Knowledge Transfer, Coordination and Reuse in Information Systems', *Organization Studies*, 27(9): 1289–1318.

Nonaka, I. and Takeuchi, H. (1995) *The Knowledge-Creating Company: How Japanese Companies Create the Dynamics of Innovation*. New York, Oxford University Press.

Orna, E. (2005) *Making Knowledge Visible: Communicating Knowledge Through Information Products*. Aldershot, Gower.

Patriotta, G. (2003) *Organizational Knowledge in the Making: How Firms Create, Use and Institutonalize Knowledge*. Oxford, Oxford University Press.

Senge, P. M. (1990) *The Fifth Discipline: The Art and Practice of the Learning Organization*. New York, Doubleday.

Tsoukas, H. (2004) *Complex Knowledge: Studies in Organizational Epistemology*. Oxford, Oxford University Press.

Glossary

Actor–Network Theory	An approach often encountered in studies of science, technology and innovation which argues that innovation depends on the successful translation of ideas into local networks (rather than the mechanical diffusion of ideas). Such networks consist of both human and non-human actors (the latter sometimes called 'actants') to which equal attention should be given.
Application specific training	Training in the operational details of a particular ICT application which often fails to deal with questions such as the purpose and potential of using the application.
Artificial intelligence	Attempts to reproduce human decision making in computer programs. Most successful in bounded area of activity with clear rules, where it is often known as *expert systems*.
Bounded rationality	Concept developed by the Carnegie school of Simon and others to describe the limits to human decision making which mean that we look for a satisfactory (satisficing) decision rather than the optimum one.
Business models	Term much associated with wilder claims for the impact of the Internet on organizational strategy, which relates to means by which strategy is going to be put into practice and value generated.
Business Process Reengineering	Advocated marrying the power of ICT to an approach which questioned why processes were undertaken in order to bring about fundamental change in organizational structures and practices. Discredited by its association with 'downsizing' and the loss of organizational knowledge.
Client-server	An arrangement of computing power which uses a network to distribute task. Intensive processing is often carried out on the client (usually a PC) with data being held on the server. An example would be an *intranet*, in which the code that determines the content of a page is held on the server, but the formatting is carried out according to instructions contained on the client.
Communities of practice	Groups at work centred on a common practice in which learning happens through experience and involves learning how to become and act as a full member of the community.

Comparative business systems perspective	A tradition which looks at clusters of characteristics that distinguish business systems. Such systems in their turn condition the form which organizations take and include legal and cultural facets as well as economic features.
Content management systems	Designed to facilitate the updating and control of material on websites, both external and internal (*intranets*). Use standard templates to maintain a common 'look and feel' while allowing for control of content by non-technical staff.
Critical realism	Philosophical tradition which argues that there is a world independent of our knowledge of it, but that we only know it through concepts. Important contributor to the *morphogenetic approach*.
Customer Relationship Management (CRM)	While there is debate over whether this refers to a process or a technology, it is often used to refer to software which will organize and analyse customer transactions with a view to managing these more effectively.
Data mining	Software based on rules which looks for patterns in large bodies of data such as those held in *data warehouses* or generated by CRM systems.
Data warehouses	Systems which take data from operational systems and store them in a fashion which is optimized for the analysis of data, often to discover trends and relationships. Often run on standalone specialist machines because of the large volumes of data.
Databases	Form of organization of data in computer systems which keeps the data apart from the programs which use them.
Disintermediation	The removal of intermediaries from a value chain, often associated with Internet developments. Often happens when technology enables direct communication between parts of a value chain when the data is clear and unambiguous.
Document management systems	Systems which facilitate the capture, storage and retrieval of documents. Often used in otherwise paper intensive industries such as insurance and financial services.
Dominant logic	A conceptualization of the world, often at the level of senior managers, which shapes action and information use.
Electronic mail (email)	ICT-enabled messaging systems with facilities for the composition, distribution and filing of messages.
Electronic Point of Sale (EPOS)	Devices (such as cash registers and barcode scanners) which enable the collection of large volumes of transaction data. Accompanied by network systems for the automatic collection and transmission of the data for further use in, for example, stock control systems. From there, often transferred to *data warehouses*.
Enterprise Resource Planning (ERP)	ICT systems that have a common database which supports different applications, such as accounting and purchasing. The aim is to have a common store of data across the organization which facilitates the sharing of information. Often very expensive and difficult to implement. The market leading application is from SAP; Oracle is another important product.

Executive Information Systems (EIS)	Systems aimed at senior managers which enable them to look at a summary of figures and then to 'drill down' into the supporting data to explore problems. Often not used by senior managers because they do not work this way (they tend to ask others to do the exploring) but have developed into 'Business Intelligence' applications often used by more junior managers to prepare reports and investigate problems.
Expert systems	Systems which, based on *artificial intelligence,* attempt to mimic the decisions an expert would reach based on data presented. Used for intensive analysis tasks where the volume of data would render the task unfeasible for human processing.
Explicit and tacit knowledge	While an area for debate, this refers to a distinction between formal bodies of knowledge, often taking the form of procedures in written form (explicit knowledge) and knowledge which is personal and gained through experience. The debate centres on the extent to which tacit knowledge can be made explicit.
Formal and informal information	Formal information is the officially sanctioned position, often produced by particular offices on a regular basis. It is compared to informal information such as gossip which travels through unofficial channels.
Genre	A particular style of communication, often expressed in an artefact such as a memo or a set of presentation slides, which becomes taken for granted and shapes the way communication takes place.
Globalization	Term used to refer to either expansion of trading (through, for example, common brands) to cover world or organization of production and other systems on global basis.
Groupware	ICT systems designed to enable collaborative working. The most well known is Lotus Notes. Can be used for discussion databases and collective editing of documents, as well as more commonly used email and shared calendar functions.
Hybrid managers	Managers who combine both business and ICT knowledge, the combination of which is hoped to facilitate more successful use of the latter.
Informate	Term developed by Zuboff to represent the potential which ICT brings to produce information about how a process has been carried out, as compared to other technologies which simply automate the process.
Information and Communication Technology (ICT)	Defined for the purpose of this book as 'technologies for the processing, storage and transmission of digital material, consisting of ensembles of hardware and software with distinctive feature sets allowing for the physical storage and logical representation of different forms of data'.
Information literacy	Body of ideas drawn largely from library and information sciences which suggests that skills of information use are, in an 'information age', of parallel importance to skills of reading and writing.
Information policy	Argument, often connected with the work of Orna and others from library-based disciplines, that organizations should make explicit their practices relating to the creation, dissemination and use of information.

Information Resource Management	Argues that information is as important a resource as land, labour and capital, but criticized for failure to distinguish the particular features of information (such as its non-exhaustion through use).
Interpretive systems	As developed by Daft and Weick, sets of assumptions held at organizational level which condition information use by organizational members.
Intranet	An internal version of the Internet, using the same techniques to present material, but restricted to the members of a particular organization. Often used to present procedures and resources like telephone directories but can also be used as a 'front end' to other systems, such as databases.
Isomorphism	Process by which organizations come to adopt similar processes or practices. Three types are often emphasized: mimetic (copying), normative (adhering to norms) and coercive (being forced), although competitive pressures should also be recognized.
Knowledge Intensive Firms (KIFs)	Organizations in which the key feature is the intensive generation and application of knowledge. Often feature very highly educated and potentially mobile workforces.
Knowledge management systems	Systems which purport to enable knowledge sharing. Based on a range of applications, from groupware to intranets to expert systems. Most successful when acting as a forum for raising and answering questions of a bounded type within a particular grouping who share similar assumptions.
Knowledge boundaries	Carlile suggests three levels of boundaries which are revealed during innovative activity – syntactic (definitions), semantic (meanings) and pragmatic (political).
Mainframe	Specialized computing equipment optimized for handling high volumes of transactions. Often at the centre of a network of input and output devices. Needs dedicated accommodation with specialized cooling plant and security arrangements.
Media Richness Theory (MRT)	Otherwise known as Information Richness Theory, an approach that seeks to rank communication media in terms of the richness of communication which they facilitate by features such as multiple cues and channels for feedback. Also suggests that managers can and should select on the basis of the suitability for the task in hand, with more ambiguous tasks requiring richer media.
Meta data	'Data about data' often particularly important in *data warehouse* applications. Tells users about how data was collected to facilitate subsequent analysis.
Morphogenetic approach	Developed by Archer, this argues that we need to hold agency (the actions of people) apart from structures (enduring patterns produced by people, such as organizations) in order to examine their changing relationship over time.
New institutionalism	A perspective which addresses the central problem of legitimacy, arguing that organizations do not act only on the basis of what is economically rational but also seek to conform to societal norms – taken for granted sets of rules which are often referred to as institutions.
Outsourcing	The contracting out of some or all of activities which are not regarded as core to organizational strategy.

Positioning view of strategy	Influential school of thought associated with the work of Porter which stresses the importance of analysing the environment and selecting a position based on the results. Often contrasted to the Resource Based View.
Power users	Those in business functions who have skills in using ICT systems of relevance which are much higher than those generally used in the function.
Product Data Management (PDM)	Systems which enable the recoding of data created during the design and manufacture of a product, data which accompany the product throughout its lifecycle.
Programmed/ unprogrammed decisions	Distinction developed by Simon. Programmed decisions are those which are routine and regular and for which the rules can be written down. By contrast, other decisions are so infrequent or different that no such process is possible.
Reification	In the sense used by Wenger (1999), the taking of learning that has arisen through interaction and rendering it in a more concrete form, such as procedure manuals or pages on an Intranet so that it can be used by others.
Resource Based View (RBV)	A perspective on strategy, often contrasted to the positioning school, which argues that what is important for competitive advantage is the nurturing of distinctive resources which cannot easily be imitated.
Shopfloor Collection and Data Analysis (SCADA)	Systems to take data generated from process control systems to monitor in real time and to facilitate subsequent analysis.
Short Messaging Service (SMS)	Commonly known as 'text'. Developed to carry technical messages, but now widely used, despite limitations on message size, for a variety of communications.
Socio-technical systems	Approach which argues for balance between individual, organizational and technological factors for optimum use of the latter.
Strategic Alignment	Attempts to recognize that developments in ICT can suggest new ways of carrying out business as well as supporting business-led approaches. Suggests four ways of achieving alignment.
Structuration theory	Developed by Giddens, this argues for the mutual constitution of agency (action by people) and structure (enduring patterns produced by people, such as organizations).
Technological determinism	Perspective which sees technology as producing certain results and only those results within organizations. Unlikely to be held in a pure form – terms such as 'condition' or 'shape' more likely.
Weightless economy	Term used to refer to a form of economic life in which the product is not physical but abstract and hence 'weightless'. Used in particular to refer to use of electronic representations of money and media which can be transferred easily across electronic networks.
Workflow management	ICT systems which route work between work teams and individuals on the basis of rules written into the software. Automatically route work based on expertise, availability and stage of the process. Used by companies such as insurance companies to handle claims which need several people to work on the same claim at the same time.

Index

An environmentally friendly book printed and bound in England by www.printondemand-worldwide.com

PEFC Certified

This product is
from sustainably
managed forests
and controlled
sources

www.pefc.org

PEFC/16-33-415

This book is made entirely of sustainable materials; FSC paper for the cover and PEFC paper for the text pages.

#0391 - 071113 - C0 - 254/178/15 - PB